Literature as Social Action

Pamela Currie

LITERATURE AS SOCIAL ACTION

Modernist and Traditionalist Narratives
in Germany in the Seventeenth
and Eighteenth Centuries

CAMDEN HOUSE

Copyright © 1995 by
CAMDEN HOUSE, INC.

Published by Camden House, Inc.
Drawer 2025
Columbia, SC 29202 USA

Printed on acid-free paper.
Binding materials are chosen for strength and
durability.

ISBN:1-57113-022-5

Library of Congress Cataloging-in-Publication Data

Currie, Pamela, 1941-
Literature as social action : modernist and traditionalist narratives in
Germany in the seventeenth and eighteenth centuries / Pamela Currie.
p. cm. -- (Studies in German literature, linguistics, and culture)
Includes bibliographical references and index.
ISBN 1-57113-022-5 (alk. paper)
1. German fiction--Early modern, 1500-1700--History and criticism.
2. German fiction--18th century--History and criticism.
3. Literature and society--Germany--History. 4. Authors, German--Political
and social views. 5. Middle classes--Germany--History.
I. Title. II. Series: Studies in German literature, linguistics, and culture
(unnumbered)
PT 756.C87 1995
833' .509--dc20   94- 34993
                                                                   CIP

Contents

Preface

This book as first conceived was a study of the reading public for eighteenth century German fiction. I wanted to find out who had read what, and started by attempting to define the public for the moral weeklies, in an article published in *Oxford German Studies* in 1968. But that enquiry soon began to seem too narrow. I realised that my true interest lay in the relationship between literature, society and politics, so the work extended beyond literary studies into neighbouring disciplines, and reached further back in time than originally intended, in an attempt to situate eighteenth-century developments within processes beginning in the early modern period. Prompted particularly by the work of Peter L. Berger and Michael J. Böhler, I have come to understand literature not as an entity with a relationship to society and politics, but as a form of action itself ineradicably social and political. The book has therefore evolved as an exploration of the ways in which the rival cultural élites of the seventeenth and eighteenth centuries employed literary narratives to construct the public consciousness of social and political issues.

My work has been greatly assisted by periods of leave granted to me by the University of Oxford and by the Principal and Fellows of Lady Margaret Hall, Oxford, who have also generously provided a personal computer which has speeded my progress in the last two or three years. I am indebted to the Schiller-Nationalmuseum at Marbach, the Staatsbibliothek der Stiftung Preuischer Kulturbesitz in Marburg, the Bayerische Staatsbibliothek in Munich and the Württembergische Landesbibliothek in Stuttgart for assistance in the early stages of my research; to the British Library and the Bodleian Library; and especially to the late Mr D. M. Sutherland, Librarian of the Taylor Institution, Oxford, his successor Mr G. G. Barber and their staff for unfailing helpfulness over many years. I am grateful, too, to the Curators of the Taylor Institution, who have made a generous grant from the Fiedler Memorial Fund toward publication of this book.

As a graduate I belonged to the generation which was supervised with such kindness and good humour by the late Professor Ernest Stahl. Since then I have received encouragement from many colleagues in the Oxford Sub-Faculty of German, but especially from Professor T. J. Reed, who has read the manuscript, offered a great deal of useful advice, and given practical help when it was most needed. Robert Currie, Fellow of Wadham College, Oxford, has shared with me his knowledge of history, theology and literature; provided constant moral support; and given unstintingly of his own time to advise and comment on successive drafts.

Needless to say, the faults of the book in its present form are entirely my own. Finally I should like to say a word of thanks both to those of my students who have taken a particular interest in my work over the years and to my son and daughter, Dan and Lizzy, who have grown up with this book and have done so with a very good grace.

P. C.
September 1994

Introduction

I

THE SEVENTEENTH AND eighteenth centuries saw great social and cultural changes in Germany. The Protestant territories, on which this book concentrates, endured a period of relative cultural stagnation in the seventeenth century, but then, starting with Gellert and Lessing, began to produce writers of European fame. By the end of the eighteenth century, Germany was experiencing a classical moment which would prove to be as significant for western Europe as had been France's *grand siècle*. Meanwhile Brandenburg-Prussia developed from a modest electorate in 1648 to a powerful centralised monarchy under Friedrich II, whose victory over Austria in the Seven Years' War established Prussia's ascendancy within Protestant Germany.

It is not surprising that such an era has been intensively studied, nor that many attempts have been made to relate its literary to its social developments. Yet in this, as in many another instance, the interconnections between literature and society remain obscure. Successive approaches have mainly served to show how complex these interconnections are.

If any one thesis has dominated discussion of the period, among Marxist and non-Marxist scholars alike, it is that the emergence of the bourgeoisie or middle class caused the development of a national literature in German. But the hypothesis of the middle class poses more questions than it answers. Marx used the term *bourgeoisie* within his general theory of history to signify the dominant class of the capitalist era, and Marxist literary studies have followed his usage.[1] Western studies of literature and society, which are mostly undertaken by literary specialists rather than sociologists, tend to apply the term, or its German equivalent, *Bürgertum*, in a broad, general way, making little or no attempt to differentiate between different possible groupings within the middle range of society.[2]

Furthermore, to say that a middle class, however defined, lies behind the development of Germany's literature of course leaves open the question of that literature's characteristics: the types of utterance in which middle-class energies are thought to issue. According to Marx's schema, feudal society corresponds with religious culture, bourgeois society with rationalism.[3] Hence Marxists have often argued that the middle-class literature of eighteenth-century Europe generally incorporates the rationalist principles asserted in the course of the struggle for emancipation from feudalism.[4] But Marxists are not alone in making a link between the middle class and rational culture. Such a link is posited in a multitude of influential surveys of occidental developments, including Weber's theory of capitalism, Troeltsch's history of religion and Mannheim's sociology of knowledge.[5] In fact the concept of the middle class as the bearer of rationalism is virtually common ground in seventeenth and eighteenth-century cultural studies.

However this leaves out of account what every observer of eighteenth century Germany knows, namely that, running alongside any rationalism in thought and literature, there is also a strong current of what is often described as irrationalism. This comprises not only the traditional Christianity which Marxists link with the feudal aristocracy, but also secular movements such as sentimentalism, or *Empfindsamkeit*, and *Sturm und Drang*. So the student of literature and society must find a bearer for non-rational cultural phenomena also. And here again, the middle class has done duty, albeit within a variety of theories. Middle-class irrationalism has been differently explained and differently evaluated according to the ideological standpoint of the commentator.

According to one theory, the German middle class of 1600 to 1800, so far from being rationalist, was always and by inclination the bearer both of irrational values — whether of Christian spirituality or of a more secularised *Innerlichkeit* — and of social traditionalism. This view has most characteristically been taken by apologists of the political right who represent the middle class not merely as carrier but as champion of these values against the onslaught of alien reason. The most developed version of the argument appears in Thomas Mann's *Betrachtungen eines Unpolitischen*.[6]

A second, overlapping theory has the middle class as bearer of cultural irrationalism — seen in the sentimental movement or in *Sturm und Drang* — but under force of circumstance rather than from some sort of natural inclination. Here Germany is seen as an aberration from normal developments in western Europe. While the English and French middle classes progressed through economic strength to political power — so the argument runs — the German middle classes remained economically weak and politically impotent in a world dominated by the nobility. In these circumstances, they turned to the private sphere for compensation. Under the maxim "Im Stillen ein König seyn,"[7] they found in the inner life and the family the satisfaction denied them in the public world. Hence the development, sometimes to the point of hypertrophy, of spirituality, self-analysis, sensibility, all of which are interpreted within this theory as resignatory rather than revolutionary: their significance is regarded as psychopathological rather than political. Norbert Elias argued in this way in the 1930s, and a line of later writers including Peter Szondi and Wolf Lepenies has taken the same view.[8]

But in recent years more support has gone to a third theory which sees irrationalism as the ally of rationalism in the process of middle-class emancipation. Here irrationalism is politically progressive. Marxists could always be found to argue, in conformity with Marx's theory of history, that sentimentalism and *Sturm und Drang* reflected the class struggle of the bourgeoisie against feudalism. Thus for Georg Lukács, Goethe's *Werther* heralded the revolution.[9] More subtly, Jürgen Habermas has argued that the development of sentimental values in the middle-class "nuclear" family was a pre-political phase of the emancipatory struggle.[10] The generality of western writers has moved steadily closer to this point of view, encouraged no doubt by Reinhard Koselleck's presentation of eighteenth-century bourgeois morality as covert opposition to absolute monarchy.[11] A large body of opinion now holds that from the 1740s onwards, reason and feeling *together* became the foundation of a middle-class self-awareness which, if it was not yet revolutionary, at least had revolutionary potential.[12]

Thus far irrationalism has been read either as endemic to the German middle class or as its response, pathological or progressive, to noble power. But if rationalism is regarded as a quintessentially bourgeois phenomenon, then logically irrationalism might well be considered anti-bourgeois. And there are schools of thought which represent the irrationalism of the late eighteenth century as a reaction, by some form of intelligentsia floating free of class, against both a bourgeois-capitalist order and an absolutist state construed as promoter of such an order. Irrationalism is again seen in two different ways, either as progressive or pathological.

One theory has irrationalism as a potentially revolutionary attack on the capitalist *haute bourgeoisie*. Marxists have argued that the sentimentalist ethic of altruism preached in domestic plays and novels attempts to subvert the rational-stoic discipline necessary to the capitalist system. In these writers' eyes, sentimentalism is a precursor of democratic socialism. Rousseau in France, and Gellert and Lessing in Germany, spoke for a proletarian revolution whose time had not yet come; their onslaught on capitalist values was therefore doomed to failure.[13] Some non-Marxists also see sentimentalism as antagonistic to the bourgeois-capitalist world; but to them Rousseau and his ilk are not progressive but conservative revolutionaries, aiming to transcend liberal humanism in a totalitarian order.[14]

The second theory identifies irrationalism as a symptom of discomfort in a bourgeois-capitalist world where natural instinct and desire must be rigidly disciplined in the interests of economic prosperity. This theory is ultimately traceable to Weber's tragic vision of the bureaucratised world as an iron cage and Freud's analysis of civilisation and its discontents.[15] So far as eighteenth-century Germany is concerned, sentimental drama or the *Sturm und Drang* appear, in the work of the "Alewyn school" or of Paul Mog, as a pathological response to modern constraints. The sentimental family, romantic love and ultimately death provide a respite from the rigid world of work.[16] Similarly, Klaus Scherpe sees Werther as a young man who refuses to submit to the laws of capitalist society.[17] And the aesthetic of autonomous art is increasingly viewed as an attempt to escape from market constraints.[18] Even writers with Marxist sympathies who persist in perceiving the *Sturm und Drang* as part of the bourgeoisie's revolutionary struggle against feudal absolutism now interpret the *Autonomieperiode* of Weimar classicism as tantamount to an escape into a new religion.[19] The bourgeois intellectuals who make such an escape are evidently not to be seen as forerunners of proletarian revolution. But if they can not be explained by way of the Marxian historical schema, neither have they been satisfactorily defined by reference to their social origins and contemporary political affiliation, or to rival intellectual groupings of the day.[20]

There is, then, no little disagreement about literature and society in Germany between 1600 and 1800, partly arising from inadequate differentiation of social groups and literary movements, partly from uncertainty about the pace of social change in the early modern period. The term *middle class* suggests a homogeneous social group where there was none. The contrast between rationalism and irrationalism conceals rather than reveals the true alliances and alignments of literary groups during the period. And the frequent appeal to a bourgeois-capitalist era seems anachronistic in relation to pre-industrial Germany. But in a sense these are superficial difficulties. The deeper source of continuing confusion lies in the inadequacy of the models of literature and society which have been used by critics of all persuasions: an inadequacy made manifest by unthinking use of the phrase "literature and society" itself.[21]

II

The conventional western model, in use from the Romantic period to the 1960s, and not entirely defunct today, incorporates the notion of literature as an ontologically distinct body of poetic or imaginative texts which, when correctly interpreted, yields morally and spiritually valuable meanings. The ontological separation of literature from utilitarian and pragmatic texts is at the same time a separation of literature from society. In order to be literature, a text must do nothing: it must not work in the world.[22] Indeed the very phrase "literature and society," which seems innocent enough, enshrines the notion of the two phenomena as separate entities. The inevitable effect of the model has been to marginalise the study of literature as a social phenomenon and to obscure its social dynamics.[23] The traditional Marxist model has hardly served better. If western liberal-humanist criticism emphasises literature at the expense of society, classical Marxism does the opposite. The theory of economic base and ideological superstructure reduces literature, along with religion or philosophy, to secondary outworkings of the various modes of production. Texts become mere reflections, if sometimes highly revealing reflections, of the progress of mankind towards communism.[24] Once again, there is no question of the literary text working on the social world and changing it.

So long as we remain within the ambit of such theories we decline to ask either who wills what literature does or whose interests it serves. And so long as those questions remain unasked, there can be no clarity about the social origins of literary texts. The starting point for a re-examination of literature's place in seventeenth and eighteenth-century German society must, therefore, be a theory of literature as social action.

Happily, such a theory need not be constructed *de novo*. Nor does it demand elaborate justification. For most of the major initiatives in post-war literary theory have, in their several ways, encouraged the idea that the texts we commonly call literature do in fact work in the world. Structuralism, reader-response criticism and discourse theory have all tended to repoliticise literature.[25] And even Derridean deconstruction, though it sometimes chooses to ignore the implications of its own arguments, has devoted its best energies to proving the rhetorical and suasive, hence political nature of all writing.[26]

However the model I wish to use derives not so much from any school of literary theory as from Durkheim's sociology of religion, which has shaped much of the thinking of modern social constructionist sociologists and neo-Marxists alike.[27] Durkheim sees religion as the source of group identity. Any given religion is a socially-constructed symbolic universe or life-world, which enables individuals to understand themselves as members of a specific society, and thus creates and sustains that society. Without religious, or comparable, structures individuals would have no common identity, hence society would have no cohesion.[28] Today, all man's edifices in language are widely understood as Durkheim understood religion. None communicates pre-existent truth, however much it may deny its fictionality. All are socially-constructed life-worlds, which fix individuals in an identity, ensure a fit between them and their society, and thus make that society possible.[29]

Symbolic universes are transmitted, and identity is shaped, in the pre-linguistic phase of the individual's development. An infant observing his parents will imitate the way they behave, and respond to the way they behave towards him: their assumptions about him, embodied in the way they treat him and the demands they make of him, make him what they expect him to be. The infant's identity is formed by reflection of the symbolic reality which exists in his immediate environment.[30] But identity continues to be formed throughout childhood and adolescence; and even adult identities, once formed, may be altered. Once the pre-linguistic phase is past, identity-formation depends to a great extent on narrative.

Storytelling is man's primal way of making sense of the world or, in other words, of bringing sense into the world. Like the Kantian forms of space and time, narrative makes the world knowable.[31] Not merely do we render our own perceptions of the outside world and of other people into narrative, but other people's narratives work on us in the same way as does our personal experience. Identity can be formed through our understanding of real people's behaviour among themselves and towards us; but so, too, can it be formed by our encounters with narrative of all kinds, oral and written, from simple sayings and anecdotes to myths, legends, folktales, written history and the literary genres of romance and novel.[32]

The behaviour of others, witnessed by us as spectators, provides us with models for imitation. Others' words, addressed to us, invite us to adopt particular attitudes in response.[33] And narrative offers the same possibilities. It is customarily analysed into story and discourse, story being the narrative of character in action, and discourse being the utterance of the narrative voice telling the story.[34] Here the story presents the reader with a spectacle akin to the observed acts of people in real life. The characters may offer models for identification, just as real people do. The discourse addresses the reader — via the intermediary of an inscribed reader — as people address him in life.[35] The address suggests a particular form of response, just as real-life conversation does. It can not force that response, any more than can a real-life interlocutor, but it can encourage it.[36] So the texts we read can help to constitute or fix individuals as subjects within an existing symbolic universe. They can reinforce the tendency, acquired through childhood socialisation, to take for granted the symbolic universe of the society into which one has been born. Equally, they may play a part in converting an individual from one symbolic universe to another.[37]

The model of narrative I have outlined here — a model of narrative as social action — should help to bring greater clarity to the analysis of literature and society. Social groups may be examined for their political aims: what kind of society they wish to form or maintain; narrative texts for their political tendency: what kind of society they are capable of forming or maintaining. It should then become possible to make meaningful correlations between social groups and texts. Groups will be found to devise the sort of text which can help to construct the type of society they desire.

III

Before the model can be successfully applied to Germany between 1600 and 1800, the society and political circumstances of that time must be more carefully analysed than has sometimes been the case in studies whose principal subject is literature. I have already indicated that the concept of the middle class or bourgeoisie has played a large part in the discussion. But this inexact term implies a social unity which the period was far from exhibiting. The middle range of society, between nobility and peasants, included a wide variety of groups: clergy, academics, officials of all kinds, military officers, professional men, financiers, large and small businessmen, master craftsmen. Some members of these groups were subjects of major and some of minor princes; some inhabited self-governing republics. Some lived in large urban centres, some in small rural market towns. Not surprisingly, these people were not conscious of themselves as a unified middle class. In fact their perceived interests often diverged very considerably, so that greater antagonisms sprang up between different groups within the middle class than existed from time to time between some of those groups and the nobility: the socio-political battles of the period were not fought on class lines.[38]

Hence the relevance to German culture and society in the seventeenth and eighteenth centuries of sociological categories whose import is precisely not that of class struggle.[39] From the sociologist's point of view, the post-medieval period in western Europe generally has been one of "modernisation," which is usually held to have begun with changes in the economic sphere, though its origins need not have been the same everywhere, and its course is recognised as varying from country to country. Whatever its starting point or points in any particular country, its tendency has been eventually to affect all aspects of life: economic, social, political, legal and cultural.[40]

Analysis of modernisation in particular contexts has greatly relied on two limiting conceptions of a pre-modern and a fully modern society. Many theorists have proposed their own contrasting pair of ideal types, using terminology dictated by their primary interest in the legal, political or economic sphere. "Status society" has been contrasted with "contract society"; "lineage society" with "civil society"; "customary society" with "market society." Perhaps the most famous pair of types is that incorporated by Ferdinand Tönnies in the title of his book *Gemeinschaft und Gesellschaft*, published in 1887.[41] Tönnies' terms have yielded no completely satisfactory English equivalents: *Gemeinschaft* translates well as *community*, but *Gesellschaft* has given either *society*, which seems too broad, or *association* and *organisation*, which seem too narrow. In this book I shall simply call the two contrasting ideal types "traditional society" and "modern society." These terms are *not* intended to imply any value-judgment in favour of one or the other type.

Life in traditional society may be likened to family life. It is lived in small, concrete collectivities — clan, village, country town — where relationships are like family relationships: personal, permanent, diffuse and affective. Members of the collectivity know one another individually, participate equally in the performance of many common tasks, and feel bound to one another by kinship, shared local allegiance, and similarity of outlook. In traditional society the individual is subordinate to the social family. He falls under its paternal authority, and is required to serve its purposes, not his own. His birth provides both his status in life and the security of a livelihood appropriate to that status. He fears no competition for the place he holds, since all other members of the social family likewise remain within the status assigned to them.[42] The individual has no legal standing *qua* individual. His civil and social rights and duties depend entirely on his status in the collectivity. He is coresponsible for its actions, and is himself judged "as a whole man, bringing with him his status...all of his history and his social relations."[43] Life for the individual in traditional society is settled and certain: he has a clear identity and function. He may not be happy — he is not immune from disease, disaster and the fear of death — but he has a certain psychological security, a sense of being at home in the social world.[44] By the same token, the individual in traditional society lacks personal freedom. He has no choices within the collectivity. Either he accommodates himself to its aims and objects, or he must leave it altogether.[45]

Modern society contrasts fundamentally with traditional society. Its characteristic structures are large and abstract: the nation-state, governmental and administrative bureaucracies, national defence forces, industrial corporations, cities. Relationships within these structures are often impersonal, intermittent, specialised and non-affective. In the public sphere, people transact single items of business, often without face-to-face contact, and without forming any emotional attachment. Family relationships are now confined to a private sphere, which has become distinct from the world of work. But though the individual may appear dwarfed by modern institutions, he has become the basic unit of modern society. His biography is no longer determined, as it was in traditional society, by family or collective. No status, no livelihood accrues to him by virtue of his birth. He does not stand or fall with the collectivity. Instead he is a legal person *qua* individual, and has the right to enter into agreements on his own account. He is confronted with a variety of possible career choices, and must compete with others for his living. He will achieve his own status in society, which may be higher or lower than that of his parents.[46] Thus in certain obvious ways the individual has greater autonomy in modern than in traditional society. But his freedom has uncertainty and insecurity on its reverse. The private sphere forms a small, possibly safe, refuge in a dangerous public world which all too often requires the individual to adopt a variety of roles. In these circumstances, one may well begin to wonder who one is: it is something of a truism that the modern condition involves a "permanent identity-crisis."[47]

In Germany, as elsewhere in western Europe, the transition from a traditional to a modern society took place over several centuries, beginning in the sixteenth. And right through the seventeenth and eighteenth centuries modernisation — unnamed as yet but perceptible in its effects — was the political issue which polarised opinion. Modernisation was wanted and indeed actively pursued by groups which were marginal to or oppressed within traditional society, and whose aspirations found no fulfilment through the structures and practices of such a society. In contrast modernisation was feared and resisted by groups which risked losing their power and even their *raison d'être* in modern society. The division between modernisers and traditionalists separated noble from noble and commoner from commoner, bringing together nobles and commoners in both opposing camps. The question to be asked about any given persons or groups is not, therefore, whether they were nobles or commoners, but whether they were modernisers or traditionalists.

A corresponding question can be asked of literary texts. It is not in fact whether texts are irrationalist or rationalist, but what kind of world they tend to construct: is it a traditional world or a modern world? The two pairs of categories might at first glance seem essentially the same. Marxists, for instance, link feudalism with the non-rational, religious world-view, capitalism with reason. And the feudal world is generally held to be traditional, the capitalist modern. Yet the case is not quite so simple. The division between traditionalist and modernising texts cuts across the other two categories as they are usually understood. Some texts commonly considered irrationalist nevertheless tend to construct a modern world, while others considered rationalist tend to construct a traditional one.

Chapters 2 to 7 use the categories of traditional and modernising groups, traditional and modernising texts, in the attempt to bring order into present confusion. When the membership and practices of social groups and the contents of literary texts are examined for indications of traditionalism and modernity, it will be suggested that traditional groups generated traditionalist texts, while modernising groups produced modernising texts. The conundrum of the rational-irrational bourgeoisie can thus be resolved in so far as the bourgeoisie proves to contain antagonistic groups consistently using opposite means to attain opposite ends.

It will also be suggested that the fortunes of the modernisers and traditionalists fluctuate throughout the seventeenth and eighteenth centuries. The two groups consciously engage in an often bitter ideological struggle to win hearts and minds for the worlds on which their power if not their very existence depends.[48] If the modernisers make gains, the traditionalists respond with all the force at their command. And the outcome is not altogether what might be expected. Ralf Dahrendorf notes that certain social groups in nineteenth-century Germany promoted a traditional ideology because they hoped to profit from it, and "contributed to hindering the advent of modernity." It was largely through their efforts that imperial Germany developed as an "industrial feudal society." And even after 1945, Dahrendorf considers, modern attitudes had still not altogether established themselves.[49] The conflict which took place in the seventeenth and eighteenth centuries between modern and traditional ideologies goes a long way towards explaining the situation that Dahrendorf describes.

In order to follow that conflict, it is necessary to attempt the identification of writers and texts as traditionalist or modernising. Chapter 1 therefore seeks to establish models with which individual examples can be compared. Each type of society has its own characteristic ideologues: theoretical experts who construct and maintain its reality. And each type of expert uses a characteristic form of narrative in the everyday performance of his tasks, a form of narrative which corresponds, it will be argued, with a larger literary form. The theoretical experts of traditional society have always been religious experts, for legitimations of traditional societies have always been legitimations "in a sacred mode." In tribal societies the expert was a medicine man or a shaman; in medieval Europe he was a priest.[50] The theoretical experts of modern society are perhaps less easy to identify. But its first apologists were lawyers: men like Bodin, Hobbes and Grotius. And its categories are legal categories: the modern individual is in the first instance the legal individual.[51] Hence Durkheim identified law as the basis of cohesion in modern societies.[52] Though, in Roger Cotterrell's words, legal ideology "is rarely 'preached' directly by lawyers," it can "be thought of as seeping into popular consciousness," where in parallel with religion it struggles "to define individuality and humanity and the relationships between collective and individual life."[53] To religious and legal experts, priests and lawyers, I shall now turn.

[1] On Marxian theory, see "Stages of development," "Bourgeoisie," "Middle class," "Capitalism," "Transition from feudalism to capitalism" and "Literature," *A Dictionary of Marxist Thought*, ed. Tom Bottomore (Oxford: Basil Blackwell, 1983).

[2] Wolfgang Martens makes wide use of the terms *Bürger* and *bürgerlich* in his major study of moral weeklies, *Die Botschaft der Tugend: die Aufklärung im Spiegel der deutschen Moralischen Wochenschriften* (Stuttgart: J. B. Metzler, 1968). See, for example, "Zum ersten Mal seit langem sieht der bürgerliche Leser sich hier in der Literatur mit seinen eigenen Angelegenheiten befaßt" (344); "Das Lebensideal des Bürgers rückt hier an die Stelle des höfischen" (346). Wilhelm Vosskamp proceeds in the same way in

Romantheorie in Deutschland: von Martin Opitz bis Friedrich von Blanckenburg (Stuttgart: J. B. Metzler, 1973). See for example the chapter title "Spannungen im Begriff...des bürgerlichen Romans" and comments such as "Seine spätere politische Vormachtstellung antizipiert das Bürgertum in einer Usurpation des Moralischen" (179). There has been a lengthy debate on the question as to whether *Empfindsamkeit* was or was not *bürgerlich*: see Gerhard Sauder, *Empfindsamkeit*, vol. 1 (Stuttgart: J. B. Metzler, 1974) xiii-xiv and "'Bürgerliche' Empfindsamkeit?" *Bürger und Bürgerlichkeit im Zeitalter der Aufklärung*, ed. Rudolf Vierhaus, Wolfenbütteler Studien zur Aufklärung 7 (Heidelberg: L. Schneider, 1981). A few writers have pointed out the dangers of assuming the existence of a simple, single *Bürgertum*: see Gerhart von Graevenitz, "Innerlichkeit und Öffentlichkeit: Aspekte deutscher 'bürgerlicher' Literatur im frühen 18. Jahrhundert," *Deutsche Vierteljahrsschrift für Literaturwissenschaft und Geistesgeschichte* Sonderheft 1975: 69*-70*; Gunter E. Grimm, *Literatur und Gelehrtentum in Deutschland: Untersuchungen zum Wandel ihres Verhältnisses vom Humanismus bis zur Frühaufklärung*, Studien zur deutschen Literatur 75 (Tübingen: M. Niemeyer, 1983) 675-76.

3 On the Marxian view of religion, see "Religion," *A Dictionary of Marxist Thought* 413-16. Bourgeois rationalism is above all economic rationality, calculation. See for example Marx's evocation of the bourgeois order in the Manifesto of the Communist Party, *The Marx-Engels Reader*, ed. Robert C. Tucker, 2nd. ed. (New York: W. W. Norton & Co., 1978) 475-78. Compare "Reification," *A Dictionary of Marxist Thought* 411-413, and Georg Lukács, "The Phenomenon of Reification," *History and Class Consciousness: Studies in Marxist Dialectics*, tr. Rodney Livingstone (London: Merlin Press, 1971).

4 See for example the volume *Aufklärung: Erläuterungen zur deutschen Literatur*, ed. Kollektiv für Literaturgeschichte im Volkseigenen Verlag Volk und Wissen (Berlin: Volk und Wissen, 1958) and, on this, Peter Pütz, *Die deutsche Aufklärung*, Erträge der Forschung 81 (Darmstadt: Wissenschaftliche Buchgesellschaft, 1978) 175-77. The same general thesis still appears in a major work of recent American Marxist criticism, see Fredric Jameson, *The Political Unconscious: Narrative as a Socially Symbolic Act* (1981; London: Methuen, 1983) 95-96.

5 For Weber's concept of rational capitalism, see Max Weber, *The Protestant Ethic and the Spirit of Capitalism*, tr. Talcott Parsons (1930; London: Unwin, 1965) 21-27. For Troeltsch on the bourgeoisie as proponent of rational explanations of the world, see his article "Aufklärung," *Realencyclopädie für protestantische Theologie und Kirche*, 3rd ed., vol. 2 (Leipzig: J. C. Hinrichs, 1897) 225-241. For Mannheim on bourgeois rationalism, see Karl Mannheim, *Ideology and Utopia: An Introduction to the Sociology of Knowledge* (1936; London: Routledge, 1960) 108-110.

6 Mann's *Betrachtungen* belong in a line of conservative criticism which begins with Herder and passes through Ferdinand Tönnies: see Michael J. Böhler, *Soziale Rolle und ästhetische Vermittlung: Studien zur Literatursoziologie von A. G. Baumgarten bis F. Schiller* (Bern: H. Lang, 1975) 222-23. See also for example Wolfdietrich Rasch, *Freundschaftskult und Freundschaftsdichtung im deutschen Schrifttum des 18. Jahrhunderts vom Ausgang des Barock bis zu Klopstock*, Deutsche Vierteljahrsschrift für Literaturwissenschaft und Geistesgeschichte, Buchreihe 21 (Halle/Saale: M. Niemeyer, 1936) 96-97, 104-5, where the German *Bürgertum* with its cult of friendship is presented as the bearer of spiritual and moral culture against the fragmenting influence of rationalism.

7 The phrase "To be a king in the peace of one's own hearth" is Gellert's: see Sauder, *Empfindsamkeit* 225.

[8] Norbert Elias, *Über den Prozess der Zivilisation: soziogenetische und psychogenetische Untersuchungen*, vol. 1 (Basel: Haus zum Falken, 1939) 8-9, 20-21; Peter Szondi, *Die Theorie des bürgerlichen Trauerspiels im 18. Jahrhundert: der Kaufmann, der Hausvater und der Hofmeister*, ed. Gert Mattenklott (Frankfurt am Main: Suhrkamp, 1973) 146-7, 167; Wolf Lepenies, *Melancholie und Gesellschaft* (Frankfurt am Main: Suhrkamp, 1969) 79-93, 99-104. See also Alberto Martino, "Barockpoesie, Publikum und Verbürgerlichung der literarischen Intelligenz," *Internationales Archiv für Sozialgeschichte der deutschen Literatur* 1 (1976): 135-44.

[9] Georg Lukács, *Goethe und seine Zeit* (Bern: A. Francke, 1947) 17-30.

[10] Jürgen Habermas, *Strukturwandel der Öffentlichkeit: Untersuchung zu einer Kategorie der bürgerlichen Gesellschaft*, Politica 4 (Neuwied: Luchterhand, 1962) 58, 60-65.

[11] Reinhart Koselleck, *Kritik und Krise: ein Beitrag zur Pathogenese der bürgerlichen Welt* (Freiburg: Karl Alber, 1959) especially 122-23, 155.

[12] See for example Vosskamp 142, 179, 184, 198, and 255, note 12; Sauder, *Empfindsamkeit* 197-98, 200-202, 204, 206-7, 225, 235; Karl S. Guthke, *Das deutsche bürgerliche Trauerspiel* (Stuttgart: J. B. Metzler, 1972) 32-35, 45-46.

[13] See *Aufklärung*, ed. Kollektiv für Literaturgeschichte 24-25; Peter Weber, *Das Menschenbild des bürgerlichen Trauerspiels: Entstehung und Funktion von Lessings* Miss Sara Sampson (Berlin: Rütten & Loening, 1970) 76, 89, 109, 116, 124, 150-51, 186.

[14] Koselleck 138-39; J. L. Talmon, *The Origins of Totalitarian Democracy* (1952; London: Sphere Books, 1970) 5, 7, 42-44.

[15] Max Weber 47-78. On Weber's "tragic vision," see Roland Robertson, "Aspects of Identity and Authority in Sociological Theory," *Identity and Authority: Explorations in the Theory of Society*, ed. Roland Robertson and Burkart Holzner (Oxford: Basil Blackwell, 1980) 226-27. For "Civilization and its Discontents" ("Das Unbehagen in der Kultur"), see *The Standard Edition of the Complete Psychological Works of Sigmund Freud*, ed. James Strachey, vol. 21 (London: Hogarth Press and Institute of Psycho-Analysis, 1961) 64-145.

[16] The work of the Alewyn school (see Sauder, *Empfindsamkeit* xiii) includes Lothar Pikulik, *"Bürgerliches Trauerspiel" und Empfindsamkeit* (Cologne: Böhlau, 1966): see especially 29, 31-32, 35-37, 93-95, 101, 123; and Paul Mog, *Ratio und Gefühlskultur: Studien zu Psychogenese und Literatur im 18. Jahrhundert* (Tübingen: M. Niemeyer, 1976): see especially 83-91, 119-138.

[17] Klaus R. Scherpe, *Werther und Wertherwirkung: zum Syndrom bürgerlicher Gesellschaftsordnung im 18. Jahrhundert* (Bad Homburg vor der Höhe: Gehlen, 1970), 30-52, 66, 71, 73, 88.

[18] See for example Bernd Jürgen Warneken, "Die relative Autonomie der Literatur: Stichworte zur Entwicklung der Kunst in der bürgerlichen Gesellschaft," *Historizität in Sprach- und Literaturwissenschaft: Vorträge und Berichte der Stuttgarter Germanistentagung 1972*, ed. Walter Müller-Seidel (Munich: W. Fink, 1974) 600-607; Kurt Wölfel, "Zur Geschichtlichkeit des Autonomiebegriffs," *Historizität* 568-70, 574-75, 577.

[19] See for example Christa Bürger, *Der Ursprung der bürgerlichen Institution Kunst im höfischen Weimar: literatursoziologische Untersuchungen zum klassischen Goethe* (Frankfurt am Main: Suhrkamp, 1977).

[20] The terms "bürgerliche Intelligenz" and "literarische Intelligenz" are now in common use to describe writers of the *Sturm und Drang* period onwards, see for example Hans

J. Haferkorn, "Zur Entstehung der bürgerlich-literarischen Intelligenz und des Schriftstellers in Deutschland zwischen 1750 und 1800," *Deutsches Bürgertum und literarische Intelligenz 1750-1800*, Literaturwissenschaft und Sozialwissenschaften 3, ed. Bernd Lutz (Stuttgart: J. B. Metzler, 1974) 113-275; Hans-Jürgen Schings, *Melancholie und Aufklärung: Melancholiker und ihre Kritiker in Erfahrungsseelenkunde und Literatur des 18. Jahrhunderts* (Stuttgart: J. B. Metzler, 1977) 225.

[21] Compare Böhler 27-28.

[22] Compare Jane P. Tompkins, "The Reader in History: The Changing Shape of Literary Response," *Reader-Response Criticism: From Formalism to Post-Structuralism*, ed. Tompkins (Baltimore: Johns Hopkins UP, 1980) 207, 210, 218-19, 221-23; Frank Lentricchia, *After the New Criticism* (1980; London: Methuen, 1983) 3, 6, 13, 83 and *Criticism and Social Change* (1983; Chicago: University of Chicago Press, 1983) 54 .

[23] Compare Böhler 20, 23, 27-28, 42-43; Karlheinz Stierle, "L'Histoire comme Exemple, l'Exemple comme Histoire," *Poétique* 3 (1972): 186.

[24] Compare Klaus Vondung, "Probleme einer Sozialgeschichte der Ideen," *Das wilhelminische Bildungsbürgertum: zur Sozialgeschichte seiner Ideen*, ed. Vondung (Göttingen: Vandenhoeck & Ruprecht, 1976) 12. For a survey of Marxist criticism including the "reflection" theory, see "Literature," *A Dictionary of Marxist Thought* 284-87.

[25] On Saussure and the early Barthes, see Lentricchia, *After the New Criticism* 119, 130, 132, 134. On reader-response criticism, see *Reader-Response Criticism*, ed. Tompkins xxv and Wolfgang Iser, "The Reality of Fiction: A Functionalist Approach to Literature," *New Literary History* 7 (1975): 7. For discourse theory, see Christopher Norris, *Deconstruction: Theory and Practice* (London: Methuen, 1982) 21, 60-61, 88; Edward W. Said, "The Text, the World, the Critic," *Textual Strategies: Perspectives in Post-Structuralist Criticism*, ed. Josué V. Harari (1979; London: Methuen, 1980) 177-78.

[26] Compare Lentricchia, *After the New Criticism* 175-76, 193-98 and *Criticism and Social Change* 50-51; Christopher Norris, *The Contest of Faculties: Philosophy and Theory After Deconstruction* (London: Methuen, 1985) 73, 80-83.

[27] For the influence of Durkheim on recent Marxist thinking about ideology, see Jameson 70, 292. Compare William C. Dowling, *Jameson, Althusser, Marx: An Introduction to* The Political Unconscious (1984; London: Methuen, 1984) 54, 83.

[28] Emile Durkheim, *The Elementary Forms of the Religious Life*, tr. Joseph Ward Swain, 2nd ed. (London: George Allen & Unwin, 1976) especially 416-427. Compare the chapter "Religion and World-Construction" in Peter L. Berger, *The Social Reality of Religion* (1967; Harmondsworth, England: Penguin Books, 1973) 13-37.

[29] Peter L. Berger and Thomas Luckmann, *The Social Construction of Reality: A Treatise in the Sociology of Knowledge* (1966; Harmondsworth, England: Penguin Books, 1971) 55; Tompkins, "The Reader in History" 224; Benjamin Nelson, *On the Roads to Modernity: Conscience, Science, and Civilizations*, ed. Toby E. Huff (Totowa, New Jersey: Rowman and Littlefield, 1981) 22-25; Richard Harvey Brown and Stanford M. Lyman, "Symbolic realism and cognitive aesthetics: an invitation," *Structure, Consciousness and History*, ed. Brown and Lyman (Cambridge, England: Cambridge UP, 1978) 1-10; Hayden White, *Tropics of Discourse: Essays in Cultural Criticism* (Baltimore: Johns Hopkins UP, 1978) 82-84, 88-89, 97-98; Stanley Fish, *Is There a Text in This Class? The Authority of Interpretive Communities* (Cambridge, Mass.: Harvard UP, 1982) 242-43.

[30] See Berger and Luckmann 149-57.

[31] Compare Dowling 95-97; Lennard J. Davis, *Resisting Novels: Ideology and Fiction* (New York: Methuen, 1987) 212.

[32] Berger, *Social Reality* 40; Berger and Luckmann 86.

[33] Berger and Luckmann 172.

[34] See for example Tzvetan Todorov, *The Poetics of Prose*, tr. Richard Howard (1971; Oxford: Basil Blackwell, 1977) 25-26, and compare Jonathan Culler, *Structuralist Poetics: Structuralism, Linguistics and the Study of Literature* (London: Routledge & Kegan Paul, 1975) 197-98; Wallace Martin, *Recent Theories of Narrative* (Ithaca: Cornell UP, 1986) 108-109.

[35] On the inscribed reader see Gerald Prince, "Introduction to the Study of the Narratee," *Reader-Response Criticism*, ed.Tompkins 7-25.

[36] Compare Althusser's suggestion that ideology works by "hailing" the individual: see Louis Althusser, *Positions* (Paris: Éditions sociales, 1976) 122-29. For a discussion of the extent to which a text can control the reader's response see Jonathan Culler, *On Deconstruction: Theory and Criticism after Structuralism* (1982; London: Routledge, 1983) 31-83.

[37] Compare Kenneth Burke, *Attitudes toward History*, vol. 1 (New York: The New Republic, 1937) 44; Lentricchia, *Criticism and Social Change* 24, 102; Catherine Belsey, *Critical Practice* (London: Methuen, 1980) 66-67; Karlheinz Stierle, "Was heisst Rezeption bei fiktionalen Texten?" *Poetica* 7 (1975): 383-86; Jonathan Potter, Peter Stringer and Margaret Wetherell, *Social Texts and Context: Literature and Social Psychology* (London: Routledge & Kegan Paul, 1984) 22-24, 93-94, 98.

[38] Compare Grimm, *Literatur und Gelehrtentum* 675-76. On divisions within the middle range of society, see Habermas 35-36; Mack Walker, *German Home Towns* (Ithaca: Cornell UP, 1971) 106, 111, 119.

[39] Compare Jameson 83-84.

[40] On modernisation, modernity and modern consciousness, see Peter L. Berger, Brigitte Berger and Hansfried Kellner, *The Homeless Mind: Modernization and Consciousness* (1973; Harmondsworth, England: Penguin Books, 1974) 15-16 and passim; Peter L. Berger, *Facing Up To Modernity: Excursions in Society, Politics, and Religion* (1977; Harmondsworth, England: 1979) 101-112; Thomas Anz, "Literarische Norm und Autonomie: Individualitätsspielräume in der modernisierten Literaturgesellschaft des 18. Jahrhunderts," *Tradition, Norm, Innovation: soziales und literarisches Verhalten in der Frühzeit der deutschen Aufklärung*, ed. Wilfried Barner, Schriften des Historischen Kollegs: Kolloquien 15 (Munich: Oldenbourg, 1989) 71-88; Hans Erich Bödeker and Ernst Hinrichs, "Alteuropa — Frühe Neuzeit — Moderne Welt? Perspektiven der Forschung," *Alteuropa — Ancien Régime — Frühe Neuzeit: Probleme und Methoden der Forschung* ed. Bödeker and Hinrichs, problemata 124 (Stuttgart: Frommann-Holzboog, 1991).

[41] For "status" and "contract" see Sir Henry Sumner Maine, *Ancient Law: Its Connection with the Early History of Society and its Relation to Modern Ideas*, introd. Sir Frederick Pollock, new ed. (London: John Murray, 1930) 180-82; for "lineage society" and "contract society" see Alan Macfarlane, *The Origins of English Individualism: The Family, Property and Social Transition* (Oxford: Basil Blackwell, 1978) 59; for "customary society" and "market society" see C. B. Macpherson, *The Political Theory of Possessive Individualism: Hobbes to Locke* (1962; London: Oxford UP, 1964) 49-58. See also Charles P. Loomis and John C. McKinney, introduction, *Community and Society (Gemeinschaft und Gesellschaft)*, by Ferdinand Tönnies, tr. and ed. Charles P. Loomis

(1957; New York: Torchbooks-Harper & Row, 1963); Berger, *Facing Up To Modernity* 169-70.

[42] Tönnies 43, 45, 55, 59, 64; Hans Gerth and C. Wright Mills, *Character and Social Structure: The Psychology of Social Institutions* (1954; London: Routledge & Kegan Paul, 1970) 100-104; Leonhard Bauer and Herbert Matis, *Geburt der Neuzeit: vom Feudalsystem zur Marktgesellschaft* (Munich: Deutscher Taschenbuch Verlag, 1988) 15, 33-77.

[43] Eugene Kamenka and Alice Erh-Soon Tay, "Beyond Bourgeois Individualism: the Contemporary Crisis in Law and Legal Ideology," *Feudalism, Capitalism and Beyond*, ed. Eugene Kamenka and R. S. Neale (London: Edward Arnold, 1975) 136. See also Gerth and Wright Mills 101; Anthony T. Kronman, *Max Weber* (London: Edward Arnold, 1983) 142-43.

[44] K. R. Popper, *The Open Society and Its Enemies*, 5th ed., vol. 1 (London: Routledge & Kegan Paul, 1966) 171-72; Berger and Luckmann 183-84; Berger, Berger and Kellner 74. For a critique of the ideology of community see Ralf Dahrendorf, *Society and Democracy in Germany* (1965; London: Weidenfeld and Nicolson, 1968) 120-32.

[45] Kamenka and Tay 136-37; Berger and Luckmann 138-40.

[46] Compare Berger, *Facing Up To Modernity* 101-112; Berger, Berger and Kellner 29-105; Bauer and Matis 315-45.

[47] Berger, Berger and Kellner 74; see also 67, 76-77, 163-68, 174-75.

[48] Cf Bertrand Russell's comment that from ancient times to the present day, "philosophers have been divided into those who wished to tighten social bonds and those who wished to relax them," *History of Western Philosophy and its Connection with Political and Social Circumstances from the Earliest Times to the Present Day*, new ed. (London: George Allen & Unwin, 1961) 21.

[49] Dahrendorf 61, 130, 203-7.

[50] Berger, *The Social Reality of Religion* 34, 36-37. Berger and Luckmann 134-35.

[51] The point is made by Althusser, 122-23; see Diane Macdonell, *Theories of Discourse: An Introduction* (Oxford: Basil Blackwell, 1986) 77-78. Compare Ernest Barker, introduction, *Natural Law and the Theory of Society: 1500 to 1800*, by Otto Gierke, tr. Ernest Barker, vol. 1 (Cambridge: Cambridge UP, 1934) xviii-xxiv; Kronman 100, 105, 112, 138, 143-44; Max Weber, "Politics as a Vocation," *From Max Weber: Essays in Sociology*, tr. and ed. H. H. Gerth and C. Wright Mills (1948; London: Routledge & Kegan Paul, 1970) 82-83, 88-89, 93-94; Notker Hammerstein, "Universitäten — Territorialstaaten — Gelehrte Räte," *Die Rolle der Juristen bei der Entstehung des modernen Staates*, ed. Roman Schnur (Berlin: Duncker & Humblot, 1986) 687-90.

[52] See especially Emile Durkheim, *De la division du travail social: étude sur l'organisation des sociétés supérieures* (Paris: F. Alcan, 1893).

[53] Roger Cotterrell, *The Sociology of Law: An Introduction* (London: Butterworth, 1984) 206, 131.

1: Priests, Lawyers and Their Narratives

The priestly role and clerical narrative

THE THEORETICAL EXPERT of western European traditional society is the priest who speaks with the authority of God and the church, and claims to provide absolute, systematic knowledge about man and the cosmos. This knowledge is conclusive and final, needing no extension. The priest's methods are ontological and dogmatic, his mode of thought is that of conceptual realism in the medieval sense. His claim to know is at the same time a claim to rule, his teaching demands unconditional acceptance. Proclamation, not dialogue, characterises the age of faith. The priest tolerates no other experts beside himself, nor any rival faiths. All those within the group, from the greatest to the least, must submit to his spiritual authority, which obtains in all spheres of life, for the public world is nowhere segregated from the private.[1]

As religious expert the priest offers a cognitive scheme that both transcends and includes man. In this scheme, the cosmos is the creation of an all-powerful God, who has made its laws to be as they are. What happens, happens at his behest, and in order to fulfil his purposes. Events must therefore be understood teleologically, and not as the product of human motives and intentions. All earthly reality is an emanation from the sacred cosmos, the *ens realissimum*. Abstract form in heaven has its counterpart in concrete matter on earth: the macrocosm is reproduced in the microcosm. The hierarchy of archangels, angels and saints in heaven is represented by the hierarchy of the estates on earth. Here, pope and emperor rule in their respective spheres with divine authority, and the entire rank-order beneath them has the sanction of God.[2]

On the basis of this cognitive scheme, the priest acts as lawgiver, issuing authoritative commands about the conduct of life. Since the social order is willed by God, the individual has a duty to accept and maintain that order. He must not question his rank in society nor seek to better it. Instead he must fulfil the duties of his station; he can not live the good life outside the community. Hence morality is not a matter of obedience to abstract rules, but of attainment to particular virtues which together form a character-ideal appropriate to a specific position: the virtues of a knight differ from those of a peasant. Yet all character-ideals are alike in requiring self-denial and obedience in the interests of the social organism. In this respect it has particularly to be noticed that each individual member of traditional Christian society must fill his place in the church

as well as in the world. The Christian character-ideal, held to be most
clearly exemplified in the person of the saviour himself, obliges the believer to practise ascetic self-discipline. He must feel as few desires as
possible, or at any rate restrain and spiritualise his desires. In particular,
he must curb his sexual appetite, chastity ranking as one of the principal
Christian virtues.[3]

When successfully inculcated, the religious ethic ensures a "fit" between individual and traditional world. It shapes the individual for the
position he must occupy, and thus acts as an agency of social control.
Wayward individual desires are thus curbed, and the natural inclination
to freedom and rebellion is restrained. Since normative teaching alone
may not suffice to attain this end, the priest will use sanctions to ensure
conformity with his doctrine of virtue as acceptance, and vice as rejection, of one's place in society. The vicious man who, by seeking to ag-
grandise himself, necessarily disrupts the social order is warned to
expect the wrath of God: damnation awaits the sinner unless he repents
and submits to the discipline of the community.[4]

However social control is not the priest's only function, and indeed
control could scarcely be sustained over the long term, even with the
help of divine sanctions, if religion did not offer something positive to
the individual as well as to society. What is offered in the sacred sphere
parallels or perhaps reinforces the assumed benefits of the secular
sphere. Traditional society requires the individual to accept its authority,
no matter what restrictions that imposes on his personal freedom. But
acceptance of authority can bring an obvious psychological compensation, in a sense of security. The peasant, for example, must accept a life
of toil with none of the comforts enjoyed by his lord: conversely, the
lord risks his life warding off enemies who might otherwise conquer the
land and take away what little the peasant has. It is a similar security
which the priest offers his congregation as the supreme value.

Religious teaching presents the world as a wild "Forrest, full of un-
knowne dangers,"[5] a place of temptation where fallen man is beset by a
host of demons which, by playing on his conflicting desires, may conquer his soul and take away for ever what little he has. The priest offers
to rescue man from outward disappointments, inner anarchy, and eternal
damnation. Since all this unhappiness has its cause in man's lower self,
his natural inclinations, the remedy lies in disciplining those inclinations.
Religion cures souls — brings happiness — through the same strict rules
which construct traditional society. Obedience to God's laws, that is, acceptance of the character-ideals of religious ethics, brings order to the
psyche and peace to the soul.[6] But these character-ideals are shaped by
the community: to be virtuous is to take one's proper part in it. So religion cures by integration of the individual into the community, whether
that be secular society properly ordered under a Christian ruler; the con-

gregation of the local church; or the stricter community of a closed order. The priest is what has been called a "commitment therapist."[7] By calling individuals to membership of the traditional community, he frees them from insecurity and the burden of choice. They know that they commit no fault so long as they obey the law of the community. In Peter Berger's words, "self-denying surrender to society and its order" stills the "anguish of separate, individual subjectivity."[8] Salvation does not strictly belong in an afterlife: it is a psychological state in the here and now, the happiness that religion procures for the believer here on earth.[9] The priest not only controls individuals, but also releases them. Religion has a utopian as well as an ideological function.

In order to carry out this dual function, the priest must proclaim his view of the world and his rule of life to the public at large. This he characteristically does by word of mouth, in regular sermons delivered from the pulpit to the assembled congregation. The sermon may incorporate biblical exegesis, doctrinal exposition and moral exhortation. It may be entirely discursive in style. But in order to reach a mixed audience of old and young, educated and uneducated people, it may also rely to some extent on narrative. At least from the early Middle Ages priests have reinforced their teaching with brief stories, usually known as *exempla*.[10] The *exempla* have distinctive features which are determined by the function they perform, and contrast clearly with those of functional narratives from non-religious contexts. These features can be seen in the work of Abraham a Sancta Clara.

Abraham, whose secular name was Johann Ulrich Megerle, was born in 1644 and died in 1709. An Augustinian friar, he became *kaiserlicher Prediger* in Vienna in 1677. Later he held various other ecclesiastical offices, and made a reputation as a writer of popular devotional books. The text which follows appeared in a collection of homilies entitled *Judas der Erzschelm*, published in 1689.[11] The sermon to which it belongs is preached against swearing by the devil. But it is a woman's sexual misdemeanour which forms the background to Abraham's narrative of diabolical intervention. A Saxon girl who has promised to marry one man frivolously breaks her promise in order to take up with another. The *exemplum* is preceded by a paragraph of discursive text:

> Jene Gäst in dem Evangelio, nachdem sie eingeladen worden, seynd nit erschinen bey der Mahlzeit, sonder sich lassen mit underschidlichen Außreden vnd Vorwandt entschuldigen, ja, sagt einer, ich wär gern kommen, aber ich hab ein Kauff eingangen wegen eines Mayrhof, vnd dessenthalben hab ich dißmahl nit können auffwarten. Der andere wendete vor, daß er Ochsen vmb sein paares Geld hab eingehandlet. Der dritte war gar starck verhindert, dann er hab ein Weib genommen, seynd also dise drey eingeladene Gäst außgeblieben; Aber der Teuffel ist gar nit vonnöthen einzuladen, es braucht kein ruffens, er kombt vngeladener, vnd wann es die Güte GOttes zuliesse, so wäre di-

ser verdambte Geist augenblicklich, vnd urplötzlich auff den Fluch, vnd bethörten Wunsch da, vnd thät dich holen, vnd gib acht, damit nit der so offt beleydigte GOtt einmahl über dich elendes Geschöpff verhenge, wie es schon mehrmahlen geschehen ist.

In Sachsen hat eine junge vnd reiche Tochter einen wackeren, jedoch wenig begüten Jüngling die Ehe versprochen, der Jüngling bedanckt sich dessen bestermassen, sagt aber, weil er dises Geschlechts Wanckelmuth wol wuste, er glaub schier, sie werde ihr Wort nit halten, ich, sagte sie, ich soll einen anderen heyrathen? wann ich einen andern nimb, als dich, so holl mich der Teuffel am Hochzeit-Tag. Was geschicht? mittler Zeit hat ein anderer ein Ansuchung gethan, vnd dise für ein Braut begrüst, weil nun Aprill, vnd Weiber-Will, sich bald ändern, also hat sie disen, weil er bey stattlichen Mittlen, das Jawort ertheilt, wessenthalben sie der erste öffters ermahnt, sie soll sich ihres Versprechen, vnd harten Schwurs erinneren, vngeacht aber alles diß, muste der erste mit dem Korb befridiget seyn, vnd führte der andere die Braut heim, der Ehrentag wird gehalten, die Mahlzeit ist herrlich, die Befreunde seynd wolauff, die Gäst lustig, die Spilleuth fleissig, die Gemüther frölich, der Wein häuffig, aber die Braut, wegen deß nagenden Gewissens-Wurm, war etwas traurig, man sucht aber auff alle Weiß solche auffzumundtern, vnderdessen kommen zwey, dem Ansehen nach edle junge Herren, in das Zimmer, welche man höfflichst empfangen, auch so gar zu der Tafel gesetzt, haben es für ein sonders Glück auffgenommen, daß solche Gäst das Hauß würdigen mit ihrer Gegenwart. Nach der Tafel gieng der gewöhnliche Tantz an, man tragte einem auß disen Herren Ehr halber die Braut an, welche er mit aller *Cortesi* angenommen, vnd zweymahl gar wacker vnd hurtig herumb getantzt, nachmahls in Gegenwart der Eltern, Befreunden, Benachbarten, vnd anderen Gästen die Braut mit einem erschröcklichen heulen vnd Geschrey in die Lufft geführt, vnd auß aller Menschen Augen entzogen; als den anderen Tag mit höchstem Wehklagen von den Eltern die Braut gesucht wurde, seynd ihnen eben die gestrige zwey Herren begegnet, der Braut Kleyder vnd guldene Ketten eingehändiget, mit disen Worten, in solche Ding haben wir von dem Allerhöchsten keinen Gewalt gehabt, aber wol in die Braut, worüber sie verschwunden.

O wie offt wurde solches traurige *Spectacul* zu sehen seyn, wann nicht GOttes Barmhertzigkeit dem Sathan ein Zaum einlegte...

When those other guests in the gospel were invited to supper they did not come, but instead made various excuses. The first said he would have liked to come but had bought a farm, so could not accept that time. The second said that he had bought oxen for cash. The third was indeed prevented, for he had married a wife. So these invited guests stayed away. But there is no need to invite the devil, no need to call him, he comes uninvited, and if God in his goodness permitted it, this accursed spirit would suddenly appear on the instant every time you curse and every time you appeal to him in your delusion and would carry you off; take heed, therefore, lest the God you have offended visit on you, miserable creature that you are, what has happened to many another before you.

In Saxony a rich girl from a good family promised to marry a decent young man of modest means. The young man thanked her kindly but, knowing as he did the fickleness of the sex, he said he believed she would not keep her word. "I," said she, "am I to marry another? If I marry anyone else but you, may the devil take me on my wedding day." So what happens? After a while another man paid his court to her and asked her to be his bride. Now women's whims change like April weather, so she accepted his proposal, because he was a man of means. The first young man repeatedly warned her to remember her promise and her solemn oath, but in the end had to content himself with a refusal, while the second young man bore his bride home. The great day came, the wedding feast was splendid, the couple's relatives were in good heart, the guests were merry, the musicians played busily, spirits were high, wine flowed freely, but the bride was sorrowful, because her conscience nagged her, and everyone tried to cheer her as best they could. While they were doing so, there came into the room two men who looked like young nobles. They were politely received, seated at table even: it was counted a mark of special good fortune that such guests should favour the house with their presence. When the wedding feast was over and the dancing began, they did one of these young men the honour of asking him to take the floor with the bride. He accepted with all due courtesy and twice circled the room with her as merrily as you please; then as parents, relatives, neighbours and all the other guests looked on, he uttered a dreadful shriek, snatched the bride up into the air and disappeared with her, no-one knew whither. The next day, when the bride's parents were searching for her with loud lamentation, they met the two gentlemen of the previous day who gave them the bride's clothes and her gold chain, saying: "The lord gave us no power over these things, but over the bride he gave us power," whereupon they vanished.

Oh how often would we see such woeful sights, if God in his mercy did not rein Satan in...

Abraham's text consists of a story in a discursive context, that of the preacher addressing his congregation. His is an authoritative discourse, demanding assent to a cognitive proposition, and obedience to a norm that follows from that proposition. The story itself is adapted, by its structure, to reinforce the injunction contained in the discourse.

The paragraph of discursive writing that precedes the story of the bride begins with a reference to Jesus's parable of the guests who fail to attend a feast.[12] The guests themselves — who attend a wedding in St. Matthew's version, but supper in St. Luke's, from which Abraham derives his details — are not, strictly speaking, central to Abraham's purpose but simply provide a striking contrast to the devil, who supplies the burden of the discourse, and who comes unbidden, even to wedding-feasts. But by mentioning the parable Abraham situates what he is saying within a specific pedagogic context. He reminds the reader that Jesus told stories which required interpretation but which, when correctly interpreted, contained a rule of life. So at the outset the reader is alerted to the possibility of finding in stories not only general truths but consequent rules of action, and is indeed invited to look for both in the story Abraham tells.[13]

The second part of Abraham's opening paragraph contains his general theoretical proposition: namely that the devil is constantly seeking whom he may devour. This proposition is presented in terms suggested by the antithesis with the wedding guests. Unlike them, the devil refuses no invitation and, but for the divine mercy, would surely come to all who, without really desiring his presence, recklessly invoke him. Abraham records this as a matter of fact, writing with priestly authority, and expecting that his statement will be accepted as truth. The statement itself is a subordinate part of his present utterance, simply preparing the way for his real message, which appears in the most prominent position, at the close of the paragraph. That message, which follows from the previous generalisation about the devil, is the injunction: "gib acht" — "take heed." Thus the reader is warned lest he suffer the fate of many another; and Abraham the preacher, who has the cure of souls, clearly intends that his injunction be obeyed.

Then follows the story of the Saxon bride. The last clause of the introductory paragraph makes the transition between introduction and narrative proper. It identifies the bride's experience both as an instance of what the reader must avoid, and as an instance among many. This establishes the logical relationship between the opening discourse and the story and, consequently, the way in which the writer wants the story to be interpreted. Abraham's general proposition and the injunction in which it issues are logically superior to the story, which exists to reinforce them. Therefore the story is to be read as confirmation of what precedes it. The reader is to treat the story as an *exemplum*, and to discover in it the selfsame proposition and injunction which have already appeared in discursive form. Any other reading would run counter to the clear intention of the writer, who requires the reader not to form his own conclusions about the meaning of the story, but simply to accept the interpretation given him on the writer's authority. In case any reader should be tempted to deviate from this interpretation, Abraham appends to the finished story of the bride a further reflection designed to fix its meaning beyond all possible doubt. Here he describes the conclusion of the story as a "traurige *Spectacul*" — a "woeful sight" — only prevented from occurring more frequently by the mercy of God. The consequent imperative is not restated, but is easily inferred: the reader must not tempt God but must take heed, as he has been told before.

Thus far we know that the bride's story is exemplary — that its meaning is a rule of action — because the authoritative writer tells us so, in discourse external to the story itself. But Abraham's comments made in his own person in the preceding and following paragraphs are also reinforced by the internal commentary from the characters. The characters themselves concur in attributing to events the meaning given them by the authoritative writer. Thus when the bride promises to marry the man of means, her former fiancé warns her to remember her oath. By so doing he reminds the reader that to break oaths is to invite evil consequences. When the bride has finally been spirited away, the two "young nobles" who caused this to happen reappear to her parents and declare that almighty God gave them power over her. In so doing they reveal themselves as the diabolical agents to whom God consigns sinners. Hence the imperative meaning of the story is inscribed in the characters' own utterances. But neither internal nor external commentary is essential to the story's imperative force, which inheres in its very structure, itself derived from the religious world of thought.

That world is teleological: what happens in it happens in order to fulfil God's purpose. But his purpose is to reward virtue and punish vice. So the world displays an ethically compensatory causality. Beginnings can thus be judged by their endings: the outcome of events tells us what to think of them. When, as cleric, Abraham a Sancta Clara constructs a story in the course of his preaching, he does so in accordance with Christian teleology. Characters do good or evil as an unexplained matter of fact which has its ineluctable, ethically appropriate sequel. The characters have no control over intervening events, which relentlessly lead to a predictable end. In Abraham's story of the Saxon bride this narrative structure of "happening-and-consequence" is worked out in three carefully-organised sentences.

The first sentence tells of an engagement, stated as a fact: a young Saxon woman has agreed to marry a young man who is less well-off than she is. We are not told why the two agree to wed, nor whether their families approve, nor whether they made their decision precipitately or not. So, too, we do not really know why the girl is moved to utter the ill-considered oath which constitutes the second major event of the first sentence. The young man is said to doubt her fidelity, though apparently for no good reason — he refers only to the supposed inconstancy of womankind in general — and she doubtless desires to reassure him. But she could surely have used other means. Her motivation is minimal and the oath itself is presented as a simple matter of fact, an unexplained happening. It appears in a prominent position, at the end of the first sentence, and stands out all the more for being rendered in direct speech. Its form is conditional: "If I marry anyone but you, may the devil take me on my wedding day." This oath clearly marks the end of the beginning of this story. Various things have happened, culminating in the oath; and now we expect matters to work themselves out to some conclusion.

The question in the historic present, "Was geschicht?" — "So what happens?" — marks the beginning of the end. It also suggests that the sequel is not of the characters' making, but "happens to" them. And in fact the sequence of events that follows runs counter to what one would suppose their own wishes to be. The second sentence of the story tells how the girl, whose life is forfeit to the devil if she marries anyone but her first fiancé, meets and weds another man, though specifically reminded of the risk she thus runs. By way of motivation we are told that she wants a richer husband; but this can not explain why she receives a fresh proposal of marriage. It is as if things must fall out this way so that the condition contained in the oath may be fulfilled. With its fulfilment, the middle of the story is finished and the second sentence ends.

Now comes the third and last sentence which completes the tight, syllogistic structure of the whole narrative. The girl made a condition for her own death; the condition has been fulfilled; now she must die. Her death is the focal point of the story. From the swearing of the oath, everything bears on it: the first fiancé's warning; the girl's own melancholia on her wedding day; and the merriment of the guests, ironically contrasting with what is to come. Once the death has occurred, the narrator turns back to comment on its significance, which is damnation. Death and damnation are by nature final; but more than that, they exhaust the possibilities contained in the oath, and so give the story a formal wholeness and completeness. Events are not lost in the flux of time, but have rounded themselves into a pattern.

Such a pattern seems as though it were meant to be: in other words it contains the possibility of meaning. *Figur* is *Sinnfigur*.[14] If the oath were but one event in a random series, we would not know its meaning. By making it part of a pattern, the author of this text *tells* us the meaning. The oath begins a sequence of events that ends, finally and unequivocally, in death and damnation; and the oath is the only event in the sequence that can account for that end. So the oath is a happening that has death for its consequence. But to any reader versed in the Christian tradition, death followed by hell is the ultimate evil that can befall a human creature. Therefore the oath that accounts for such disaster inevitably appears in an equally negative light. It is judged by its consequence as a mortal sin, and its perpetrator as a sinner deserving damnation. The Saxon bride is the antithesis of the saint of legend. Instead of a character-ideal, she is a cautionary figure. The story says, unequivocally, "Do as she did and you will die; therefore take heed...." The imperative prefaced to the story is embedded in its narrative structure.

The closure of the story communicates knowledge to the intellect: the knowledge that a specific act is sinful. But the story depends for its effect not so much on the intellect as on the emotions. The tight structure creates a sense of impending doom, and the girl's disappearance happens with awful suddenness and chilling finality. For all its economy, the narrative appeals powerfully to the apprehensions engendered in its audience by Christian culture. The girl and her oath become associated with fear, and are thus made objects of aversion. Emotional reflexes are made to serve the purpose of moral training.

This text has a very distinct manner of working in the world. The narrator addresses his reader as a teacher addresses a pupil. The reader is encouraged, by the mode of address, to behave *as* a pupil, and to defer to the teacher's authority. The story embodies the conventional Christian world-picture and invites the reader to regulate his conduct in accordance with models from that picture. The reader who responds as invited accepts the preacher's discipline and so integrates himself into the community founded thereon. He thus enters into the happiness of membership in a community united by condemnation of sin, and partakes of the consolation of knowing himself to be one of God's people.

Abraham's text is but a minor instance of clerical storytelling. An apparently insignificant sample of pragmatic religious teaching, it might seem rather irrelevant to literature as usually understood. But it is to be regretted that few scholars have followed the lead of André Jolles in exploring the possible connections between simple pragmatic texts and complex literary genres.[15] Here something of a critical lacuna requires to be filled. For broad agreement exists on the possibility of identifying a great category of texts which has romance as its principal genre. This category has received a wide variety of names: Erich Auerbach calls it "figural," Northrop Frye "thematic," Angus Fletcher "allegorical," and Frank Kermode "mythical."[16] But there seems to be little recognition of the fact that under these headings scholars have been describing romance, and related genres such as fable, moral tale, and chivalric epic, in terms highly reminiscent of the pragmatic *exemplum*.

Thus romance, like the *exemplum*, is identified as a vehicle of ideas, as a philosophical not a historical form. Frye's "thematic" texts are those in which the idea or poetic thought is primary, rather than the story of characters in action.[17] Furthermore the starting point for romance is an external authority: that is, a story about the world which has apodictic value within a culture or sub-culture, and which is known from pre-existing texts, as the Christian view of the world, for instance, has been known from the New Testament and from commentaries and devotional books. Romance incorporates the "standard story" in allegorical form. In religious epochs, when there are "total and adequate explanations of things," romance or "myth" is the major fictional mode.[18] The standard story provides everything that is necessary to the interpretation of any romance which is based on it, just as general knowledge of Christian doctrine tells us how to understand particular parables.[19]

Romance achieves a high degree of verisimilitude merely from correspondence with the standard story. Everything that takes place in romance, and everything said in it, will appear entirely plausible to a reader who inhabits the world of thought created by that story. A tale of abduction by the devil would ring true enough for unsophisticated audiences of the early modern period. But romance may need a more complex, and therefore less easy, verisimilitude. If the standard story on which it depends competes with another story of a different kind, romance will have to make a gesture towards the latter if it is not to lack credibility for all those who are influenced by the rival story, and thus achieve a merely incomplete effect. Attempting to solve this problem, an eighteenth-century Christian apologist will overlay a plot of virtue triumphant with motives derived from the stereotypes of contemporary psychology. Yet what he gains by this more complex verisimilitude may be offset by a loss of ideological clarity.[20]

Further points of contact between romance and example appear when character and plot are considered. The theme of romance is a proposition drawn from the standard story: usually the proposition that some particular form of behaviour, belief or personality is desirable and its opposite undesirable. The theme is inscribed in both characters and plot. Thus the hero of romance is exemplary. He possesses all those qualities which are held by the standard story to be good; and he possesses them in perpetuity. His character is simple and unchanging.[21] Being unchanging, it has something iconographic about it: the hero is an image of the praiseworthy. Often he is surrounded by his attributes, like the saint of religious art.[22] The consistency of his motives means that, if he is regarded psychologically, he appears almost obsessive.[23] The hero's adversary is his antitype, the embodiment of all evil; like the hero he is simple and unchanging.

The plot of romance is of the "happening-and-consequence" type. Causation is supernatural or magical: the characters are propelled by a higher power toward their appropriate destiny. The good ones triumph because they are good; the wicked ones are defeated because they are wicked.[24] The actual shape of the plot will most commonly consist of a journey or quest. In what Frye considers the archetypal form of romance, the hero journeys to a distant land, does battle with an adversary, disappears, returns and is recognised as hero.[25] In a common variant the hero dies in his struggle and does not reappear but can still claim a spiritual or moral victory simply by being in the right.[26] Often enough, romance has no closure but, undetermined by anything more than the failure of authorial invention, merely replicates the exemplary conflict of good and evil in a structural parataxis as inevitabilistic as the syntactical parataxis of scripture.[27]

Sometimes the events of romance are accompanied by an authoritative narrative voice which relates them to the theme and ensures as far as possible that the reader does not miss the point.[28] But even when this is not the case, romance allows the reader very little freedom of reaction.[29] Its positive characters carry a strong emotional charge and invite an emotional response. The reader is encouraged not only to identify but to sympathise with them.[30] As Frye has said, romance does not purge but arouses and sustains feeling; this genre's effect is not cathartic but ecstatic.[31] The reader rises to new heights of emotion, he becomes elated, he experiences a sense of triumph. Romance is, in this respect, a species of the sublime.[32] And in raising spirits, it gives comfort and sustenance; it integrates its hearer or reader into the company of all who are capable of responding to it.

It is thus an instrument of control. By enlisting the reader's emotions on behalf of the positive values it embodies, it seeks to win him for those values and ensure that he acts in accordance with them.[33] If romance succeeds in winning the reader's assent to the story on which it is based, it helps to perpetuate that story and the community of those who believe in it. So romance is often regarded as a conservative force, an agent of stability.[34] This remains true in a sense even when romances are put to the apparently revolutionary task of replacing one form of authority by another, or of replacing a pluralist society by a new community.[35] In these cases they still work to bring individuals under a single, uniform rule.

The features of romance, as described by a wide range of literary scholars, are thus so like those of the *exemplum* that romance may be regarded as a more or less highly developed, literary equivalent of this simple form. Like the *exemplum*, though often in a much more complex and sophisticated fashion, romance provides a "clerical" and an "imperative" form of fiction adapted to proclaim an authoritative world-view and to enjoin action in conformity with that view.

The lawyer's role and legal narrative

As the chief theoretical expert of early modern society, the civil lawyer inhabits an entirely different world of thought from that of the cleric. The cleric, relying on divine authority, claims to possess absolute truth. The lawyer appeals to no supra-human source of knowledge and denies that absolute truth is attainable by the human intellect working in the empirical world. He regards existing knowledge not as complete and final but as capable of revision and extension. His methods are epistemological and critical, his assumptions nominalistic. He offers his conclusions as approximations to the truth; his judgments are cast in the form of probabilities rather than certainties; he asserts no authority over other men's minds. His preferred approach, institutionalised in the adversarial system of justice, is to submit his arguments to public scrutiny. He values dialogue as a safeguard against the dogmatisation of error.[36]

The civil lawyer's cognitive universe centres not on God and the social order ordained by him but on man as individual.[37] In the world of law the individual human being is an autonomous subject. The essential thing about him is that he possesses the power of will. He can act purposively: in other words he can represent to himself in advance both a goal he wishes to attain, and a method by which to attain it.[38] And in the legal cognitive universe purposive action is a principal determinant of events. Consequences arise not by divine fiat but because of the conscious will of man, helped or hindered by the powers of physical nature.[39] The universe is not a material representation of ideal form but must be understood in terms of mechanical cause and effect. Nor is it inherently harmonious. Individuals are free to pursue their own interests, and those interests differ. Hence the legal universe involves competition and conflict.[40] But conflict is not a cause of regret. The legal world of thought contains no primeval harmony which conflict negates. Conflict, when properly regulated, is a force for good. According to the legal world-view it is so regulated by two social contracts: one between government and citizens which establishes authority; and another between the citizens themselves, which establishes the rules by which the "game" of conflict will be played. The most fundamental of these is that all participants must enter the game on an equal footing. Thus regulated, conflict is deemed to be the "moving force of social development" and the guarantor of liberty: "by conflict alone the multitude and incompatibility of human interests and desires find adequate expression."[41]

The norms of individual conduct in the universe so conceived bear little resemblance to those operative in traditional society. There religion proposed absolutes of conduct for the whole man, required that everyone attain the character appropriate to his status in the community, and specified the virtues which that character was to embody. The lawyer as theoretical expert of modern society does not concern himself with the traditional virtues, which now recede into the private sphere. The law itself treats character purely as a circumstance of action. The imperative which governs the public sphere of modern society is that of participation. The individual must enter the competition which is modern society and abide by its rules. He must turn himself into a player of the game, setting aside all irrelevant aspects of himself such as his traditional rank and his private emotional life. The most prominent sphere of competition in modern society is commerce, where goods are bought and sold and men vie for the greatest profit. But the world of thought is also competitive, whether individuals are thought of as bringing their ideas to the stadium for prizes or to market for custom. In either case the locus of competition is conversation, and its rules are the rules of politeness, which require that participants treat each other as equals, respect each other's feelings and keep their own feelings under strict control.[42]

The ethic of participation according to man-made rules is a major means of social control in the modern world, inducing individuals to accept the conditions of that world and thus to sustain it. Without participation, there could be no competition, and without competition, so the ideology would have it, no progress. Traditional teaching of virtue was reinforced by the threat of punishment for vice. As the ethic of participation no longer employs the religious concepts of virtue and vice, sin and guilt, its sanctions are different. Refusal to participate is not a matter for punishment but for ridicule. The individual who flees the competitive society of his fellows risks the barbs of satire. Public censure directs itself not against the sinner but against the eccentric, and all non-participation — political, economic, social, sexual or intellectual — now ranks as eccentricity.[43]

In modern as in traditional society, norms and sanctions alone may not suffice to persuade individuals to fit themselves into the existing social structures. Competition, even according to the rules, is only a modified form of the war of all against all. For the individual any competition can mean uncertainty instead of freedom. The legal expert therefore presents men with a vision of earthly happiness to be obtained in modern society, and law tends to supply in the modern world the therapeutic function which was formerly fulfilled by religion. Instead of salvation it offers justice.[44] As Thurman W. Arnold points out, "the function of law is not so much to guide society, as to comfort it." Law acknowledges ideals unrealised in existing society. It "develops the structure of an elaborate dream-world where logic creates justice." Law holds out hope to all sorts and conditions of men. In the realm of the law, Arnold suggests, "the least favoured members of society are comforted by the fact that the poor are equal to the rich and the strong have no advantage over the weak. The more fortunately situated are reassured by the fact that the wise are treated better than the foolish, that careless people are punished for their mistakes." Thus law, like religion, is not merely ideological but utopian. It knits modern society together through its promise of reckoning with all aspirations, weighing all claims, and adjudicating according to "rational" or "scientific" principles.[45] Yet to remain credible, law must of course admit criticism. Though predictability is essential to law, it is nevertheless embedded in society and subject to social pressures. Changes may take place in society which make changes in law seem necessary or desirable. So lawyers not only judge in individual cases by existing norms, but also engage in criticism of those very norms, in the attempt to approximate ever more closely to the ideal of justice.[46]

In the everyday world of law, as in that of the church, narrative has an important part to play. Briefs for counsel, and pleas before the bench in court, are presented, in many legal systems, in story form. In German courts, narrative pleading became the norm about the middle of the seventeenth century.[47] The narrative of facts in the legal context is a distinctive form, known as the *casus*, which differs in crucial respects from the *exemplum*. The *exemplum* was an instance of a known rule; the *casus* is an instance in search of a rule.[48] The business of the adjudicator — counsel or judge — is to find the rule which covers the case.[49] This form of narrative constitutes not a command but a question to the reader, who is called upon to supply an answer. The answer, when given, may provoke further questions as to its acceptability according to possible higher criteria.[50]

A case published by J. H. Böhmer in his *Consultationes et Decisiones Iuris* illustrates the nature and function of narrative within the legal context.[51] Böhmer (1674-1749) was a member of the Halle law faculty and one of the last great exponents of the tradition of case law known as *usus modernus*, which dominated German legal life during the seventeenth and early eighteenth centuries.[52] The *Consultationes et Decisiones Iuris* is a *Consiliensammlung*, a collection of legal opinions given by Böhmer. The opinions are set out in a standard form: first, the conclusions to be drawn from the case are summarised in Latin; then the various items in the opinion are indexed; then follows the narrative of the facts in the case; and the whole concludes with questions put by the enquirer, the arguments which may be adduced pro and contra, and the answer given to each.[53] The opinion from which this extract is drawn dates from 1728.

> Als uns derselbe eine *facti speciem* nebst sechs Fragen zugeschicket, und...Hat *Christianus* sich mit Dorothea einer tugendhafften Person von 24. Jahren in ein Ehe-Verlöbnis eingelassen, welches nicht nur mit seiner leiblichen Mutter *consens*, und ihres *curatoris* Genehmhaltung vollenzogen, sondern auch durch einen auf die Vollziehung der Ehe abzielenden Brief-Wechsel bestätiget, und bey der *notification* ihrer Mutter Ablebens *renovi*ret worden, dabey auch sonst nichts übereiltes vorgegangen, vielmehr jeder, des andern Gemüths-Eigenschafften und Beschaffenheit derer Güter zu beurtheilen, hinlängliche Gelegenheit gehabt, und dahero er nach einiger Zeit zu der Dorothea, um nähere Verabredung der Ehe wegen mit ihr zu nehmen, eine Reise vorgenommen, auch nach gehaltener Unterredung von beyden Theilen beliebet worden, daß sich *Christianus* um eine Bedienung bewerben, Dorothea hingegen mit ihrer Baarschaft ihm an die Hand gehen, und inzwischen, weil ihre übrigen Güter meistentheils in *immobili*en bestünden, für deren Verkauff sorgen wollte, dabey denn jener derselben zum

Mahlschatz, weil sie nichts kostbares verlanget, sein gar zierlich einge-
faßtes und in einer künstlich ausgearbeiteten Elffenbeinernen Schachtel
verwahrtes *portrait* geschencket, wofür sie ihm ein ander *portrait* nach-
zuschicken versprochen. Ist hierauf *Christianus* sich um einen Dienst
zu bewerben davon gereiset, und hat derselbe sogleich gute Hoff-
nung dazu bekommen, auch endlich nach einiger Zeit die *function* erhalten, davon der Dorothea Nachricht gegeben, und zugleich wegen
Verkauffung derer *immobilien* Anfrage gethan, dieselbe ihm auch durch
einen guten Freund wegen ihrer Unpäßlichkeit dazu *gratuli*ren, und
versichern lassen, daß jemand ihr den gebauten Wein abkauffen wolte,
und ihm nachgehends das Geld, nebst dem was ihm *loco dotis consti-
tui*ret worden, zu Dienste stehen würde, nachgehends aber binnen etli-
chen Monathen kein Schreiben noch Geld von ihr eingelauffen, auch
Christiano zu Ohren gekommen, daß *Martinus* sich bey seinem Daseyn
schon heimlich daselbst aufgehalten, und darauf öffters bey ihr aus und
eingegangen, und mit ihr gespeiset, folglich den Verdacht gehabt, daß
er dieselbe, die Ehe mit ihm zu vollziehen, verleiten würde, und
deßfalls, ob sie ihm ungetreu werden wollte, an sie geschrieben, darauf
aber die Antwort erhalten, daß sie zwar nach ihrer [sic] Abreise ihren
Stand bey einer *profitabl*en Parthey ändern können, aber ihre Tage
nicht zu heurathen, bey sich beschlossen hätte, wo es nicht Gottes
Wille wäre, daß sie mit ihm die Ehe vollziehen könte, diesem ohngeachtet aber derselbe nachgehends erfahren müssen, daß sie durch
Vermittelung einer gewissen Matrone, *Martinum* zu heurathen, sich
habe verleiten lassen, und daß die Trauung im Hause auf zweymaliges
Aufgeboth wider die Kirchen-Ordnung und Sächsische Gewohnheit in
der Stille vollzogen worden, dem ohngeachtet *Christianus* seine Ver-
lobte zu unvermeidlichem Aergerniß der Kirchen und des *publici*, auch
ihrer Beschimpfung und Schaden, nicht rügen wollen, inmittelst es sich
sogleich zugetragen, daß *Martinus* kräncklich worden, und nach Ver-
lauff zweyer Jahre an der Wassersucht gestorben, und daher derselbe
nach Verfliessung eines Theils des Trauer-Jahres ihr abermals durch
einen guten Freund, was ihm vor Recht wegen der gehaltenen Ver-
lobung zustünde, vorstellen, und ob sie sich nicht nach Verfliessung
des Trauer-Jahres, die Ehe mit ihm zu vollziehen, bequemen wollte,
anfragen lassen, Dorothea aber sich dazu nicht verstehen wollen, sondern dawider, daß ihr vornehmlich ein Versprechen an ihren seeligen
Ehe-Herrn, als welcher von einer Zeit zur andern immer gesaget hätte,
er gönne sie keinem andern, im Wege stünde, eingewendet, zumal sie
auch in einem *testamento reciproco* bey Verlust einer Summe Geldes
von seiner Verlassenschaft noch mehr dazu *vinculi*ret worden, als
welches sie bey Verrückung ihres Witwen-Stuhls herausgeben müste,
bey welchem Vorhaben sie auch nach einer zweyten Abschickung
eines guten Freundes und dessen gethanen Vorstellung beständig be-
harret, er hingegen von seinem Rechte nicht abstehen, und dahero über
folgende Fragen belehret seyn will:....

According to the facts he submitted, together with six questions,... Christianus entered with Dorothea, a decent woman aged 24 years, into an engagement which was made not only with the consent of his own mother and the approval of her guardian, but was confirmed by an exchange of letters aiming to bring about the marriage, and was renewed along with her notification to him of her mother's death. Neither was there anything precipitate about this engagement in any other respect; on the contrary, each had had sufficient opportunity to judge of the other's temperament and financial position. So after a time he journeyed to Dorothea to make more detailed arrangements with her about the marriage and following some discussion both parties agreed that Christianus would apply for an appointment, that Dorothea would assist him with the cash at her disposal and that meanwhile, since most of her remaining resources consisted in real estate, she would arrange for their sale. At the same time, since she did not ask for a costly betrothal present, Christianus gave her an attractively framed portrait of himself, enclosed in an elaborately carved ivory box, in return for which she promised to send him a portrait. After this Christianus went away to apply for a position, was immediately given expectations of one, and in fact after a while received it. He informed Dorothea, and also enquired about the sale of the property. Dorothea congratulated him through a friend because she was unwell, and assured him that she had a purchaser for her vines and that the money as well as what had been promised him in lieu of a gift would soon be made available to him. But when after several months Christianus received no money and no word from Dorothea, and it came to his ears that Martinus had already been present in secret at Dorothea's when Christianus was there, and had subsequently visited her often and taken meals at her house, Christianus began to suspect that Martinus would suborn her into marrying him. So Christianus wrote to her asking whether she meant to break faith with him, but received the reply that although it was true that after he left she had had the opportunity to make an advantageous marriage, she had resolved never to wed unless it was God's will that she should wed him. But despite this Christianus later learned that through the intervention of a certain matron she had been suborned into marrying Martinus, and that, contrary to church regulations and Saxon custom, the wedding ceremony had taken place quietly in her private residence after the banns had been called twice. However Christianus did not wish to censure his fiancée, which would inevitably cause offence to church and public, and shame and damage to her. It then transpired that Martinus took sick and after two years died of dropsy. So when her year of mourning was partly over, Christianus reminded her, through a friend, of the rights he possessed by virtue of their betrothal, and enquired whether she would not consent to marry him after the expiry of the year of mourning. But Dorothea would not agree to this, and objected that she was prevented in particular by a promise she had made to her late husband, who had always said he would not permit her to marry another man. She was also bound to her refusal under the terms of a reciprocal testament on pain of losing a sum of money from his estate, which she would forfeit if she ceased to be a widow. She persisted in this attitude even after a second visit by a friend of Christianus, and the friend's representations. But Christianus does not wish to relinquish his rights, and therefore seeks clarification of the following questions...

The events in this story are much the same as those in Abraham's: a young woman promises to marry one man, breaks her promise and marries another. Yet the form of address to the reader, and the structure of the narrative are quite different. The fixed discursive formulae at the beginning ("According to the facts he submitted together with six questions") and at the end ("therefore seeks clarification of the following questions...") show that the enquirer, Christianus, has presented the narrative of events, presumably through a solicitor, to Böhmer for his opinion. The narrative is not offered by an authoritative speaker to a subordinate audience, as established truth, but by a subordinate member of the legal profession to a higher authority as an open question for decision. Now it is the original reader of the material, not the writer, who has the most powerful position. The drafting solicitor defers to the faculty professor.

The surrounding formulae indicate the interrogative nature of the story. Indeed the events themselves are structured in such a way that they demand to be read as a question. Their structure derives from the legal world of thought. Here human volition is the main motive force. And human wills, being independent, are wont to cross one another, just as they are wont to be crossed by natural forces. A man's good intentions may produce bad results, and his bad intentions good results. Human events do not form meaningful wholes but disjunctive and intrinsically meaningless sequences. So it is axiomatic in law that events must not be judged by their outcome, but by the motives and intentions that precede them.[54] The beginning of a story tells the lawyer what to think of the end. For the end is not the answer, as in the clerical *exemplum*, but a question to be answered, according to the evidence of the beginning. So it is the motives and intentions which precede each act that are emphasised in the telling, and not the conclusion. This causal structure may be described as "motive-and-action," in contrast to "happening-and-consequence."

The structure is visible in the first phase of the story, which deals with Christianus' and Dorothea's engagement. The narrator does not take the engagement for granted and pass on to its consequences. Instead, he notes all the attendant circumstances: the consent of Christianus' mother and Dorothea's guardian; the exchange of letters between Christianus and Dorothea; Dorothea's renewal of her promise at the time of her mother's death; Christianus' visit to Dorothea to plan their future; their reciprocal financial undertakings on that occasion; and their exchange of gifts. The term *engagement*, used at the start of the story, thus proves to have been a general, indeed a provisional, description for what is in fact a multiplicity of different events, each of which is open to different interpretations. The question for Böhmer as counsel, and for any other reader, is "What do these various events add up to?" Is it in fact correct to say that what has taken place amounts to an engagement? This implicit question is partly answered by the narrative itself. If Dorothea had been coerced by Christianus, or tricked by him, or otherwise taken advantage of, then in law the engagement would be simply null and void. But this is not the case. There was no indecent haste, and both parties were able to judge of one another's character and circumstances. Thus informed by the narrator, the reader may legitimately conclude that Christianus and Dorothea freely entered into a valid engagement: the use of the term *engagement* does appear to be justified by the facts of the case.

The circumstances of the engagement occupy the first sentence, and constitute the first phase, of the story. The second sentence begins a second phase. Now the matter at issue is Dorothea's marriage — not, as it happens, to Christianus but to someone else, Martinus. Once again the text sets out all the circumstances. The reader learns that Christianus obtained the appointment he had promised to seek, whereas Dorothea failed to fulfil her reciprocal obligation, entertained Martinus while assuring Christianus of her continuing intention to marry him, and eventually went through a wedding ceremony with Martinus, in the privacy of her own home. A final material circumstance is that Christianus raised no objection to this procedure, for fear of bringing Dorothea into disrepute. As with the original engagement, a multiplicity of factors creates and maintains this "marriage": there are acts of omission or commission by Dorothea, Martinus, Christianus himself, and the unnamed woman who influences Dorothea. These various agents have their several motives. So a question arises once more: are Dorothea and Martinus married, taking all the circumstances into account? And it is likewise possible to ask, over and beyond this, whether it is *right* that they should be married, considering all the circumstances.

So far as Christianus and Dorothea are concerned, this question would never come into the open, were it not for the death of Martinus. In Abraham's story death formed part of a pattern. Conceivably it might have done so in the lives of Christianus and Dorothea. Had Dorothea said, "If I marry anyone but Christianus, may I be a widow in two years," and had Martinus died accordingly, Dorothea's loss of her husband could have been represented as a consequence of her breach of promise, and the couple's story could have been treated as an *exemplum*. But the narrative of Christianus and Dorothea as presented up to this point is patternless. An engagement seems to have occurred, followed by what may be a valid marriage of one of the parties to a third person; now these ambiguous undertakings are followed by a death which happens, not as part of some design, but completely by chance, as appears from the manner of its introduction: "inmittelst es sich sogleich zugetragen." Martinus dies from dropsy, a physical cause outside his and the other characters' control. In short, far from terminating a sequence of events which can be perceived as a meaningful pattern, his death continues a sequence which has no pattern and hence no meaning.

This does not imply that his death is unimportant. On the contrary, it turns the question implicit in the story into an open conflict between the principal characters. Christianus considered Dorothea bound to marry him; she considered herself bound in marriage to Martinus. Now Martinus is dead, Christianus is prepared to assert the claim he formerly waived in order to spare Dorothea disgrace. He asks Dorothea to marry him in fulfilment of her earlier promise; she refuses on account of her undertakings to Martinus. At this point in the text, two voices are audible, each putting a case which conflicts with that of the other. So counsel is left with the question of whether Christianus has any legal or moral claim on Dorothea. The text is essentially interrogative.

Lest it seem that open-endedness and explicit conflict are essential to the interrogative effect, we should note that this would persist even if the story of Christianus and Dorothea were concluded on the death of one or other party, or on their permanent separation; and even if there were no open disagreement between the two of them. If, for instance, Christianus made no further approach to Dorothea after Martinus' death, and she remained a widow while he married another woman, the circumstances narrated would still leave a question in the mind of the reader. Given Dorothea's prior obligation to Christianus, and given Christianus' failure to assert his claim, it is unclear whether Dorothea's marriage to Martinus was valid, or whether she remained bound by her undertaking to Christianus. It is the inclusion of all the circumstances that gives the story its interrogative quality. Where more than one motive shapes an action, the action will be ambiguous and the reader will be obliged to weigh the motives in order to judge the action.

Böhmer's legal opinion on this case revealed his response, as a professional judicial reader, to the questions contained in the story. In order to decide the issue between Christianus and Dorothea, Böhmer went back to the beginning of the story, to see whether their engagement was a genuine one. From the repeated indications of the two parties' intention to marry, he concluded that both entered freely into the engagement which was therefore binding on both.[55] Next he considered the marriage of Dorothea and Martinus, which was contracted by Dorothea when she was legally bound to Christianus, but was not contested by Christianus at the time. Böhmer concluded that Christianus had forfeited the rights he acquired by his engagement. But Böhmer's consideration of the case did not stop there. Having made his legal judgment he proceeded to a moral one, which fell out differently. Legally, Dorothea had no case to answer, but Böhmer felt she must answer to God and her conscience both for her wilful breach of faith, and for her continued refusal to make amends to a man who allowed his legal claim to lapse out of consideration for herself. In short even when the text's particulars have been subsumed under the correct legal head, one still needs to consider whether the legal outcome is acceptable from the point of view of general ethics or social policy.

The *casus* of Christianus and Dorothea is a single instance of legal narrative in professional practice which may seem to have little to do with literary fictions. But, as with the *exemplum*, this appearance requires deeper scrutiny. Many of the writers who identify a category of thematic or mythical narratives centred on romance contrast that with a second category of "realist," "fictional" or "mimetic" narratives which includes the eighteenth and nineteenth-century novel in particular and which they usually identify by features typical of the *casus*.[56]

If romance was perceived and defined as a philosophic genre — a vehicle for ideas — then the novel is perceived as a relative of "pragmatic" history-writing as distinct from legend or chronicle.[57] The novel is held to resemble the kind of history which consists for the most part of "singular causal propositions" and which began to be written in modern Europe in the seventeenth century.[58] The standard story for the novel is the mechanical-causal world-view of modern history; verisimilitude in the novel consists in approximation to this world-view and some commentators have even suggested that the novel actually evolved out of history-writing.[59] But the view of the historian is also that of the lawyer, and in so far as the novelist approximates to history, he adopts the assumptions of the law courts: the common-sense approach to responsibility and liability which is indispensable if conflict is to be regulated and due compensation given.[60]

The novel therefore equates the self with the legal *persona*, the public self which is the *locus* of rights and duties. Frye describes the characters of writers like Henry Fielding and Jane Austen as "wearing their *personae* or social masks."[61] Like legal *personae*, such characters are treated as discrete individuals with coherent, permanent identity. In the terminology of structuralism and post-structuralism, they are the "centred subjects" of the "western humanist" tradition.[62] They possess such combinations of character-traits as are available within the legal-historical culture. The seventeenth-century natural law tradition provided a set of psychological stereotypes, which give backbone to fiction's "lifelike characters."[63] These characters are acted upon by physical circumstances and by other human agents, but subject to such constraints they are free, in other words capable of purposive action. They can choose their objectives, and devise means by which to attain them.[64] It follows that events in the novel are caused not by supernatural forces but very largely by human will. The novel's plot has the structure here called motive-and-action. The writing concentrates on the antecedents of actions: the thoughts and feelings of the principal agents, their moral and physical circumstances at the time, and the part played by others, whether helpers or opponents. The sequence of motives for action is as coherent as the sequence of the actions themselves. The whole is "well-motivated."[65]

But the motive-and-action plot does not of itself entail any particular shape. Precisely because its basic characteristic is coherence, it can progress in linear fashion from any beginning to any end, provided only that it hangs together. It is even claimed that the novel, like history, or like life itself, tends towards plotlessness.[66] But written history is in truth far from plotless;[67] — and so are many novels. Critics have noted that the conventions of typical novels, especially eighteenth-century novels, resemble those of comedy.[68] But this is to imply a further connection with the legal universe, for comedy often looks remarkably like a completed court case.[69] There is no better intuitive evidence of this than stage comedies, such as *Measure for Measure* and *Der zerbrochene Krug*, which incorporate some sort of trial. Comedy begins in a bad world ruled by deceivers; when their deceit is penetrated and dispelled a new, good order is established. So, too, through the action of the court, falsehood gives way to truth, an unjust world gives way to a just one: or such, at least, is the aim of the law. And even when comedy reaches its *dénouement* by way of a sudden twist in the plot which ruptures the threads of natural causation, and produces a happy ending that seems to belong to an ideal world rather than to quotidian reality,[70] there is perhaps an analogy with the function of justice as an ideal, sustaining the legal universe if never quite achieved in juridical actuality.

The novel's appeal to the reader is perceptibly different from that of romance. Instead of giving injunctions, the novel is said to ask questions. Susan Suleiman's contrast between the *roman à thèse* which "offers certainties," and the novel which proposes "not definitive answers but questions," identifies the essential characteristic of realist fiction.[71] It approaches its reader as pragmatic legal narratives approach counsel, judge or jury, by asking the reader to construe sets of "facts," to weigh allegations as to motive, and to pass judgment on human agents. Jolles noted a similarity between the weighing and measuring of motives required of the novel-reader, and the demands made by the *casus*, and particularly by Catholic casuistry.[72] Much more recently, Christopher Norris has commented: "What goes on in a court is rather like what happens in

novels. Where motive is in question, the process of arriving at a just or
equitable verdict may strike the observer as something like the experience of reading a complex 'psychological' novel."[73] The reader of such a
novel decides what the characters are actually like. Some of their personality traits are told him directly, as matters of fact; others he infers
from their actions, using available cultural stereotypes to guide him. As
he encounters new evidence he continually modifies his interpretation.[74]
Then he judges the characters he has constructed by the moral norms
that the narrative makes available. And as he does so, he finds that different norms produce different verdicts, and starts to choose which
norms best decide the case before him. In short, he engages in the com-
parative criticism of laws.[75]

Structuralists deny that narrative poses genuine ethico-legal questions
for the reader's consideration and fundamentally reject readings addressed to such questions. By contrast they hold that motives in realistic
fiction are merely a veneer of efficient causation superimposed on the
final causation which determines all plotting. In other words, the end of
the story as pure story determines what must happen in it, and the motives attributed to the characters are there merely to distract us from this
narrative teleology, by producing an effect of commonsense verisimilitude.[76] But fictional motivation may be deeper and more open than
structuralists imply. The analogy between narrating and pleading stands.
Legal adversaries agree on the same facts, but prosecuting counsel emphasises one set of possible motives in order to secure conviction, while
defence counsel emphasises another in order to secure acquittal. The
novelist, for his part, tells a story with a particular conclusion in mind,
but his conclusion does not of itself determine which motives are necessary to it. The novelist himself still has to choose how to motivate his
story, and does so with a certain indeterminacy and in the knowledge
that different choices of motivation will invite different responses from
his reader. It is therefore difficult to conclude that fictional motivation is
either superficial or arbitrary, and those critics who affirm the interrogative effect of realistic fiction would seem to have right on their side.[77]

Because such fiction invites the reader to weigh evidence and reach
decisions, in short, to think for himself, it is sometimes considered subversive of authority and hence liberating in an absolute sense.[78] But this
is to misapprehend its true nature. If it hails the reader as a judge, and
invites him to accept, as a case for judgment, a story about autonomous
individuals making free choices, it thereby integrates the reader into the
legal world of thought. It socialises him into the symbolic universe of the
law. The more he reads interrogative fiction and the more he answers its
questions on its own terms, the more he takes for granted that the world
is really like the legal world.[79] Yet the legal world-view is as much an
ideology as any other, and interrogative fiction questions the norms of

other symbolic universes, such as that of religion, only to replace them with its own. As Fredric Jameson has said, the novel combines a critical mission *vis à vis* other life worlds with the mission of producing a new life-world of its own, and affirming a new form of social solidarity.[80]

If romance appears to be a relative of the *exemplum*, the novel seems in many respects to be an equivalent in the literary sphere of the pragmatic *casus* form. Like the *casus* it may be considered a legal and an interrogative form of narrative. The contrasting models of the priest's role and imperative fiction on the one hand, and the lawyer's role and interrogative fiction on the other suggest the possibility of attempting to explicate the relationship of social groups and texts in seventeenth and eighteenth-century Germany during a social and cultural conflict occurring in three phases, in each of which "lawyerly" proponents of modernisation challenge "priestly" guardians of traditional community.[81] This conflict begins at the level of government, spreads to the institutions of higher learning, and is finally fought out in the forum of public opinion.

[1] See Peter L. Berger and Thomas Luckmann, *The Social Construction of Reality: A Treatise in the Sociology of Knowledge* (1966; Harmondsworth, England: Penguin Books, 1971) 138-39; Peter L. Berger, *The Social Reality of Religion* (1967; Harmondsworth, England: Penguin Books, 1973) 56-57, and *Facing Up To Modernity: Excursions in Society, Politics and Religion* (1977; Harmondsworth, England: Penguin Books, 1979) 235-36; Charles P. Loomis and John C. McKinney, introduction, *Community and Society (Gemeinschaft und Gesellschaft)*, by Ferdinand Tönnies, tr. and ed. Charles P. Loomis (1957; New York: Harper & Row, 1963) 28.

[2] Berger and Luckmann 111, 113-15, 127-30; Max Weber, "Religious Rejections of the World and their Directions," *From Max Weber: Essays in Sociology*, tr. and ed. H. H. Gerth and C. Wright Mills (1948; London: Routledge & Kegan Paul, 1970) 350, 355; V. H. H. Green, *Renaissance and Reformation: A Survey of European History between 1450 and 1660*, 2nd ed. (London: Edward Arnold, 1964) 13-16.

[3] Berger and Luckmann 111; Philip Rieff, *The Triumph of the Therapeutic: Uses of Faith After Freud* (1966; London: Chatto & Windus, 1966) 49, 59, 67-68; Alasdair MacIntyre, *After Virtue: A Study in Moral Theory* (London: Duckworth, 1981) 114-122, 123-136.

[4] Berger, *Social Reality* 44-46, 48-49; Erik H. Erikson, *Childhood and Society* (1950; Harmondsworth, England: Penguin Books, 1965) 269-70.

[5] The phrase is Lewis Bayly's, *The Practice of Pietie: Directing a Christian how to walke that he may please God*, 15th ed. ([London]: Printed for Iohn Hodgets, 1624) 275. See Max Weber, *The Protestant Ethic and the Spirit of Capitalism*, tr. Talcott Parsons (1930; London: Unwin, 1965) 223, note 25.

[6] See William James, *The Varieties of Religious Experience: A Study in Human Nature* (London: Longmans, Green, and Co., 1902) 166-75, 267-71, 507-511; Max Weber, "The Social Psychology of the World Religions," *From Max Weber* 270-73; Rieff 49-51.

[7] Rieff 71, 73, 76-77. See also Weber, "The Social Psychology of the World Religions" 282-83; Berger and Luckmann 177-78; John H. Marx, "The Ideological Construction of Post-Modern Identity Models in Contemporary Cultural Movements," *Identity and*

Authority: Explorations in the Theory of Society, ed. Roland Robertson and Burkart Holzner (Oxford: Basil Blackwell, 1980) 185-86.

[8] Berger, *Social Reality* 63-64. See also James 312-13.

[9] Weber, "The Social Psychology of the World Religions" 278; cf. James 504-7.

[10] See Franz Dornseiff, "Literarische Verwendungen der Fabel," *Vorträge der Bibliothek Warburg* 4 (1927): 207, 219-20; Hans Robert Jauss, *Ästhetische Erfahrung und literarische Hermeneutik*, vol. 1 (Munich: W. Fink, 1977) 150-51, 156, 160.

[11] See Pr. Abraham à S. Clara, Augustiner, "Judas der lasterhaffte Gesell wird durch Einrathung / Anspohrung / mit Hülff und Anlaß deß Sathans zu solcher Verrätherey / und gröster Untreu angetrieben," *Judas Der Ertz-Schelm*, part 2 (Salzburg: Melchior Haan, 1689) 164-65.

[12] Matt. 22, 1-10; Luke 14, 15-24.

[13] Compare Susan Rubin Suleiman, *Authoritarian Fictions: The Ideological Novel As a Literary Genre* (New York: Columbia UP, 1983) 28-45.

[14] For the concept of *Sinnfigur* see Ulrich Fülleborn, *Das dramatische Geschehen im Werk Franz Grillparzers: ein Beitrag zur Epochenbestimmung der deutschen Dichtung im 19. Jahrhundert* (Munich: W. Fink, 1966) 136, 165. Compare Otto Görner, *Vom Memorabile zur Schicksalstragödie*, Neue Forschung 12 (Berlin: Junker und Dünnhaupt, 1931) 10, 27-29, 31-32, 66.

[15] André Jolles, *Einfache Formen*, 2nd ed. (Halle/Saale: VEB M. Niemeyer, 1956).

[16] Northrop Frye, *Anatomy of Criticism: Four Essays* (Princeton: Princeton UP, 1957) 52; Erich Auerbach, *Mimesis: The Representation of Reality in Western Literature*, tr. Willard R. Trask (1946; Princeton: Princeton UP, 1968) 48-49, 73-76, 116, 119-20, 156-162, 555; Angus Fletcher, *Allegory: The Theory of a Symbolic Mode* (Ithaca: Cornell UP, 1964) 2-4 and passim; Frank Kermode, *The Sense of an Ending: Studies in the Theory of Fiction* (1967; Oxford: Oxford UP 1968) 39.

[17] Frye 52-53.

[18] Kermode 39; Fletcher 345.

[19] Jonathan Culler, *Structuralist Poetics: Structuralism, Linguistics and the Study of Literature* (London: Routledge & Kegan Paul, 1975) 230; Suleiman 10, 44, 84, 274; Fletcher 368.

[20] Suleiman 202-3.

[21] Auerbach 19-20, 116, 121, 136-37; Frye 187, 304; Fletcher 7, 22, 35, 222; Suleiman 56, 58, 69, 102, 106, 108, 113, 188.

[22] Jolles 26, 43; Auerbach 116; Fletcher 98, 110, 125.

[23] Frye 304-5; Fletcher 65, 67, 340-41.

[24] Fletcher 182, 187-88, 307; Suleiman 93, 98, 100.

[25] Frye 187-88, 192, 215. Compare Fletcher 151, 157-58.

[26] Suleiman 112.

[27] Fletcher 174-77; Suleiman 113.

[28] Suleiman 10, 69-72, 184-85.

[29] Fletcher 128, 192, 304-5, 323.

[30] Compare Suleiman 73, 147.

[31] Frye 66-67.

[32] Fletcher 244, 251, 267, 307, 314.

[33] Kenneth Burke, *Attitudes Towards History*, vol. 1 (New York: The New Republic, 1937) 44; Suleiman 37, 58, 146, 243.

[34] Fletcher 331-2; Kermode 39.

[35] Compare Jauss 138, 141-43, 233-34.

[36] See Hanns Ernst von Globig, *Versuch einer Theorie der Wahrscheinlichkeit zur Gründung des historischen und gerichtlichen Beweises* (Regensburg: Montag und Weiss, 1806) vi and part 1, section 1, par. 2, 3; section 2, par. 2; Loomis and McKinney, introduction, *Community and Society (Gemeinschaft und Gesellschaft)* by Ferdinand Tönnies 28; Ralf Dahrendorf, *Society and Democracy in Germany* (London: Weidenfeld and Nicolson, 1968) 147, 162-63, 210-11; Anthony T. Kronman, *Max Weber* (London: Edward Arnold, 1983) 23. I am aware that in attempting to sketch the "legal" view underlying modern society I risk minimising the differences which have been perceived to exist between different legal traditions. The ideology I describe is that of legal individualism, which centres on the legal person or legal subject, "the foundation, in a sense, of all legal ideology": see Roger Cotterrell, *The Sociology of Law: An Introduction* (London: Butterworth, 1984) 130-31.

[37] See Ernest Barker, introduction, *Natural Law and the Theory of Society: 1500-1800*, by Otto Gierke, tr. Ernest Barker, vol. 1 (Cambridge, England: Cambridge UP, 1934) 40, 78, 108; Eugene Kamenka and Alice Erh-Soon Tay, "Beyond Bourgeois Individualism: the Contemporary Crisis in Law and Legal Ideology," *Feudalism, Capitalism and Beyond*, ed. Eugene Kamenka and R. S. Neale (London: Edward Arnold, 1975) 129, 134, 137; Cotterrell 125-30; Leonhard Bauer and Herbert Matis, *Geburt der Neuzeit: vom Feudalsystem zur Marktgesellschaft* (Munich: Deutscher Taschenbuch Verlag, 1988) 467-73.

[38] Kronman 21, 24, 105, 141-44, 156, 165, 168-69.

[39] Compare Carl Hinrichs, ed., *Die Entstehung des Historismus*, by Friedrich Meinecke (Munich: R. Oldenbourg, 1959) 60, vol. 3 of *Werke*; Kronman 168; Cotterrell 126, 209; Bauer and Matis 208.

[40] Max Weber, "Religious Rejections of the World and their Directions," *From Max Weber* 355; Richard Taylor, "Causation," *The Encyclopedia of Philosophy*, ed. Paul Edwards, 1967; Hayden White, *Metahistory: The Historical Imagination in Nineteenth-Century Europe* (Baltimore: Johns Hopkins UP, 1973) 61-65; Bauer and Matis 321, 379-85.

[41] Dahrendorf 128, 147-48, 210-11.

[42] Ferdinand Tönnies, *Community and Society (Gemeinschaft und Gesellschaft)*, tr. and ed. Charles P. Loomis (1957; New York: Torchbooks-Harper & Row, 1963) 78; Dahrendorf 300-301, 318-19; Bauer and Matis 466-67; Manfred Riedel, "Gesellschaft, bürgerliche," *Geschichtliche Grundbegriffe: historisches Lexikon zur politisch-sozialen Sprache in Deutschland*, ed. Otto Brunner, Werner Conze and Reinhart Koselleck, vol. 2 (Stuttgart: Klett, 1975) 747-48.

[43] "Pedantism" and "melancholia" were regarded as forms of eccentricity and were often attacked in the seventeenth and eighteenth centuries: see for example Wilhelm Kühlmann, *Gelehrtenrepublik und Fürstenstaat: Entwicklung und Kritik des deutschen Späthumanismus in der Literatur des Barockzeitalters* (Tübingen: M. Niemeyer, 1982) and Hans-Jürgen Schings, *Melancholie und Aufklärung: Melancholiker und ihre Kritiker*

in Erfahrungsseelenkunde und Literatur des 18. Jahrhunderts (Stuttgart: J. B. Metzler, 1977).

[44] Thurman W. Arnold, "Law as symbolism," *Sociology of Law: Selected Readings*, ed. Vilhelm Aubert (Harmondsworth, England: Penguin Books, 1969) 46-47, 50; Bauer and Matis 472.

[45] Arnold 46-47, 50-51; Cotterrell 80, 108.

[46] Arnold 51; Harry C. Bredemeier, "Law as an integrative mechanism," *Sociology of Law*, ed. Aubert 60-61; Philip Selznick, "Sociology of Law," *The Encyclopedia of Philosophy*, ed. Paul Edwards, 1967; Cotterrell 180.

[47] See Benedict Carpzov, *Processus Juris in Foro Saxonico* (Jena: n.p., 1675) 181-82; Erich Döhring, *Geschichte der deutschen Rechtspflege seit 1500* (Berlin: Duncker & Humblot, 1953) 135-36, 201; G. Buchda, "Gerichtsverfahren," *Handwörterbuch zur deutschen Rechtsgeschichte (HRG)*, ed. Adalbert Erler and Ekkehard Kaufmann, vol. 1 (Berlin: E. Schmidt, 1971) col. 1558.

[48] Compare Jolles 144, 148.

[49] See "Beweis und Beweislast," *Handwörterbuch der Rechtswissenschaft*, ed. Fritz Stier-Somlo and Alexander Elster, vol. 1 (Berlin: W. de Gruyter, 1926) 735.

[50] Jolles 158-64, 227.

[51] My text is taken from "Responsum CXLVII" of Justus Henning Böhmer, *Consultationum et Decisionum Iuris*, 2nd ed., vol. 1 (Halle, 1756) 481-486.

[52] Döhring 296, 298-99, 315; Gertrud Schubart-Fikentscher, "Hallesche Spruchpraxis: Consiliensammlungen Hallescher Gelehrter aus dem Anfang des 18. Jahrhunderts," *Thomasiana* 3 (1960); G. Buchda, "Fallrecht," *HRG*, vol. 1.

[53] On the submission of cases to law faculties, and the standard form in which opinions were given, see Eckhardt Meyer-Krentler, "'Geschichtserzählungen': zur 'Poetik des Sachverhalts' im juristischen Schrifttum des 18. Jahrhunderts," *Erzählte Kriminalität: zur Typologie und Funktion von narrativen Darstellungen in Strafrechtspflege, Publizistik und Literatur zwischen 1770 und 1920: Vorträge zu einem interdisziplinären Kolloquium, Hamburg, 10.-12. April 1985*, ed. Jörg Schönert with Konstantin Imm und Joachim Linder, Studien und Texte zur Sozialgeschichte der Literatur Band 27 (Tübingen: M. Niemeyer, 1991).

[54] For a discussion of this principle in the context of seventeenth-century legal theory, see Sieghart von Köckritz, "Die Bedeutung des Willens für den Verbrechensbegriff Carpzovs in der Practica Nova Imperialis Saxonica Rerum Criminalium," diss., U of Bonn, 1955, 24, 30-31, 38-39. For the role of motive in legal narratives, see Meyer-Krentler 142-43; Thomas-Michael Seibert, "Erzählen als gesellschaftliche Konstruktion von Kriminalität," *Erzählte Kriminalität*, ed. Schönert 82; Ludger Hoffmann, "Vom Ereignis zum Fall: sprachliche Muster zur Darstellung und Überprüfung von Sachverhalten vor Gericht," *Erzählte Kriminalität*, ed. Schönert 99-100.

[55] Contemporary opinions contain many contrasting instances of "engagements" which were held to be void because one or other party had acted under duress, cf. Schubart-Fikentscher 39.

[56] The term "realist fiction" is used by Suleiman, *Authoritarian Fictions* 189. "Fictional" is used by Frye, *Anatomy* 33 and frequently; also by Kermode, *Sense of an Ending* 39. "Mimetic" is used by Fletcher, *Allegory* 150, 192.

[57] See Frye 306-307; Robert Scholes and Robert Kellogg, *The Nature of Narrative* (New York: Oxford UP, 1966) 211, 214, 229, 232. Compare Hayden White, *Tropics of Discourse: Essays in Cultural Criticism* (Baltimore: Johns Hopkins UP, 1978) 89, 98.

[58] Morton White, *Foundations of Historical Knowledge* (New York: Harper & Row, 1965) 222-23.

[59] See for example Georges May, "L'Histoire a-t-elle engendré le roman?: Aspects français de la question au seuil du siècle des lumières," *Revue d'Histoire Littéraire de la France* 55 (1955).

[60] Richard Taylor, "Causation," *The Encyclopedia of Philosophy*, vol. 2. The link between the *casus* and the aesthetics of the "realist" novel is made by Meyer-Krentler, "'Geschichtserzählungen'" 121, 135.

[61] Frye 305.

[62] Compare Fredric Jameson, *The Political Unconscious: Narrative as a Socially Symbolic Act* (1981; London: Methuen, 1983) 153-54; Catherine Belsey, *Critical Practice* (London: Methuen, 1980) 67, 73-74; Lennard J. Davis, *Resisting Novels: Ideology and Fiction* (New York: Methuen, 1987) 102-117.

[63] Frye 171-72. On natural law psychology, compare Eberhard Kessel, ed., *Zur Theorie und Philosophie der Geschichte*, by Friedrich Meinecke (Stuttgart: K. F. Koehler, 1959) 222, 225, 227, vol. 4 of *Werke*.

[64] Fletcher 66; Belsey 67.

[65] On the causal chain of motive and action, see for example R. S. Crane, "The Concept of Plot," *The Theory of the Novel*, ed. Philip Stevick (New York: Free Press; London: Collier Macmillan, 1967) 141-42; Norman Friedman, "Forms of the Plot," *The Theory of the Novel*, ed. Stevick 146, 155.

[66] Scholes and Kellogg 13, 232.

[67] See Hayden White, *Tropics*, 82, 84, 88, 98, 123; and *Metahistory* x, 7-11, 29.

[68] Frye 304; Scholes and Kellogg 234.

[69] See Frye 166.

[70] Frye 75, 170; Jameson 154.

[71] Suleiman 242-43.

[72] Jolles 157-64, 226-27.

[73] Christopher Norris, *The Contest of Faculties: Philosophy and Theory After Deconstruction* (London: Methuen, 1985) 167.

[74] Compare Culler 225-29, 230-38.

[75] Jolles 148; Wolfgang Iser, "The Reality of Fiction: A Functionalist Approach to Literature," *New Literary History* 7 (1975): 14.

[76] See for example Gérard Genette, *Figures II* (Paris: Éditions du Seuil, 1969) 79-99. Compare Culler 230.

[77] For the view that the "realistic" novel does invite the reader to assign responsibilities, see for example Jameson 165; Suleiman 59. For a discussion of "Inference, Causality, and the Levels of Narrative," see Roy Jay Nelson, *Causality and Narrative in French Fiction from Zola to Robbe-Grillet* (Columbus: Ohio State UP, 1990) 80-99.

[78] Kermode argues (*Sense of an Ending* 39) that "fictions" as opposed to "myths" are "agents of change." Iser (23, 25-29) suggests that novels cast doubt on dominant norms.

[79] cf. Cotterrell 130-31, 206.

[80] Jameson 152; and see also 291-92. The life-world for which the novel programmes its readers is, according to Jameson and other Marxist critics, that of bourgeois capitalism: see also Belsey 67-69; Davis 102-161.

[81] cf. Cotterrell 306 on "law's antipathy to community."

2: The First Phase of Modernisation: Princely Courts and Court Romance

Princes, lawyers, *Amadis* and *Argenis*

IN THE MIDDLE Ages, the Holy Roman Empire was a traditional society with a fixed order of ranks. This society was structured vertically by the feudal obligations of master to man and man to master, and horizontally by the corporate bonds between the members of the various estates. At both imperial and territorial level the monarch shared political power with the estates, by far the most powerful of which was the landed nobility. In the imperial diet the electors and the remaining princes could easily outvote prelates, counts and cities. In the territories the noble estate usually outweighed cities and peasantry in the diet and staffed the privy council as of right. The Catholic clergy provided the medieval social order with its theoretical legitimation: Thomism, the period's most elaborate doctrinal statement, represented feudal relationships as a divinely-appointed reflection of the heavenly hierarchy.[1]

By the middle of the sixteenth century, the Empire's religious unity had been shattered: in 1555, the Peace of Augsburg gave princes the right to introduce Lutheranism into their territories. The church now found a new position in the state: Lutheran territorial churches came under the princes' control and the clergy were no longer represented in the territorial diets.[2] But the social order of the newly Lutheran parts of the Empire remained largely unchanged. The Lutheran princes still acknowledged the emperor as feudal overlord and continued to participate, with their Catholic peers in the imperial diet, in the government of the Empire according to its existing constitution. In their own principalities they continued to govern with the assistance of the local estates meeting in the territorial diet.[3] And this traditional order continued to receive its traditional religious justification, but from Lutheran instead of Catholic priests. For Lutheranism remained close to Catholicism not only in its theology, ecclesiastical organisation and observances but also in its social teaching. Adopted by princes and estates of the old order, it endorsed that old order: the overlordship of the emperor, paternal rule by the princes in the interests of their people, and participation of the estates in government.[4]

Real social and political change only began in Germany after the Lutheran reformation had been completed, and threatened the Lutheran world as much as the Catholic. Change came from the princely order itself. The somewhat uneasy position of the major princes in the Empire had been a cause of conflict since the Middle Ages. The emperor had never been able to control the ambitions of his greatest vassals, as the monarchy had gradually done in France and England; but neither had those vassals been able to turn the Empire into an aristocratic federation.[5] In the latter part of the sixteenth and the early seventeenth century, some Protestant princes now made determined efforts to remodel their role, by making themselves more independent both of the emperor above them and of the territorial estates below. These princely innovators included elector Friedrich III of the Palatinate; prince Christian I of Anhalt-Bernburg, governor of the Upper Palatinate under electors Friedrich IV and Friedrich V; landgraves Wilhelm IV and Moritz of Hessen; duke Friedrich I of Württemberg; and duke Heinrich Julius of Brunswick-Wolfenbüttel.[6]

These men received support and encouragement from certain commoner scholars who tended to be lawyers and historians rather than theologians or representatives of theology's ancillary disciplines, philosophy and *literae humaniores*. Commoner lawyers first came to prominence early in the sixteenth century because the Lutheran princes needed technical assistance in setting up the new territorial churches. When that was done, the lawyers took on a more general role, whether as advisers to progressive princes or as advocates of social and political change in the territories of conservative or reactionary rulers.[7] This latter course was adopted, for example, by the Palatine jurists Loefenius and Lingelsheim during the reign of the traditionalist elector Friedrich IV, some years before the reforming Christian of Anhalt became governor of the Upper Palatinate in 1595.[8]

Most commoner lawyers who entered princely service in the sixteenth century were sons of well-placed city families with a history of membership in merchant and craft guilds.[9] But these men cannot simply be interpreted as representatives of a rising middle class since, as opponents of Marx and Weber have convincingly argued, the sixteenth century witnessed a decline rather than a rise in the relative influence of towns and merchants.[10] The new men did not attempt to act as spokesmen of larger urban and commercial interests. They did not even wish to identify with the larger *Lehrstand*, the body of professionals and intellectuals which in the Middle Ages had included both clergy and teachers in school and university regardless of faculty or specialism.[11] Then of course all scholars had been clerics. But now lawyers and historians drew a distinction between themselves as secular scholars or *Gelehrte* and the clergy as *Geistliche*.[12] *Gelehrte* had every reason to hasten the passing of traditional society, in which military nobles exercised political power, while the clergy claimed a monopoly of knowledge, leaving secular scholarship, such as it was, to marginal figures whose lack of an established function forced them to compete for influence with these two entrenched élites. As *Gelehrte* increased in numbers they asserted their own claims: they were neither mere practitioners — like the purely military nobility — nor mere theoreticians — like the clergy — but a combination of the two: *politici*, practical statesmen with a thorough training in law and historical wisdom.[13]

Such wisdom encouraged them to assist in dismantling, so far as they could, the traditional order which had existed at the end of the Middle Ages and was still largely in place at the time of the Peace of Augsburg. The Palatinate in particular pursued a policy of independence from the emperor, and from the institutions of the Empire, which precipitated the Thirty Years' War, and eventually led by way of foreign intervention to the Peace of Westphalia. This granted such freedoms to the princes that the structures of the Empire largely ceased to have significance except for the smallest and weakest member-states which were incapable of independent existence.[14] After 1648 the term *Reich* became synonymous with the patchwork of free cities and small ecclesiastical and secular principalities in southern and western Germany; the larger principalities went their own way.[15]

Meanwhile princes and lawyers attacked traditional institutions and traditional social groups within the individual territories. The greatest counterweight to princely power was the noble estate, which had corporate representation in privy councils and diets, and the power to raise taxes. In Württemberg, where the knights had ceased to be subjects of the duke, the burgher notables formed the strongest estate. Around 1600 bitter struggles occurred in Saxony, the Palatinate, Württemberg, Hessen and Brunswick-Wolfenbüttel, as princes and lawyers, or lawyers on their own, tried to diminish estate power by replacing traditional privy councils with personal rule and abolishing or circumventing the territorial diets. These struggles did not end estate power: in Saxony in 1592 the noble estate beat off the threat altogether and elsewhere, in Brunswick-Wolfenbüttel for instance, a compromise was reached. At this stage, princes and lawyers did not so much establish an ascendancy over the traditional estates as signify an intention to do so.[16]

Innovating princes and lawyers also came into conflict with the Lutheran clergy who, as Protestant successors to the medieval Catholic intellectual élite, naturally resisted attempts to dismantle a traditional order which still gave them their *raison d'être*, and made common cause with the noble estate or the burgher notables in their struggles against monarchism. This led to draconian measures by some princes against the Lutheran clergy of their territorial churches: duke Friedrich I of Württemberg restricted their freedom of speech; landgrave Moritz of Hessen removed them from office.[17]

At the same time, the princely camp made a more subtle attack on the traditional *Lehrstand* as a whole: clerics, philosophers and classical philologists. While promoting their own claims as a new political-intellectual élite, lawyer-historians also denigrated their traditional rivals. Around 1600 lawyers and clergy, the two principal groups of educated commoners, began a lengthy struggle for the exclusive privilege to function in Germany as accredited experts and constructors of symbolic universes. The lawyers rapidly adopted the argument that the members of the old *Lehrstand*, formerly both theoretical experts and providers of practical political advice to emperor and princes, were but schoolmen out of touch with the practical world of affairs: idealistic inventors of irrelevant moral and metaphysical systems, and antiquated guardians of a useless rhetorical and literary culture. Satire was added to argument. Clerics, philosophers and *poetae-philologi* were portrayed as eccentrics incapable of integration into contemporary society, and *pedant* began its long career as a term of abuse hurled at commoner clerics by commoner lawyers.[18]

The princes profited from these attacks on traditional structures and traditional groups. Men like Friedrich III of the Palatinate, Moritz of Hessen and Heinrich Julius of Brunswick-Wolfenbüttel concentrated power in central institutions, attempted to introduce a uniform legal system for the whole of their territory, created new governmental and administrative agencies, staffed to a significant extent by commoner lawyers, founded new schools and universities which taught the skills needed in the secular state, and recruited militias from among their own subjects.[19] As the princes expanded their activities, princely courts grew in size and importance. The court, which had been little more than the household of the princely family, now became the principal centre of political, social and cultural life for the territory, and the visible symbol of growing princely power.[20] The movement towards royal ceremonial and display, which reached its European peak in the Versailles of Louis XIV, was beginning in Germany by 1600. One symptom of this was the new building done at the time: the *Friedrichsbau* and the *Englische Bau* at the Heidelberg palace; the *Neue Bau* in Stuttgart; and duke Heinrich Julius' palace at Gröningen.

In short, between 1550 and 1650 the princes and their advisers and supporters sought to shift German society from a traditional to a modern order. Since this shift urgently demanded some sort of legitimation, princes, lawyers and historians came forward as theoretical experts, formulating a new legal world-view with which they intended to reshape the consciousness of their contemporaries.

Calvin was one of the guiding spirits of this enterprise. Of those princes who departed furthest from traditional forms of government, Friedrich III and Friedrich V of the Palatinate, Christian I of Anhalt and

Moritz of Hessen were Calvinists, while Friedrich I of Württemberg and Heinrich Julius of Brunswick-Wolfenbüttel were Calvinist sympathisers. Lawyer-historians in princely governments around 1600 were often professing Calvinists.[21] For Calvin himself had been a lawyer and a humanist, and many of his later sixteenth and early seventeenth-century German followers looked to him not so much for ammunition in the confessional struggle with Lutheranism and Counter-Reformation as for guidance in matters of secular government.[22] Germans who read Calvin in this practical-political way also readily absorbed the ideas of Jean Bodin and the "third party" in the French religious disputes, the so-called *politiques*. Bodin's secular theory of history and his argument (from Aristotle rather than the natural law tradition) for the separation of politics and religion influenced the Strasbourg historian Matthias Bernegger and the teaching of Henning Arnisaeus at the law faculty in Helmstedt, the university founded in 1576 by duke Julius I of Brunswick-Wolfenbüttel.[23] Bodin's historical and political thought also inspired a group of late humanist scholars in the Netherlands, foremost among whom was Justus Lipsius: neo-stoic, editor of Tacitus, Tacitean stylist, and theorist of monarchical absolutism. Lipsius' work was widely read in Germany and attracted many German scholars to study in the Netherlands.[24]

Drawing variously on these sources, German lawyer-historians abandoned teleology and sought to explain history as a product of earthly forces operating according to the laws of cause and effect. Human affairs now became a matter for human management, with goals set and procedures chosen by the light of human reason. History itself was to teach both ends and means. The historian ceased to be a hagiographer, as many a medieval chronicler had been. Taking his cue from ancient historians such as Tacitus, he was to weigh evidence, reconstruct the past using his general knowledge of human psychology, and arrive at probabilistic judgments about the participants' responsibility for them. In other words, he was to treat historical events as legal cases and the participants in those events as equal before the law. From his verdicts he could derive general precepts for the practical conduct of affairs: this and this form of action brings success; this and this form brings failure in any given task. In schools and universities in the Palatinate, Hessen, or Brunswick-Wolfenbüttel, historians presented students of government and administration with cases from the ancient historians, to help them draw their own practical conclusions. The younger generation began to be inculcated with the modern, this-worldly, causal-mechanical view of experience.[25]

The supreme lesson which the lawyer-historians drew from history, in France, Holland and Germany, was that the sectional and confessional divisions of traditional society caused conflict and threatened anarchy. The solution to this problem was the development of a strong sovereign state as guarantor of peace and order. Secular authority, backed by force, was to provide a legal and political structure in which legitimate economic, social and cultural activities might be peaceably pursued by groups or individuals. German legal theorists held that such a state could best be embodied in monarchy: kingship would optimise the transition from fragmented traditional forms to more centralised, modern ones. But strong monarchical government was to be introduced only at the territorial level. The emperor, stripped of the trappings of sacral kingship, was to survive into a more modern world only as titular head of a loose federation of sovereign states.[26]

The idea of a non-sectional, competitive society accompanied that of the modern state, though the former was even less of a reality than the latter in the years around 1600. The new "legal experts" called on the prince not only to head a new kind of state but to involve all sections of society in common activity for the good of that state. Prince Friedrich Ulrich of Brunswick-Wolfenbüttel accepted the call in a textbook discussion published by his history professor at the Tübingen *Collegium illustre*, Thomas Lansius.[27] The context was highly significant. Any such programme required the local nobles, the most powerful social group in the territories, to integrate themselves into the monarchic state. The nobles were independently-minded military men, many of whom regarded a military training as the only one appropriate to their station, and despised any of their number who studied in the traditional universities.[28] The princes therefore gave them new educational opportunities. A variety of new universities, noble academies and schools such as the *Collegium illustre* began to offer nobles modern courses in statecraft and administration, to encourage and enable them to take their place in government alongside commoner graduates.[29]

This opened the way for closer association between nobles and educated commoners. Elsewhere in Europe, the development of the monarchic state with its recruitment of all the talents contributed to the levelling of traditional social distinctions.[30] The rigid status society, where each group had its own decorum, began to move, slowly and in part, towards a more open society with a single code of politeness for all participants. The principal *locus* of this development was the princely court, the centre for *conversatio* in both its senses. At court nobility, royal household, governmental and administrative élites and all men of significance and talent in the realm at large were thrown together. And at court, therefore, there could be talk, the expression of a mixed society as well as the means of sustaining it. The Italian Renaissance courts were the first to produce a common cultural ideal, that blend of knightly and humanist manners which was most elegantly exemplified in the dialogues of Baldassare Castiglione's *Libro del Cortegiano*, and which was later systematised in courtesy manuals like Stefano Guazzo's *La civil con-*

versazione.[31] This ideal in turn contributed to the evolution in French court society of the concept of the *honnête homme*. German Protestant courts of the early seventeenth century were modest by European standards, and many have left scant evidence of association across barriers of rank, but some did strive to emulate foreign models in this respect. Prince Ludwig I of Anhalt-Köthen, who spent long periods in Italy from 1597 to 1602, reorganised his own court on Italian lines, and succeeded so well in creating a polite society in Köthen that the Tuscan ambassador professed himself perfectly at home there.[32]

In 1617 Ludwig became the founding president of the *Fruchtbringende Gesellschaft*, an institution which extended its influence far beyond the boundaries of his own small court. The new society's declared purpose was to promote the German tongue and encourage Christian virtue. Its membership included reigning princes, nobles, and commoners, most of them broadly sympathetic to the politics of territories like the Palatinate and Hessen. Until 1641, the commoner members of the *Fruchtbringende Gesellschaft* were all secular scholars holding court offices. Ludwig feared clerical dogmatism, and admitted only two clergymen while he was president. Precedence in the society was determined solely by date of entry. On admission, each member received a descriptive sobriquet by which he became known for society purposes. These *Gesellschaftsnamen* were intended to foster "confidence, equality and friendship" across barriers of rank. To the same end, the society's rules required members to observe the courtly code, in particular its injunction to cheerfulness and good humour, in dealings with each other.[33] As Ludwig made clear, noble pride of caste was unwelcome in the society. In 1648, in response to a suggestion that membership be confined to the nobility, he insisted that "knightly exploits alone" were not its aim.[34] Though the *Fruchtbringende Gesellschaft* may not have entirely succeeded in effacing the social distinctions that obtained in the outside world, it did create an environment in which nobles and commoners could associate in relative freedom.

The attempt by princes and lawyers to remodel traditional society had significant consequences for German literature. The reformers, who had a high opinion of the power of fictional narrative to keep social systems in being as well as to change them, first attacked the literary culture of their chief adversary, the traditional nobility, and especially a late product of this culture, the Amadis romance. The text of *Amadis* originated in Spain, increased in size as it passed through Italy and France, and appeared in German in twenty-four books between the years 1569 and 1595, under the title *Amadis ausz Frankreich*.[35] The story, profusely illustrated with woodcuts, introduces its reader to a marvellous world of knights and ladies, jousts and battles, giants, dragons and enchantments. The principal personages are Amadis and his lineal descendants, whose adventures involve a host of other figures: 248 characters appear in the first five books alone. The heroes fight with their peers, according to the rules of chivalry, or with monsters that recognise no rules; they fight on land, at sea and even in the air.[36]

Amadis himself is a true hero of romance, inferior to the gods, but surpassing in power even the mightiest of mortals: for him "the ordinary laws of nature" are, at the very least, "slightly suspended."[37] His origin is mysterious: a king's illegitimate son, entrusted to the waves in earliest infancy, he is washed ashore in a foreign land with only a talisman to identify him. When he reaches adolescence, the enchantress Urganda gives her patronage to him, so identifying him as the agent of a higher power. But he is not simply a magical figure, for he embodies the knightly virtues. Brave and courteous, loyal to his friends, respectful of his peers, faithful in love, and swift to succour the oppressed, he always and only acts from the desire for knightly honour. Hence his behaviour manifests the asocial, almost feral quality of many heroes of romance, who pursue their goal with a singlemindedness amounting to obsession. The reader is never invited to ask whether Amadis's motives are pure, or his actions right or indeed appropriate or reasonable in any particular situation; for he knows but one motive and one code and his conduct is never ambiguous.[38]

The plot of *Amadis* therefore consists in the ritualistic repetition of a single element: the knightly adventure in which the hero proves himself constant in love, and unequalled in feats of arms. As Erich Auerbach remarked, the "world of knightly proving...contains a practically uninterrupted series of adventures;.... Nothing is found in it which is not either accessory or preparatory to an adventure."[39] Every conflict Amadis enters is shaped by the dualism of good and evil; and every time, good wins. Events are governed "from above" to produce this happy outcome — usually by deliberate violation of natural probabilities. Amadis' longing to prove himself can never be satisfied, for no matter how great his triumphs, there is always still more honour to be had. So the text multiplies his adventures, linking them paratactically in a loose chronological sequence which has no necessary limit. Amadis eventually dies, but the knightly quest then continues through six generations of his descendants. Nothing but the eventual exhaustion of the *Amadis*-writers prevents it continuing indefinitely.[40]

The episode of the Irish war, which appears in the first book of the romance, illustrates this fictional parataxis. Here, despite overwhelming odds, Amadis conquers the usurping Irish king Abies.[41] Though, as is often the case, Amadis is taking part in a complex military operation involving multitudes of fighting men, he acts as an individual, pursuing a personal quest rather than common policy. And the rhetoric of the text is designed to shed lustre on him as individual, both by praising him, and by heaping dispraise on all who dare to oppose him. Abies, king of Ireland, and his allies Daganil and Gallin besiege Perion, the rightful king of France, who has recently dubbed Amadis knight. Daganil and Gallin plan to lure Perion into a trap laid by Abies. In the opening skirmish, Amadis unhorses Gallin, then singlehandedly hacks his way through Daganil's forces, killing and maiming many men. Surrounded, Amadis is rescued in time to disarm Daganil, who is slain by Perion. When the French nevertheless fall into the ambush, Amadis holds back the enemy and covers their retreat.

His greatest glory comes when, in order to decide the dispute between Perion and Abies, Amadis engages, at his own suggestion, in single combat with the Irish king. In order to shed all the greater lustre on Amadis, Abies is represented as a formidable adversary, a veritable giant of a man and a greathearted combatant. But there is no doubt as to his moral status: though beloved of his own people he has led them into an aggressive war, and as a fighter in an unjust cause, he rides to his encounter with Amadis on a black charger. The two fall on each other with a mercilessness which strikes terror into all the assembled spectators, and are soon unhorsed. The struggle continues on foot, with shattering blows being exchanged in the fierce heat of the day. When both are forced to pause, Abies admits that Amadis is the most valiant adversary he has ever encountered. Amadis, for his part, takes the opportunity to reproach Abies for the wanton destruction that he in his wickedness has brought on the people of France. When the fight recommences, Amadis' knightly skills, his boldness and fleetness of foot eventually give him the upper hand, and he deals Abies a mortal blow. With death approaching, Abies acknowledges that pride has been responsible for his fall, restores the territory he has usurped from Perion, and professes himself content to die by the hand of such a noble fighter as Amadis, who is duly acclaimed by the French as their deliverer.

The Amadis romance, being an exemplary narrative in which good always triumphs, has a positive imperative force, just as Abraham a Sancta Clara's story had a negative one. But the copiousness and the intensity of *Amadis* generate a much more powerful imperative than that achieved by a sermon example. The appropriate analogy within religious literature is the saint's legend.[42] Here the saint, whose goodness is manifested by his miracle-working power, is invested with all the religious fervour of his chronicler, and stands forth as an ideal for imitation. Similarly Amadis, whose knightly excellence is repeatedly proclaimed by his victories in battle, carries a strong emotional charge. He is a projection of his creators' desire: their attachment to their hero, as well as their aversion from his enemies, can everywhere be felt. Amadis, like the saint, is an ideal to be imitated. He invites noble readers to identify with him, to be of his party, to rejoice in his triumphs, and feel them as their own. By identifying themselves in this way with knightly success, readers could assure themselves of their own knightly worth. As André Jolles suggested, the knight of romance resembled the sporting heroes of the twentieth century, who give their supporters a sense of greatness by association.[43]

But the text could do more than instil a sense of individual greatness. Written when the traditional warrior caste was threatened by princely centralisation and military reorganisation, it sprang from anxiety, "the fertile ground from which allegorical abstractions appear."[44] *Amadis* was calculated to combat the nobles' anxiety and keep them in tolerable mental health through its idealised image of the fighting man on horseback, armed with lance and axe. Identification with the pattern knight could give noble readers a sense of belonging "to a community of the elect, a circle of solidarity…set apart from the common herd,"[45] and could thus help to sustain their belief in the excellence of their social order and its continuing meaningfulness. For this reason, *Amadis* was a powerful political document that seemed calculated to assist the traditional nobility in its struggle against the princes.[46] Those who supported the princes made it a favourite target of their cultural polemics.

Jean Bodin, for instance, thought the work neither history nor poetry. In his *Methodus ad facilem historiarum cognitionem* of 1566 he cited the phrase "as true and as probable as *Amadis*" as a form of insult.[47] Justus Lipsius agreed. In the notes to his *Six Books of Politics* he described *Amadis* as a pestilential book, to be avoided by truth-loving and serious-minded people. "Fugite Princeps et Aulici," he wrote, "qui vera & seria amatis."[48] German lawyers and historians such as Bernegger, Lansius and J. H. Boecler also condemned this specimen of the traditional chivalric ethic so objectionable to the legal world-view.[49] In his discourse "De Elegantia Moris civilis et aulici," Boecler pointedly remarked that the manners and morals portrayed in *Amadis* diverged so far from the standards of decorum appropriate to public men that the romance should play no part in their education.[50]

Yet the lawyer-historians believed they could use romance to cast out romance. While deploring *Amadis* they united in their praise of John Barclay's *Argenis*.[51] Published in Latin in 1621, *Argenis* was avidly read in the circle around the Palatine councillor G. M. Lingelsheim, as the historian Janus Gruter related in his letters.[52] Lingelsheim may even have had a hand in encouraging the book's translation into German, since the work was done by Martin Opitz, who had been Lingelsheim's protégé during his stay at Heidelberg in 1621.[53] Boecler explained the book's appeal when, alongside his condemnation of *Amadis*, he eulogised *Argenis* as a handbook for princes and their advisers, a romance which treated affairs of state seriously and court manners accurately.[54]

The author of *Argenis* was himself a scholar-statesman, the son of the Scottish lawyer William Barclay, who defended the French monarchy against its Huguenot opponents. Born in 1582, John Barclay was educated in France by the Jesuits at Pont à Mousson, but by 1606 had left for the service of his compatriot James I of England, in whose court he became gentleman of the bedchamber. Barclay apparently carried out various diplomatic missions for James, but may have hoped for a post in France, since he cultivated relations with French statesmen and dedicated his *Icon animorum*, which was published in 1614, to Louis XIII. Despite having offended the Catholic church by his early *Satyricon Euphormionis*, Barclay installed himself in Rome in 1616, with a post at the papal chancellery under Paul V. He began writing *Argenis* in 1618, and died in 1621, just after it was published.

Barclay indicated that his object in writing *Argenis* was to hold up a mirror to his own times: a mirror in which contemporaries might see themselves, and learn from what they saw.[55] But though his confessed purpose was mimetic, he interpreted mimesis in neo-classical terms, as imitation of what is typical in nature. Barclay's mirror does not reflect individuals' particular traits of appearance or character, so much as the way they perform generalisable roles. Yet Barclay's stereotypes strongly suggest historical figures. His Meleander, king of Sicily, a typical weak ruler, would remind contemporaries of Henry III of France; Lycogenes, the rebellious vassal, recalls the duke of Guise; and Poliarchus, the strong ruler, Henry of Navarre. The title-heroine Argenis stands for France.[56]

Barclay plots his story as a comedy following the Greek form of romance, best known from Heliodorus' *Aethiopica*, which itself derived from New Comedy.[57] Argenis loves Poliarchus, and he her: they are the young lovers of the comedy. But as is always the case in comedy, their world is full of hostile or troublesome figures who ensure that the course of true love does not run smooth. The blocking characters of comedy are often fathers, and Meleander, Argenis' father, does indeed stand in the way of her happiness, but through incompetence rather than direct opposition. He is not the only obstacle: Lycogenes (the vassal turned rebel), Radirobanes — a foreign ruler — and even Archombrotus — the hero's own friend and ally — in turn try to wrest Argenis from Poliarchus. But eventually Poliarchus and Argenis marry, and a new, legitimate order crystallises around them, just as France, misgoverned by Henry III, rent by warring factions and threatened from outside, is eventually rescued and pacified by Henry IV.[58]

Barclay's story sets out his own politics. Poliarchus is a prince of strong monarchical convictions; the establishment of absolutist rule supplies the happy ending. Here, then, is a new fictional hero: a military man, certainly, yet one who is not the knight-at-arms of *Amadis*, but an

ideal ruler, equipped with neo-stoic virtues. When Poliarchus and Archombrotus first meet, at the beginning of the book, they stare at each
other with wonderment in a nice example of the cynosure which Frye
regards as a central image in seventeenth-century literature of heroic
kingship.[59] But ambiguity soon clouds this blazing clarity. While the
knightly hero of chivalric romance establishes by endlessly repeated
victories the supremacy of himself and the virtue he stands for, in *Argenis*, as in comedy generally, the triumph of virtue flashes only briefly on
the eye, in a swift and unexpected happy ending. For when that ending
comes at last, it does so by a sudden twist in the plot, against the logic
of events: rival claims to the heroine's hand seem all too likely to prevent her marriage to the hero indefinitely, then suddenly it is revealed
that the latest and most formidable claimant, Archombrotus, is permanently ineligible because her own half-brother.

In the interim between the opening cynosure and the final twist in
the plot that reveals an ideal realm of peace, order and justice, *Argenis*
evokes the disorderly political actuality determined by mechanical causation: the real world of conflicting forces, in which might usually obscures right. This narrative displays the motive-and-action structure. A
story within the story exemplifies the whole. Poliarchus tells Archombrotus of recent events in Sicily, where the nobleman Lycogenes has re-
belled against king Meleander.[60] Poliarchus, the convinced monarchist,
believes that the king's cause is just, but is far from uncritical of Meleander the man. Though good, Meleander lacks judgment. By surrendering
power to Lycogenes' supporters he has allowed this nobleman, moved
by envy and ambition, to raise the standard of revolt. When Poliarchus
meets Archombrotus, Meleander has already done battle with the rebels
and indeed forced them to retreat, but he has completely failed to pursue and crush them. Why this is so is uncertain. Poliarchus suggests
three possible explanations: that the king wished to spare his subjects;
that he feared an ambush; or that he anticipated defections from his own
side. In any case, Meleander is now in a precarious situation, unable to
trust his own counsellors who betray his plans to his enemies, desirous
of peace at any price, naively hopeful that once the war is over, the rebels will disperse, allowing measures to be taken to set them against
each other or to discredit them with the people. Poliarchus thinks it
wrong as well as unwise to make peace with men guilty of *lèse-
majesté*.[61]

He represents all this as a contemporary historian or political adviser
might do. He does not set out a mere chronicle of what has taken place
but tries to suggest how each circumstance has arisen, using the method
of Tacitus, as described by Auerbach: he "does not see forces," he "is not
concerned with historical developments either intellectual or material,"
but looks at human agents. From their actions he infers such motives as

are suggested by contemporary conceptions of human behaviour. And having inferred motives, he passes ethical judgments: he "sees vices and virtues, successes and mistakes."[62] Thus rebellion can be traced to excess ambition, or civil war to lack of resolve. Poliarchus' analysis exempts no-one, of however exalted a rank, from judgment. He presents Meleander the king not as an unambiguous hero but as a mixed character with both good and bad qualities. The analysis once made, and judgment passed, Poliarchus offers his own opinion of the course the king ought to have taken *qua* king.

This account of rebellion against a legitimate monarch parallels the account in *Amadis* of Abies' usurpation of legitimate power. But whereas *Amadis* demands emotional identification with the hero, and repudiation of his adversary, *Argenis* by contrast gives the reader food for thought. The text puts questions as well as presenting evidence to support various possible answers.[63] Does Meleander act rightly in temporising with the rebels? Or ought he to pursue them relentlessly, as Poliarchus suggests? Is the civil war in Sicily the grandees' fault or that of the king himself? Opinions may differ, though certain opinions are favoured over others since Barclay, like counsel in a court of law, guides his audience towards one view of events rather than another. Poliarchus, presented as a reliable narrator, is not undecided. His analysis suggests that king Meleander has been at fault, and is indeed largely responsible for the disorder in his realm. But Poliarchus also suggests that some responsibility must be borne by Lycogenes and his supporters who have acted purely from selfish motives. This sort of fictional case study closely resembles the materials used by contemporary teachers of statecraft, and by linking together a number of such studies Barclay organised into a single connected narrative many of the problems which were treated separately in teaching manuals like Thomas Lansius' *Mantissa consultationum et orationum.*[64]

Argenis reinforces its status as political and legal manual by means of a series of text-book debates offering a very clear picture of Barclay's rhetorical technique. Each of the five books contains at least three such debates, which interrupt the action of the story and make further intellectual demands on the reader. In places Barclay openly seeks to control the reader's response by disproportionately weighting each side of the argument, for example by presenting a brief statement from one character and then a lengthy exposition of the contrary view from another character. Elsewhere, conflicting points of view are given more equal treatment. This is the case, for instance, when several of the characters discuss whether a republic or an elective or a hereditary monarchy would be the best form of government.[65] True, Barclay indicates where his own sympathies lie by attributing ulterior motives to the opponents of hereditary monarchy. Yet he supplies the reader with ample material to allow independent thought on the subject. Rigid control of the reader's responses is abandoned for an essentially interrogative approach. The world of absolute verities gives way to a world of probabilities.[66]

The contrast between *Amadis* and *Argenis* illustrates the struggle between the old feudal nobility, the traditional first estate of Empire and territories, and the princes and commoner counsellors who were seeking to acquire the supreme political power in Germany in the hundred years from 1550 to 1650. The nobles hoped to maintain the preeminence which had been theirs by right of birth. Princes and counsellors wanted to replace sectionalism with a more integrated social order. But the reader's ability to put down the last volume of *Amadis* and open the pages of *Argenis* belies the complexities of this social and political conflict. The transition from traditional to modern structures, from the outlook and values epitomised in *Amadis* to the world-view embodied in *Argenis*, was neither smooth nor complete: it took place, over centuries, in fits and starts. Modernising initiatives suffered successive defeats and distortions, and therefore needed repeating, by different agents operating under different social conditions in a historical sequence the beginnings of which were clearly discernible by the mid-seventeenth century, when the lawyer-historians had proved incapable of defeating the traditionalist nobility outright.

Indeed the commoner graduates were, in a sense, their own worst enemies. As the princes, with their new advisers' assistance, gradually escaped from the tutelage of the Empire and began to play a part on the European political scene, they came to need diplomatic skills far more readily acquired by nobles than by commoners.[67] The eighteenth-century historian L. T. Spittler described the peace negotiations at Münster in 1648 as the last great appearance of commoner lawyers on the political stage: "die letzte große Doktorszene."[68] After that, they all but disappeared from high government office in the territories, to be replaced by nobles who now combined privilege of birth with nearness to the throne.[69] However this reconfirmation of status society did not preclude further cultural change, and well after the end of the Thirty Years' War there belatedly appeared a native German successor to Barclay, a successor who was eventually to inherit the duchy of Brunswick-Wolfenbüttel.

Anton Ulrich

Duke Anton Ulrich began his career as a writer of romances by refashioning a text begun by his sister, Sibylle Ursula. In its finished form *Die Durchleuchtige Syrerinn Aramena* was a vast work comprising 3,882 numbered octavo pages in the original edition, which appeared in five volumes at the rate of one a year from 1669 to 1673, and was reprinted once, between 1678 and 1680. He then produced *Octavia. Roemische Geschichte*, the first three volumes of which were published from 1677 to 1679, and later reprinted once. Publication of the rest of the text did not begin until 1703, and the work was only completed, in six volumes containing almost seven thousand quarto pages, in 1707. Three further printings of the whole romance followed shortly thereafter.[70]

Despite the bulk of his published work, which included poetry and plays as well as *Aramena* and *Octavia*, Anton Ulrich remains a somewhat enigmatic figure. His early upbringing seems in some ways to have fitted him for the traditional world. His father, duke August, was, like many of the reforming lawyer-historians, an irenicist. But his willingness to overlook confessional differences arose not from the rationalism many of them espoused, but from the conviction that true Christianity consisted in spiritual fervour rather than ecclesiastical loyalties. In fact August, whose Lutheranism was that of Johann Arndt, expected everyone at his court, where Arndt's most notable follower, Joachim Lütkemann, was chaplain, to profess it also.[71] The young Anton Ulrich was raised in his father's faith, performed the appropriate religious exercises, corresponded with the Swabian divine J. V. Andreae, and wrote religious verse. Both the correspondence and the lyrics eventually appeared in print. But Anton Ulrich stopped writing religious verse after his father's death.[72] And though religious faith undoubtedly continued to play an important part in his later life — he was not the indifferentist that his apparently political conversion to Catholicism might make him out to be — he became notable as a representative of secular rather than of spiritual culture.

Duke August would not necessarily have disapproved. Though renowned for his piety and knowledge of divinity, he was a man of wide interests who published books on law and politics as well as on theology.[73] In 1638, when Anton Ulrich was five, the duke, like other German princes of the early seventeenth century, chose not a theologian but a lawyer, J. G. Schottel, then still a student, as his son's tutor. Schottel had sole charge of Anton Ulrich's education until 1645, thereafter sharing this responsibility with Sigmund von Birken. Schottel spent the rest of his life at Wolfenbüttel, holding various court offices, and maintaining his interest in Anton Ulrich's work.[74] However these commitments did not prevent Schottel from keeping abreast of current legal thinking. His dissertation, completed in 1643, concerned the principles of sentencing, a subject of great contemporary interest since its airing during the previous decade by the eminent Saxon lawyer Benedict Carpzov.[75] Carpzov had argued in his *Practica*, published in 1635, that when determining whether or not to apply the statutory penalty for any given misdemeanour, judges should consider the motives of the perpetrator. This practical application of the concern with individual psychology shown by historians like Bodin was a crucial stage in the development from traditional to modern law, which Schottel showed every sign of approving.[76] His *Ethica*, published in 1669, enlarged the purely legal concern with motive by arguing that the goodness and badness of actions generally must be judged not according to their outcome but according to the intentions of the agent.[77]

It therefore seems likely that Anton Ulrich was aware of modern legal-historical thinking from a very early age. In any event his further education was such as to reinforce his tutor's influence. Between 1650 and 1655, Anton Ulrich attended the university of Helmstedt, where he heard the lectures of Schottel's associate, the professor of politics Hermann Conring. Duke Heinrich Julius had first encouraged the teaching of a neo-Aristotelian theory of absolutism at Helmstedt, and Conring carried on this tradition, advocating strong government by the secular authority, and strict subordination of church to state. Influenced to no small extent by Machiavelli, Conring has been described, quite surprisingly for a man of what was still an essentially pious era in Germany, as a thoroughgoing empiricist and sceptic.[78] In him, therefore, Anton Ulrich encountered a hardheaded analyst with a strong interest in political processes.

Another element in Anton Ulrich's early experience was the *Fruchtbringende Gesellschaft*. His mother's uncle was prince Ludwig of Anhalt-Köthen, the society's first president,[79] while Anton Ulrich's father was himself a member of the society, as were several of his courtiers, including Schottel, who was the society's chief grammarian. Indeed Wolfenbüttel, a very literary court, was one of the two or three principal centres of the *Fruchtbringende Gesellschaft*, and as such an early example of the small court as the scene of co-operation between nobles and commoners in a joint cultural endeavour.[80] Anton Ulrich himself was admitted to the society, as "Der Siegprangende," in 1659.[81] Though the *Fruchtbringende Gesellschaft* did not admit women, they participated actively in the literary and cultural life of the German courts, especially those with Calvinist and French connections,[82] and Anton Ulrich's stepmother, Sophie Elisabeth of Mecklenburg, translated a French romance under the title *Historie der Dorinde*, while his sister Sibylle Ursula translated La Calprenède's *Cassandre* and *Cléopâtre*.[83] Anton Ulrich enlarged his experience of a mixed society of *gens de lettres* of both sexes when he visited Madeleine de Scudéry in Paris on the grand tour,[84] and in Italy, at a later stage of his travels, he seems to have delighted in a still greater freedom of association between people of different rank, for he returned there three times when co-regent of Brunswick-Wolfenbüttel, and once wrote wistfully of his fondness for Venice, where princes and commoners were all alike.[85] In his literary life, at any rate, he was able to work and correspond with men and women of lower rank than his own: his tutors

Schottel and Birken, the poet Catharina Regina von Greiffenberg, the philosopher G. W. Leibniz.

Anton Ulrich the writer of romance has proved no less difficult to place than Anton Ulrich the man. Birken wrote a preface for *Aramena* which defends the text in traditional terms.[86] To protect Anton Ulrich, the princely author, from post-humanist noble prejudice against purely imaginative literary activity by the second estate, Birken classifies *Aramena* as a *Geschicht-Gedicht* — a *historical* fiction — thus appealing to the neo-classical argument that fiction can reveal the truth of history better than the historical record itself, which obscures truth in the flux of events.[87] That truth, claims Birken, is God's work in the world, rewarding virtue and punishing vice. But this providential, teleological reading of *Aramena* as imperative fiction reveals rather less of Anton Ulrich than of Birken whose spirituality led him, for example, to convert the *Pegnesischer Blumenorden* from a predominantly secular to a clerical society.[88] Those of *Aramena*'s modern readers who, following Birken, have understood the text primarily as a theodicy, a grandiose attempt to represent the divine world-order in fiction, seem to fall short of an adequate historical analysis of Anton Ulrich's mental universe, which was neither systematic nor dogmatic.[89] He was a political figure who inhabited the probabilistic, legal-historical world of thought; it is this above all which takes fictional shape in *Aramena*.[90]

The story recounts the struggle of the three children of the Syrian king Aramenes to overthrow the Assyrian usurper Belochus in the time of the patriarch Jacob. The action is structured as comedy: in this respect, Anton Ulrich follows the example of *Argenis*.[91] Delbois of Syria (whose real name, Aramena the Elder, gives the book its title) and Marsius of Basan are the principal young lovers. Belochus and his allies are the older characters whose illegitimate rule blocks the lovers' legitimate desires. When Belochus' tyranny is finally overthrown, a new and better world forms around Delbois and Marsius, who of course marry, as do all the many pairs of lovers who have supported them.[92]

This comedy ending invites belief in a just world-order, a meaningful universe where all things work together for good to them that love God. Leibniz considered that Anton Ulrich's work embodied the conviction he himself expressed in the *Monadologie*: "Ainsi il n'y a rien d'inculte, de sterile, de mort dans l'univers, point de Chaos, point de confusions qu'en apparence."[93] Yet the providential ending is only the ending; and the meaningfulness of events in *Aramena* belongs to what Adolf Haslinger has called the story's "deep structure."[94] At this level, *Aramena* embodies the ideal of justice which sustains the legal world of thought. But the surface structure of the romance, with which the reader is most likely to concern himself, at least for the greater part of the text, is precisely that world of appearance, that phenomenal world, in which there is chaos and confusion. Anton Ulrich evokes with fascination a causal-mechanical world in which there is conflict of wills, a world that only legal-historical habits of thought are likely to elucidate. He presents his characters as striving to understand that world, and he encourages his reader to join the attempt.

Precisely because Anton Ulrich wishes to suggest a world of competition and conflict, his cast of characters is large. Chivalric romance often had a multiplicity of characters; but since it was an episodic form, they appeared successively in time. Comedy, though a closed form, can extend in space, by proliferation of characters within the same action. *Aramena* multiplies both blocking characters and lovers: the narrative follows the fortunes of almost thirty couples.[95] So many are the participants in the story, and so involved are their family connections, that the reader needs genealogical tables as badly as the courtier needs his almanach.[96] Furthermore the characters are not differentiated psychologically but are schematic and typical, as is so often the case in stage comedy.[97] For like comic writers generally, Anton Ulrich is interested in his characters not as individuals but as social beings. He shows them "wearing their *personae* or social masks," and forming a web of social relationships, that is, a design in space rather than a progression in time.[98] This, too, reveals Anton Ulrich's comic vision. He shows his characters "manoeuvering around a central situation" in the manner of comedy, rather than proceeding in a straight line forwards, as did the knights of romance.[99] The central situation is the archetypal situation of comedy: the elimination of the false suitors and the success of the true one. Meanwhile these social *personae* who circle around the question of marriage are also legal *personae* who seek to uphold the contracts into which they have freely entered.

To this extent, Anton Ulrich's narrative is very like *Argenis*. What is new in *Aramena* is the extreme opacity of its fictional world of disguises, substitutions and mistaken identities. The characters crucially do not understand the pattern of relationships in which they are involved. Like Anton Ulrich himself and his fellow-participants in the intricate dynastic politics of the seventeenth-century European courts, they struggle to perceive — and risk misperceiving — each other's motives and intentions. Anton Ulrich thus comes much closer to the conventions of comedy than Barclay did. For comedy's subject-matter *par excellence* is human blindness, and the comic reversal, when it finally comes, brings a change from blindness to sight, false opinion to true knowledge, *pistis* to *gnosis*.[100] *Aramena* explores the theme of blindness with extraordinary ingenuity.

Anton Ulrich does not merely tell of blindness, he shows it. Following the conventions of Heliodoran romance which opens *in medias res*, he begins by narrating without preamble a salient experience of one of his principal characters. The main thread of the narrative develops from this, and important events which have taken place before the beginning of the story are recapitulated by participants in them. But these narratives of past history, of which there are many, are introduced into the main story only as circumstances allow. When a character is thrown together with others who are ignorant of his background, he will relate what has happened to him. In this way, different participants become acquainted with different parts of the story as a whole. Those who hear more have a relatively good understanding of everything that has taken place, and of the true relationship of the characters in general; those who have heard less understand correspondingly little.[101]

In any event none of the characters knows the whole story. They usually learn what has happened without knowing to whom it has happened. Sometimes identities are simply not divulged. A character may relate how a prince sought a certain princess in marriage, or rescued another from a wild animal. But different princes may have done either of these things, and in the absence of individualising features in the narrative, it is difficult to tell which did what.[102] Sometimes identities are given, but incorrectly, and remain difficult to verify, for a variety of reasons. Some characters are given, or take for themselves, names other than their own. The Aramena of the title grows up as Delbois, knowing neither her true name nor her parentage. Her sister, the younger Aramena, takes the name of prince Dison of Seir, who is himself masquerading as Aramena the Younger. Marsius of Basan calls himself Cimber; but so, too, does Tuscus Sicanus. In such circumstances news of an "Aramena" or a "Cimber" has, to say the least, no very obvious referent.

This confusion often places the characters in situations as equivocal as those of stage comedy. In general, Anton Ulrich's tone is one of high seriousness: he hardly encourages laughter at the predicament of his princely heroes and heroines. But the comic element in the story is unmistakable. It is impossible not to smile at the incapacity of the characters to penetrate the mysteries in which they are involved. Haslinger points out the tragicomic perplexity of Hemor when he thinks he has no fewer than four rivals for the woman he loves, and the comic situation into which Ahalibama manœuvres Mehitabeel when she intrigues to bring about the marriage of Aramena the Younger and Dison of Seir.[103] Not even the heroine is spared. Aramena the Elder, wise in her counsel to others, cannot recognise her own happiness. Throughout the story she loves "Cimber," who is in reality Marsius of Basan, but whom she believes to be Tuscus Sicanus. When finally called on to marry the man she loves, she thinks she is being forced to renounce him. Her blindness here is complete, but it is comic not tragic, because her friends know the truth, and enlighten her at last.[104]

Understanding the facts merely facilitates the more important business of judging behaviour. In *Aramena*, the characters must distinguish
friends from enemies in order to formulate their own future policies. The
thought-processes they use are the historian's and the lawyer's. As in the
legal practice of Anton Ulrich's day, judgments of guilt or innocence depend entirely on motive, so misunderstanding of motive leads to wrong
judgments. Characters whose behaviour is imperfectly understood may
fall under suspicion of disloyalty; but discovery of their true motive will
rehabilitate them. Aramena refuses to rescue Marsius from prison and he
thinks her treacherous, until he discovers that her refusal was motivated
by the mistaken belief that he was not Marsius but her enemy Ninias.[105]

The importance of judgment according to motive is expressly stated
in the legal proceedings which occur in *Aramena*. During the course of
the narrative, various characters act the part of defence counsel. Their
pleas are founded on the conventions of the contemporary law courts,
and the points at issue were among those decided by the justices of Anton Ulrich's own day. The story of Chersis and Amphilite, which contains
a submission to Aramena as judge of final appeal, raises the same questions as the case of Christianus and Dorothea.[106] A lower court had decided that Amphilite be required to marry Abinael, basing its decision on
the alleged ending of her relationship with her former friend, Chersis;
her father's wish that she marry Abinael; Abinael's testimony that she
returned his love; and witnesses' testimony that Amphilite was seen embracing Abinael. But Sandenise, as counsel for Amphilite, offers a different version of events. The supposition that Amphilite and Chersis had
parted was based on false appearances; Abinael's testimony was motivated by self-interest, and therefore unreliable; and the person seen embracing Amphilite was in fact Eunome, who had dressed in Abinael's
clothes, in order to compromise her. Thus Sandenise argues that Amphilite has been the victim of circumstances and intrigue. The defence
borrows tactics and phraseology from the contemporary lawyers to
whose language Anton Ulrich was generally indebted for his narrative
style.[107] As required by court rules, Sandenise sets out all the circumstances of the case in order that the appellant's true mind may be
known. In accordance with contemporary verdicts, Aramena reverses the
judgment against Amphilite because no intention to wed Abinael can be
imputed to her. Amphilite's motives are decisive, not any undertaking
given by her father.

Anton Ulrich's narrative of illusion and confusion does not appeal to
the reader's emotions as does an imperative romance in which good
continually triumphs over evil. In *Amadis* emotional expectations are
created and swiftly satisfied, episode by episode. But *Aramena* can
hardly be read for emotional satisfaction. There is indeed a happy ending. But the narrative is of such length and intricacy as to defuse the

reader's emotions long before the conclusion, while there is little suggestion en route of a serious attempt to arouse sympathy for the characters. Anton Ulrich's narrative is not as neutral as has sometimes been maintained, since his use of epithets implies certain value-judgments. Yet he does not polarise the reader's responses by heavily antithetical characterisation. Nor does he offer repeated or emphatic instances of the punishment of evil.[108]

Anton Ulrich's programme is in fact to offer the reader not emotional satisfaction but an intellectual challenge. For the problems of evidence and judgment which confront the characters confront the reader also. Narrative by recapitulated life-histories ensures not just that the characters only partially comprehend the events in which they are involved but that the reader too knows only in part. He may at any given moment know more than a particular character, since he has access to all the life-histories which together form the truth of the story as a whole. But since, at the time of their telling, the reference of these life-histories is not much clearer to him than it is to the characters, he still has to puzzle out the meaning of what he reads as he reads. The text continually throws up questions of agency and motive which he needs to answer. Many of the clues he is given are far from immediately relevant and have to be remembered till their significance becomes apparent dozens of pages later. Some clues are so hidden in an elaborate *salon* game involving several characters that only the most alert reader can work out the true relationships between the participants.[109]

Anton Ulrich presents puzzles; he entertains his reader; he offers the satisfactions of a detective story. But he also does something more, which is taken for granted by readers of interrogative fiction today, but was by no means self-evident when he wrote. By inventing his puzzles and posing his questions, he invites the reader to adopt legal-historical habits of mind. So he sustains, during the high Baroque period, the contested world-view of the princes and lawyers of the beginning of the century.

---

[1]Leonhard Bauer and Herbert Matis, *Geburt der Neuzeit: vom Feudalsystem zur Marktgesellschaft* (Munich: Deutscher Taschenbuch Verlag, 1988) 15, 19, 21, 31-32, 41, 44-45; Hajo Holborn, *A History of Modern Germany: The Reformation* (London: Eyre & Spottiswoode, 1965) 25-26, 40; V. H. H. Green, *Renaissance and Reformation: A Survey of European History between 1450 and 1660*, 2nd ed. (London: Edward Arnold, 1964) 13-18.

[2]Gerhard Ritter, *Die Neugestaltung Deutschlands und Europas im 16. Jahrhundert: die kirchlichen und staatlichen Wandlungen im Zeitalter der Reformation und Glaubenskämpfe*, Deutsche Geschichte: Ereignisse und Probleme, ed. Walther Hubatsch (1950; Frankfurt am Main: Ullstein, 1967) 143-44, 147, 381-82; Holborn 263.

[3] Holborn 262-63; Hellmuth Rössler, *Europa im Zeitalter von Renaissance, Reformation und Gegenreformation 1450-1650* (Munich: F. Bruckmann, 1956) 495.

[4] Rössler 584; Ritter 144, 174, 380, 386, 406, 408-9; Holborn 261-266, 372.

[5] Holborn 22-33.

[6] Rössler 522-31.

[7] Gerd Heinrich, "Amtsträgerschaft und Geistlichkeit: zur Problematik der sekundären Führungsschichten in Brandenburg-Preussen 1450-1786," *Beamtentum und Pfarrerstand 1400-1800: Büdinger Vorträge 1967*, ed. Günther Franz, Deutsche Führungsschichten in der Neuzeit vol. 5 (Limburg/Lahn: Starke, 1972) 196-97; Albrecht Eckhardt, "Beamtentum und Pfarrerstand in Hessen," *Beamtentum und Pfarrerstand 1400-1800* 86-87; Harald Schieckel, "Die Pfarrerschaft und das Beamtentum in Sachsen-Thüringen," *Beamtentum und Pfarrerstand 1400-1800* 161-62; Herbert Helbig, "Der Adel in Kursachsen," *Deutscher Adel 1555-1740: Büdinger Vorträge 1964*, ed. Hellmuth Rössler, Schriften zur Problematik der deutschen Führungsschichten in der Neuzeit 2 (Darmstadt: Wissenschaftliche Buchgesellschaft, 1965) 231; Friedrich Hermann Schubert, *Ludwig Camerarius 1573-1651: eine Biographie*, Münchener Historische Studien Abteilung Neuere Geschichte, ed. Franz Schnabel, vol. 1 (Kallmünz Oberpfalz: Lassleben, 1955) 56; Volker Press, *Calvinismus und Territorialstaat: Regierung und Zentralbehörden der Kurpfalz 1559-1619*, Kieler Historische Studien 7 (Stuttgart: Klett, 1970) 37. On the relative importance of lawyers, historians and others among the advisers to the princes, see Michael Stolleis, "Grundzüge der Beamtenethik (1550-1650)" and Notker Hammerstein, "Universitäten — Territorialstaaten — Gelehrte Räte," *Die Rolle der Juristen bei der Entstehung des modernen Staates*, ed. Roman Schnur (Berlin: Duncker & Humblot, 1986) 273-302, 687-735.

[8] Press 367-68, 383-394, 411, 426-27, 451, 457-58.

[9] See for example Hans Joachim von der Ohe, *Die Zentral- und Hofverwaltung des Fürstentums Lüneburg (Celle) und ihre Beamten 1520-1648* (Celle: Pohl, 1955) 211-217; Heinrich 195.

[10] G. R. Elton, *Reformation Europe 1517-1559* (1963; London: Collins, 1967) 305-11; Andreas Dorpalen, *German History in Marxist Perspective: The East German Approach* (Detroit: Wayne State UP, 1988) 124.

[11] Erich Trunz, "Der deutsche Späthumanismus um 1600 als Standeskultur," *Deutsche Barockforschung: Dokumentation einer Epoche*, ed. Richard Alewyn (Cologne, Kiepenheuer & Witsch, 1965) 149-51, 156.

[12] Gunter E. Grimm, *Literatur und Gelehrtentum in Deutschland: Untersuchungen zum Wandel ihres Verhältnisses vom Humanismus bis zur Frühaufklärung*, Studien zur deutschen Literatur 75 (Tübingen: M. Niemeyer, 1983) 17-19.

[13] Wilhelm Kühlmann, *Gelehrtenrepublik und Fürstenstaat: Entwicklung und Kritik des deutschen Späthumanismus in der Literatur des Barockzeitalters* (Tübingen: M. Niemeyer, 1982) 48, 240-41, 334-35, 338, 350-51, 356. See also Stolleis, "Beamtenethik" 286-88.

[14] Holborn 371-72; Fritz Hartung, *Deutsche Verfassungsgeschichte vom 15. Jahrhundert bis zur Gegenwart*, 5th ed. (Stuttgart: K. F. Koehler, 1950) 156; Gerhard Oestreich, *Geist und Gestalt des frühmodernen Staates: ausgewählte Aufsätze* (Berlin: Duncker & Humblot, 1969) 262.

[15] Hartung 159.

[16] Rössler 527-28, 530-31; Thomas Klein, *Der Kampf um die zweite Reformation in Kursachsen 1586-1591*, Mitteldeutsche Forschungen 25 (Cologne: Böhlau, 1962) 20, 28, 68,

70-71, 87-89, 92, 119, 122, 149-50 and passim; Press 367-68, 383-86, 394, 411, 426-27, 451, 457-58; Horst Dreitzel, *Protestantischer Aristotelismus und absoluter Staat: die Politica des Henning Arnisaeus (ca. 1575-1636)* (Wiesbaden: Steiner, 1970) 105-108.

[17] Rössler 530-31; Dreitzel 107.

[18] Kühlmann 338, 341, 356, 372-376. Notker Hammerstein, "Res publica litteraria — oder Asinus in aula? Anmerkungen zur 'bürgerlichen Kultur' und zur 'Adelswelt'," *Respublica Guelpherbytana: Wolfenbütteler Beiträge zur Renaissance- und Barockforschung*, Festschrift Paul Raabe, ed. August Buck and Martin Bircher, Chloe 6 (Amsterdam: Rodopi, 1987) 59.

[19] Rössler 522-32. Compare Stolleis, "Beamtenethik" 276-78.

[20] On the early modern court, see Ronald G. Asch, "Court and Household from the Fifteenth to the Seventeenth Centuries," *Princes, Patronage and the Nobility: The Court at the Beginning of the Modern Age c. 1450-1650*, ed. Ronald G. Asch and Adolf M. Birke, Studies of the German Historical Institute London, ed. Adolf M. Birke (Oxford: Oxford UP; London: German Historical Institute, 1991) 1-38.

[21] Rössler 522-532, 535; Ritter 408-11; Holborn 259; Klein 30-31; Press 399-400; Jürgen Moltmann, *Christoph Pezel (1539-1604) und der Calvinismus in Bremen*, Hospitium Ecclesiae: Forschungen zur bremischen Kirchengeschichte 2 (Bremen: Verlag Einkehr, 1958) 11; Notker Hammerstein, "Schule, Hochschule und Res publica litteraria," *Res Publica Litteraria: die Institutionen der Gelehrsamkeit in der frühen Neuzeit*, part 1, ed. Sebastian Neumeister and Conrad Wiedemann, Wolfenbütteler Arbeiten zur Barockforschung 14 (Wiesbaden: Harrassowitz, 1987) 93-110.

[22] Rössler 588; Ritter 234-36; Klein 128; Press 334; Moltmann 11-14; Gerhard Oestreich, "Calvinismus, Neustoizismus und Preussentum," *Jahrbuch für die Geschichte Mittel- und Ostdeutschlands* 5 (1956).

[23] Rössler 373, 377; Ritter 361-62; Julian H. Franklin, *Jean Bodin and the Sixteenth-Century Revolution in the Methodology of Law and History* (New York: Columbia UP, 1963) passim; Kühlmann 45, note 82; Dreitzel 427.

[24] On Lipsius, see Gerhard Oestreich, "Justus Lipsius als Theoretiker des neuzeitlichen Machtstaates," *Historische Zeitschrift* 181 (1956); Gerhard Oestreich, "Politischer Neustoizismus und Niederländische Bewegung in Europa und besonders in Brandenburg-Preussen," *Geist und Gestalt des frühmodernen Staates*, by Gerhard Oestreich; Kühlmann 221-42. On German students in the Netherlands, see Heinz Schneppen, *Niederländische Universitäten und deutsches Geistesleben*, Neue Münstersche Beiträge zur Geschichtsforschung 6 (Münster in Westfalen: Aschendorff, 1960).

[25] Conrad Bursian, *Geschichte der classischen Philologie in Deutschland von den Anfängen bis zur Gegenwart*, Geschichte der Wissenschaften in Deutschland: Neuere Zeit 19, part 1 (Munich: Oldenbourg, 1883) 325-337; Oestreich, "Justus Lipsius" 33-34, 38-42; Kühlmann 55-66; Dreitzel 312, 427-28; Wilfried Barner, *Barockrhetorik: Untersuchungen zu ihren geschichtlichen Grundlagen* (Tübingen: M. Niemeyer, 1970) 378-80. See also Wilhelm Vosskamp, *Untersuchungen zur Zeit- und Geschichtsauffassung im 17. Jahrhundert bei Gryphius und Lohenstein* (Bonn: Bouvier, 1967).

[26] Oestreich, "Justus Lipsius" 47-49; Dreitzel 80, 211, 310-11, 420, 424-428; Friedrich Hermann Schubert, "Die pfälzische Exilregierung im Dreissigjährigen Krieg: ein Beitrag zur Geschichte des politischen Protestantismus," *Zeitschrift für die Geschichte des Oberrheins* 102 (1954): 593, 616, 618; Friedrich Hermann Schubert, *Die deutschen Reichstage in der Staatslehre der frühen Neuzeit*, Schriftenreihe der historischen Kom-

mission bei der bayerischen Akademie der Wissenschaften 7 (Göttingen: Vandenhoeck & Ruprecht, 1966) 216-218, 347-49, 356, 358, 392, 540.

[27] Kühlmann 359; cf. Barner 379.

[28] See Gerd Heinrich, "Der Adel in Brandenburg-Preussen," *Deutscher Adel 1555-1740* 292-93; "Adel und Konfession: ein Rundgespräch," *Deutscher Adel 1555-1740* 140-41; F. W. Barthold, *Geschichte der Fruchtbringenden Gesellschaft* (Berlin: A. Duncker, 1848) 46; Barner 380.

[29] On the appeal of Helmstedt university to the nobility, see Dreitzel 104; "Adel und Konfession: ein Rundgespräch," *Deutscher Adel 1555-1740* 133. On *Ritterakademien* see Friedrich Paulsen, *Geschichte des gelehrten Unterrichts auf den deutschen Schulen und Universitäten vom Ausgang des Mittelalters bis zur Gegenwart*, 2nd ed., vol. 1 (Leipzig: Veit & Comp., 1896) 457, 502-9; Wilhelm Roessler, *Die Entstehung des modernen Erziehungswesens in Deutschland* (Stuttgart: Kohlhammer, 1961) 129-31; Barner 377-84.

[30] Compare Erich Auerbach, *Mimesis: The Representation of Reality in Western Literature*, tr. Willard R. Trask (1946; Princeton: Princeton UP, 1968) 308-9; Hans-Georg Gadamer, *Wahrheit und Methode: Grundzüge einer philosophischen Hermeneutik* (Tübingen: Mohr, 1960) 32-33.

[31] See Erich Loos, "Baldassare Castigliones 'Libro del Cortegiano'," *Analecta Romanica* 2 (1955); Otto Brunner, *Adeliges Landleben und europäischer Geist: Leben und Werk Wolf Helmhards von Hohberg 1612-1688* (Salzburg: O. Müller, 1949) 109-11; Barner 369-72. On the education of German princes and the manners of the German courts, see Barthold passim, and Berthold Haendcke, *Deutsche Kultur im Zeitalter des dreissigjährigen Krieges: ein Beitrag zur Geschichte des 17. Jahrhunderts* (Leipzig: E. A. Seemann, 1906). Hammerstein, "Res publica litteraria" 38 notes that the significance of the court as a training-ground for the modern world has not yet been fully recognised; see also his further comments, 44-46, 54-55.

[32] On prince Ludwig see Haendcke 124.

[33] On the *Fruchtbringende Gesellschaft* see Karl F. Otto, *Die Sprachgesellschaften des 17. Jahrhunderts* (Stuttgart: J. B. Metzler, 1972) 14-33. On its social composition and ethos, see in particular Klaus Conermann, "War die Fruchtbringende Gesellschaft eine Akademie? Über das Verhältnis der Fruchtbringenden Gesellschaft zu den italienischen Akademien," *Sprachgesellschaften, Sozietäten, Dichtergruppen: Arbeitsgespräch in der Herzog August Bibliothek Wolfenbüttel, 28. bis 30. Juni 1977: Vorträge und Berichte*, ed. Martin Bircher and Ferdinand van Ingen, Wolfenbütteler Arbeiten zur Barockforschung 7 (Hamburg: Hauswedell, 1978); Ferdinand van Ingen, "Aus der Frühzeit der Fruchtbringenden Gesellschaft," *Jahrbuch der deutschen Schillergesellschaft* 22 (1978): 65. For the view that the *Fruchtbringende Gesellschaft* did not level social distinctions, see Volker Sinemus, *Poetik und Rhetorik im frühmodernen deutschen Staat: sozialgeschichtliche Bedingungen des Normenwandels im 17. Jahrhundert*, Palaestra 269 (Göttingen: Vandenhoeck & Ruprecht, 1978) 214-228.

[34] "Ritterliche thaten alleine": *Der Fruchtbringenden Gesellschaft ältester Ertzschrein: Briefe, Devisen und anderweitige Schriftstücke*, ed. Gottlieb Krause (1855; Hildesheim: G. Olms, 1973) 98.

[35] On the romances of Amadis see John J. O'Connor, *Amadis de Gaule and its Influence on Elizabethan Literature* (New Brunswick, NJ: Rutgers UP, 1970); Hilkert Weddige, *Die Historien vom Amadis auss Franckreich: Dokumentarische Grundlegung zur Entstehung*

und Rezeption, Beiträge zur Literatur des XV. bis XVIII. Jahrhunderts, ed. Hans-Gert Roloff, vol. 2 (Wiesbaden: Franz Steiner, 1975). For a synopsis of Books 1 to 4, see Felix Bobertag, *Geschichte des Romans und der ihm verwandten Dichtungsgattungen in Deutschland*, part 1, vol. 1 (Berlin: L. Simion, 1881) 303-331.

[36] O'Connor 85-105.

[37] Northrop Frye, *Anatomy of Criticism: Four Essays* (Princeton: Princeton UP, 1957) 33.

[38] Auerbach 18-20; Frye 305; Angus Fletcher, *Allegory: The Theory of a Symbolic Mode* (Ithaca: Cornell UP, 1964) 65.

[39] Auerbach 136.

[40] Compare Frye 186-87, 192, 304; Fletcher 171, 175; Adolf Haslinger, *Epische Formen im höfischen Barockroman: Anton Ulrichs Romane als Modell* (Munich: Fink, 1970) 113-116.

[41] The final encounter of the Irish war is related in book 1, chapter 10 of the German romance, see *Amadis*, book 1, ed. Adelbert von Keller, Bibliothek des Litterarischen Vereins in Stuttgart 40 (Stuttgart: Litterarischer Verein, 1857) 100-103.

[42] Compare André Jolles, *Einfache Formen*, 2nd ed. (Halle/Saale: VEB M. Niemeyer, 1956) ix-x; 225.

[43] Jolles x, 48.

[44] Fletcher 37.

[45] Auerbach 137. Compare Fletcher 244-49.

[46] Norbert Elias, *Die höfische Gesellschaft: Untersuchungen zur Soziologie des Königtums und der höfischen Aristokratie* (Neuwied: Luchterhand, 1969) 322.

[47] Jean Bodin, *Methodus ad facilem historiarum cognitionem* (Lyon: J. Mareschal, 1583) 54. Compare Weddige 237-38.

[48] Justus Lipsius, *Politicorum, sive civilis doctrinae libri sex, qui ad principatum maxime spectant, additae notae auctiores, tum et de una religione liber*, part 2 (Antwerp: Plantin, 1610) 24. Compare Weddige 244.

[49] Compare Weddige 189-90, 200-201, 244.

[50] Johann Heinrich Boecler, "De Elegantia Moris civilis et aulici," *Opera*, vol. 1 (Frankfurt am Main: Joh. P. Schmidt, 1733) 492.

[51] Compare Weddige 272 on *Argenis* as antitype of *Amadis*.

[52] Alexander Reifferscheid, *Quellen zur Geschichte des geistigen Lebens in Deutschland während des 17. Jahrhunderts*, vol. 1 (Heilbronn: Henninger, 1889) 125, 127.

[53] See Georg Schulz-Behrend, "Opitz' Übersetzung von Barclays *Argenis*," *Publications of the Modern Language Association of America* 70 (1955): 455-73. Schulz-Behrend notes (458) that Lingelsheim, Zincgref and Gruter were eagerly awaiting Opitz' translation, according to their letters of 1626. For Opitz's *Argenis* see Martin Opitz, *Gesammelte Werke*, ed. Georg Schulz-Behrend, vol. 3, parts 1 and 2, Bibliothek des Litterarischen Vereins in Stuttgart 296 and 297 (Stuttgart: Hiersemann, 1970). My references are to this text. On *Argenis*, see Günther Müller, "Höfische Kultur," *Deutsche Barockforschung*, ed. Alewyn 196-202; Dietrich Naumann, *Politik und Moral: Studien zur Utopie der deutschen Aufklärung*, Frankfurter Beiträge zur Germanistik 15 (Heidelberg: Carl Winter, 1977) 22-67.

[54] Boecler 491-92.

[55] *Argenis*, book 2, chapter 14: 178-82.

[56] Albert Dupond, *L'Argenis de Barclai* (Paris: E. Thorin, 1875) 47. Early seventeenth-century editions of the text appeared with a key: see for example John Barclay, *Argenis cvm clave, hoc est, nominum propriorum elucidatione hactenus nondum edita* (Frankfurt am Main and Leiden, 1634).

[57] See Albin Lesky, *A History of Greek Literature*, tr. James Willis and Cornelis de Heer (London: Methuen, 1966) 858, 866-67.

[58] For a synopsis of the text see Bobertag, part 1, vol. 2.1, 30-42.

[59] "Es stallte jhm einer deß andern Gestalt für Augen / vnd stunden als bestürtzt vber solcher jhrer Beschawung," *Argenis*, book 1, chapter 1:14. See Frye 153-54; Haslinger 163-65.

[60] *Argenis*, book 1, chapter 2: 16-22.

[61] Compare Naumann 27-29, 35.

[62] Auerbach 38.

[63] Compare Paula Kettelhoit, *Formanalyse der Barclay-Opitzschen* Argenis, diss., U Münster (Bottrop i. W.: W. Postberg, 1934) 21.

[64] See Barner 379, 386; Kühlmann 65-66.

[65] *Argenis*, book 1, chapter 18: 89-101.

[66] Compare Naumann 54-56, 58.

[67] See for example Press 486.

[68] See Joachim Lampe, *Aristokratie, Hofadel und Staatspatriziat in Kurhannover: die Lebenskreise der höheren Beamten an den kurhannoverischen Zentral- und Hofbehörden 1714-1760* (Göttingen: Vandenhoeck & Ruprecht, 1963) 218-221.

[69] On office-holding by the nobility in Brandenburg-Prussia see Gerd Heinrich, "Der Adel in Brandenburg-Preussen," *Deutscher Adel 1555-1740* 299-300; F. L. Carsten, *The Origins of Prussia* (Oxford: Clarendon Press, 1954) 264-65.

[70] For a brief account of Anton Ulrich's life and work see Blake Lee Spahr, "Herzog Anton Ulrich von Braunschweig-Lüneburg," *Deutsche Dichter des 17. Jahrhunderts: ihr Leben und Werk*, ed. Harald Steinhagen and Benno von Wiese (Berlin: Erich Schmidt, 1984). Volker Meid, *Der deutsche Barockroman* (Stuttgart: J. B. Metzler, 1974) contains a bibliography of work on Anton Ulrich.

[71] On August, see *Sammler, Fürst, Gelehrter: Herzog August zu Braunschweig und Lüneburg 1579-1666: Niedersächsische Landesausstellung in Wolfenbüttel: 26 Mai bis 31 Oktober 1979* (Brunswick: Herzog August Bibliothek, Wolfenbüttel, 1979). On the religious culture of the Wolfenbüttel court, see Jörg Jochen Müller, "Fürstenerziehung im 17. Jahrhundert: am Beispiel Herzog Anton Ulrichs von Braunschweig und Lüneburg," *Stadt–Schule–Universität–Buchwesen und die deutsche Literatur im 17. Jahrhundert: Vorlagen und Diskussionen eines Barock-Symposions der Deutschen Forschungsgemeinschaft 1974 in Wolfenbüttel*, ed. Albrecht Schöne (Munich: Beck, 1976) 256; Jörg Jochen Berns, "Justus Georg Schottelius," *Deutsche Dichter des 17. Jahrhunderts* 422-23.

[72] Spahr 605, 598; Étienne Mazingue, "Réflexions sur la création romanesque chez Anton Ulrich," *"Monarchus Poeta": Studien zum Leben und Werk Anton Ulrichs von Braunschweig-Lüneburg: Akten des Anton-Ulrich Symposions in Nancy (2.-3.Dezember 1983)*, ed. Jean-Marie Valentin (Amsterdam: Rodopi, 1985) 48.

[73] Spahr, "Herzog Anton Ulrich" 597.

[74] Jörg Jochen Müller 250-54; Berns 416, 418; Giles Reid Hoyt, *The Development of Anton Ulrich's Narrative Prose on the Basis of Surviving Octavia Manuscripts and Prints* (Bonn: Bouvier, 1977) 21.

[75] Berns 418.

[76] Sieghardt von Köckritz, "Die Bedeutung des Willens für den Verbrechensbegriff Carpzovs in der Practica Nova Imperialis Saxonica Rerum Criminalium," diss., U of Bonn, 1955, 8-9, 24, 52-54, 96.

[77] Justus Georg Schottelius, *Ethica: die Sittenkunst oder Wollebenskunst*, ed. Jörg Jochen Berns (1669; Bern: Francke, 1980) 54-55, 278-281.

[78] Dreitzel 80, 424-25. On Conring, his work at Helmstedt and his connections with the ruling family, see also Jörg Jochen Müller 250-51; Schottelius 54; "Hermann Conring," *Handwörterbuch zur deutschen Rechtsgeschichte (HRG)*, ed. Adalbert Erler and Ekkehard Kaufmann, vol. 1 (Berlin: E. Schmidt, 1971) col. 633-34; Michael Stolleis, "Die Einheit der Wissenschaften — Hermann Conring (1606-1681)," and Günter Scheel, "Hermann Conring als historisch-politischer Ratgeber der Herzoge von Braunschweig und Lüneburg," *Hermann Conring (1606-1681): Beiträge zu Leben und Werk*, ed. Michael Stolleis (Berlin: Duncker & Humblot, 1983) 11-31, 271-301.

[79] Anton Ulrich's mother, Dorothea (1607-34), was a daughter of Rudolf of Anhalt-Zerbst, who was a brother of Ludwig of Anhalt-Köthen.

[80] Jörg Jochen Müller 256.

[81] Spahr 602.

[82] See Otto 19; Barthold 114-116, 136-145.

[83] Blake Lee Spahr, *Anton Ulrich and Aramena: The Genesis and Development of a Baroque Novel*, University of California Publications in Modern Philology 76 (Berkeley: U of California Press, 1966) 7, 43; Berns 20.

[84] Spahr, "Herzog Anton Ulrich" 598, 600.

[85] Spahr, "Herzog Anton Ulrich" 603; Berns 29.

[86] "Vor-Ansprache zum Edlen Leser," *Die Durchleuchtige Syrerinn Aramena*, part 1 (Nuremberg: J. Hofmann, 1669). For a reprint of the preface, see *Theorie und Technik des Romans im 17. und 18. Jahrhundert*, vol. 1, ed. Dieter Kimpel and Conrad Wiedemann (Tübingen: M. Niemeyer, 1970) 10-15. For a discussion of the preface, see Wilhelm Vosskamp, *Romantheorie in Deutschland: von Martin Opitz bis Friedrich von Blanckenburg* (Stuttgart: J. B. Metzler, 1973) 7-28.

[87] Klaus Heitmann, "Das Verhältnis von Dichtung und Geschichtsschreibung," *Archiv für Kulturgeschichte* 52.2 (1970): 252-53, 267-270, 273-74.

[88] Richard van Dülmen, "Sozietätsbildungen in Nürnberg im 17. Jahrhundert," *Gesellschaft und Herrschaft: Forschungen zu sozial- und landesgeschichtlichen Problemen vornehmlich in Bayern*, Festschrift Karl Bosl (Munich: Beck, 1969) 175, 180; Blake Lee Spahr, "Nürnbergs Stellung im literarischen Leben des 17. Jahrhunderts," *Stadt–Schule–Universität–Buchwesen* 78.

[89] See Meid 34; Vosskamp, *Romantheorie* 13-17.

[90] Compare Heinz Otto Burger, *"Dasein heißt eine Rolle spielen"* (Munich: Hanser, 1963) 103.

[91] Günther Müller noted the affinity between *Argenis* and Anton Ulrich's romances in "Barockromane und Barockroman," *Literaturwissenschaftliches Jahrbuch der Görres-Gesellschaft* 4 (1929): 2, 20.

[92] The content of *Aramena* is summarised in Leo Cholevius, *Die bedeutendsten deutschen Romane des 17. Jahrhunderts: ein Beitrag zur Geschichte der deutschen Literatur* (1866; Stuttgart: B. G. Teubner, 1965) 178-208.

[93] G. W. Leibniz, *Die philosophischen Schriften von Gottfried Wilhelm Leibniz*, ed. C. J. Gerhardt, vol. 6 (Berlin: Weidmann, 1885) 618-19. On the relationship of Anton Ulrich's romances and Leibniz's philosophy, see Haslinger 380-83.

[94] Haslinger 26, 33, 36 and elsewhere.

[95] See Günther Weydt, "Der deutsche Roman von der Renaissance und Reformation bis zu Goethes Tod," *Deutsche Philologie im Aufriss*, 2nd ed., ed. Wolfgang Stammler, vol 2 (Berlin: Erich Schmidt, 1960) col. 1267, 1269. Compare Haslinger 319 on "Das Darstellungsprinzip der Fülle."

[96] Haslinger 379.

[97] On the schematic treatment of the characters' responses, see Haslinger 352. On comic characters, compare Robert Scholes and Robert Kellogg, *The Nature of Narrative* (New York: Oxford UP, 1966) 225-26.

[98] Frye 305; Haslinger 330 (on "Das Darstellungsprinzip der menschlichen Beziehungen") and 26, 165, 371.

[99] Frye 304.

[100] Frye 169-70.

[101] See Haslinger's discussion of the "Ausschnitte" of the characters, 31-65.

[102] A prince of Gerar seeks Ammonide's hand. Aramena takes him for Abimelech, when he is really Ahusath. See *Aramena*, vol. 4: 347-48 and Haslinger 56. Cimber rescues Aramena from lions; but she takes Cimber to be Tuscus Sicanus, when he is in fact Marsius of Basan. See *Aramena*, vol. 2: 180-84; vol. 4: 368-69, and Haslinger 63-64.

[103] Haslinger 356, 52. See *Aramena*, vol 1: 482-83; vol. 3: 172-176.

[104] *Aramena*, vol.5: 857-62. On the origins of Aramena's confusion, see Haslinger 56-64.

[105] For Aramena's confusion of Ninias with Cimber-Marsius, see vol. 4: 390-97.

[106] *Aramena*, vol. 5: 153-78. Compare Haslinger 285-88.

[107] Compare Hoyt 21, 24, 43-45, 47-48, 219.

[108] Compare Haslinger 27-28, 129, 309-310. The same restraint is characteristic of Anton Ulrich's second romance, *Octavia*: see Fritz Martini, "Der Tod Neros: Suetonius, Anton Ulrich von Braunschweig, Sigmund von Birken oder: historischer Bericht, erzählerische Fiktion und Stil der frühen Aufklärung," *Probleme des Erzählens in der Weltliteratur*, Festschrift Käte Hamburger, ed. Fritz Martini (Stuttgart: Klett, 1971) 68-69.

[109] Haslinger 36, 228-29, 373.

3: The Traditionalist Response: Orthodox Revival and Exemplary Fiction in the Seventeenth Century

THE LAWYER-HISTORIANS' world view was contested not least by the Lutheran clergy who, at the end of the sixteenth century, still sought to exercise in the Lutheran territories a monopoly of knowledge comparable to that enjoyed by the Catholic establishment in the medieval world, controlling the people from the pulpit and, increasingly, by means of the printed word. Like the Catholic clergy before them, they used the sermon *exemplum* to reinforce their teaching.

The Catholic *exemplum* was a brief narrative of righteousness rewarded or — as in Abraham a Sancta Clara's tale of the Saxon bride — sin punished. Such narratives contributed to the teaching of salvation through works, by indicating what to do, and what to leave undone, in order to earn a place in heaven. Their relevance to Lutheranism is less obvious. Catholic doctrine drove Luther first to despair over his inability to earn salvation, and then to the liberating realisation that he was not in fact required to do so. The jealous God he feared thus became the loving father whose grace was available to all that had the faith to receive it.[1] But though this discovery might seem to destroy the traditional teaching of the church on sin and righteousness by indicating the possibility that a man might act as he pleased so long as he had faith, neither Luther nor his church fell into antinomianism, even if the precise relationship between faith and law was never clearly defined in the Lutheran tradition. In *Von der Freiheit eines Christenmenschen*, Luther expounded the Christian's continuing obligation to do good works, for which he offered several justifications, most persuasively perhaps the argument, favoured by all Protestant churches, that since repentance and new birth in faith bore good works as their fruit, faith without works was no true faith.[2] Philipp Melanchthon, who became the principal pedagogue of the Lutheran church despite, or perhaps because of, his temperamental and doctrinal differences from its founder, then contrived to invert this general understanding of the relationship of faith and works. Works were for Luther the inevitable result of faith; faith was for Melanchthon the necessary condition of works. The reform of doctrine thus became the mere means to a reform of life, and the Lutheranism over which Melanchthon presided continued the ascetic teachings of the medieval church, and reinforced them with the selfsame system of reward and punishment.[3]

Luther himself had urged that, when teaching from the pulpit, the clergy should illustrate precepts by examples. Such examples were to come not from the imagination but from history, which was for Luther the totality of God's acts in the world, a "monument of God's acts and judgments, showing how he maintains, rules, prevents, furthers, punishes and rewards the world and especially men, according to each man's deserts."[4] Melanchthon concurred. History, he declared, exhorted the Christian believer "to the faith and fear of God, for in very truth, the things that happen in history are a terrible image of God's anger and his judgment against all unrighteousness."[5]

Lutheran clergy drew their admonitory examples from the Bible, the Fathers and the classics, from humanist historians, and from the lives of the reformers.[6] By the 1560s clergymen were beginning to collect examples for publication. Among the earliest collections to appear in print were Andreas Hondorff's *Promptuarium Exemplorum*, published in 1568, and Wolfgang Bütner's *Epitome Historiarum* of 1576.[7] As their Latin titles suggest, these early collections, some of which were vast works published in folio, were primarily intended to serve the professional needs of the sermon-writing clergy, for whose benefit the *exempla* were arranged under the main heads of Christian doctrine or according to the church calendar.[8] But even the earliest compilers of Protestant examples appealed to the general reader as well as students of theology by offering the public at large a new genre of devotional books. Hondorff said in his preface to the *Promptuarium* that he had compiled it for simple, ordinary people who did not otherwise read much and had few books at their disposal. Bütner intended his *Epitome* to be not only a *miroir des princes* for heads of state but a domestic manual for heads of households.[9]

This marketing strategy seemed to succeed for the seventeenth-century public received a steady supply of example collections from clergy and schoolmasters, most of whom drew freely on the work of their predecessors while adding new items from hitherto untapped literary sources or from contemporary news sheets. Typical volumes from the latter part of the century included Matthäus Hammer's *Rosetum Historiarum* of 1657; J. D. Ernst's *Historisches Bilder-Haus* of 1674; Martin Grundmann's *Geschicht-Schule* of 1677; and Zacharias Hermann's *Historisches Blumen-Gepüsch* of 1680. These later compilations abandoned the systematic arrangement of the material under heads of doctrine and appeared in a handier octavo or even duodecimo format. *Exempla* were in fact now being offered primarily to a lay reading public, as an alternative to fiction. One clerical compiler even allowed himself a fashionable pseudonym, "Misander," in order to keep abreast of trends in secular publishing around 1700.[10]

But despite these changes in the outward appearance of the example collections, the example form remained substantially unaltered from the Reformation to the end of the seventeenth century. Its most striking feature was the distinguishing mark of all clerical storytelling, the claim to truth. Christian preachers maximised their effects by asserting the facticity of their *exempla*, which they presented as sections of the historical record of God's work in the world. Hence the use by writers such as Hammer, Ernst and Grundmann, of the terms *Historia, historisch* and *Geschichte* in the titles of their collections, and the widespread authentication of examples by names, dates and places.

With the claim to truth went explicit condemnation of fiction. Christianity had followed Plato in opposing truth to falsehood and outlawing literary invention as false.[11] Seventeenth-century Lutheran clerics regularly contrasted their own edifying veridical narratives with the corrupting fictions of secular authors. In the increasingly competitive struggle for readers, clerics often prefaced their *Historienbücher* with attacks on these rival productions. Matthäus Hammer presented his true stories as an alternative to the tales of Marcolphus, Eulenspiegel and Melusina.[12] Christoph Richter insisted that his *exempla* came from the works of world-famous historians rather than from books like Johannes Pauli's *Schimpf und Ernst*.[13] The verse preface to Martin Grundmann's *Geschicht-Schule* asked what benefit could be had from *Amadis*, d'Urfé, Sidney, or Jörg Wickram's *Rollwagenbüchlein*.[14]

As "true stories," clerical narratives were exempt from the conventions governing seventeenth-century fiction, not least the *Ständeklausel*, which required the "serious" literary forms, tragedy and romance, to take their characters from the highest social ranks, and comedy and satire to deal only with members of the middle and lower orders.[15] *Exempla* dealt with salvation and damnation, serious subject-matter indeed, but did not confine themselves to the vicissitudes of personages of any particular social class. God acted in history without respect to persons, his mercy and his wrath falling on both high and lowly, according to their deserts. *Exempla* therefore recorded notable divine judgments on men and women of high and low estate, as Zacharias Rivander announced in the title of his *Promptuarium*.[16]

The clergy intended true *exempla*, taken from the lives of all sorts and conditions of men, not to entertain but to edify the public, not least by terrifying sinners into obedience to God. Hence the Lutheran compilers' tendency to dwell in their titles and prefaces on the fear, horror and revulsion to be inspired by the tales of swift and violent retribution they promised.[17] Yet *exempla* were addressed not merely to sinners beyond the pale but also and perhaps chiefly to the children of God who already belonged to the community of the faithful, for whom they were to provide consolation in adversity. Clerics repeatedly used the words *Trost* and *tröstlich* in describing the benefit to be had from their examples. Wolfgang Bütner, for instance, offered his collection to "sorrowful and wretched Christians who are despised and rejected of men" as a source of "reichen Trost" — "plentiful consolation."[18]

Consolation flows most readily from examples of God's succour to his faithful people, especially if their suffering is great. A typical *Trost-exempel* thus tells of an upright man who, Job-like, endures repeated tribulations for which he is finally rewarded on earth or in heaven. The suffering reader is expected to identify with the upright man, reflect that his own sufferings are not unique and learn to see righteous suffering as part of God's testing and perfecting plan for his children here on earth. So the reader gains strength to endure. He knows he deserves better and indeed can hope for better, even if only in the life after death.[19] He can also take consolation from examples of the punishments meted out to the ungodly, who may triumph for a spell, yet must in the end pay the price for their sins, an eventuality which perhaps consoles less by satisfying a thirst for revenge than by reinforcing the Christian view, so often refuted by immediate experience, of a divine order ultimately manifest in things.

Examples, whether oral or printed, constituted the simplest form of popular appeal and, as such, supplied the stock-in-trade of the Lutheran clergy, whose reliance on them well into the later seventeenth century is symptomatic of an institutional continuity, the continued functioning of the territorial churches in the community at large. But this continuity is only one part of the picture. While many of the clergy continued to preach familiar doctrines by familiar means, the religious and secular upheavals of the first half of the century were prompting new forms of faith — and new forms of narrative in which to embody them.

The *Lehrstand* viewed the development of the early modern state, the rise of lawyer-historians as its theoretical experts, and their polemics against the traditional experts as a series of threats to its position. Texts from the first decades of the seventeenth century show traditional scholars on the defensive. Men whose studies had no immediate practical application, and indeed historians who lacked court office and merely professed their subject at university, began to feel a need to justify their existence. Some, noting the way in which scholarship had lost respect and scholars had lost status, concluded that traditional academic studies had reached the end of their life: this was the "Greisenalter der Studien." Those who had formerly enjoyed high esteem in the traditional world as part of the clerical profession now registered apprehension and gloom. Social change appeared to threaten a whole status-group with melancholia.[20] Such developments would have seemed alarming enough had they taken place in peace-time. The protracted war which in fact accompanied them necessarily intensified the sense of despair they engendered. Yet despair did not cause the religious world-view to collapse but, on the contrary, stimulated a religious revival.[21]

The starting-point for this revival was the *Lehrstand*'s own alienation from the modern age. Erudite *Zeitklagen* identified the seventeenth century as an era of worldly ambition in which men pursued material advantage to the neglect of their true happiness. This analysis largely restated traditional clerical mistrust of the world as a wild forest full of dangers, a place to be renounced by all who would save their souls. But the renunciatory melancholia of these years led not to a renewed eschatology, centred on the future, but to forms of utopianism that idealised the past. The *Lehrstand* now contrasted the conflict and disorder of the unacceptable present with what it saw as the orderliness and harmony of past ages, and the *laudatio temporis acti* became the typical literary exercise of the period.[22] Yet those who found themselves disorientated in the present, longing for an idealised past, did not resign themselves to their fate but, on the contrary, called for an intensification of the ascetic self-discipline implicit in both the traditional imitation of Christ and the teaching of the Stoics; by such means the devout might recreate the utopia of the past in a future human order truly capable of reflecting the divine.[23]

Because the evolution of Christian-stoic ideas of *Ordnung* coincided with the initiation of the absolutist state, the *Lehrstand* has sometimes been identified as the pioneer of absolutism, preparing the way for reforming princes by socialising contemporaries into a *Policeystaat*.[24] But this is to mistake both the position of the *Lehrstand* and the nature of the state. Traditional experts — clerics, philosophers and arts men — risked losing function and status as a result of increasing modernisation, which they had no intention of supporting. The *Lehrstand*'s new credo was designed, like the old, to sustain a traditional society, and not to promote an increasingly modern one which, even in its dynastic absolutist phase, still drew on pragmatic, legal-historical thinking.[25]

The new pattern of religious thought is visible in the revival of Lutheranism which took place during the Thirty Years' War. This revival, sometimes called pre-Pietism, combined mysticism with asceticism. Its intellectual ancestors were Johannes Tauler, Luther himself, and especially Johann Arndt, author of *Vier Bücher vom wahren Christentum*, published in 1609. Arndt, a monkish figure, melancholic and mistrustful of the world, sought consolation in a spirituality nourished by strict personal discipline in imitation of Christ.[26] One of Arndt's most notable followers was J. V. Andreae, who headed the Lutheran church in Württemberg from 1639. While remaining firmly within the orthodox Lutheran tradition, Andreae professed a utopian religion of world-rejection, mystic communion of the faithful, and personal asceticism.[27]

The Lutheran revival found a narrative vehicle in the exemplary novellas of G. P. Harsdörffer, who published hundreds of pieces in several collections, and achieved one of the greatest bookselling successes of the seventeenth century with *Der große Schau-Platz jämmerlicher Mord-Geschichte* and *Der große Schau-Platz lust- und lehrreicher Geschichte*, which date from 1649 and 1650, and which went through seven editions by 1700.[28] At first sight Harsdörffer may seem to be an unlikely spokesman of the religious world-view. A prolific writer in several genres and a well-connected figure in the cultural world of his day, he has appeared to some to be an astute follower of literary fashion rather than a man of conviction. In any event one can point to various circumstances that might suggest he was a moderniser rather than a traditionalist.[29] He came from one of the patrician families of Nuremberg, whose city council was noted at the start of the Thirty Years' War for pragmatic politics, confessional indifferentism, and sympathy with the Palatinate.[30] He made his name with the *Frauenzimmer Gesprächspiele*, a compilation of word-games intended to initiate its readers into the mysteries of polite conversation.[31] The first volume, published in 1641, was addressed to the *Fruchtbringende Gesellschaft*, which a year later duly responded by admitting Harsdörffer to membership as "Der Spielende." Thereafter, he tried to involve himself in the society's linguistic work, and acted as recruiting agent for south Germany and Austria.[32] Nevertheless, despite these connections with the sphere of the courts and of legal-historical thought, Harsdörffer was deeply rooted in the traditional world.

Precisely as a Nuremberg patrician, Harsdörffer considered himself first and foremost a member of the imperial nobility, a feudal vassal of the emperor.[33] Furthermore he allied himself with the clerical party which opposed the indifferentism of the city council and exerted a growing influence over cultural life during the war years.[34] The reconquest of Nuremberg for orthodox Lutheranism was begun by Johannes Saubert, who headed the clergy from 1637. At the insistence of Saubert, an Arndtian and a close friend and associate of J. V. Andreae, the city council adopted the unaltered Augsburg confession of 1530, instead of the altered, Melanchthonian humanist version of 1540.[35] After Saubert's death in 1646, the pre-Pietist form of Lutheranism continued to flourish under his successor, J. M. Dilherr, who had come to Nuremberg in 1642. Dilherr and Harsdörffer formed a close association which was to last sixteen years until the latter's death in 1658.[36]

During those sixteen years, Harsdörffer assisted Dilherr in his successful attempt to introduce sabbatarian laws despite opposition from the city council.[37] Dilherr, for his part, encouraged the work of Harsdörffer's *Pegnesischer Blumenorden*, though he did not himself become a member.[38] Harsdörffer meanwhile attempted to persuade prince Ludwig of Anhalt to admit Dilherr into membership of the *Fruchtbringende Gesell-*

schaft but could not overcome Ludwig's fears of clerical intolerance.[39] This setback did not dissuade Harsdörffer from increasing his output of religious and devotional work. He published original lyrics and meditations, as well as a large number of translations from several languages. Unusually for a Protestant of his time, he did not restrict himself to Lutheran and Calvinist writers, but also translated the work of St. Bernard, St. John of the Cross, the Jesuit Paul de Barry and the Theatine monk Luigi Novarini.[40] It is not surprising therefore that Harsdörffer's modern biographer J.-D. Krebs represents him as a man of strong Christian convictions, and specifically as a Christian ascetic who subjected himself to a rigorous discipline of spiritual exercises.[41]

Harsdörffer's novellas have sometimes been taken for secular fictions designed simply to entertain, but should rather be seen as didactic works disguised as entertainments.[42] Various of his immediate predecessors had offered such productions to a public now too sophisticated for *exempla*. Encouraged by the advice of St. François de Sales, who had urged Christians to write their own stories to compete with secular authors, J.-P. Camus, archbishop of Belley, had published several collections of exemplary novellas.[43] The example of J. V. Andreae, who approved de Sales' programme of "humanisme dévot" and tried to introduce it into Germany, may have prompted Harsdörffer to do what Camus had done.[44] In any event, Harsdörffer's letter to Andreae of 2 April 1649, requesting friendship, was accompanied by a copy of *Der große Schau-Platz jämmerlicher Mord-Geschichte*, much of the material for which Harsdörffer had taken from Camus' *L'Amphithéâtre sanglant*. Harsdörffer promised to send Andreae, as soon as it was ready, a copy of *Der große Schau-Platz lust- und lehrreicher Geschichte*, the second part of which bore an explicit clerical endorsement in the form of an epistolary preface by Dilherr on the usefulness of *exempla*.[45]

Camus was but one of Harsdörffer's sources. In the late sixteenth and early seventeenth centuries various Italian and French writers including Matteo Bandello, Simon Goulart and François de Rosset had published collections of novellas, some comic in the Renaissance manner, but the great majority of them "tragic" tales of passion, crime, and violent death, revealing what Northrop Frye has called "a world of shock and horror in which the central images are images of…cannibalism, mutilation and torture."[46] These foreign novellas were usually longer and more highly-wrought pieces of writing than the *exempla* in German clerical collections, from which they were often distinguished by dramatic dialogue and descriptive detail — not least of hideous crimes.[47] Yet the striking thing about Harsdörffer as novella-writer is not that he abandons the unadorned native *exemplum* tradition but that on the contrary he seeks to consolidate it by the use of such foreign materials.

Thus, so far from offering his novellas as fictions, Harsdörffer presents them as *exempla* by insisting on their historical veracity. His preface to *Der große Schau-Platz jämmerlicher Mord-Geschichte* claims that the contents of the work are all true — "alle wahre Geschichte" — authenticated by the date and place of their occurrence, and recounting "nothing incredible or impossible."[48] A similar claim appears in the preface to the second part of *Der große Schau-platz lust- und lehrreicher Geschichte.*[49] Harsdörffer further signalled his fidelity to the *exemplum* and his distance from fiction by pointing out that he had taken serious subject-matter from the lives of ordinary people rather than public figures. The preface to the *Mord-Geschichte* promises remarkable stories of private persons: "der privat Personen merckwürdige Geschichte"; other tales present the experiences of private persons — "die Begebenheiten der Privat-Personen" — since their vicissitudes can so often teach a moral or give a warning to posterity.[50]

Harsdörffer also followed the practice of those clerical compilers of *Exempelbücher* who bolstered their claims to be telling true stories by attacking the self-confessed fictions of others, even though in so doing he was obliged to contradict the positive evaluation of fiction expressed in the *Frauenzimmer Gesprächspiele*, written under the influence of the courtly tradition of Castiglione and Guazzo.[51] The preface to the *Mord-Geschichte* criticised Cervantes and Diego Agreda for being long-winded, Vicente Espinel's *Obregón* for containing obscenities and Boccaccio for giving bad rather than good examples and dwelling excessively on love-stories. Such inventions, Harsdörffer maintained, were scarcely more valuable than the stories of love and war commonly called romances: "die Liebs- und Helden Geschichte / welche man *Roman* nennet."[52]

The structure and form of address of Harsdörffer's novellas thus bear a close resemblance to the traditional *exemplum*, while their plots aptly conform to the "happening-and-consequence" pattern. Sometimes this pattern appears in its simplest form of one single event followed by another: a soldier frightens a comrade to death by firing an unloaded gun at him and then dies of fright when put in front of a firing squad which shoots wide.[53] Sometimes the sequence of events is prolonged: Cratis marries his friend Politian's fiancée, Phebe; Cratis and Phebe quarrel, and she reproaches him with his deceit of Politian; Cratis strikes Phebe, and she revenges herself by sleeping with Politian; Cratis surprises them; Politian kills Cratis; Politian and Phebe are both executed.[54] Neither tale is impossible in the natural order of things, for on the whole Harsdörffer does not follow traditional *exempla* in recounting self-evidently super-natural manifestations such as the appearance of the devil. Yet the symmetry of his stories does suggest the operation of an ethically compensatory causality. The soldier's death has the appearance of design in that it replicates the death he caused. The story of Cratis also seems too organised to be fortuitous. Things need not have fallen out that way after he stole his friend's fiancée: the fate of all three again suggests design.[55]

Harsdörffer leaves the reader in no doubt as to the author of the design; like sermon *exempla*, his novellas illustrate the workings of God in the world. Indeed as Brückner has pointed out, the title *Schauplatz* which Harsdörffer, like many clerical compilers of *Exempelbücher*, chose for his principal collections of stories, derives from the notion of history as theodicy, the play God presents for man's edification.[56] Moreover Harsdörffer's prefaces expressly interpret the events he narrates not in terms of the order of nature or of reason but in terms of Christian theology. Murder, adultery, theft and all the rest are sins. The man who commits them forsakes God for the devil, and must pay the price, which is damnation. Meanwhile by letting the devil into his life he becomes an agent of evil in the world around him. The "Zuschrifft" to the *Mord-Geschichte* introduces, as the "director" of these "murder-plays," the "Meister dieser Mordspiele," none other than Satan himself, who on the world's stage tempts young men with the pleasures of the flesh, men in their prime with power, and old men with money.[57]

Each story then develops these general themes in its own explicit self-interpretation. For Harsdörffer takes the greatest care to ensure that each narrative is read in one way only, as an illustration of an express precept. The titles of his stories usually indicate the point on which they turn: the story of Cratis, for example, is entitled "Der falsche Freund"; that of a husband who prostitutes his wife is "Der ehrlose Ehemann."[58] The title is usually followed by a statement of the precept to be illustrated: thus "Der falsche Freund" begins with the declaration that "Treachery is an evil in the eyes of God and men, and is linked with many vices."[59] Having reinforced his precept by citations from scripture or from proverbial wisdom, Harsdörffer then indicates the relationship of narrative to precept by a standard formula such as "as will be seen from the following story" ("wie aus folgender Geschichte zu ersehen seyn wird"), or "and there is an example of this in the following story" ("wie dessen ein Exempel in folgender Geschichte"). Being but one possible example among many — "unter vielen andern" — the narrative is always firmly subordinated to the precept it illustrates.[60]

As the story develops, the narrative voice analyses the spiritual condition of the characters. The epithets chosen indicate to the reader in the clearest possible fashion how each character and each action is to be judged. The narrator also comments at crucial moments on the progress of the story as a whole, with such announcements as "But the time had come for this deception to be revealed and for the criminals to receive due punishment."[61] By these means Harsdörffer leads his narrative to an ineluctable conclusion, from which he sometimes returns to the moral significance of the whole, once again using fixed formulae such as "From this follows the precept..." ("Hierauß fließet die Lehre...") or "In connection with this act we should notice in particular..." ("Es ist aber bey dieser That sonderlich zu beobachten..."), followed by a restatement of the precept.[62] Thus the same truth is often formulated twice over, at both the beginning and the end of the narrative. And when Harsdörffer ends a story with a prose precept, he often also appends a four-line verse summary of its significance.[63] Where his source offered no moral, he frequently supplies one.[64]

The teachings thus attached to each story continue the theme of the struggle between God and the devil for the soul of man. Though some stories simply offer a piece of prudential wisdom, Harsdörffer's moralising is usually mixed with a measure of eschatology. When hidden crimes come to light through unusual agencies and are punished by strange coincidences, the reader is reminded that the eye of God is ever open on the doings of men.[65] As minor transgressions lead step by step to all-engulfing catastrophes, the reader is warned that neglect of the simple safeguards of religion will deliver him over to the powers of darkness.[66] Yet though the world is a place of desperate danger, and the passions are a devilish snare, the Christian believer receives the consoling message that he does indeed belong to a divinely-ordered universe, and that salvation will await the practitioners of a strict, world-renouncing asceticism.

Intent on this religious message, Harsdörffer made few concessions to entertainment. He shortened the foreign novellas he adapted, omitting precisely those details which were most likely to entertain the reader and to involve him in the events and with the characters of the story. Camus, for instance, went to some trouble to give his stories an appearance of truth to life and often incorporated direct speech and dialogue to create a dramatic effect. Harsdörffer ruthlessly excised such superfluous circumstances — "überflüssige umstände" — so as to avoid detaining readers anxious to come to the end of the story.[67] "Der falsche Freund" illustrates Harsdörffer's method. Camus' version occupies more than ten pages of text; Harsdörffer's is half as long, and summarises all the events following Cratis' marriage to Phebe in two paragraphs.[68] Similarly, Camus' "Le puant concubinaire," a story of some 1,800 words, is reduced by Harsdörffer to about 850. The central figure in Camus' story, a lecherous scholar, is steeped in Greek and Latin eloquence and in philosophy but in Harsdörffer's is merely "learned." Camus details the elaborate but ineffectual measures taken to contain the stench of a corpse: the coffin is treated with pitch, wax and mastic, and strips of leather are stuck over the joints with glue. Harsdörffer simply states that all manner of steps were taken in vain.[69] Camus' "La sanglante chasteté," in which a young man is tempted by a prostitute on the orders of his father, who wishes to prevent him entering a monastery, contains an impassioned address by the young man to the woman; Harsdörffer's version leaves it out.[70] All that is left of some of Camus' sensational narratives is a bare outline far better fitted to instruct than to entertain.[71]

Apart from sermon examples Harsdörffer's novellas are therefore the simplest and shortest form of imperative fiction imaginable. But longer imperative texts had already proved viable in France, where Camus had published some thirty separate novel-length stories designed to teach Christian principles and to combat the influence of secular fiction in general, and *Amadis* in particular.[72] Andreae took up the theme in Germany. His *Mythologiae Christianae Libri Tres*, published in 1619, declared that *Amadis* "passed off the worst form of criminal magic as divine wisdom, and polluted the beds of virgins and spouses with impure lusts and filled generous souls with animal ferocity and broke the chains of religion and the laws of the land, and occupied pure minds with futile fictions."[73] Andreae may also have encouraged a German Lutheran cleric, A. H. Bucholtz, to follow the example of archbishop Camus in competing with *Amadis*.[74] Bucholtz was a native of Brunswick-Wolfenbüttel who studied at Wittenberg, and then taught in schools and universities before being called in 1647 to join the ministry in Brunswick, which then held a status similar to that of the free imperial cities. Bucholtz rose to the position of *Superintendent* in 1664. Though begun in the 1640s, his two romances were published much later, *Des Christlichen Teutschen Groß-Fürsten Herkules Und Der Böhmischen Königlichen Fräulein Valiska Wunder-Geschichte* in 1659-1660, and *Der Christlichen Königlichen Fürsten Herkuliskus Und Herkuladisla... Wunder-Geschichte* in 1665.[75] Despite Bucholtz's appointment to Brunswick, there seems never to have been any close personal or literary contact between him and duke Anton Ulrich, with whom he had little in common.[76] Bucholtz was a political traditionalist, faithful to the idea of the Empire, and his manner of writing romance was equally traditional.[77]

Bucholtz prefaced his *Herkules und Valiska* with a direct attack on the infamous *Amadis*: the "schandsüchtige Amadis Buch." His criticism indicated a fundamental repudiation of chivalric romance. He found immorality in the heroes' conception out of wedlock, irreligion in the pagan magic on which the plot often turned, and improbability both in individual episodes, and in the departure of the entire narrative from the known course of world history. What Bucholtz offered his readers instead of *Amadis* was not merely a morally unimpeachable romance — Barclay's *Argenis* was that, as Bucholtz conceded — but one which was specifically Christian. Bucholtz's preface not only identifies his hero Herkules as an image of Christian perfection in layman's estate, but carefully explains the theological significance of the other characters: Ninisla, for example, is described as an audacious villain who prospers for a spell, only to be overtaken at last by divine justice. The reader is adjured to note the Christian teachings contained in the text, and especially to peruse a summary of Christian doctrine set out under its principal headings at the end of the book.[78] Having denounced *Amadis* for its lack of truth (among much else), Bucholtz boldly authenticates his own efforts by intimating that an ancient manuscript version of his romance had come to light during the recent war, after having lain hidden for over 1,400 years.[79] Thus the traditional truth-claim of the religious moralist fulfils the elementary requirements of the genre. A slightly more sophisticated literary form appears in *Herkuliskus und Herkuladisla*, the preface to which expresses the belief that it no less than *Herkules und Valiska* will foster religion and virtue, and does indeed provide notes on the precepts contained in the text to follow, but openly defends the use of fiction for religious-didactic purposes by appealing to the example of the parables of Jesus.[80]

Bucholtz delivers the teaching he promises. The hero of *Herkules und Valiska* is an ideal character, an unambiguously positive figure who remains true to himself throughout the action. A warrior knight like Amadis, he displays the chivalric virtues. But he also manifests an exemplary traditional piety by his faith in providence, acknowledgement of God's help, and the virtuous love which fills him with an earnest desire for the conversion of his intended bride to Christianity.[81] The story has the episodic form familiar from chivalric romance, instead of the closed narrative structure achieved by Barclay and Anton Ulrich. Like Amadis, Herkules and his friends are knights errant who seek to prove themselves in a succession of adventures.[82] Though Ladisla believes his royal father has died, he prefers to wander in search of adventure rather than succeed to the throne and assume a sedentary life.[83] Herkules seeks Valiska through roughly one half of the book, but this quest fails to unify the work and seems to begin and end fortuitously. Valiska is stolen away by robbers, not by any usurping antagonist of comparable stature with the hero; and she is eventually rescued from the hands of Artabanus of Parthia without any fatal consequences to him.[84] After her safe return, the story is prolonged by means of new martial incursions from hitherto insignificant quarters. A summary of Christian belief at the end of the book merely emphasises the lack of any real conclusion.[85]

Each adventure in this episodic narrative is an allegory of the conflict between good and evil. Because Bucholtz's hero is a knight, most of the moral allegories necessarily belong to the realm of knightly combat. Good takes the form of Christian valour, evil is aggression against it, and retribution is defeat or death by the sword. The ordeal in which Herkules engages to prove the virtue of Euphrosyne against slanderous accusations from eight Greek knights is a paradigm of all the battles in the romance. Euphrosyne believes that "a just God" will not let her slanderers, "these godless and dishonourable knaves," go unpunished; and as Herkules defeats them one by one she reiterates to those still capable of hearing that "God eventually avenges evil" — "Gott endlich der Boßheit vergilt."[86] Thus sin is punished directly, swiftly and ruthlessly through God's chosen agent. No doubts deter Herkules from torture and execution in furtherance of the just cause. But on one occasion the knightly code stays his hand and Bucholtz the clerical romancer reverts to the homiletic *Exempel* tradition. A Jew blasphemes the Chistian God. Though an evident sinner, he is no worthy opponent for the Christian knight, and his punishment comes by supernatural means, as it might have done in a Reformation *exemplum*. Three mysterious black dogs appear, tear the Jew in pieces, and disappear again without harming any of the onlookers.[87]

When adapted for Christian purposes, the chivalric romance form in effect reverts to the saint's legend, from which it had originated. As practised by Bucholtz this fictional regression proved moderately successful with the public. *Herkules und Valiska* went into a second, third and fourth edition, in 1666, 1676 and 1693; *Herkules und Herkuliskus* appeared in a second edition in 1676.[88] But Bucholtz's impact was slight compared with that of H. A. von Ziegler und Kliphausen, the last of Germany's major seventeenth-century romancers.

Ziegler's *Die asiatische Banise* appeared in 1689, and went through ten further editions by 1764. A continuation by J. G. Hamann, published in 1724, had four further editions by 1766. Numerous imitations appeared, several incorporating the name *Banise* in their title.[89] Ziegler's immense success might suggest skill in manipulating the market rather than seriousness of purpose. But though not himself a cleric, Ziegler was, like Harsdörffer, associated by origin and inclinations with Lutheran traditions and more or less consciously attempted to translate Lutheran thought patterns into narrative prose.

Ziegler was born in 1663 in the Oberlausitz — then a possession of electoral Saxony — into one of the oldest noble families in the Electorate. Educated from 1679 to 1682 at the Gymnasium in Görlitz, and from 1682 at the university of Frankfurt on the Oder, he studied history, languages and poetry as well as law. On the death of his father in 1684 he left university to administer the lands he inherited. H.-G. Roloff maintains that Ziegler had good connections with the courts of Dresden and Weissenfels, and supposes that he will have made frequent visits to Dresden, but Ziegler never took office at court, and has left no evidence that he spent any time there. The only public appointment he held, as *Assessor* of the *Stift* at Wurzen, was that of judge in an intermediate, formerly episcopal, court. He died in 1697, at the early age of 34, on his estate at Liebertwolkwitz near Leipzig.[90]

As a Saxon noble, Ziegler belonged to the traditional rather than the modern world. The Saxon nobility, like the noble estate in the other German principalities, was hostile to monarchic centralisation, which it had resisted with considerable success. The Electorate continued to be governed according to a traditional, dualist constitution. Saxon nobles who exercised court office in the latter part of the seventeenth century did so less in the interests of the prince than in those of the noble estate, whose powers the "Bible" of Saxon statecraft at this period, V. L. von Seckendorff's *Teutscher Fürstenstaat* of 1656, stoutly defended.[91] The Saxon nobility was at the same time a bastion of Lutheran orthodoxy against both humanistic and Calvinistic beliefs, and not surprisingly very few Saxon nobles had joined the *Fruchtbringende Gesellschaft*, which began as a grouping of Calvinists and their sympathisers.[92] All this would suggest a community of interests with the Lutheran clergy in Saxony which Ziegler's work in fact indicates.

His *Täglicher Schauplatz der Zeit* of 1695 is a two-volume folio collection of *Historien*, most of which recount in calendar order historic battles, natural disasters, and the deaths of kings and public figures.[93] As the term *Schauplatz* suggests, these episodes are presented as instances of divine reward and punishment for good or evil deeds. Like clerical *exempla*-writers, Ziegler expressly indicates how his historical characters should be judged. Thus Ziegler regards Wallenstein, who plotted against the emperor and the traditional order of the Empire, as a villain. Hence what Wallenstein renders up, on receiving his death-blow, is not simply his spirit but his "vengeful spirit" — "rachgierigen Geist."[94] For the reader who fails to notice such epithets, Ziegler appends to his stories a verse *Epitaphium* containing a summary of their content, and their moral — a "kurtzen Inhalt der Historie nebst dem Morale."[95] Such indications of a spiritual affinity with the Lutheran clerics who compiled *Exempelbücher* are reinforced by the inclusion in the *Täglicher Schauplatz* of a congratulatory poem addressed to Ziegler by the Leipzig theology professor Valentin Alberti, a leading representative of Lutheran orthodoxy at the end of the seventeenth century, and inveterate opponent of Pufendorf's natural law theory.[96]

Ziegler's *Banise* has rightly been described as a *miroir des princes*.[97] It preached not dynastic aggrandisement but a traditional ideal of kingship as responsibility to the common weal. Kings are mortals under God, bound by the same moral rules as their subjects. And what happens to them is a lesson for the whole world. For *Die asiatische Banise* is addressed not simply to kings nor indeed to those who govern, but to all regardless of station, to whom it teaches a traditional, self-denying morality expounded according to the conventions of imperative storytelling. In his preface Ziegler declines to enter the debate on the morality of fiction and admits to neglecting what he calls the real task of romance —

the task assigned to it by the *Fruchtbringende Gesellschaft* — of refining the German language. His only claim is that of the religious storyteller to historical authenticity: *Banise* narrates events, says Ziegler, which occurred at the end of the fifteenth century and are attested by various authorities whom he mentions by name.[98]

Despite the book's title, Ziegler's chief character is in fact prince Balacin of Ava who, as the story begins, denounces the tyrant Chaumigrem for usurping the kingdom of Pegu. At the outset an unambiguous rhetoric of praise controls the reader's response to Balacin, "this valiant prince." The reader's sympathy is increased by Balacin's servant Scandor's recapitulation of his master's life emphasising his youthful exploits in the war between Ava and Pegu.[99] Balacin's heroism arouses not only respect but a touching devotion from Scandor, who therefore has no difficulty in presenting his master to the reader as an ideal figure, comparable with Amadis or Bucholtz's Herkules. Like them he is indeed a warrior, whose battles fill much of the book, whether he appears as general in command of large armies, or as single knight on horseback.

This latter, more traditional military role suits Balacin who, though a product of the late seventeenth century, most closely resembles the heroes of the old chivalric romances.[100] He slays a giant when his rival Zarang, too cowardly to risk single combat, sends as his substitute a black knight who, according to Scandor, bears on his left arm a shield big enough to cover Balacin from head to foot. In the course of his quest for Banise, Balacin receives special assistance from dye or ointment given to him by the priest at the temple in Pandior where he is vouchsafed a vision of his princess. The priest's gift, like that of a benevolent wizard of romance, so alters Balacin's appearance that he is able to visit Banise, unrecognised by his and her enemies.[101] Yet while slaying giants and associating with benevolent wizards Balacin also has his all-too-human servant Scandor, a comic figure who has been explained as an intruder from the *Schelmenroman*, or even a forerunner of "realistic" narrative.[102] But the comic servant was quite at home in the old chivalric romances, where dwarves or fools of the race which eventually gave birth to Sancho Panza were "licensed to show fear or make realistic comments," as Frye remarks.[103] Describing his own sensations when first he fights alongside his prince, Scandor admits he "wished very heartily I was a girl, so I could stand a chance of escaping such bloodshed." Later experiences, such as his narrow escape from drowning, are related by Scandor with humour that verges on the grotesque and provides in the approved manner of the old chivalric romances a contrast with, and a relief from, the lofty adventures of the knightly characters, which are narrated in a sustainedly elevated tone.[104]

Against the unambiguous hero Balacin are set equally unambiguous villains. Thus Chaumigrem's three emissaries, who encounter Balacin at the start of the story, are described as three audacious Brahmans, "frightful," "vile," "blind and insane" rogues. Balacin condemns Chaumigrem himself as a tyrant who deserves to be exterminated, along with his followers who are "hated of gods and men." Nor is Balacin anxious to avoid his own responsibilities in the matter. On the contrary his dearest wish is to come upon the murderous king, kill him and despatch his wicked soul to its proper place, as indeed it finally befalls when by divine retribution the mortally wounded Chaumigrem, who has "so often sullied his hands with innocent blood," is "forced to writhe screaming in his own welling gore, and with many complaints to render his evil spirit to the fires of hell."[105]

The plot of Ziegler's narrative exemplifies Northrop Frye's "central form of quest romance," where "a land ruled by a helpless old king is laid waste by a sea-monster, to whom one young person after another is offered to be devoured, until the lot falls on the king's daughter: at that point the hero arrives, kills the dragon, marries the daughter, and succeeds to the kingdom."[106] In this instance the land is Pegu, the king Xemindo, who does indeed become helpless and old, his land laid waste by the monstrous Chaumigrem. Banise is the daughter of this unfortunate king, who finally rides to his execution in beggar's rags on a wretched, broken-down mare.[107] During most of the action Banise is little more than the passive object of various suitors' desires, imprisoned by her enemies, her whereabouts unknown, and her very survival in doubt. When Chaumigrem fails to make her his wife, he agrees that this immaculate virgin should be sacrificed to propitiate the war-god Carcovita, who claims a maiden victim annually. Balacin performs a last-minute rescue as his bride is about to be ritually slain and, having despatched the "monster," marries her.[108]

In relating a successful quest which ends in the establishment of a new kingly order, Die asiatische Banise bears a superficial resemblance to the "closed" form of the court romance exemplified in Anton Ulrich's Aramena. But Aramena was a Gesellschaftsroman with a comedy-like structure, employing mistaken identities, disguises and conscious deceptions to create an intricate web of interconnected narratives which invites both characters and reader to "see face to face" even as it obliges them to "see through a glass, darkly." Ziegler uses mistaken identity and the rest to quite a different purpose. With him such conundrums are merely episodic and rarely create much suspense. On one occasion Balacin conceals his identity from Talemon, a friend to his cause; but the deception lasts only a few hours, and has no consequences. On another occasion, at the court of Xemindo, Balacin passes for Pantoja of Tannassery, but this disguise, adopted merely to avoid the repercussions of old enmities, is eventually abandoned without having in any way complicated let alone developed the plot. Abaxar, who more than once rescues Banise, is finally revealed as prince Palekin of Prom; but his true identity is immaterial, and makes no difference to his or anyone else's prospects. Sometimes characters overhear misleading conversations, but neither they nor the reader are left in much doubt about what is going on: when Balacin suspects Banise of infidelity, he is instantly reminded by Scandor that she is acting a part. Chaumigrem attempts to deceive Balacin's sister Higvanama with a letter supposedly containing her dying fiancé Nherandi's last farewell. But Ziegler makes no effort to sustain this motif: far from using it as the starting-point for a long chain of misunderstandings and narrative complications, he immediately allows Higvanama (and with her the reader) to see that Chaumigrem's communication is a fictitious report: "erdichtete Zeitung."[109] In short Ziegler sets his readers no intellectual puzzles. On the contrary he presents moral absolutes in an allegory of reassuring simplicity.

Certain episodes in *Die asiatische Banise* are even handled as *exempla*, in the manner of Ziegler's *Täglicher Schauplatz*. Thus king Xemindo's ignominious death is glossed with the comment, "Here we see how futile are the efforts of us poor mortals when we take it on ourselves to escape the decrees which fate has written in the heavenly book."[110] The wicked king and queen of Siam come to an equally exemplary end. The queen, who dies from a self-administered dose of poison, becomes a "pallid witness to divine vengeance against all unjust stepmothers,"[111] and is even given a verse like those in the *Täglicher Schauplatz*:

> Gott zahlet zwar nicht täglich aus:
> Doch ist er keinem je was schuldig blieben,
> Sein langsam Zorn drückt gar in Graus,
> Und sein Gemerk ist in Metall geschrieben.[112]

No *Exempelbuch* could be more explicit about the divine mills' tendency to grind slowly, yet also exceedingly small.

The lawyer-historians' mills may have ground faster; they certainly ground less small. Had their political challenge to the traditional *Lehrstand* succeeded, the clergy would have been eliminated as theoretical experts, and interrogative fictions would have disseminated legal thought-forms. But the seventeenth century witnessed the disappearance neither of the clerical world-view nor of the imperative fictions in which that world-view could be embodied. On the contrary, especially in the main Lutheran strongholds of Saxony and the free imperial cities, the *Lehrstand* dedicated itself to a highly effective revival of religious values, in the course of which both the clergy and their lay associates not only maintained the *Exempel* tradition, but successfully applied secular genres to their own purposes. The fictions of Harsdörffer and Ziegler offered their readers the comfort of a pre-modern symbolic universe, achieved immense success on the book market, and in so doing helped keep traditional habits of thought alive.

[1] Compare William James, *The Varieties of Religious Experience: A Study in Human Nature* (London: Longmans, Green, & Co, 1902) 128, 244-46, 382-83; Heinrich Boehmer, *Martin Luther: Road to Reformation*, tr. John W. Doberstein and Theodore G. Tappert (London: Thames & Hudson, 1957) 87-117; Erik H. Erikson, *Young Man Luther: A Study in Psychoanalysis and History* (London: Faber & Faber, 1958) 207-212, 249-50.

[2] Max Weber, *The Protestant Ethic and the Spirit of Capitalism*, tr. Talcott Parsons (1930; London: Unwin University Books, 1965) 80-81 and 211-12 (note 6), 126, 238-40 (note 104).

[3] Gerhard Ritter, *Die Neugestaltung Deutschlands und Europas im 16. Jahrhundert: die kirchlichen und staatlichen Wandlungen im Zeitalter der Reformation und Glaubenskämpfe*, Deutsche Geschichte: Ereignisse und Probleme, ed. Walther Hubatsch (1950; Frankfurt am Main: Ullstein, 1967) 224-25, 403-4; Hellmuth Rössler, *Europa im Zeitalter von Renaissance, Reformation und Gegenreformation 1450-1650* (Munich: F. Bruckmann, 1956) 262-64; Hajo Holborn, *A History of Modern Germany: The Reformation* (London: Eyre & Spottiswoode, 1965) 194-200; Jürgen Moltmann, *Christoph Pezel (1539-1604) und der Calvinismus in Bremen*, Hospitium Ecclesiae: Forschungen zur bremischen Kirchengeschichte 2 (Bremen: Verlag Einkehr, 1958) 13.

[4] "...merckmal Göttlicher werck und urteil, wie er die welt, sonderlich die Menschen, erhelt, regiert, hindert, fördert, straffet und ehret, nach dem ein jedlicher verdienet": Martin Luther, *Werke*, Kritische Gesamtausgabe, vol. 50 (Weimar: Böhlau, 1914) 383-84. Luther's attitude to the example is discussed in Wolfgang Brückner, "Historien und Historie: Erzählliteratur des 16. und 17. Jahrhunderts als Forschungsaufgabe," *Volkserzählung und Reformation: ein Handbuch zur Tradierung und Funktion von Erzählstoffen und Erzählliteratur im Protestantismus*, ed. Wolfgang Brückner (Berlin: E. Schmidt, 1974) 38-40.

[5] "...zu Glauben und Gottesfurcht..., wie denn in Warheit die Historien ein schrecklich Bild seind göttliches Zorns und Gerichtes wider alle Laster": Philipp Melanchthon, *Opera quae supersunt omnia*, ed. C. G. Bretschneider, vol. 3 (Halle: Schwetschke, 1836) col. 881. See Brückner, "Historien" 36-45.

[6] See for example Ernst Heinrich Rehermann, "Die protestantischen Exempelsammlungen des 16. und 17. Jahrhunderts: Versuch einer Übersicht und Charakterisierung nach Aufbau und Inhalt," *Volkserzählung*, ed. Brückner 598-99.

[7] Heidemarie Schade, "Andreas Hondorffs Promptuarium Exemplorum," *Volkserzählung*, ed. Brückner 646-703; Rehermann 633.

[8] See Brückner, "Historien" 53-75; Rehermann 580-83, 611, 614, 620-21.

[9] See Schade 655; Rehermann 599.

[10] See Brückner, "Historien" 110-120, 120-123; Rehermann 630-45, 622-25, 641-44.

[11] Compare Hans Robert Jauss, *Ästhetische Erfahrung und literarische Hermeneutik*, vol. 1 (Munich: W. Fink, 1977) 156.

[12] Matthäus Hammer, *Rosetum Historiarum...* (Leipzig: Göpner & Scheibe, 1657) Vorrede.

[13] Brückner, "Historien" 108. I have not been able to see a copy of Richter's text.

[14] Martin G[r]undmann, *Geist- und Weltliche Geschichtschule...* (Dresden: A. Löffler, 1655) prefatory poem.

[15] See C. Träger, "Ständeklausel," *Wörterbuch der Literaturwissenschaft*, ed. Claus Träger (Leipzig: Bibliographisches Institut, 1986) 489-90, 663; Bernhard Asmuth, *Einführung in die Dramenanalyse* (Stuttgart: J. B. Metzler, 1980) 25, 27-29. The separation of styles is discussed in Erich Auerbach, *Mimesis: The Representation of Reality in Western Literature*, tr. Willard R. Trask (1946; Princeton: Princeton UP, 1953) 23, 31, 41-49, 72-73, 151-55, 312-18, 362-64, 554-55.

[16] See Rehermann 633.

[17] For example, Wolfgang Bütner's *Epitome Historiarum* (1576) was offered "Den sichern aber und rohem Weltpöbel / zum schrecken und abschewe," see Rehermann 633. Compare Schade 660-61 on Hondorff's "Vorrede an den Leser" in his *Promptuarium Exemplorum* (1568).

[18] Rehermann 633. See also Brückner, "Historien" 40, 50-51; Schade 661.

[19] See Herbert Wolf, "Erzähltraditionen in homiletischen Quellen," *Volkserzählung*, ed. Brückner 754; Melanchthon col. 879.

[20] Walter Benjamin, *Ursprung des deutschen Trauerspiels*, ed. Rolf Tiedemann (1928; Frankfurt am Main: Suhrkamp, 1978) 119-137. Wilhelm Kühlmann, *Gelehrtenrepublik und Fürstenstaat: Entwicklung und Kritik des deutschen Späthumanismus in der Literatur des Barockzeitalters* (Tübingen: M. Niemeyer, 1982) 54, 267-71, 276-77.

[21] Compare Kühlmann 184, note 117.

[22] Benjamin 72-75; Kühlmann 272.

[23] Kühlmann 275-76.

[24] Thus Conrad Wiedemann, who is indebted to the work of Gerhard Oestreich on Justus Lipsius and the theory of the absolutist state, thinks of *Gelehrten*, meaning both clergy and lawyers, as humanists and projectors of a poetic utopia which prefigures the absolutist state: see Wiedemann, "Barocksprache, Systemdenken, Staatsmentalität: Perspektiven der Forschung nach Barners 'Barockrhetorik'," *Internationaler Arbeitskreis für deutsche Barockliteratur: erstes Jahrestreffen in der Herzog August Bibliothek Wolfenbüttel 27. bis 31. August 1973: Vorträge und Berichte*, Dokumente des Internationalen Arbeitskreises für deutsche Barockliteratur 1, 2nd. ed., ed. Paul Raabe and Barbara Strutz (Hamburg: Hauswedell, 1976) 38, 40-41. Even Kühlmann, who carefully distinguishes between clerics, philosophers and poets on the one hand, and lawyer-politicians on the other, seems at 320-28 to be regarding the traditional *Lehrstand* as educating the people for an absolutist *Policeystaat* founded on rigid social order. Elsewhere Kühlmann clearly documents the antagonism between *Lehrstand* members and the "princes' men," mainly lawyers, who supported the new regimes, see 240, 242, 285-87, 292-94, 338, 341-43, 350-51, 356, 362, 375-76.

[25] On *Lehrstand* opposition to court and absolutism, see Benjamin 77-79, 106-109, 122-25. On traditional political thinking among clergy and scholars, see Kühlmann 47-48, note 89; 52, note 106; 103, note 105; 151; 343; 365. For doubts about Oestreich's theory of *Ordnung* and *Sozialdisziplinierung* as the guiding principles of the early absolutist state, see Notker Hammerstein, "Reichspublicistik und humanistische Tradition," *Aufklärung und Humanismus*, ed. Richard Toellner, Wolfenbütteler Studien zur Aufklärung 6 (Heidelberg: L. Schneider, 1980) 77. On *Sozialdisziplinierung*, see W. Schulze, "Gerhard Oestreichs Begriff 'Sozialdisziplinierung in der frühen Neuzeit'," *Zeitschrift für histori-*

sche Forschung 14 (1987); Hans Erich Bödeker and Ernst Hinrichs, "Alteuropa — Frühe Neuzeit — Moderne Welt? Perspektiven der Forschung," *Alteuropa — Ancien Régime — Frühe Neuzeit: Probleme und Methoden der Forschung*, ed. Hans Erich Bödeker and Ernst Hinrichs, problemata 124 (Stuttgart: Frommann-Holzboog, 1991) 37-38.

[26] On Arndt, see Hans-Jürgen Schings, *Melancholie und Aufklärung: Melancholiker und ihre Kritiker in Erfahrungsseelenkunde und Literatur des 18. Jahrhunderts* (Stuttgart: J. B. Metzler, 1977) 78-79, 330. Jörg Jochen Berns, "Justus Georg Schottelius," *Deutsche Dichter des 17. Jahrhunderts: ihr Leben und Werk*, ed. Harald Steinhagen and Benno von Wiese (Berlin: Erich Schmidt, 1984) 422 notes the importance of Arndt's form of piety at the court of duke August of Brunswick-Wolfenbüttel.

[27] On Andreae see Richard van Dülmen, "Sozietätsbildungen in Nürnberg im 17. Jahrhundert," *Gesellschaft und Herrschaft: Forschungen zu sozial- und landesgeschichtlichen Problemen vornehmlich in Bayern*, Festschrift Karl Bosl (Munich: Beck, 1969) 162-64, 169-70; Kühlmann 103, 151, 172, 184, 394.

[28] For a brief account of Harsdörffer's life and work, see Irmgard Böttcher, "Der Nürnberger Georg Philipp Harsdörffer," *Deutsche Dichter des 17. Jahrhunderts*, ed. Steinhagen and von Wiese 289-346. For a fuller discussion of Harsdörffer's religion and poetics, see Jean-Daniel Krebs, *Georg Philipp Harsdörffer (1607-1658): Poétique et Poésie*, 2 vols (Berne: Peter Lang, 1983). The bibliography of the *Schau-Platz* collections can be found in Heinz Zirnbauer, "Bibliographie der Werke Georg Philipp Harsdörffers," *Philobiblon* 5 (1961): 12-49. On the novellas see Günther Weydt, *Nachahmung und Schöpfung im Barock: Studien um Grimmelshausen* (Bern: Francke, 1968) 47-57, 59-72.

[29] On Harsdörffer's "ambivalence," see Gunter E. Grimm, *Literatur und Gelehrtentum in Deutschland: Untersuchungen zum Wandel ihres Verhältnisses vom Humanismus bis zur Frühaufklärung*, Studien zur deutschen Literatur 75 (Tübingen: M. Niemeyer, 1983) 132, note 107. Differing views of Harsdörffer's position may be found in Karl Viëtor, *Probleme der deutschen Barockliteratur*, Von deutscher Poeterey 3 (Leipzig: J. J. Weber, 1928) 46-47; Rössler 628; van Dülmen 172-175; Dietrich Jöns, "Literaten in Nürnberg und ihr Verhältnis zum Stadtregiment in den Jahren 1643-1650 nach den Zeugnissen der Ratsverlässe," *Stadt-Schule-Universität-Buchwesen und die deutsche Literatur im 17. Jahrhundert: Vorlagen und Diskussionen eines Barock-Symposions der Deutschen Forschungsgemeinschaft 1974 in Wolfenbüttel*, ed. Albrecht Schöne (Munich: Beck, 1976) 90, 92.

[30] van Dülmen 154, 164; Krebs, vol. 1, 330-31.

[31] The text has been reprinted as Georg Philipp Harsdörffer, *Frauenzimmer Gesprächspiele*, ed. Irmgard Böttcher, Deutsche Neudrucke Reihe Barock 13-20 (Tübingen: M. Niemeyer, 1968-69). See Georg Adolf Narciss, *Studien zu den Frauenzimmergesprächspielen Georg Philipp Harsdörffers (1607-1658)* (Leipzig: H. Eichblatt, 1928); K. G. Knight, "G. P. Harsdörffer's 'Frauenzimmergesprächspiele'," *German Life and Letters* ns 13 (1959).

[32] On Harsdörffer and the *Fruchtbringende Gesellschaft*, see Narciss 34, 159; Krebs, vol. 1: 28-41.

[33] Hanns Hubert Hofmann, "Nobiles Norimbergenses," *Zeitschrift für bayerische Landesgeschichte* 28.1-2 (1965): 141 and Krebs, vol. 2: 22, note 150; Böttcher 299 and 339, note 67. Justus Georg Schottel, *Ausführliche Arbeit von der Teutschen Haubt Sprache...* (Brunswick: C. F. Zilliger, 1663) 1175 lists Harsdörffer as "ein Nürnbergischer vom Adel."

[34] van Dülmen 154.

[35] van Dülmen 162-64; Krebs, vol. 1: 331-32; vol. 2: 190-91, notes 7-9. See also Richard van Dülmen, "Orthodoxie und Kirchenreform: der Nürnberger Prediger Johannes Saubert (1592-1646)," *Zeitschrift für bayrische Landesgeschichte* 33.2 (1970).

[36] Krebs, vol. 1: 333-35; vol. 2: 191-92, note 13. For the view that Dilherr took the side of the city council against Saubert, see Thomas Bürger, "Der Briefwechsel des Nürnberger Theologen Johann Michael Dilherr," *Barocker Lust-Spiegel: Studien zur Literatur des Barock*, Festschrift Blake Lee Spahr, ed. Martin Bircher, Jörg-Ulrich Fechner and Gerd Hillen, Chloe 3 (Amsterdam: Rodopi, 1984) 140.

[37] Krebs, vol. 1: 334, 338. On asceticism and sabbath-reform, see F. Fritz, "Luthertum und Pietismus," *Aus dem Lande von Brenz und Bengel*, ed. Julius Rauscher (Stuttgart: Quell-Verlag, 1946) 132.

[38] *Festschrift zur 250jährigen Jubelfeier des Pegnesichen Blumenordens*, ed. Theodor Bischoff and August Schmidt (Nuremberg: J. L. Schrag, 1894) 215; Thomas Bürger 148.

[39] Böttcher 309; Krebs, vol. 1: 29; vol. 2: 16, note 108; Karl F. Otto, *Die Sprachgesellschaften des 17. Jahrhunderts* (Stuttgart: J. B. Metzler, 1972) 18.

[40] van Dülmen, "Sozietätsbildungen" 172; Böttcher 322. Compare Max Wieser, *Der sentimentale Mensch, gesehen aus der Welt holländischer und deutscher Mystiker im 18. Jahrhundert* (Gotha: Perthes, 1924) 78.

[41] Krebs, vol. 1: 336-341.

[42] Brückner, "Historien" 103-4 and 107-110 suggests that Harsdörffer's novellas are a new form of "bürgerliche Leseliteratur," satisfying an "Unterhaltungskitzel." But see Guillaume van Gemert, "Geschichte und Geschichten: zum didaktischen Moment in Harsdörffers 'Schauplätzen'," *Georg Philipp Harsdörffer: ein deutscher Dichter und europäischer Gelehrter*, ed. Italo Michele Battafarano (Bern: P. Lang, 1991) 313-331.

[43] Ruth Murphy, *Saint François de Sales et la civilité chrétienne* (Paris: A. G. Nizet, 1964) 186-87. On Camus, see Maurice Magendie, *Le Roman français au XVIIe siècle, de l'Astrée au Grand Cyrus* (Paris: E. Droz, 1932) 45, 64-65, 140-149, 329-33, 383-94.

[44] On Andreae and St. François de Sales, see Rössler 522.

[45] The letter is reproduced in van Dülmen, "Sozietätsbildungen" 185-86. (van Dülmen assumes that Harsdörffer is referring in the letter to the first and second volumes of *Heraclitus und Democritus*, but the first volume of this collection did not appear until 1652.) The "Sendschreiben" of Dilherr is dated 1648. See Georg Philipp Harsdörffer, *Der Grosse Schauplatz Lust- und Lehrreicher Geschichte: das erste Hundert* (1664; Hildesheim: G. Olms, 1978) 4. Rehermann points out (618) that clergymen drew on Harsdörffer's compilations when making their own collections of examples.

[46] Northrop Frye, *Anatomy of Criticism: Four Essays* (Princeton: Princeton UP, 1957) 222. On the novella collections, see Magendie 44-46; Frédéric Deloffre, *La Nouvelle en France à l'âge classique* (Paris: Didier, 1967) 15, 17-18; Brückner, "Historien" 47, 106-7, 122.

[47] Magendie 45, 330.

[48] "...nichts ungläubiges/ das nicht geschehen könte": G. P. Harsdörffer, *Der Grosse SchauPlatz Jämerlicher Mordgeschichte*, parts 1 and 2 (Hamburg: Johann Nauman, 1650) "Vorrede," para. 17. I refer to the individual stories in this text (*JMG*) by number only, as the pagination of the various contemporary editions differs.

[49] *Der Grosse Schauplatz Lust- und Lehrreicher Geschichte: das zweyte Hundert,* "Vorrede."

[50] *JMG,* "Vorrede," par. 2; *Der Grosse Schauplatz Lust- und Lehrreicher Geschichte: das erste Hundert,* "Zuschrifft."

[51] "Das Verlangen," *Frauenzimmer Gesprächspiele,* ed. Böttcher, part 1: 232-272.

[52] *JMG,* "Vorrede," par. 7 and 8.

[53] "Die tödtliche Einbildung," *Heraclitus und Democritus* (Nuremberg: M. Endter, 1661) no. 199. (This story is reprinted in Weydt 70-71.)

[54] "Der falsche Freund," *JMG* no. 8.

[55] Compare Otto Görner, *Vom Memorabile zur Schicksalstragödie,* Neue Forschung 12 (Berlin: Junker & Dünnhaupt, 1931) 8, 10, 27-29, 31-32; Angus Fletcher, *Allegory: The Theory of a Symbolic Mode* (Ithaca: Cornell UP, 1964) 187-88.

[56] Brückner, "Historien" 103-106.

[57] *JMG,* "Zuschrifft."

[58] The latter story is no. 13 of *Heraclitus und Democritus.* It is reprinted in Georg Philipp Harsdörffer, *Jämmerliche Mord-Geschichten: Ausgewählte novellistische Prosa,* ed. Hubert Gersch (Neuwied: Luchterhand, 1964) 74-78.

[59] "Die Falschheit ist für Gott und den Menschen ein Greuel und mit vielen Lastern verknüpffet": *JMG* no. 8.

[60] "Der stinckende Hurenhengst," *JMG* no. 10 (Gersch 14); "Der verzagte Fechter," *JMG* no. 39 (Gersch 31); "Die verzweiffelte Rache," *JMG* no. 185 (Gersch 63).

[61] "Es war aber die Zeit vorhanden/ daß solcher Betrug solte offenbaret/ und die Verbrecher zu gebührlicher Straffe gezogen werden": "Die Zauberlieb" *JMG* no. 36 (Gersch 26).

[62] "Die verwundte Keuschheit," *JMG* no. 3 (Gersch 13); "Ungeborner Kinder Hertzen," *JMG* no. 182 (Gersch 61).

[63] "Der stinckende Hurenhengst," *JMG* no. 10 (Gersch 18).

[64] Compare *JMG,* "Vorrede," par. 14.

[65] See, for example, "Die unverhoffte Rache," *JMG* no. 165 (Weydt 89-90); "Die bestraffte Unschuld," *Der Geschichtsspiegel...* (Nuremberg: W. & J. A. Endter, 1654) no. 25 (Weydt 129-30).

[66] "Der ehrlose Ehemann," *Heraclitus und Democritus* no. 13 (Gersch 74-78); "Die bestraffte Unzucht," *JMG* no. 110 (Weydt 135-36).

[67] *JMG,* "Vorrede," par. 14.

[68] *JMG* no. 8; J.-P. Camus, "Le faux Amy," *L'Amphitheatre sanglant ou sont representees plusieurs actions Tragiques de nostre temps,* book 1 (Paris: J. Cottereau, 1630) 116-128.

[69] "Der stinckende Hurenhengst," *JMG* no. 10 (Gersch 14-18); Camus, "Le puant concubinaire," *Amphitheatre* 148-161.

[70] "Die verwundte Keuschheit," *JMG* no. 3 (Gersch 9-13); Camus, "La sanglante chasteté," *Amphitheatre* 33-50.

[71] Against this view it has recently been argued that Harsdörffer's novellas or at least some of them resemble the *casus* form and are intended to exercise the intellect: see

Winfried Theiss, "'Nur die Narren und Halßstarrigen die Rechtsgelehrte ernehren...': zur Soziologie der Figuren und Normen in Georg Philipp Harsdörffers *Schauplatz*-Anthologien von 1650," *Literatur und Volk im 17. Jahrhundert: Probleme populärer Kultur in Deutschland*, ed. Wolfgang Brückner, Peter Blickle and Dieter Breuer, part 2, Wolfenbütteler Arbeiten zur Barockforschung 13 (Wiesbaden: Harrassowitz, 1985) 907-8.

[72] Magendie 140-43, 384-85; Walter Ernst Schäfer, "Hinweg nun Amadis und deinesgleichen Grillen!: die Polemik gegen den Roman im 17. Jahrhundert," *Germanisch-Romanische Monatsschrift* 46, New Series 15 (1965): 370.

[73] "Nam & scelestissima Necromantiam pro divina sapientia venditabat, & impuris libidinibus virgineum & conjugalem thorum polluebat, & ferocitate bestiali animos generosos imbuebat, & religionis legumque vincula dissolvebat, & vanis fabulis puriorem mentem occupabat": Johann Valentin Andreae, *Mythologiae Christianae...Libri Tres* (Strasbourg: L. Zetzner, n.d.) 46-47. Cf. François de la Noue, *Discours politiques et militaires*, ed. Philippe Canaye (Basle: F. Forest, 1587) 136-145.

[74] Schäfer 373-375 suggests that Bucholtz knew the work of Camus, perhaps through Harsdörffer, and used it as his model. Bucholtz was in close touch with duke August of Brunswick-Wolfenbüttel, who was an admirer and patron of Andreae: see *Sammler, Fürst, Gelehrter: Herzog August zu Braunschweig und Lüneburg 1579-1666: Niedersächsische Landesausstellung in Wolfenbüttel: 26 Mai bis 31 Oktober 1979* (Brunswick: Herzog August Bibliothek, Wolfenbüttel, 1979) 228-30.

[75] On the date of composition of Bucholtz' romances, see Ulrich Maché, "Die Überwindung des Amadisromans durch Andreas Heinrich Bucholtz," *Zeitschrift für deutsche Philologie* 85 (1966): 545. The content of the two romances is summarised in Leo Cholevius, *Die bedeutendsten deutschen Romane des siebzehnten Jahrhunderts: ein Beitrag zur Geschichte der deutschen Literatur* (1866; Stuttgart: B. G. Teubner, 1965) 119-123, 139-143.

[76] The differences between the two writers have been noted by Günther Weydt, "Der deutsche Roman von der Renaissance und Reformation bis zu Goethes Tod," *Deutsche Philologie im Aufriss*, 2nd. ed., ed. Wolfgang Stammler, vol. 2 (Berlin: E. Schmidt, 1960) col. 1263; and Adolf Haslinger, *Epische Formen im höfischen Barockroman: Anton Ulrichs Romane als Modell* (Munich: Fink, 1970) 118-19, 146-50, 205-6, 275-76, 329.

[77] On Bucholtz's politics, see Volker Meid, "Absolutismus und Barockroman," in *Der deutsche Roman und seine historischen und politischen Bedingungen*, ed. Wolfgang Paulsen, Neuntes Amherster Kolloquium zur deutschen Literatur (Bern: Francke, 1977) 64-66.

[78] Herkules is "ein Ebenbilde eines nach Vermögen volkommenen Christen der im weltlichen Stande lebet" — see Andreas Heinrich Bucholtz, "Freundliche Erinnerung An den Christlichen...Leser," *Des christlichen teutschen Gross-Fürsten Herkules und der böhmischen königlichen Fräulein Valiska Wunder-Geschichte*, facsimile of the 1659 ed., ed. Ulrich Maché, 4 vols., Nachdrucke deutscher Literatur des 17. Jahrhunderts, ed. John D. Lindberg 6 (Bern: Herbert Lang, 1973-79). All of my references to this text are to Maché's edition. On Bucholtz's condemnation of *Amadis*, compare Maché, "Die Überwindung" 545-47, 550, 553-54.

[79] *Herkules*, part 2: 960.

[80] "An den gewogenen gottseligen Leser," *Der Christlichen Königlichen.Fürsten Herkuliskus und Herkuladisla...Wunder-Geschichte* (Brunswick: Zillinger & Gruber, 1665).

[81] Compare Weydt, "Der deutsche Roman" col. 1263; Maché, "Die Überwindung" 552.

[82] Compare Weydt, "Der deutsche Roman" col. 1264-65; Haslinger 118-19.

[83] *Herkules*, part 1: 5 and 12-13.

[84] The text is divided into 8 books. Valiska is abducted roughly half-way through book 2 (part 1: 354) and rescued at the end of book 5 (part 2: 250).

[85] For the summary, see *Herkules*, part 2: 951-57.

[86] *Herkules*, part 1: 400 and 405.

[87] *Herkules*, part 1: 687.

[88] Maché's claim ("Die Überwindung" 559) that Bucholtz's romances superseded *Amadis* seems exaggerated.

[89] The content of the story is summarised in Cholevius 154-161.

[90] Hans-Gert Roloff, "Heinrich Anshelm von Ziegler und Kliphausen," *Deutsche Dichter des 17. Jahrhunderts*, ed. Steinhagen and von Wiese 798-818. On the *Stift* at Wurzen and Ziegler's position there, see J. H. Zedler's *Grosses vollständiges Universal-Lexicon*, vol. 60 (Leipzig: Zedler, 1749) col. 334, 337.

[91] See Herbert Helbig, "Der Adel in Kursachsen," *Deutscher Adel 1555-1740*, Büdinger Vorträge 1964, ed. Hellmuth Rössler, Schriften zur Problematik der deutschen Führungsschichten in der Neuzeit 2 (Darmstadt: Wissenschaftliche Buchgesellschaft, 1965) 235-37, 240-42; F. L. Carsten, *Princes and Parliaments in Germany* (Oxford: Clarendon Press, 1959) 224-57; Hans Haussherr, *Verwaltungseinheit und Ressorttrennung vom Ende des 17. bis zum Beginn des 19. Jahrhunderts* (Berlin: Akademie-Verlag, 1953) 45-52; Heinz Schilling, *Höfe und Allianzen: Deutschland 1648-1763*, Siedler Deutsche Geschichte (Berlin: Siedler, 1989) 136-140.

[92] See "Sprachgesellschaften," *Sachwörterbuch zur deutschen Geschichte*, ed. Hellmuth Rössler and Günther Franz (Munich: R. Oldenbourg, 1958).

[93] Heinrich Anselm von Ziegler und Kliphausen, *Täglicher Schau-Platz der Zeit...* (Leipzig: J. F. Gleditsch, 1695).

[94] *Täglicher Schau-Platz* 146.

[95] *Täglicher Schau-Platz* "Vorbericht."

[96] On Alberti's opposition to Pufendorf, see Karl Freiherr von Ledebur, *König Friedrich I von Preussen: Beiträge zur Geschichte seines Hofes, sowie der Wissenschaften, Künste und Staatsverwaltung seiner Zeit* (Leipzig: Otto Aug. Schulz, 1878) 65.

[97] Roloff 802, 805, 808.

[98] Heinrich Anselm von Zigler und Kliphausen, "Nach Standes-Gebühr Geehrter Leser!" *Asiatische Banise: Vollständiger Text nach der Ausgabe von 1707 unter Berücksichtigung des Erstdrucks von 1689*, ed. Wolfgang Pfeiffer-Belli (Munich: Winkler, 1965) 12-14. My references to *Die Asiatische Banise (AB)* are to this edition.

[99] "diesen tapfern Printzen," *AB* 12. For Scandor's narrative, see *AB* 43-92, 102-179.

[100] Compare Weydt, "Der deutsche Roman" col. 1270; Haslinger 126-27.

[101] See *AB* 159, 250-52, 395.

[102] Volker Meid, *Der deutsche Barockroman* (Stuttgart: J. B. Metzler, 1974) 53; Haslinger 174-77.

[103] Frye 197.

[104] "Ja, ich wünschte wohl herzlich gar ein Mädchen zu sein, so dörfte es noch eher ohne sonderliches Blutvergießen ablaufen," *AB* 45. For Scandor on drowning, see *AB* 37.

[105] *AB* 15-17. "der tödlich verwundete Chaumigrem, welcher sich so ofte mit unschuldigem Blute besudelt, sich in dem häufigen Blute brüllende herumwälzen, und mit Ach und Weh seinen schwarzen Geist der flammenden Hölle zuschicken mußte," *AB* 408.

[106] Frye 186, 189.

[107] *AB* 202.

[108] For Banise's perils and rescue, see especially *AB* 236-37, 241-42, 247-48, 272, 275, 373-75, 398-408.

[109] *AB* 21-24; 161; 412-13; 259-60 (for instances of eavesdropping, see 76, 162-65, 253-60); 78, cf. Haslinger 208.

[110] "Hier sehen wir, wie vergebens wir arme Menschen bemühet sind, wenn wir uns unterstehen, den Schluß zu meiden, welchen das Verhängnis in das Himmels-buch...eingeschrieben hat," *AB* 203.

[111] "ein blasses Zeugnis der göttlichen Rache gegen alle ungerechte Stiefmütter," *AB* 337.

[112] *AB* 338. An approximate equivalent might be:

> God pays not ev'ry day, it's said:
> Yet he with just deserts has never stinted.
> His patient wrath is stamped in dread,
> And his great works on earth in bronze are printed.

4: The Second Phase of Modernisation: Thomasius and the Psychological Novel

THE CLERICAL WORLD-VIEW and the imperative tradition of narrative did not go completely unchallenged by the younger generation at the close of the seventeenth century. The publication of *Die asiatische Banise* coincided with the early work of Christian Thomasius, who became the leading thinker of the second phase of modernisation in Germany. The first had been a struggle for control of the state, a struggle between princes and court lawyers on the one side and territorial estates on the other. In that struggle, the lawyers had been political winners but social losers: though most Protestant territories moved towards princely absolutism, the lawyers had lost their hold on government by the end of the Thirty Years' War. The second phase of modernisation was to be a struggle between lawyers and clergy for control of the universities and the intellectual life of educated commoners.[1] The antagonism between lawyers and clergy, already apparent in the early seventeenth century, thus became yet more pronounced and, so far from forming a united middle class front against the nobility, these two principal groups of educated commoners put their best energies into attacking one another.

The academic lawyers' most forthright spokesman was Christian Thomasius, who graduated from the Leipzig philosophy faculty, where his father was a professor, at the age of seventeen in 1672. The young Thomasius then turned to jurisprudence, completing his doctorate in civil and canon law at Frankfurt on the Oder in 1679. After practising law for a while, he returned to Leipzig university as a jurist.[2] In 1687 he both published his first major legal work, the *Institutiones jurisprudentiae divinae*, a textbook of natural law theory based on Grotius and Pufendorf, and broke with convention by lecturing in the vernacular instead of Latin. During the next two years he published a German periodical, the *Monats-Gespräche*, which reviewed recent publications in law, theology and *belles lettres* and commented on topics of current interest in a series of dialogues between a nobleman, a scholar, a merchant and a schoolteacher, all of them members of a fictitious "Gesellschafft derer Müßigen."[3] The *Institutiones*, the vernacular lectures and the *Monats-Gespräche* were all calculated to loosen the hold of the theology faculty on the intellectual life of the university and to promote the legal-historical world-view.

By attacking the Lutheran clergy in Leipzig, Thomasius was meeting the enemy head on. If electoral Saxony was the Lutherans' stronghold, then the universities of Wittenberg and Leipzig could be taken for their guardhouses. Both universities required their theologians to take an oath of loyalty to Luther's teaching. The leading figures in the Leipzig theology faculty — J. B. Carpzov, August Pfeiffer and Valentin Alberti — were vehement controversialists who engaged in famous disputes and controlled both the manner and the matter of teaching in the university's other faculties, over which they exercised the right of censorship. Philosophy in all its branches was taught according to Aristotle, following a decree of 1591 which remained in force until the eighteenth century. The disputation was the central academic exercise, and the sole approved language of scholarship was Latin.[4]

As far back as the late sixteenth century, lawyer-historians had begun to think of themselves as revealing the ugly faces hidden behind public men's prepossessing masks. Bodin wanted the historical analysis of motive and intention to supersede hagiographical chronicles of great men, while the desire to unmask inspired a series of notable sceptics from Montaigne to La Rochefoucauld, the first edition of whose *Maximes* appeared in 1665 with a frontispiece in which a child, symbolising love of truth, tore from a bust of Seneca the mask hiding his real features.[5] Thomasius set himself the task of unmasking the theologians and philosophers of Leipzig, and exposing what he saw as the sinister reality behind their respectable public face.

The first issue of the *Monats-Gespräche* carried a satirical dedication to "Monsieur Tarbon Et Monsieur Bartuffe," a fairly obvious recombination of those literary types of hypocrisy and pedantry, Molière's Tartuffe and J.-L. Guez de Balzac's Barbon.[6] The conceit had a double purpose. The allusion to Tartuffe, who used his appearance of piety to tyrannise over others, was a thrust not only at theologians in general but at Valentin Alberti in particular.[7] He and his colleagues presented the public face of men of religion. Thomasius identified their religion as the claim of traditional experts to absolute knowledge, and the mask of intellectual tyranny. He viewed the Leipzig theology faculty as a monopolistic craft guild applying strict rules of entry — orthodoxy, Aristotelianism, latinity — and replenishing itself largely from its own members' children.[8] And the faculty did indeed show many signs of attempting to stifle all dissenting opinion from outside its ranks, and of insisting on an exclusive right to pronounce not only on theological but also on political issues.[9] So far as Thomasius was concerned, here was the head and front of a Lutheran establishment no less papistical than the Catholic hierarchy.[10] The reference to Barbon was intended to expose the academic philosophers, whose public face was that of men of learning, but whose erudition, according to Thomasius, was a mere mask for Aristotelian obscurantism. For Thomasius ranked Aristotle, still the presiding genius of German philosophy faculties, as the founding father of pedantry, who exhibited (as did his modern followers) all the characteristics enumerated

by that tradition of satirical writing which, from the Renaissance onwards, condemned in the would-be wise their appetite for abstruse concepts and rebarbative terminology, their repellent dress and manners,
their anti-social disposition and their persistent melancholia.[11]

Thomasius's attacks on the Leipzig academic establishment provoked
the theology faculty into a series of increasingly hostile responses, culminating in 1689 in a ban on his teaching and publishing in Saxony.
However a dispute with the Leipzig theologians about an inter-
confessional marriage between the princely houses of Saxony and
Brandenburg had commended Thomasius to Friedrich III, elector of
Brandenburg, who now invited him to lecture at the *Ritterakademie* in
Halle.[12] Thomasius was as much at home in Halle, where Brandenburg
nobles trained for posts in government and administration, as he had
been out of place in Leipzig. Brandenburg had been drawn into the
sphere of the modernising Calvinist princes early in the seventeenth
century. Elector Johann Sigismund converted to Calvinism in 1613. The
Great Elector Friedrich Wilhelm I, who succeeded to the throne in 1640,
had outdone all his German Protestant rivals in establishing central monarchical rule in the period after the Thirty Years' War. The estates' powers had been drastically curtailed; new government agencies had been
established to collect the taxes necessary to support a powerful standing
army; and a policy of religious toleration had been pursued in order to
attract skilled craftsmen into the region[13] Hence Brandenburg in 1690
was the most modern of the German Protestant territories, and the one
best suited to someone with Thomasius's cast of mind.[14]

Following a brief but successful career at the *Ritterakademie*, Thomasius was given a much larger academic audience when that institution
expanded into a full university, the Fridericiana, in 1694. The university
of Helmstedt, founded by a modernising prince some hundred years
earlier, had already begun to shift the emphasis of academic study from
theology to history and law. But Halle carried this process further: here
traditional clerical experts ceded their place to modernising, legal experts. Halle was a Lutheran foundation, and one of its principal functions
was still to train clergy for the Lutheran territorial church of Brandenburg. But no stringent test of Lutheran orthodoxy was applied to the
faculty members, and the university's theologians were prohibited by
statute from engaging in confessional polemics. The first holders of theology chairs were not themselves orthodox Lutherans but pietists, whom
the state preferred over their doctrinally uncompromising brethren.[15]
Philosophy and *literae humaniores* also lost ground at Halle, along with
theology: Christoph Cellarius, professor of eloquence and history in the
1690s, lectured to small audiences, and despaired of keeping Greek
studies alive in an institution whose ethos he rendered as "ius, ius, ius et
nihil plus."[16]

For Halle was above all a school of law. Law was the largest faculty, with 64% of matriculations by 1700, compared with 30% for theology.[17] Moreover, whereas in the older universities theology, as the senior faculty, headed the institution as a whole, at Halle responsibility for the general welfare of the university was vested by statute in the senior law professor.[18] This striking innovation not merely institutionalised the separation of sacred and secular spheres demanded by modern political thought but affirmed that preeminence of secular over sacred which is so generally assumed in the modern world-view. Thomasius may well not have been fully conscious of the historic significance of this transition. Indeed so far from being a thoroughgoing secularist he always considered himself a Protestant believer and was even influenced, between 1692 and 1702, by the Halle pietists.[19] Nevertheless the lawyer who had been driven from traditional Leipzig because he presumed to differ from theologians on political issues now received the state's support for the doctrine that general responsibility for the common weal — "die gantze Vorsorge für das gemeine Wesen" — rested with the legal profession.[20] His lectures, his legal opinions and his many published works rapidly made Thomasius the best-known member of the Halle law faculty. In the public eye he, more than any other contemporary, embodied the notion of the legal expert as adviser to the age. If in former times Melanchthon ranked as *praeceptor Germaniae*, that position now passed for a while to Thomasius.[21]

Thomasius rejected systematic theology for empiricist jurisprudence. He found the only valid source of knowledge in personal experience supplemented by other people's experience as recorded in history.[22] Thomasius, who held the lawyer's maxim to be "*little theory* and *much practice*" — "*kurtze Theorie* und *lange Praxin*"[23] — belongs in large part to the jurisprudential tradition exemplified by Oliver Wendell Holmes's well-known dictum that "The life of the law has not been logic: it has been experience."[24] According to that tradition legal knowledge, being empirical, must take the form of probabilistic statements. Even if other faculties regarded their dicta as infallible and incontrovertible, lawyers — Thomasius held — were "sufficiently modest to represent theirs as no more than probable."[25] Given this sceptical view of truth, critical eclecticism was the only possible philosophy for a lawyer. In his *Introductio ad philosophiam aulicam* of 1688, which specifically identifies eclecticism as a court phenomenon, in contrast to the dogmatism of the schools, Thomasius advised his readers to select the finest flowers from all the different philosophical sects.[26] Reason not authority should govern the choice.

The general picture of the world which most commended itself to Thomasius was that adopted by earlier legal-historical writers like Bodin or the Dutch humanists. Thomasius understood human affairs in terms not of final but of efficient causes, among which the weightiest was purposive action by human agents. Like many of his contemporaries in an age of court politics, Thomasius attached great importance to nonrational impulses as motives for action. The idea of the ruling passions, traceable as far back as the Bible and the Fathers, had persisted into Thomasius's time as the typology of three dominant psychological humours — lust, ambition, and avarice — employed by writers in the natural law tradition, such as Pufendorf, and by the Spanish Jesuit Baltasar Gracián, who gave a thoroughly sceptical and pessimistic account of human motivation.[27] Thomasius himself believed that men were governed by one or other of the three humours, and developed a theory of the behavioural, linguistic and gestural signs by which any individual's dominant humour might be recognised.[28] Secretiveness and jealousy in love indicated an ambitious man, for example; indiscretion and carelessness of rivals indicated a lustful one.

As a young man, Thomasius believed that an ethical order might be imposed on the chaos of the conflictual universe. In the *Einleitung zur Sittenlehre*, published in 1692, he argued that reason could so overcome the passions in the realm of private morality, the realm of *honestum* which the law could not regulate, that the human race might ultimately attain harmony. However the *Ausübung der Sittenlehre* of 1696 and the definitive *Fundamenta Juris Naturae et Gentium* of 1705 took the more sceptical view that individuals might merely achieve such an equilibrium of the passions as to prevent the worst excesses of any single one of them.[29] This ethical pessimism, sometimes thought to reveal a Lutheran loyalty to the doctrine of original sin, is perhaps best seen merely as an anticipation of the eighteenth century Enlightenment theory, held for instance by David Hume, of world history as a losing battle between reason and unreason.[30] For all his scepticism about the sphere of unenforceable private morality, Thomasius envisaged that the conflictual universe could be successfully regulated in the sphere of enforceable public rights and duties, or *iustum*. Earlier German legal experts, such as Conring, who assisted the modernising princes had relied for the most part on Aristotelian principles mediated through Bodin. Thomasius turned instead to the tradition of natural law. Following Grotius rather than Pufendorf, he elaborated a system of civil law based on individual rights instead of obligations within a divinely-ordered universe, and thus contributed to the formation of modern society.[31]

Thomasius concerned himself not merely with the legal instruments by which such a society might be regulated but also with the code of politeness by which its members might be guided. As early as his Leipzig lecture of 1687 on the question "Welcher Gestalt man denen Frantzosen in gemeinem Leben und Wandel nachahmen solle?" he commended the French ideal of *galanterie*, which he defined as a combination of the famous "je ne sais quoi" of the courtesy tradition with good style, the manners of the courtier, wit, knowledge, and a cheerful disposition: the courtly opposite of the schoolman's reputed melancholia.[32] Much of this could be traced to courtesy books based on Castiglione. But the lecture on French manners also mentions "bon goût," an idea central to the work of Gracián, whom Thomasius was to treat at length in subsequent lectures, with the aid of Amelot de la Houssaie's annotated French edition of the *Oráculo manual y arte de prudencia.*[33] Gracián's rules of taste mark, as Gadamer has argued, a decisive stage in the seventeenth-century courts' replacement of the sectional values of traditional élites by a common standard of politeness.[34] Such a standard remained a central concern of Thomasius who, in his later Halle years, incorporated the concept of *decorum* into his natural law theory alongside *honestum* and *iustum* in the belief that, whether or not men do justice, a society without politeness is unworthy of the name.[35]

Politeness was above all the art of conversation, for conversation both embodies and sustains the mixed society.[36] Thomasius expected lawyers, as custodians of *decorum*, to exemplify it in their own lives by entering into civilised dialogue with each other and all men of good will. The lawyers were to model themselves on Socrates, whose method Thomasius considered to be the ideal of dialogic, non-authoritarian education. Members of a Socratic faculty of law would not merely reject the methods of the clerics and philosophers whom Thomasius regarded as exponents of an austere, authoritarian Aristotelianism, but by practice and example would transform the university as a whole from a gaggle of feuding status groups into a truly polite society.[37] Halle under Thomasius, Notker Hammerstein suggests, engaged in enough of such dialogue to achieve, uniquely in Germany at this time, the quality of society attained in Paris *salons* or London clubs.[38] A picture of Thomasian dialogue emerges from the four-cornered discussions between men of different rank published in the *Monats-Gespräche*. The genial Hamburg merchant Christoph typically engages Augustin the travelled nobleman and Benedict the scholar in a friendly discussion, while the narrator anticipates the reactions of his readers in an attempt to involve them also. The fourth participant, the schoolmaster David, ignores the conventions, discourteously repudiates the others' views, seeks to impose his own, and so plays the part of fool among wise men that he provokes justified protests from his companions. Their complaints, by embodying much of Thomasius' own thinking, enable him to advance his own ideas without appearing dogmatic, and thus to practise the politeness which he preached.[39]

Thomasius's belief in dialogue made him a sympathetic reader of Daniel Casper von Lohenstein's *Großmütiger Feldherr Arminius*, published in 1689.[40] In *Arminius*, Lohenstein makes Hermann's battle against

Rome into a framework for extended analysis of political and philosophical subjects. This synthesis of fiction and discourse superficially resembles Barclay's *Argenis* but in fact introduces a kind of dialogue more innovative than Barclay's, or indeed Thomasius's. For while neither Barclay's nor Thomasius's dialogue conceals their sympathies from the reader, Lohenstein's allows each speaker to contribute an unprivileged — or equally privileged — opinion in turn. No-one refutes anyone else, or emerges as the author's spokesman, nor does the ensemble reach anything approaching an agreed conclusion: the reader has to decide which if any of the characters' various opinions commands his assent. Such a technique characterises Lohenstein as the proto-*Aufklärer* of Dieter Kafitz's interpretation, affirming free enquiry as the only possible means to truth, and adopting a value system which precisely excluded authoritative teaching.[41] Lohenstein's technique won him high praise from Thomasius, who reviewed *Arminius* for the *Monats-Gespräche*. "I can truly say," Thomasius wrote, "that...I have never read a romance which requires more thought than *Arminius*." The text's power to provoke thought resided not in any obscurity of style but in the importance of the issues raised and in the manner of their presentation. For "having considered the rights and wrongs of an issue," Thomasius explained, Lohenstein "does not decide it, but leaves the decision to the reader."[42] In *Arminius* Lohenstein had created a new form of interrogative writing, and Thomasius's appreciation of it has been recognised as a milestone in the theory of the novel in Germany.[43]

However the *Arminius* review was by no means Thomasius's only contribution to the contemporary debate about fiction. In the first conversation between the four members of the "Gesellschafft derer Müßigen," and in a series of sometimes lengthy reviews of German and French novels, Thomasius ranged far beyond the erudite fictional dialogue exemplified by *Arminius*, and showed himself to be a knowledgeable reader with a well-developed theory of fiction in general.[44] As might be expected of the most prominent German legal expert of the late seventeenth century, he saw the capacity of less unconventional narrative forms than Lohenstein's for asking their readers questions and inducting them into the legal-historical view of the universe.

Thomasius's theory followed from his idea of "public" and "secret" history. By public history, he understood the hagiographical mode which continued to flourish in the seventeenth century despite the criticisms of men like Bodin. The public historian confronted with the task of recording the events of a particular reign showed the monarch forming alliances, waging wars and concluding treaties to the advancement of his kingdom. In short, such a historian presented events as a design completed by a powerful — and sometimes all-powerful — will. For the kings of public history tend always to become figures of more-than-human stature fulfilling a divinely-appointed destiny.[45] Thomasius, with his sceptical view of human nature, rejected this mode of history-writing which, by observing the *bienséances* of the aristocratic genres of imaginative literature, and omitting everything which might be considered ignoble, sordid or trivial, presented monarchs as heroes of romance. In Thomasius's judgment this effort was both deceptive and misconceived, for heroism was but the public mask concealing the reality of private passions.[46]

Hence the historian's proper task was precisely to reveal the working of the passions in the lives of great men, to tell the "secret" history behind public events. The maxim of public history was: "Tell no lies." That of secret history was: "Omit no truth." Secret history would show private intrigues, ambitions and jealousies as moving forces in political conflict. Once their heroic masks were stripped away, great men would often appear more childish than children, more womanish than women, and more servile than slaves;[47] and this disclosure, however disconcerting it might seem to some, was essential to an understanding of history. For only by laying bare these secrets of the heart could the historian enable the reader to form a valid opinion on the rights and wrongs of the actions of great men, and on their responsibility for the fate of their people.[48] This historical theory was by no means peculiar to Thomasius, a number of whose contemporaries also accepted the "scandalous chronicle" as a valuable historical tool. Pierre Bayle for instance argued that, given what he took to be the depraved state of human nature, truth must necessarily have the appearance of slander.[49] Doctoral dissertations were written in German universities on the value as historical evidence of books like *Les Anecdotes de Pologne* and *Les Mémoires de Mr L.C.D.R.*, and scholars shelved such titles in the history section of their libraries.[50]

The special interest of Thomasius's approval of scandalous chronicle lies in his application of the historical model it implied to the development of a para-historical theory of fiction, which he divided into two categories, the one corresponding to public and the other to secret history. Fictional romance corresponded to public history, and of course shared its vices and deficiencies. In romance a perfect hero triumphs over all obstacles. However, in Thomasius's judgment, the fiction-writer had no business to represent his characters as angels or even demigods, and ought not to model them on "an idea of human perfection" — "eine ideam hominis perfectissimi." Homer and Virgil might have initiated the romance tradition of semi-divine heroes, but even their authority could not justify it.[51] *Amadis* and the pastoral romances had represented an impossible perfection rightly ridiculed by Cervantes in *Don Quixote* and Charles Sorel in *Le Berger extravagant*.[52] Yet even in Thomasius's own time, he found some fiction writers continuing to idealise human behaviour in general and, above all, to posit a form of love between the sexes which was no more real than Plato's republic.[53] As Thomasius developed this analysis, he modified his critical judgments accordingly. Whereas in 1688 he gave A. H. Bucholtz a favourable mention, by 1710 he was condemning the author of *Herkules* for imagining men to be other than they are.[54]

Thomasius specifically associated idealising romances with the schoolmen, as his remark about *The Republic* suggests. In fact he was one of the first commentators to identify such texts as vehicles of clerical teaching, a function which only served as far as Thomasius was concerned to damn romance more deeply, as the replication, in fictional narrative, of that intellectual arrogance and remoteness from reality for which he so vehemently attacked the theologians of Leipzig.

Theologians had used exemplary romance to influence their readers' moral conduct. Now Thomasius fundamentally challenged the validity of example-teaching. While others might more cautiously have left such a venerable institution unscathed, he preferred to brave the moralists' wrath by listing its defects. As a philosopher, Thomasius concluded that examples could illustrate propositions but not prove them.[55] As a lawyer, he distrusted examples on the ground that actions must not be judged by their consequences.[56] As a moralist, he found examples in practice unable to move the will.[57] A man would no more seek good and shun evil without direct, personal experience of both than he would seek or shun a food of which he had read but never tasted. Therefore, concluded Thomasius, controversially enough for his day and contrary, as he put it, to the teaching of sour-faced stoics, no-one can live a moral life unless he has experienced the passions in his own person.[58]

If Thomasius was remarkable among contemporaries for his dissatisfaction with romance — the fictional equivalent of public history — he was no less unusual in his enthusiasm for the sort of fiction which approximated to the secret history. At a time when many moralists still regarded fiction as altogether sinful or, at the very most, justified it as a narrowly exemplary device, Thomasius went out of his way to recommend, in articles and reviews, stories which he considered not exemplary at all, but rather "true to life,"[59] the life of the conflictual, causal-mechanical universe moved by human passion. Thomasius wanted the writer of fiction to let human — that is, all-too-human — nature everywhere show through events: "überall Menschheit vorblicken lassen."[60] His business was therefore to reveal, in any given work, the "characteristics of one or other of the passions."[61] Fictional narrative would thus resemble the narratives of facts presented in law cases, where the aim was above all to elucidate the motives of the agents involved.

Just as Thomasius associated exemplary fiction with schoolmen lacking experience of the great world, he insisted that fiction which was true to life could only be written by men — or women — with a knowledge of the world of affairs: "Politische Welt-Klugheit."[62] Good novels would therefore be expected to issue from the courts, as the centres of political and diplomatic activity, and novelists would be court nobles, ministers, statesmen, or court ladies. Here, as elsewhere, Thomasius relied on the notion of mimesis, and assumed a pre-existent reality available to the imitative fiction-writer. Those who knew the "reality" of court life and court intrigue were best placed to reproduce it in their texts. He might equally well have argued that those who inhabited the legal-historical world of thought were best situated to write fiction predicated on that world.

Thomasius's idea of fiction as a mimesis of reality by writers close to reality would seem to place the novel at the opposite end of the spectrum from conventional literary forms. And of course Thomasius condemned the remoteness from life of romance, the most highly conventionalised of literary patterns. But Thomasius's vision of a conflictual world which might ultimately be capable of regulation naturally inclined him towards comedy, although a somewhat darker form of comedy than Barclay's or Anton Ulrich's. Judging by the texts Thomasius reviewed favourably, he set no store by comic resolution. The novelist might choose to remain in the topsy-turvy world of intrigue, rather than rising out of it to an ideal world at the end. All Thomasius required of narrative structure was cogent motivation, and he more than once criticised plots which hinged on unconvincing novelistic devices such as telltale words spoken in sleep.[63] The real attraction of comedy for Thomasius was its treatment of character. In the classical canon stage comedy was the genre which was free of the *bienséances* and able to explore human nature — if only as manifested in the middle and lower orders of society — in all of its peculiarities.[64] Therefore the comic tradition could assist the novelist in his task of representing the whole range of *Affekte* or psychological humours. Thomasius thought of many characters in the novels he valued as being akin to comic humours and complimented novelists by comparing their creations with one or other of Molière's most admired figures: Alceste, Tartuffe or Célimène.[65] The anonymous but Thomasian treatise entitled *Raisonnement über die Romanen*, published in 1708, appeals to Molière as model for the novelist, calling him the "wonder of the age" — 'Wunder des Seculi" — who "knew how to present all the humours so vividly."[66]

Thomasius felt he knew not merely who could write but also who would read the kind of realistic fiction he advocated. Thus a satirical piece on Aristotle in the *Monats-Gespräche* begins with an episode in which a philosophy student takes a law student to task for his interest in novels.[67] Elsewhere in that publication, Thomasius observes that it would be ridiculous for a clergyman to give a courtier a stack of devotional books, and equally ridiculous for someone to give the clergyman *Liebes-Historien*.[68] The young Thomasius, at least, viewed the novel as essential reading for the man of law and the man of affairs. And despite his Pietist period, when he turned away from "satirical books" ("Satyrischen Schriften"), in later years he continued to recommend novels to his students and to young people wanting to get to know the world.[69]

While Thomasius plainly knew what he wanted lawyers to read, the more interesting question, how he wanted them to read, remains to be answered. If fiction was not to teach morality by example, what was it to do? The *Monats-Gespräche* suggest that inexperienced young men can get from novels an armchair introduction to human nature: intelligent novels depict character-types as a bestiary depicts exotic animals, thus enabling the intelligent novel-reader to get a good idea of his fellow men's infinite variety without wasting time or endangering life in risky social encounters.[70] This pedagogical, or informational, notion of the novel could be seen as casting the novelist in the part of authoritative teacher to the reader's docile pupil, and Thomasius has in fact been described, by Woitkewitsch for instance, as using the realistic novel for dogmatic teaching, rather than stimulating the reader's own thought processes, in the manner adumbrated by the *Arminius* review.[71]

Yet other comments, and Thomasius's own practice as reader, indicate that he did not regard novel-reading as a mere passive absorption of psychological facts. His understanding of the reading process almost certainly owes something, as Hans Hinterhäuser notes, to the French theorist P. D. Huet, who remarked in his *Traité de l'origine des romans* that "nothing can de-rust the mind so well as reading good novels."[72] Thomasius wrote of the mind being "sharpened" by fiction.[73] Novels were particularly valuable for the man of affairs, because they taught "the art of analysing character."[74] Such art or skill is not acquired by mere absorption of factual information but depends on experience and practice not always readily available given the restricted opportunities which the averagely various and extended social circle will offer for investigating the mysteries of other people's minds. Novel-reading, as understood by Thomasius, would greatly increase the quality as well as the quantity of experimental human contact by equipping the reader with a sort of societal simulator. With the aid of this device he could practise his psychological skills by bringing his mind actively to bear on highly adapted motivational and attitudinal data about which he was precisely obliged to form his own conclusions. The novel, in short, so far from simply providing the reader with the bald facts of modern legal-historical investigation, could assist him to engage in such investigation and thus to perform the mental processes required in a world based on legal-historical thought: to perceive individuals as agents, understand their motives, and assess their responsibilities.

These processes are now taken for granted in connection with realist novels, which are customarily read for the characters' motives, and those motives' interaction with the course of events. The reader starts with few clues and modifies his reading of character as he acquires more. In order to make sense of the text, he must understand its conventions, and above all the notions of agent, motive and intention. Given that understanding he can analyse the characters and judge the actions about which he reads. Both exercises will be essentially open-ended, for different readers will interpret clues in different ways and draw different conclusions from characters' behaviour: and it is this possibility of independent analysis and judgment which leads Thomasius to recommend the novel to lawyers wishing to learn how to weigh evidence and pass judgment and to statesmen desirous of calculating each other's intentions and policies.

Thomasius's reaction to Catherine Bernard's *Éléonore d'Yvrée*[75] shows how he approached the business of reading, namely by asking himself the sort of questions that a lawyer must try to answer in the courtroom: what kind of people were the actors in the story, what were their real motives, and who was responsible for the outcome of events. In *Éléonore d'Yvrée* the duke of Meissen's mother has the eponymous heroine betrothed to the elderly count de Retelois, while tricking Meissen into thinking that Éléonore has taken a young husband. Meissen engages himself to Mathilde, but learning of his mother's deception, wishes to break his engagement. Éléonore marries de Retelois in the hope of making Meissen keep his word to Mathilde, but he deserts her, and she dies in despair. Thomasius saw in Éléonore a woman whose reason triumphed over passion, and in Mathilde one whose passions overwhelmed her reason. Éléonore did not find happiness but her self-control protected herself and others; Mathilde's lack of control intensified her own and others' misery.[76] That quite another verdict on *Éléonore d'Yvrée* would be possible is indicated by Bernard de Fontenelle's contemporary judgment that none of the three principal characters in the story could be blamed for their predicament.[77]

As a writer of fiction Thomasius chose satire, the form that Northrop Frye particularly associates with the empiricist and the pragmatist.[78] In his polemics Thomasius often evoked not merely Guez de Balzac's Barbon, but the pedant Hortensius in Charles Sorel's comic romance, *Francion*.[79] Thomasius's own contribution to the tradition of anti-pedant satire was the character of David, the schoolmaster of the "Gesellschafft derer Müßigen." David, the orthodox Lutheran and Aristotelian, likes to distinguish himself from the common herd by a display of erudition, but his syllogisms and technical terms merely render him unfit for polite society. He generally cuts a poor figure among men of the world, and becomes the butt of broad farce when pitched out of a carriage head-first into the snow, or attacked by a cat at an inn.[80]

Thomasius attempted a longer piece of fiction on the subject of the arch-pedant Aristotle in the April 1688 issue of the *Monats-Gespräche*, which contains sketches for a satirical novel "von des *Aristotelis* seinen Courtesien."[81] The philosophy student Cyllenio mocks the law student Cardenio for reading novels, and challenges him to write one on the life of Justinian. Cardenio turns the joke against Cyllenio by writing instead on Aristotle. But the interest of the piece lies in the way that Cardenio tells the story. First he sketches the outline of Aristotle's life as known to history. Then he starts a new text, concentrating on Aristotle's love-life, and supplying motives for his behaviour, that of Pythias, his first wife, and that of Olympias, whom Cardenio shows as falling in love with Aristotle. Finally Cardenio converts his story into a burlesque novel in which Aristotle falls in love with Olympias, using intrigue and blackmail to win her for himself. The three different versions of the story show Thomasius the lawyer-historian ranging over a set of facts for which he envisages different possible explanations.

Though Thomasius's own attempts at fiction-writing were satirical, he did not give priority to satire in his recommendations to the readers of the *Monats-Gespräche*.[82] His psychological and juridical interest led him to court romance and especially the work of duke Anton Ulrich, which is mentioned in the general discussion of fiction by the "Gesellschaft derer Müßigen" and in the *Arminius* review. Thomasius did not greatly concern himself with the metaphysical implications of Anton Ulrich's comic structures, but was fascinated by the duke's portrayal of human nature and human action. Since Thomasius himself understood psychology as a study of basic types, he found much that he considered true to life and revealing of human behaviour in Anton Ulrich's schematic and typical characterisation. Thomasius's Hamburg merchant Christoph asserts that virtues and vices are so well portrayed in *Aramena* that full appreciation requires more than one reading. Indeed Christoph claims that Anton Ulrich shows the ways of the world as if in a mirror: and conveys a true impression of political life.[83]

When Thomasius published the *Monats-Gespräche* Anton Ulrich's second romance *Octavia* was not yet complete. Only three of the six books had thus far appeared; but, according to Thomasius, the reading public eagerly awaited the remainder. *Octavia*, he suggested in his review of *Arminius*, contained more wisdom than Aristotle's *Ethics* and *Politics* combined, particularly concerning human psychology — "die Lehre von affecten."[84] What interested him most was Anton Ulrich's treatment of the characters of Messalina and Locusta.[85] *Aramena* had contained an example of rehabilitation in the successful plea on behalf of Amphilite; facts alleged against her were explained in such a way as to vindicate her honour: an "inside story" made public events appear in a new light. In *Octavia*, much the same thing happens to Messalina, who is the mother of the heroine, and must for her sake be rehabilitated. Annius Vivianus enters a plea in her defence, omitting none of the facts related by the Roman historians, but interpreting them so as to establish Messalina's innocence. This plea shifts the responsibility for her supposed crimes to a serving woman who allegedly contrived to implicate Messalina and drive her to her death. Benedict, the scholar member of the "Gesellschafft derer Müßigen," claims greatly to have enjoyed the ingenious invention of this narrative, which he has compared with the historical accounts of Messalina's life.[86] Annius Vivianus' plea, if not contradicted by historical evidence, is not supported by it either. But Anton Ulrich's treatment of Messalina is interrogative writing of the type Thomasius valued for its effect of stimulating thought by putting the reader in the position of a juryman confronted with two conflicting accounts of a case and required to decide which is the more probable given the established facts and the known character of the participants.

Apart from court romances it was the *nouvelle*, the characteristic fictional form of Louis XIV's reign, which was best calculated to place the reader in this position and which most aroused Thomasius's interest. Whereas the earlier *romans à longue haleine* ran to thousands of pages of complex and stylised prose telling the intertwined stories of numerous couples ranging over huge distances in remote periods as well as places and subject to seemingly endless vicissitudes, the French *nouvelles* of the later seventeenth century usually narrated in no more than a couple of hundred pages the outwardly uncomplicated affair of a single pair of lovers living in France in the period of the religious wars or even the reign of Louis XIII or XIV.[87] By using the middle register of style, narrating events chronologically, and representing men's weaknesses rather than their strengths, the *nouvelle* drew ever closer to contemporary history-writing.[88] While the writers of *nouvelles* often took their characters from history — as witness *La Princesse de Clèves* — and sometimes passed off pure invention as historical truth, historians for their part felt free to supply from imagination the thoughts and feelings their subjects might have had, and the conversations they might have held. Hence by Thomasius's time the conventions of the two genres were barely distinguishable, and contemporary readers had such difficulty telling fact from fiction that Pierre Bayle felt called upon to deplore the intellectual confusion caused by the "mélange de la vérité et de la fable" in large numbers of recent publications.[89]

The *nouvelle*'s very closeness to the model of the secret history naturally appealed to Thomasius: *nouvelles* contributed as much as any other form to his general ideas on the nature and working of narrative. His estimate of the genre appears in the debate on fiction in the "Gesellschafft derer Müßigen." The judicious and broadminded Christoph confesses himself an avid reader of "little French novels" — "kleinen Frantzösischen Werckgen."[90] With surprising candour, he explains that the portrayal of "illicit love" ("unerbare Liebe") in the *nouvelle* fascinates him; in this respect he very much shares the taste of his creator, who penned several lengthy and considered reviews of *nouvelles* dealing with excesses of love.

As late as the romances of Honoré d'Urfé or Madeleine de Scudéry love had still been understood as an absolute desire for the good, which knew no aberrations but existed only in proportion to the nature of its object. A lover whose mistress was faithful expected that others would also love her virtue. A lover whose mistress proved unfaithful immediately ceased, on that account, to love her. By the latter half of the century, however, love was no longer understood as the appetite of reason but as unreasoning passion. It could demand exclusive rights in a worthy object or attach itself to an unworthy one. In other words it could, by any rational standard, become excessive; and love in excess was jealousy, the salience of which in the late seventeenth century imagination is exemplified by the tragedies of Racine.[91] Jealousy also preoccupied the *nouvellistes*, whose treatment of the subject seems to have impressed Thomasius as the most significant aspect of their work. Jealousy was a central theme in *Éléonore d'Yvrée*,[92] and played an equally important part in two other *nouvelles* which he chose to review during 1689. He thought that Louise Gillot's *Le Mary jaloux*, besides presenting a perfect figure of a coquette, portrayed the boundless jealousy of the comte de Villesevran "thoroughly and with a nice attention to detail."[93] The anonymous *Agnes de Castro* contrasted the different emotions aroused by Don Pedro's love for his wife's waiting-woman, Agnes: his wife controlled her jealousy out of affection for the girl; but Elvira, also in love with Pedro, let herself be ruled by what Thomasius described as "unreasonable jealousy" — "*irraisonnable* Eyffersucht."[94]

Thomasius's work for the *Monats-Gespräche* indicates his conviction that a modern, legal-historical culture would be a literary culture, founded on French rather than classical materials, and favouring fiction in the "legal" mode: that is, the *casus*-like psychological novel. Much evidence exists to suggest that Thomasius's contemporaries in the law and in politics read the kind of stories he valued: Anton Ulrich's and Lohenstein's romances; and above all the whole range of French "secret histories" and *nouvelles*. Clerical opponents of fiction associated the novel-reading habit with lawyers and statesmen: Gotthard Heidegger discovered it "bey dem größesten Theil der Politicorum," Michael Lilienthal among "Nobilibus inprimis & hominibus Politicis."[95] And the libraries of many leading lawyers did in fact contain large quantities of fiction, much of which was in French.[96] J. P. Ludewig, a colleague of Thomasius at

Halle, owned several well-known *nouvelles* in the original French — including *La Princesse de Clèves*, Jean de Préchac's *L'Héroïne mousquetaire* and Edme Boursault's *Ne pas croire ce qu'on voit* — as well as German translations, including that of *Agnes de Castro* under the title of *Wettstreit der Liebe, der Tugend, und der Eifersucht*.[97] E. G. Rinck, law professor at Altdorf, owned stories by Madame de Villedieu and the abbé de Saint-Réal, as well as other *nouvelles*.[98] These holdings indicate that legal-historical narrative, which had taken over the small sphere of the German courts in the earlier seventeenth century, spread during Thomasius's time to a rather wider circle comprising both university lawyers and their pupils, who later pursued careers not only at court but in government and administration generally.

But this sort of fiction was by no means generally read. Though the fact that much of it remained in French suggests its influence was limited, the main reason for regarding it as the interest of a small élite among Germans is that psychological fiction did not develop within native German literature. The "gallant" novels of August Bohse and C. F. Hunold, written between 1685 and 1710, were in no sense equivalent to the contemporary French *nouvelle*. The low esteem in which they were held by the legal élite is suggested by Thomasius's comments on Bohse's *Liebes-Cabinet der Damen*. Bohse offered the novel as a study of female psychology, but Thomasius, whose taste had so largely been formed by the French writers, found Bohse's women vulgar, and his story devoid of all moral and political interest.[99] Lawyers who possessed French *nouvelles*, and even Bohse's and Hunold's own stylistic manuals, often ignored German gallant novels almost entirely.[100] In fact the gallant novel owed more to the established German tradition of moralising romance and the *exemplum* than to the French *nouvelle*.[101] It can best be understood as an adaptation of the *Banise* model for a relatively unlettered German public consisting mainly of women and students and subscribing to different values from those advocated by Thomasius. His initiatives, far from firmly establishing the legal-historical manner of thought in Germany, in fact provoked a vigorous counter-attack from traditionalists which threatened even the ascendancy he had gained among academics.

[1] For the university as cultural successor to the court, see "Diskussionsbericht zum Beitrag Notker Hammerstein, 'Der Wandel der Wissenschafts-Hierarchie und das bürgerliche Selbstbewusstsein: Anmerkungen zur aufgeklärten Universitätslandschaft'," *Tradition, Norm, Innovation: soziales und literarisches Traditionsverhalten in der Frühzeit der deutschen Aufklärung*, ed. Wilfried Barner, Schriften des Historischen Kollegs: Kolloquien 15 (Munich: Oldenbourg, 1989) 295.

[2] On Thomasius's life and work, see Christian Thomas, *Kleine deutsche Schriften*, ed. Julius Otto Opel (Halle a. d. Saale: O. Hendel, 1894); Roderich von Stintzing and Ernst Landsberg, *Geschichte der deutschen Rechtswissenschaft*, section 3, part 1 (Munich: Old-

enbourg, 1898) 76-109; Georg Witkowski, *Geschichte des literarischen Lebens in Leipzig* (Leipzig: B. G. Teubner, 1909) 204-19; Notker Hammerstein, *Jus und Historie: ein Beitrag zur Geschichte des historischen Denkens an deutschen Universitäten im späten 17. und 18. Jahrhundert* (Göttingen: Vandenhoeck & Ruprecht, 1972). Thomasius' publications are listed in Rolf Lieberwirth, *Christian Thomasius: sein wissenschaftliches Lebenswerk: eine Bibliographie*, Thomasiana 2 (Weimar: Böhlau, 1955).

3 See Witkowski 203-218; Heinz Schulz-Falkenthal, "Christian Thomasius — Gesellschafts- und Zeitkritik in seinen *Monatsgesprächen* 1688/89," *Wissenschaftliche Zeitschrift der Martin-Luther-Universität Halle-Wittenberg: Gesellschafts- und sprachwissenschaftliche Reihe* 4.4 (1955).

4 On Leipzig university, see Hammerstein, *Jus* 267-91.

5 See Antoine Adam, *Histoire de la littérature française au XVII° siècle*, vol. 4 (Paris: Domat, 1954) 102.

6The dedication, which is unpaginated, precedes the paginated text for January, 1688, in the collected edition of the *Monats-Gespräche*, which was published as Christian Thomasius, *Freymüthige Lustige und Ernsthaffte...Gedancken Oder Monats-Gespräche...* (Halle: Salfeld, 1690). This edition contains the issues for 1688 in two volumes, and those for 1690 in one. My references to the *Monats-Gespräche (M-G)* are to this edition, and are given in the form of year date, volume (in the case of 1688), and page number.

7 Compare Witkowski 204.

8 See especially Christian Thomasius, "Erfindung der Wissenschaft anderer Menschen Gemüt zu erkennen: Schreiben an Friedrich III., Kurfürst von Brandenburg, zu Neujahr 1692," *Aus der Frühzeit der deutschen Aufklärung: Christian Thomasius und Christian Weise*, ed. F. Brüggemann, Deutsche Literatur...in Entwicklungsreihen: Reihe Aufklärung 1 (Leipzig: Reclam, 1928) 66. Compare Witkowski 199; Hammerstein, *Jus* 47.

9 See for example Thomasius's dispute with H. G. Masius: *Kleine deutsche Schriften*, ed. Opel 10, 15.

10 See for example Christian Thomasius, *Kurtzer Entwurff der Politischen Klugheit / sich selbst und andern in allen Menschlichen Gesellschaften wohl zu rathen* (Frankfurt and Leipzig, 1710) 62. On Thomasius's anticlericalism, see Stintzing and Landsberg 83-84; Schulz-Falkenthal 546-47; Hammerstein, *Jus* 143.

11 See Irmgard Wedemeyer, "Das Menschenbild des Christian Thomasius," *Wissenschaftliche Zeitschrift der Martin-Luther-Universität Halle-Wittenberg: Gesellschafts- und sprachwissenschaftliche Reihe* 4.4 (1955): 524; Schulz-Falkenthal 548-49; Hans-Jürgen Schings, *Melancholie und Aufklärung: Melancholiker und ihre Kritiker in Erfahrungsseelenkunde und Literatur des 18. Jahrhunderts* (Stuttgart: J. B. Metzler, 1977) 39, 43, 58; Wilhelm Kühlmann, *Gelehrtenrepublik und Fürstenstaat: Entwicklung und Kritik des deutschen Späthumanismus in der Literatur des Barockzeitalters* (Tübingen: M. Niemeyer, 1982) 423; Gunter E. Grimm, *Literatur und Gelehrtentum in Deutschland: Untersuchungen zum Wandel ihres Verhältnisses vom Humanismus bis zur Frühaufklärung* (Tübingen: M. Niemeyer, 1983) 356-61.

12 On Thomasius and Friedrich III, see *Kleine deutsche Schriften*, ed. Opel 18; Heinrich Rüping, "Thomasius und seine Schüler im brandenburgischen Staat," *Humanismus und Naturrecht in Berlin — Brandenburg — Preussen: ein Tagungsbericht*, ed. Hans Thieme, Veröffentlichungen der Historischen Kommission zu Berlin 48 (Berlin: de Gruyter, 1979) 76.

[13] On Brandenburg under the Great Elector, see F. L. Carsten, *The Origins of Prussia* (Oxford: Clarendon Press, 1954) 179-277.

[14] Hammerstein, *Jus* 154; Rüping 78. It is worth noting that, whereas the Prussian *ancien régime* has often been represented as authoritarian, modern analysts argue that it in fact allowed considerable scope to individual liberty: see for example Rainer C. Baum, "Authority and Identity: The Case for Evolutionary Invariance," *Identity and Authority: Explorations in the Theory of Society*, ed. Roland Robertson and Burkart Holzner (Oxford: Basil Blackwell, 1980) 78, 92.

[15] On Halle university, see Hammerstein, *Jus* 153-61; Notker Hammerstein, "Zur Geschichte der deutschen Universität im Zeitalter der Aufklärung," *Universität und Gelehrtenstand 1400-1800: Büdinger Vorträge 1966*, ed. Hellmuth Rössler and Günther Franz, Deutsche Führungsschichten in der Neuzeit 4 (Limburg/Lahn: Starke, 1970) 145-65. On the decline of literary studies at Halle, see Friedrich Paulsen, *Geschichte des gelehrten Unterrichts auf den deutschen Schulen und Universitäten*, 2nd ed., vol. 1 (Leipzig: Veit & Comp., 1896) 531-34.

[16] Hammerstein, "Zur Geschichte der deutschen Universität" 159.

[17] Rüping 77.

[18] Hammerstein, *Jus* 161.

[19] See Werner Schneiders, "300 Jahre Aufklärung in Deutschland," *Christian Thomasius 1655-1728: Interpretationen zu Werk und Wirkung*, ed. Werner Schneiders, Studien zum achtzehnten Jahrhundert 11 (Hamburg: Meiner, 1989) 13-14; Grimm 347-48.

[20] Thomasius, *Kurtzer Entwurff der Politischen Klugheit...* 64-65; Hammerstein, *Jus* 65.

[21] Hammerstein, *Jus* 375-76. On Thomasius's influence, see also Stintzing and Landsberg 109; Hammerstein, "Zur Geschichte der deutschen Universität" 164.

[22] See Hammerstein, *Jus* 127.

[23] Thomasius, *Kurtzer Entwurff der Politischen Klugheit...* 93.

[24] Oliver Wendell Holmes, Jr., *The Common Law* (Boston: Little, Brown & Co., 1881) 1; cf. 213, 312.

[25] "so bescheiden, daß sie die ihrigen nur für wahrscheinlich ausgeben": Christian Thomasius, *Höchstnöthige Cautelen Welche ein Studiosus Juris...zu beobachten hat* (Halle: Renger, 1710) ch. 10, par. 52, note 10. See Hammerstein, *Jus* 133; Luigi Cataldi Madonna, "Wissenschafts- und Wahrscheinlichkeitsauffassung bei Thomasius," *Christian Thomasius 1655-1728*, ed. Schneiders 115-136.

[26] See the German translation under the title *Einleitung Zur Hoff-Philosophie...*, 2nd ed. (Berlin: Rüdiger; Leipzig: J. L. Gleditsch and M. G. Weidmann, 1712) 20-21. On the nature of Thomasius's eclecticism, see Michael Albrecht, "Thomasius — kein Eklektiker?" *Christian Thomasius 1655-1728*, ed. Schneiders 73-94.

[27] See L. B. Walton, introduction, *The Oracle: A Manual of the Art of Discretion: Oráculo manual y arte de prudencia*, by Baltasar Gracián (London: Dent, 1953).

[28] Thomasius outlines his semiotic theory in his "Erfindung der Wissenschaft anderer Menschen Gemüt zu erkennen" (see note 8, above). Compare Hammerstein, *Jus* 66-67; Heinrich Rüping, *Die Naturrechtslehre des Christian Thomasius und ihre Fortbildung in der Thomasius-Schule*, Bonner Rechtswissenschaftliche Abhandlungen 81 (Bonn: Röhrscheid, 1968) 36-39, 48. Interesting contemporary material on the dominant passions

can be found in Johann Georg Walch, *Philosophisches Lexicon*... (Leipzig: Gleditsch, 1726-): see the articles "Caracterisiren," "Temperament," "Wille."

[29] Compare Hans M. Wolff, *Die Weltanschauung der deutschen Aufklärung in geschichtlicher Entwicklung* (Bern: Francke, 1949) 27-46; Rüping 39.

[30] Compare Hayden White, *Metahistory: The Historical Imagination in Nineteenth-Century Europe* (1973; Baltimore: Johns Hopkins UP, 1975) 55, 62-64.

[31] Stintzing and Landsberg 93-94; Rüping 44; Klaus Luig, "Das Privatrecht von Christian Thomasius zwischen Absolutismus und Liberalismus," *Christian Thomasius 1655-1728*, ed. Schneiders 148-172, especially 151-52. On the ideas of Grotius as the basis of the modern state, see Leonhard Bauer and Herbert Matis, *Geburt der Neuzeit: vom Feudalsystem zur Marktgesellschaft* (Munich: Deutscher Taschenbuch Verlag, 1988) 467-472.

[32] "Christian Thomas eröffnet Der Studierenden Jugend zu Leipzig in einem Discours, Welcher Gestalt man denen Frantzosen in gemeinem Leben und Wandel nachahmen solle?" Christian Thomasius, *Allerhand bisher publicirte kleine Teutsche Schrifften*... (Halle: Salfeld, 1701) 15. In a discussion in the *Monats-Gespräche*, it is said that "allezeit die aller galantesten und gelehrtesten Leuthe grosse Spötter gewesen," but that "die *Pedanten* gemeiniglich melancholisch und von gezwungenem Schertz sind" (*M-G* 1688, vol. 1: 661). On clerical opposition to Thomasius's reception of Gracián, see Helmuth Kiesel, *"Bei Hof, bei Höll": Untersuchungen zur literarischen Hofkritik von Sebastian Brant bis Friedrich Schiller* (Tübingen: M. Niemeyer, 1979) 186-97.

[33] Baltasar Gracián, *L'Homme de Cour*, trans. Amelot de la Houssaie (Paris: Martin & Boudot, 1684).

[34] Hans-Georg Gadamer, *Wahrheit und Methode: Grundzüge einer philosophischen Hermeneutik* (Tübingen: Mohr, 1960) 32-33. See also Karl Borinski, *Baltasar Gracian und die Hoflitteratur in Deutschland* (Halle a. S.: M. Niemeyer, 1894) 39-52. For a somewhat different view of Gracián, see Otto Brunner, *Adeliges Landleben und europäischer Geist: Leben und Werk Wolf Helmhards von Hohberg 1612-1688* (Salzburg: O. Müller, 1949) 131-32.

[35] For detailed discussions of Thomasius's theory of *decorum* see Rüping, *Naturrechtslehre* 44, 48, 50-52; Hammerstein, *Jus* 58-62; Wedemeyer 527-28; Manfred Beetz, "Ein neuentdeckter Lehrer der Conduite: Thomasius in der Geschichte der Gesellschaftsethik," *Christian Thomasius 1655-1728*, ed. Schneiders 199-222.

[36] On the importance which Thomasius attached to conversation see for example "Christian Thomas eröffnet Der Studierenden Jugend einen Vorschlag, Wie er einen jungen Menschen, der sich ernstlich fürgesetzt, Gott und der Welt dermahleins in vita civili rechtschaffen zu dienen...binnen dreyer Jahre Frist...zu informiren gesonnen sey," *Allerhand bißher publicirte Kleine Teutsche Schrifften* 259-60. Compare Claudia Henn-Schmölders, "Ars conversationis: zur Geschichte des sprachlichen Umgangs," *Arcadia: Zeitschrift für vergleichende Literaturwissenschaft* 10 (1975).

[37] See Christian Thomasius, trans., *Das Ebenbild eines wahren und ohnpedantischen Philosophi oder das Leben Socratis*, by Charpentier (Halle: Salfeld, 1693). Compare Borinski 77-78; Benno Böhm, *Sokrates im 18. Jahrhundert: Studien zum Werdegange des modernen Persönlichkeitsbewusstseins*, 2nd ed., Kieler Studien zur deutschen Literaturgeschichte 4 (Neumünster: Wachholtz, 1966) 28-34; Schulz-Falkenthal 549; Gertrud Schubart-Fikentscher, "Unbekannter Thomasius," *Wissenschaftliche Zeitschrift der Martin-Luther-Universität Halle-Wittenberg: Gesellschafts- und sprachwissenschaftliche Reihe* 3.1

(1953-54): 143, 145. On Thomasius's conception of university society, see Wedemeyer 523-29.

[38] Notker Hammerstein, "Reichspublicistik und humanistische Tradition," *Aufklärung und Humanismus*, ed. Richard Toellner, Wolfenbütteler Studien zur Aufklärung 6 (Heidelberg: L. Schneider, 1980) 77.

[39] *M-G* 1688, vol. 1: 245. See Thomas Woitkewitsch, "Thomasius' 'Monatsgespräche': eine Charakteristik," *Archiv für Geschichte des Buchwesens* 10 (1970): especially 665-66.

[40] "Daniel Caspers von Lohenstein Grossmüthiger Feld-Herr Arminius," *M-G* 1689: 646-686.

[41] On Lohenstein's text see Dieter Kafitz, *Lohensteins Arminius: disputatorisches Verfahren und Lehrgehalt in einem Roman zwischen Barock und Aufklärung* (Stuttgart: J. B. Metzler, 1970) 71-77; Adalbert Wichert, *Literatur, Rhetorik und Jurisprudenz im 17. Jahrhundert: Daniel Casper von Lohenstein und sein Werk: eine exemplarische Studie* (Tübingen: M. Niemeyer, 1991) 350-364.

[42] "Ich kan wohl sagen /...daß ich keinen Roman gelesen / der mehr nachsinnen braucht als der Arminius. Aber hieran ist nicht die Dunckelheit des Schreibers / sondern die Wichtigkeit der entworffenen Sachen schuld / und die Art und Weise / daß der Herr von Lohenstein mehrentheils / nachdem er eine Sache auff beyderley Recht erwogen / nichts determiniret / sondern dem Leser dasselbige zuthun überläst," *M-G* 1689: 667-68. Compare Kafitz 36-39.

[43] Wilhelm Vosskamp, *Romantheorie in Deutschland: von Martin Opitz bis Friedrich von Blanckenburg* (Stuttgart: J. B. Metzler, 1973) 116-18.

[44] *M-G* 1688, vol. 1: 1-112; 1689: 99-154, 687-805.

[45] Compare Orest Ranum, *Artisans of Glory: Writers and Historical Thought in Seventeenth-Century France* (Chapel Hill: University of North Carolina Press, 1980) 3-5; 15, 19, 114-15; 118-19.

[46] Christian Thomasius, *Naevorum Jurisprudentiae Romanae Antijustinianeae Libri Duo* (Halle: Salfeld, 1695) preface and par. 5-6; Christian Thomasius, *Diss. de Fide Juridica*, respondent Matthaeus Lupin (Halle: Salfeld, 1699) par. 38, 44.

[47] Thomasius, *Diss. de Fide* par. 38, 41, 44; *Naevorum...Libri Duo* preface and par. 5-6.

[48] Thomasius recommended the reading of secret histories in *Höchstnöthige Cautelen*, ch. 5, par. 68.

[49] Hayden White 49.

[50] J. B. Mencke, *Dissertationum academicarum...Decas* (Leipzig: M. Blochberger, 1734) contains a dissertation "De commentariis historicis, quos Galli Memoires vocant," in which various late seventeenth-century titles are discussed. The catalogue of the library of the lawyer and Leipzig city councillor F. B. Carpzov (1649-99), published under the title *Bibliotheca Carpzoviana...* (Leipzig, 1710) lists *Mémoires de Mr de Pontis*, *Mémoires de Mr L. C. D. R.* and *Mémoires de Madame la Comtesse R** avant sa retraite* as "Libri historici" (73), rather than "Literatores."

[51] *M-G* 1689: 731.

[52] *M-G* 1689: 732-33. Compare *Höchstnöthige Cautelen*, ch. 8, par. 40, note a).

[53] *M-G* 1689: 115.

[54] *M-G* 1688, vol. 1: 45; *Höchstnöthige Cautelen*, ch. 8, par. 40, note a).

[55] *M-G* 1688, vol. 2: 682: "Exempla illustrant, exempla non probant."

[56] *Kurtzer Entwurff* 26, 30.

[57] See Hammerstein, *Jus* 146.

[58] See the review of *Éléonore d'Yvrée*, *M-G* 1689: 113-21.

[59] For the use of *Wahrscheinlichkeit* as a criterion of judgment see for example *M-G* 1688, vol. 1: 25, 27-28; 1689: 135, 150-51, 730, 734. Truth to life is regarded as the distinguishing mark of the novel by P. D. Huet in his *Traité de l'origine des romans* (1670), see Vosskamp 79, and note 72, below.

[60] *M-G* 1689: 731.

[61] "den *Character* eines und andern gewissen *Affects*": *M-G* 1688, vol. 1: 49; compare 1689: 100, 660-61.

[62] *M-G* 1689: 101. See also 1688, vol. 1: 49.

[63] *M-G* 1689: 150-51; see also 135.

[64] Compare Chapter 3, note 15 on the separation of styles.

[65] *M-G* 1688, vol. 1: 50; 1689: 130. See also the reference to Molière at *M-G* 1688, vol. 1: 59 and Borinski 137 note 2 on the importance of Molière to seventeenth-century *politici*.

[66] "...alle Affecten...so lebhaft abzumahlen gewust": *Raisonnement über die Romanen* (n. p., 1708) 27-28.

[67] The term Thomasius uses is *Liebes-Historien*: *M-G* 1688, vol. 1: 449-50.

[68] *M-G* 1689: "Zueignungs-Schrifft an meine Feinde."

[69] Thomasius refers to a warning against satire given him by P. J. Spener: see Borinski 84, note 5. For Thomasius's renewed recommendation of satirical pieces after his Pietist period, see *Höchstnöthige Cautelen*, ch. 8, par. 38.

[70] *M-G* 1689: 100, 660.

[71] See Woitkewitsch 673.

[72] "rien ne dérouille tant l'esprit...que la lecture des bons Romans": Pierre Daniel Huet, *Traité de l'origine des romans*, ed. Hans Hinterhäuser (1670; Stuttgart: J. B. Metzler, 1966) 95-96. On Thomasius's debt to Huet, see 26*-27*.

[73] "der Verstand vortrefflich...geschärffet wird": *M-G* 1688, vol. 1: 43.

[74] "die Kunst derer Leute Gemüther zuerforschen": *M-G* 1688, vol. 1: 50.

[75] *Éléonore d'Yvrée, ou les malheurs de l'amour* was first published in Paris in 1687. It has been reprinted as Catherine Bernard, *Les Malheurs de l'Amour: première Nouvelle, Éléonore d'Yvrée* (Genève: Slatkine, 1979). It was praised in *Le Mercure galant* August 1687: 288. The same periodical published an anonymous review of the novel by Bernard le Bouvier de Fontenelle, who may have helped Catherine Bernard to write it: see *Le Mercure galant* September 1687, part 1: 324-29. On this *nouvelle*, see Alain Niderst, *Fontenelle* (Paris: Plon, 1991) 115-17. For Thomasius's review, see *M-G* 1689: 110-127. Thomasius probably knew the Fontenelle review, since he comments (112) in a similar way to Fontenelle (325) on the absence from the story of complicated intrigue. Thomasius's mouthpiece Christoph mentions his liking for *Le Mercure galant*, see *M-G* 1688, vol. 1: 23, 32-34.

[76] *M-G* 1689: 111, 122, 124-25.

[77] *Le Mercure galant* September 1687, part 1: 327.

[78] Northrop Frye, *Anatomy of Criticism: Four Essays* (Princeton: Princeton UP, 1957) 229-30.

[79] See for example "Programma lectiones illas determinans: Defensio Momi et Zoili adversus Hypocritas et Pedantas, 1690," *Programmata Thomasiana* (Halle and Leipzig, 1724) 122, where Thomasius refers to Tartuffe and Hortensius.

[80] *M-G* 1688, vol. 1: 62-63, 87-88, 116, 214-217. Compare Schulz-Falkenthal 547.

[81] *M-G* 1688, vol. 1: 449-585. See Gerhart Hoffmeister, "'Aristoteles und Olympias" — Christian Thomasius' dynamischer Entwurf eines heroi-komischen Kurzromans (1688)," *Argenis: internationale Zeitschrift für mittlere deutsche Literatur* 2 (1978).

[82] He did commend Cervantes, Scarron and Sorel, see *M-G* 1688, vol. 1: 58-59; 1689: 661-64.

[83] *M-G* 1688, vol. 1: 46.

[84] *M-G* 1689: 658-59.

[85] *Die Römische Octavia...* (Nuremberg: Hofmann and Streck, 1711) vol. 1: 231-297; vol. 2: 418-476. (The pagination of earlier printings is the same.) See Adolf Haslinger, *Epische Formen im höfischen Barockroman: Anton Ulrichs Romane als Modell* (Munich: Fink, 1970) 284-85, 291.

[86] *M-G* 1688, vol. 1: 47.

[87] On the distinction between romance and *nouvelle*, see Dorothy Frances Dallas, *Le Roman français de 1660 à 1680* (Paris: J. Gamber, 1932) 10-26, 139-143; Daniel Mornet, *Histoire de la littérature française classique 1660-1700: ses caractères véritables ses aspects inconnus*, 2nd ed. (Paris: A. Colin, 1942) 301-317; Adam 171-214; Frédéric Deloffre, *La Nouvelle en France à l'âge classique* (Paris: Didier, 1967) 33-44.

[88] On the proximity of fiction and history-writing in this period, see Gustave Dulong, *L'Abbé de Saint-Réal: étude sur les rapports de l'histoire et du roman au XVII° siècle* (Paris: É. Champion, 1921); Dallas 150-56; Georges May, "L'Histoire a-t-elle engendré le roman? Aspects français de la question au seuil du siècle des lumières," *Revue d'Histoire Littéraire de la France* 55 (1955); Deloffre 53-59; Claudette Delhez-Sarlet, "'La Princesse de Clèves': roman ou nouvelle?" *Romanische Forschungen* 80 (1968); Klaus Heitmann, "Das Verhältnis von Dichtung und Geschichtsschreibung," *Archiv für Kulturgeschichte* 52.2 (1970): 250-53; Hayden White 123.

[89] May 160.

[90] *M-G* 1688, vol. 1: 43, 25. See also 23 for a further reference to "little French novels."

[91] See Anthony Levi, *French Moralists: The Theory of the Passions, 1585 to 1649* (Oxford: Clarendon Press, 1964) 184-85, 190; Claudette Delhez-Sarlet, "Les jaloux et la jalousie dans l'œuvre romanesque de Mme de Lafayette," *Revue des Sciences Humaines* 1964: 307-8.

[92] *M-G* 1689: 110-127.

[93] "außführlich und mit artigen Umbständen": *M-G* 1689: 129. See also 130, 133.

[94] *M-G* 1689:149.

[95] Gotthard Heidegger, *Mythoscopia Romantica: oder Discours von den so benanten Romans...* (Zürich, 1698) "Vorbericht"; Michael Lilienthal, *De Machiavellismo literario...*, diss., Königsberg and Leipzig, 1713, 117-18.

[96] Rolf Engelsing, "Der Bürger als Leser: die Bildung der protestantischen Bevölkerung Deutschlands im 17. und 18. Jahrhundert am Beispiel Bremens," *Archiv für Geschichte des Buchwesens* 3 (1960-61): 262, 286 contains evidence on French books in the libraries of seventeenth and early eighteenth-century lawyers.

[97] On Ludewig (1670-1743), see Hammerstein, *Jus* 169-73. Ludewig's library was catalogued under the title *Catalogus...Librorum...Joannis Petri de Ludewig...* (Halle: Lüderwald, 1745). For his fiction titles see 1481-87. *Wettstreit...* appeared in 1689, with a preface by August Bohse, who was also responsible for *Le Mary jaloux, oder der Eyfersüchtige Mann* (1689). Bohse's work was presumably inspired by Thomasius's reviews. On Bohse's mediation of French *nouvelles* to Germany, see Otto Heinlein, *August Bohse-Talander als Romanschriftsteller der galanten Zeit* (Bochum-Langendreer: H. Pöppinghaus, 1939) 23-24, 27-28.

[98] For Rinck's fiction library, see *Bibliotheca Rinckiana...* (Leipzig, n.d. [c. 1746]) 955-56, 960, 965-66, 972-74, 1010.

[99] *M-G* 1689: 654-58. Bohse's novel was published as *Talanders Liebes-Cabinet der Damen...* (Leipzig: C. Weidmann, 1685). Vosskamp (109-110) and Hoffmeister (250 and note 5) wrongly assume that Thomasius's comments refer to a pastoral romance or specifically to a work of Zesen. Thomasius's review is discussed by Ernst Schubert, *August Bohse genannt Talander*, Breslauer Beiträge zur Literaturgeschichte 27 (Breslau: F. Hirt, 1911) 27-28.

[100] Ludewig apparently owned only Hunold's *Der Europäischen Höfe Liebes- und Helden-Geschichte* (*Catalogus...Librorum* 1485). Rinck owned only Melissus' *Adelphico* (*Bibliotheca Rinckiana* 966).

[101] On Bohse's moralising, see Heinlein 17-18, 30, 35-39, 92. On exemplary elements in Hunold-Menantes, see Herbert Singer, "Die Prinzessin von Ahlden: Verwandlungen einer höfischen Sensation in der Literatur des 18. Jahrhunderts," *Euphorion* 49 (1955): 319, and Herbert Singer, *Der deutsche Roman zwischen Barock und Rokoko* (Cologne: Böhlau, 1963) 81, 103. For instances of moral didacticism in Hunold, see Christian Friedrich Hunold, *Die liebenswürdige Adalie*, reprint of the 1702 ed., ed. Herbert Singer (Stuttgart: J. B. Metzler, 1967) 328-34; Menantes [C. F. Hunold], *Der Europäischen Höfe Liebes- und Helden-Geschichte* (Hamburg: C. W. Brandt, 1744) 836-41.

5: The Traditionalist Response: Wolffian Philosophy and Exemplary Fiction in the Eighteenth Century

Rationalist Philosophers and the Moral Weeklies

THE GRADUAL MODERNISATION of Brandenburg, evidenced by the foundation of Halle and the rise of Thomasius, necessarily threatened the position of the traditional experts.[1] By 1700, clerics had become aware of a still greater loss of status than that which their forebears had endured a century earlier. The Berlin theologian Theophil Grossgebauer acknowledged this development in complaining that the secular power had grown "earthly and fleshly" and no longer cared for "the kingdom of the Lord Jesus Christ here on earth." Since, as Grossgebauer conceded, the authorities now worried most about "how to secure the state, increase revenues, raise taxes and staff administrative offices," they no longer turned to clergymen for assistance and advice but to "ingenious statesmen, clever finance ministers, and astute lawyers."[2] In consequence, commoner legal and administrative officials were paid higher salaries and enjoyed higher social status than clergymen of comparable seniority. Even before king Friedrich Wilhelm I acceded to the throne in 1713, a career in the church was beginning to lose its attraction. One clergyman observed: "It is well known that in this country no-one whose rank is at all high allows his sons to study theology."[3] Traditional religion was beginning to contemplate a rather bleak future. But a threatened cult rarely acquiesces in its own destruction. On the contrary, the experts who maintain the cult and depend on it for their *raison d'être* will defend it as best they may. When coercion is no longer available and simple revivalism has little chance of success, they will try adaptation, modifying the cult by incorporating whatever it is that threatens it, in order to maintain its following and their own power and status.[4] Hence the response to Thomasius' *Aufklärung*.

Adaptation is a collective enterprise that needs a man of vision to direct it: in eighteenth-century Germany this task fell to Christian Wolff, whose principal philosophical works in German, the *Vernünfftige Gedancken* on logic, metaphysics, ethics and politics, appeared between 1712 and 1721.[5] Wolff reworked Christianity to suit the changing times. Clergy, doctrine, the church as community: he reconsidered them all, eliminating what would not suit the new age, preserving what did, and giving the whole an apt contemporary appearance. In so doing he heartened the beleaguered clergy, and encouraged those people who felt called to the clerical role but doubted whether it remained viable in its traditional form.

Wolff very often figures in discussions of eighteenth-century culture simply as a successor to Thomasius in the struggle for enlightenment. But each criticised the other's way of thinking.[6] Thomasius came to philosophy as a lawyer and a historian; Wolff, by contrast, came from theology. When he took up mathematical philosophy, which he first taught from the mathematical chair he held at Halle between 1707 and 1723, he did so, as he said, to set theology on a firm footing.[7] He saw the philosopher as a new "religious" expert who, by means of mathematical logic, could come at truth, and possess it whole and entire. Wolff's intellectual ancestors included the great systematisers, Aristotle and the scholastics;[8] proceeding by syllogistic reasoning from simple premises, he created a vast theoretical edifice of his own, which has been described as a model of mathematical precision and logical consequence.[9] He used the vernacular (though he also published Latin versions of his principal treatises), but was not on that account in any sense a "popular" philosopher. His work had more in common with the *Summa* of Saint Thomas Aquinas than with the essayistic philosophising which was coming into fashion in the eighteenth century. Indeed far from fighting shoulder to shoulder in a common struggle, Thomasius and Wolff were the leaders of two bitterly opposed élites. For as Werner Schneiders has argued, Germany between 1680 and 1750 had not one *Aufklärung* but two.[10] One was the pluralist *Aufklärung* of the lawyers, and the other the authoritative *Aufklärung* of the philosophers. The legal experts had made their bid for supremacy under Thomasius; under Wolff, the theoretical experts struck back.

In Wolff's system the functions of the theoretical expert remained unchanged but passed from theology to philosophy, from the senior faculty to its traditional ancillary.[11] Wolff took on himself the primary expert function of constructing a cognitive and normative system. His cognitive scheme displayed many characteristics of a religious world-view. The Wolffian universe was grounded in nature rather than divine will, but according to Wolff the two coincided and nature, no less than God, decreed a traditional order for mankind. Wolff upheld the familiar notion of community, that is, of human society organised according to the model of the patriarchal family. The community's specific form in Wolff's scheme was that of a monarchic state, with the prince acting the part of father to his people.[12] Within such a state Wolff, like the seventeenth-century German schoolmen before him, expected to see the theoretical expert at the helm of government. For Wolff identified the claim to know with the claim to rule: the king would be a philosopher, the philosopher would be king. Hence Wolff's treatise "De Rege philosophante et Philosopho regnante." The ruler would be sustained not so much by a feudal rank-order of military vassals as by a bureaucratic rank-order of philosopher-administrators, reaching right down to local level. Wolff could legitimate such ideas by reference to Plato's *Republic* and to Aristotle but also found a fresh authority on government in China. His "Rede von der Sittenlehre der Sineser" extolled the Confucian mandarin state, in which a philosopher emperor acted as father to his people and a hierarchy of highly-trained officials ruled paternally over the communities in their charge.[13]

Wolff proposed to integrate the individual into the community by reshaping traditional norms. Since the Wolffian system substituted nature for the personal God, its ethical imperatives were formulated in terms of nature's law. According to Wolff, the law of nature was progress towards perfection: he was Aristotelian in envisaging perfection as a goal ahead of man, rather than a past ideal from which he has fallen.[14] Wolff's rule of life was "Do what makes you and your and others' condition more perfect; leave undone that which makes it less perfect."[15] From this general maxim he derived certain specific, and not unfamiliar, precepts. The law of God revealed in the Bible reappears as the law of nature discerned by reason. The theological virtues disappear from the canon, but Christian moral virtues are retained. Wolff reaffirmed the ascetic catalogue of private virtues — sobriety, modesty, contentedness, industry, and patience — as the ethical foundation of community.[16] The public virtues of co-operation, tolerance and adaptation advocated by Thomasius had no place in such a list but ranked merely as counsels of prudence or were treated as part of the now suspect science of politics.[17]

In Wolff's as in all traditional systems the rule which maintains the community at the same time ensures the happiness of the individual. Like the Lutheran priest before him, the Wolffian philosopher is a commitment therapist. Without membership in a well-ordered state there can be no cure for unhappiness, while to obey the philosopher-king and do one's duty in the state is to be cured.[18] Wolff's understanding of the human condition reveals a markedly religious consciousness. The world is still a dark forest full of dangers, a place where men war with themselves and others, and constantly face destruction. His images recall Baroque anxieties: nothing is certain but uncertainty; Fortune raises men to the limit of her wheel's travel only to crush them on its descent.[19] Religious melancholia is never far away, though Wolff attributes men's ills not to sin against God but to failure to obey nature's law. This is the fault of the senses, which interfere with man's perception of the good and cause him to pursue false goals: sexual gratification, power, and wealth. That way lies only pain, for such things are outside man's control: he lusts after things he can not have, and fears to lose what he has.[20] To man enslaved by the senses Wolff teaches the gospel of reason. The light of reason perceives the true good, which is obedience to the law of nature. He who pursues that good — the man who acts virtuously — will be happy. He will enjoy perfect tranquillity of mind, regardless of outer circumstances.[21] This is very much the consolation of philosophy offered by Stoic teaching, and Wolff's efforts to turn the philosopher into a therapist drew heavily on the Stoics, who had also given the philosopher cure of souls and appointed him mentor and guide at every stage of life's pilgrimage.[22]

As such the philosopher teaches a gospel of reason comparable to the clergyman's gospel of Christ. But while Christian moralists would argue that knowledge of the good does not suffice to make a man act rightly, Wolff struggled to maintain the Greek rational-intellectual position that the will follows the known good: to know the good is to do it.[23] The philosopher who can impart knowledge to his fellow men will thereby enable them to leave the night of ignorance for a new world of light. Yet there remains a problem of transmission. While knowledge may be embodied in precepts these may transmit only "theoretical knowledge" ("figürliche Erkenntnis"), and Wolff, for all his intellectualism, conceded that this may not move the will, if powerfully opposed by the promptings of sensory appetite. Theoretical knowledge must therefore be reinforced with "intuitive knowledge" ("anschauende Erkenntnis") able to move the will even against the opposition of sense.[24] Intuitive knowledge is that gained from experience, and therefore takes the form of examples. While Wolff's rationalist ethics diverge from the Christian tradition his educational method, which reinstates the example in the moral pedagogic function denied it by Thomasius, remains substantially that employed by the orthodox clergy.

Christian examples — instances of God's work in the world, rewarding righteousness and punishing sin — identified acts, by their sequel, as either pleasing or abhorrent to God, and attempted to condition the fallen will to right conduct through hope of reward and fear of punishment. The Wolffian example is an instance of nature's work in the world, improving the lot of those who act according to its law, and degrading the condition of those who do not. Without abandoning the laws of ordinary earthly causation — without appeal to miracles or magic — it establishes an evident narrative link between (for instance) honesty, truthfulness or obedience and prosperity on one hand; between dishonesty, untruthfulness or disobedience and adversity on the other. It identifies acts, by their sequel, as pleasing or abhorrent to nature: in other words, as good or bad. It thus gives the understanding intuitive knowledge which moves the will to seek the good and avoid the bad. Wolffian examples work through the intellect: they do not condition the will through the emotions of hope and fear.[25]

Christian examples claimed to be true instances of God's work in the world: and it was precisely on their truth that their power to encourage or terrify depended. Wolff expected the historical record to furnish him with examples of nature's working in the world but, conceding that these were not always easy to come by, allowed departures from history in the cause of man's improvement. If the philosopher could not find, in the apparently meaningless tangle of events, examples which clearly and unambiguously conveyed knowledge, then he might invent his own. Where the clergy followed Plato in rejecting works of the imagination, Wolff showed himself the true disciple of Aristotle, who provided him with both the authority for invention and the term which he used for the invented example, *Fabel*.[26] So Wolff deserves something of a reputation for encouraging the writing of fiction. But he set stern limits on the practice. The *Fabel*, or invented *exemplum*, was the root and branch of all imaginative literature, and no story had the right to exist unless it demonstrated a moral truth. Thus Wolff sought to annex all literary invention to his own didactic, rationalist purposes. Narrative was once the handmaid of Christian orthodoxy. Now it was to serve the Wolffian "religion."[27]

Wolff's system contained everything necessary both for a renewal of the *Lehrstand* and for a revival of imperative fiction. His work gained a wide audience; dismissal from his post at Halle, in 1723, only increased his fame.[28] As his ideas spread, the status of philosophy rose. The philosophy faculty, as Gunter Grimm observes, now shed the odium of handmaid to theology and became what theology itself had been: the principal source of theoretical knowledge.[29] Increasingly men chose to exercise their teaching function from philosophy rather than theology posts.[30] Meanwhile dynastic rulers, whose interests by no means coincided with those of Wolffian traditionalists, nevertheless welcomed philosophers as educators in place of the clergy.[31] Philosophy began to influence theology, as theology had once influenced it;[32] academic theologians adopted Wolffian ideas and began training generations of philosopher-clerics for the church.[33] Simultaneously Wolffian philosophy permeated the arts faculties, which began to serve its purposes as they had formerly served those of theology.[34]

The only major discipline which escaped this permeation was jurisprudence. Wolff wanted to restore the situation that had obtained at orthodox universities like Leipzig, where the traditional theoretical experts had controlled law teaching. He argued in a paper entitled "Wie die bürgerliche Rechtsgelehrsamkeit nach einer beweisenden Lehrart einzurichten sey" that law should have a philosophical-theoretical basis.[35] But the jurists were not impressed, and Wolff's natural law textbook seems not to have been widely used.[36] Nevertheless the advent of Wolffianism, and the prestige it conferred on philosophy faculties, blocked the lawyers' advance within the universities, thus halting a process which had begun in the early years of Halle. Law failed to dominate German culture from the 1720s onwards; the traditional *Lehrstand* reasserted itself in and through the philosophers.

As theorists and therapists, Wolffian philosophers were duty-bound to make their expert knowledge available to the laity;[37] and Wolff had shown how they could use examples to do so. The spread of Wolffian ideas and the reinvigoration of the *Lehrstand* thus increased the possibility of a new phase of exemplary narrative. In fact no new long forms emerged in the early eighteenth century; seventeenth-century favourites such as *Banise*-imitations, "gallant" novels and imaginary voyages continued to hold their own.[38] Yet one notable innovation in publishing, the *moralische Wochenschrift*, did coincide with Wolff's ascendancy. The inspiration for moral weeklies was drawn from England where Joseph Addison and Richard Steele had enjoyed great success with two papers, the *Tatler*, which appeared thrice weekly, and the daily *Spectator*. Both were printed on a folio half-sheet and contained a variety of short pieces: essays, poems, anecdotes, letters, and stories.[39] Apart from periodicity, the German papers were superficially very similar to the English. With the exception of a publication which appeared in 1713, most German weeklies, about fifty in all, were published between 1721 and 1750.[40] The most notable titles appeared during the 1720s: Bodmer's and Breitinger's *Die Discourse der Mahlern* from 1721 to 1723; *Der Patriot* from 1724 to 1726; and Gottsched's two papers *Die vernünftigen Tadlerinnen* from 1724 to 1726 and *Der Biedermann* from 1727 to 1729.[41]

Many weeklies appeared in Leipzig, one of Germany's principal publishing centres. Commercial cities, mainly in the north and east, produced others: Hamburg alone was responsible for nine weeklies between 1713 and 1750.[42] Commentators have therefore associated the commercial bourgeoisie with the publication of the weeklies, which have been identified as a symptom of growing self-confidence among those engaged in trade, and an earnest of their determination to win recognition for themselves in a society dominated by the nobility.[43] Yet to situate moral weeklies on the side of modernisation is to mistake the origin and real nature of these publications, which did not coincide with an era of commercial expansion and burgher self-confidence. On the contrary the weeklies appeared while the agrarian depression which lasted until the middle of the century continued to restrict demand for craft products, and during a period when the symptoms of municipal malaise which characterised the second half of the seventeenth century still persisted: when city patricians assimilated themselves to the country nobility, long-established business families lost control of city government to princely appointees, and young men forsook trade for bureaucratic posts.[44]

One weekly in particular — *Der Patriot* — has frequently been linked with the commercial bourgeoisie. *Der Patriot* was produced in Hamburg by the so-called "Patriotische Gesellschaft," eleven men who as prominent figures in Protestant Germany's largest trading city, which was then almost alone among the old commercial centres in enjoying a spell of prosperity, might seem likely spokesmen for commercial interests.[45] Yet only one of the "Patriotische Gesellschaft" — the philosopher J. A. Hoffmann, who had an interest in diamonds[46] — was personally involved in commerce and, taken together, the eleven look much the sort of conservative alliance that the clergyman Dilherr and the patrician Harsdörffer formed in mid-seventeenth-century Nuremberg.[47] Five of the eleven Hamburg writers were theologians, philosophers or arts graduates, four of whom held office in church or school: Michael Richey, who was one of the principal contributors, taught at the Gymnasium Academicum in Hamburg. Of the remaining six, who all read law, five achieved high office in the city council: B. H. Brockes, like Richey a major contributor, was a senator; J. J. Surland was senior syndic to the council.[48] These council office-holders belonged to a small — though by no means closed — élite which ruled Hamburg according to a medieval constitution and as recently as 1712 had needed the emperor's assistance to defeat a revolutionary challenge from the city's trading classes.[49] According to his own account, Brockes adopted a style of life which earned him some disapproval in a town "where everyone was intent on trade." He lived as a patrician, *procul negotiis*, and associated with the imperial and foreign nobles who formed Hamburg's diplomatic circle.[50] Had not the city debarred nobles from the council, he would presumably have applied for imperial patents of nobility, as patricians in the southern *Reichsstädte* often did.[51] In any event the social message of *Der Patriot* was thoroughly conservative. The term *patriot* chosen for the title derives from the slogan of the Athenian anti-democratic movement: "Back to the old paternal state."[52] The fictional figure of the Patriot who appears in the paper's pages is a thinly-disguised Brockes, living a leisured life, enjoying a substantial private income and, interestingly enough, bearing — as *Reichsfreiherr* — the imperial title the real Brockes lacked.[53]

Evidence of conservatism or neo-traditionalism among the authors of the moral weeklies can also be found outside the *Patriot* group. Though the weeklies appeared anonymously, at least twenty-five individuals have so far been identified as writers of weeklies during the first half of the century. Of these, no fewer than nineteen were or later became members of the *Lehrstand*, as clergymen, tutors, or teachers of philosophy or arts subjects in schools or universities.[54] Many of these *Lehrstand* writers were professed Wolffians. Bodmer, who began his career as a grammar-school teacher, and Breitinger, an ordained minister, eventually rejected Wolffian aesthetics but in 1721, when they launched *Die Dis-*

course der Mahlern, they considered themselves disciples of Wolff and preachers of his doctrine, and indeed asked him for support, which they duly received in the form of an encouraging letter.[55] Gottsched, who had just started lecturing in philosophy at Leipzig when he began his first weekly, was chiefly responsible for the spread of Wolffian ideas in arts faculties. His *Erste Gründe der gesammten Weltweisheit*, published in 1733-34, was a popularisation of the Wolffian system in which he amplified Wolff's theory of the *Fabel* by recommending that philosophers exhibit ethical truths in fictional form in the manner adopted in England by the *Spectator* and in Germany by *Die Discourse der Mahlern, Der Patriot, Die vernünftigen Tadlerinnen* and *Der Biedermann*.[56] Perhaps because of this recommendation many weeklies were in fact written by pupils and associates of Gottsched. J. F. Lamprecht of *Der Menschenfreund* (1737-39), J. A. Cramer of *Der Schutzgeist* (1746-47) and *Der Jüngling* (1747-48), and Christlob Mylius of *Der Freygeist* (1746) all studied under Gottsched in Leipzig and at some time or other associated themselves with his literary views. J. J. Spreng of *Der Eidsgenoß* (1749) was one of Gottsched's most effective supporters in the Swiss universities. J. G. Altmann, another supporter, wrote *Der Brachmann* (1740), which he dedicated to Gottsched and his wife. Some weekly-writers of the 1740s, such as J. E. Schlegel, author of *Der Fremde* (1745-46), and G. F. Meier, co-author of *Der Gesellige* (1748-50), notoriously deviated from strict Wolffian principles.[57] But the fact remains that they were academics engaged in a form of discourse stimulated by Wolff's ideas.

These academic and conservative writers used the weeklies as a substitute for the sermon. Wolff had secularised both the clergyman and his *exemplum*, but he had not suggested a vehicle by which rightthinking philosophers could deliver their new examples to a receptive lay public. The academic lecture, addressed to a specialist student audience, was no substitute for the clergyman's address from the pulpit to a gathered community of young and old, male and female, educated and uneducated. The weekly could to some extent fill this gap. Of course as printed matter sold on the book market, weeklies presupposed a literate and relatively prosperous audience.[58] But they did otherwise allow the new-style philosopher to address that audience as the clergyman addressed his congregation: regularly and frequently, with a short, selfcontained piece on any one of a wide choice of moral texts.

The weekly-writers exploited this opportunity to the full: their publications adopted very much the tone of the sermon, and in this respect contrasted markedly with the best-known English papers. The pioneers among these, the *Tatler* and the *Spectator*, used the urbane, conversational style typical of the London clubs from which they originated, and by printing readers' letters extended, beyond the confines of the clubs, the free debate for which they were famous.[59] German weekly-writers, by contrast, spoke with the authority of experts. They proclaimed the truth, instead of entering into dialogue with their readers. German weeklies purported to publish readers' letters but usually did no such thing. The authors supplied the publishers with a whole year's issues in advance, including appropriate "readers' letters" which they had written themselves.[60] It is also noticeable that the English papers carried advertisements, but their German equivalents did not: the English writers were engaged in a commercial enterprise aimed at the general reader, the Germans in an almost exclusively pedagogical activity, within the narrow confines of the academic book trade.[61]

The weekly-writers propounded traditional morality as restated in Wolffian philosophy, even though they rarely mentioned Wolff by name, let alone discussed his work in any detail.[62] Readers were adjured to practise the private virtues held to be essential to traditional community, and to avoid vices such as hypocrisy, profligacy and ambition, which were represented as symptomatic of non-traditional social formations such as court and city.[63] Short narratives modelled on Wolff's idea of the example taught this ethic. Most weeklies filled many numbers with exemplary stories; some even ran miniature serials over two or more issues.[64]   Together these publications generated a very considerable quantity of short prose fiction which marked a new phase of imperative story-telling.

The influence of earlier exemplary fiction has been traced in some of this material. Indeed Gottsched, the leading literary arbiter at the time of the early weeklies, advised other authors to borrow from H. W. Kirchhof's *Wendunmuth*, a universal compendium of Protestant homiletic examples published from 1563 to 1603.[65] Gottsched's own story of Marianne, in *Der Biedermann*, has some motifs in common with one of Kirchhof's, though its even greater similarity with an English novella, Mrs Aphra Behn's *The History of the Nun: or, The Fair Vow-Breaker*, suggests the possibility of another source, common to both Behn and Gottsched, in the huge body of narrative material circulating in the seventeenth century.[66] Whatever that source may be, the conventions of exemplary narrative had hardly altered in eighty years: the tale as told by Gottsched closely resembles Harsdörffer's pieces in his collections of *Tragica-Historien*.

Gottsched observes the Christian convention of historical authenticity by beginning his tale with an indication of time and place: it happened in France and Holland during Louis XIV's Dutch campaigns. Marianne's newly-wed husband Florimund goes to war and falls ill. His friend and comrade Poliander gives him up for dead, returns home, and persuades Marianne to marry him. Of course Florimund is not dead, and when in due course he returns also, young Marianne resumes her marriage with him. Having acquired two husbands she proceeds to rid herself of both.

Telling Florimund that Poliander plans to murder him, she urges Florimund to strike first, and helps him kill Poliander. Then she sews Florimund's clothes to Poliander's so that, when Florimund hurls the corpse into a river, he too is drowned. Finally Marianne is executed for this double murder. Like Harsdörffer before him, Gottsched subordinates the story-material to its didactic purpose, narrating events economically and without sensationalism, in such a way as to imply inevitability in the way they work themselves out: the law of nature is taking its course. In the Christian tradition such a story would be used as a warning against letting the devil into one's life through some venial sin. Gottsched exploits the idea of an apparently trivial weakness of character giving rise to catastrophic consequences, since it is Marianne's "fickle disposition" which accounts for the disastrous sequence of events.

This story illustrates a single-minded, if not simplistic, revival of earlier fictional techniques. Contemporary English papers adopted a much more innovative, and indeed open-ended, approach to narrative. These publications — some of which could be acquired in French translation by Germans incapable of reading the original[67] — contained, among numerous short fictional pieces, some of considerable significance for the development of the English novel: Addison showed particular skill in his sketches of members of the Spectator Club, the fictitious association which was supposed to have given birth to the paper. Sir Roger de Coverley is the best but by no means the only instance. Addison intended him partly for a satirical portrait of the Tory squire: dully conservative, incompetent, quixotic. But the *Spectator* was designed to reconcile the landed and moneyed interests in English society and, apparently influenced by this general purpose, Addison also gave Sir Roger many amiable qualities as well, thus obliging the reader to make up his own mind both about the knight and about the standards commonly used to judge men of his sort. A wealth of circumstantial detail, scenic presentation, frequent use of dialogue and absence of narrative comment all helped to give the de Coverley papers, and many other pieces by Addison and Steele, an interrogative rather than an imperative quality.[68]

When German weekly journalists borrowed from English papers, they were inclined to do what Harsdörffer had done to Camus' stories three generations before: they pruned away what they regarded as unnecessary detail in order to make an unambiguous moral point. *Der Patriot* was valued in Germany precisely because of its simplification of English models. Albrecht von Haller commented that in its portrayal of vice it was "less specific than the English" and therefore "correspondingly more useful."[69]

The story of Tanaquil von Stolzbergen, "a beautiful but extremely haughty woman," told in *Der Patriot* for 14 May 1726, exemplifies the process. Details of the first part of the story strongly suggest that the writer, probably Brockes, had read the tale of Jack Anvil in the *Spectator*: in both narratives the husband retreats to the attic to escape his wife's contempt; and the wife tells her husband that he, being inferior by birth to his own children, should not associate with them. The second part of the story, in which Tanaquil is tamed by a new husband, borrows from the shrew story in the *Tatler*, Number 231.[70]

The *Spectator*'s Jack Anvil paper is introduced by a brief observation on the vividness of examples compared with moral maxims. The narrator then offers his reader a letter on which, he says, he will not comment. The writer of the letter, "John Enville, Knt.," offers a piquant confession. He begins: "I am a person of no Extraction, having begun the World with a small parcel of Rusty Iron, and was for some Years commonly known by the Name of Jack Anvil." On acquiring a fortune — the amount of which is specified — and a knighthood, he married Lady Mary Oddly, "an Indigent young Woman of Quality." Once wed, she tried to keep him out of public view while she lived on his money as befitted her birth. Sir John's account of Lady Mary's domestic arrangements includes a wealth of distinctive detail which causes the reader to smile at both the wife's pretensions and the husband's vicissitudes. Lady Mary has "glazed all my chimney-pieces with Looking-glass, and planted every Corner with such heaps of China," that Sir John finds himself "obliged to move about my own House with the greatest Caution and Circumspection, for fear of hurting some of our Brittle Furniture." What is more, she "makes an Illumination once a Week with Wax-candles in one of the largest Rooms" in order "as she phrases it, to see Company."

This English story brings the ancient theme of the henpecked husband to life through memorable individual detail in a narrative which leaves the reader to draw his own inferences from the conduct of the characters. The German version sacrifices both detail and its comedy to didactic clarity, and guides the reader's response before showing how the characters behave. At the outset the woman and her husband are briefly described as, respectively, "haughty" and "very deficient in resolve"; their relationship is summed up as that of master and servant. Moreover the colourful but socially subversive *mésalliance* of noblewoman and ironmonger becomes a marriage of nobles. The tale is told in the third person, instead of by the protagonist, and such direct speech as is recorded has no characteristic quality. The nearest approach of the German story to local and individual detail is the wife's insistence on giving her family coat of arms precedence over her husband's.

The English source of the second part of the Tanaquil story, though inferior to the Anvil letter in detail, still contains some comedy of character. The *Tatler* tells how one of four daughters of a Lincolnshire gentleman long remains single because of her reputation for a tempestuous nature. The man who eventually takes up the challenge of marrying her resolves to cure her by a fearsome display of his own temper. Carrying his bride home, he shoots a favourite dog dead and runs his ancient horse through with his sword, because these animals have given minor offence. At a family party soon afterwards, he cheerfully claims that none of his brothers-in-law has a wife as docile as his. Amid much comical mortification on the part of husbands disappointed by their wives the claim is tested and the former shrew shows by her exemplary obedience that it is amply justified. In *Der Patriot*, the husband's brutality is increased and the wife's humiliation deepened, lest the moral point be missed. The "very obliging, but somewhat positive manner" in which the husband in the *Tatler* invites his lady to mount the horse behind him is changed in *Der Patriot* to a peremptory command, and when the wife fails to obey, the husband orders his servants to manhandle her on to the animal. After the killing of the horse, the wife not only has to carry the saddle home, but do it at the double. She is so cowed by all this that she obeys her husband's command to take his boots off for him. *Der Patriot* carefully describes how the wife gradually submits until she is "completely reduced" ("gäntzlich gebogen"). While the *Tatler* had the husband end the struggle by assuring his wife that, since she has determined to behave reasonably, he will behave reasonably too, *Der Patriot* has a lengthy exposition of the husband's intention to treat his wife as she treats him. Finally she understands "that she could be very happy if she were to follow the dictates of reason"; she acts accordingly, and reaps her just reward in being "henceforward as much valued by all as she had previously been despised and ridiculed." The entertaining family party and the test of wifely obedience are simply omitted. The humorous tale has become a rationalist moral tract.

The English weeklies' efforts at sentimental storytelling received a very similar revision. In one of Richard Hughes' contributions to the *Spectator* — "a picture of distress in low life" — he tells how a rake attempts to purchase a young girl's virtue, but is persuaded by her and her impoverished parent's goodness to marry the girl and retrieve the family's fortunes.[71] Though Hughes prefaced the story with Seneca's remark that "a Virtuous Person struggling with Misfortunes, is an Object on which the Gods themselves look down with Delight," and concluded with a comment on the satisfaction the reformed rake found in upright behaviour, he otherwise avoided stressing the moral implications of the tale, aiming rather to arouse the reader's sympathetic emotions. One contemporary commented that "as the paper was generally read at breakfast, it mixed tears with a great deal of the tea, which was that morning drunk in London and Westminster."[72]

Gottsched retold the story for German readers in *Die vernünftigen Tadlerinnen*, closely following the original, but setting it in a different context, underlining the rights and wrongs of the case, and extracting an extra moral from it at the last.[73] The paper in which his tale appears has a motto from the poet F. R. von Canitz: "Take good care of your hearts!" ("Nehmt eure Herzen wohl in Acht!") Calliste, one of the "Tadlerinnen" and narrator of the piece, warns her sex about dangerous effects of spring weather. To put vice to shame and illustrate the challenges seasonally offered to women's honour, she tells the story of Amanda, "a good example of a virtuous woman." This lengthy preamble, filling about a quarter of the paper, establishes that here is a story of chastity and its rewards; during the course of the narrative Calliste continually draws attention to Amanda's moral triumph. The landowner's attempt on the girl's virtue — narrated without comment in the English original — is glossed as "a great temptation" ("eine starke Versuchung"). Gottsched renders the mother's plea to her daughter not to increase the family sorrows by yielding to something which Hughes simply described as "worse than all" as a request to avoid "such a shameful complaisance towards a bestial creature" ("eine so schändliche Gefälligkeit gegen einen viehischen Menschen"). Finally the rake's conversion is said to show "how swift is the action of virtue even in vicious souls, provided that it is not mischievously stifled."[74] Narrative comment has made an *exemplum* out of the story, reducing its emotional impact to nothing.

The early weeklies which used *exempla* in the clerical tradition remained true to that tradition by attacking the long fiction then in print. Harsdörffer the novella-writer had condemned Cervantes and *Obregón*; now weekly-writers distanced themselves, in satirical pieces on love-stories and their obsessive readers, from both seventeenth-century romance and the "gallant" novel. The writers objected not to the fictionality of these texts — after all Wolff's code admitted fiction — but to their tendency to debauch: love-stories at best wasted their readers' time, and at worst corrupted their morals.[75] Bodmer and Breitinger appealed to the authority of the most savage seventeenth-century clerical critic of fiction, the Swiss Calvinist Gotthard Heidegger, in a piece ridiculing the romances of A. H. Bucholtz.[76] *Die Discourse der Mahlern, Der Patriot*, and Gottsched's two papers all pilloried what they saw as the enthusiasm of empty-headed women and youths for the novels of such writers as August Bohse and C. F. Hunold.[77] Yet changes were to follow. By the 1740s weekly papers were recommending love-stories to their readers, as aids to the moral life.[78] Wolffian thinking and the role of the philosopher had undergone significant modifications.

Sentimental Philosophers and Domestic Romance

Christian Wolff had engineered the theoretical expert's transformation from clergyman into rationalist philosopher, together with a corresponding shift of emphasis from revealed to natural religion. His initiative enabled a *Lehrstand* under serious threat from modernisation to accommodate itself to changed conditions and continue to preach a traditionalist gospel. However Wolff's system did not long survive unaltered. The likely reason is that by the 1740s it was proving inadequate to the psychological needs of the *Lehrstand*, which was showing signs of continuing stress.

One such sign was the high incidence in eighteenth-century Germany of what was known at the time as "melancholia" or "hypochondria," and would now be described as depression. Some modern commentators, associating melancholia with the bourgeoisie in general, have assigned a social cause to the condition, namely the exclusion of this group from political power.[79] But contemporary evidence suggests that melancholia was especially concentrated among the *Lehrstand*. Reputed melancholics among theologians, philosophers and writers born during the first four decades of the century included Albrecht von Haller, J. F. W. Jerusalem, C. F. Gellert, N. D. Giseke, J. G. Hamann and C. M. Wieland.[80] Moreover, while history may well have failed to record many a melancholic who did not put his experiences on paper, contemporaries had little doubt that here was a disease of scholars rather than officials, businessmen or indeed the rural population.[81] Admittedly this opinion often concealed an element of propaganda, as Hans-Jürgen Schings has demonstrated in his study of *Aufklärung* disapprobation of melancholics.[82] But eighteenth-century thinkers and writers do appear to Schings to have been particularly prone to a condition whose antecedents he finds in the religious melancholia of the seventeenth century.[83] His observations by no means preclude the possibility that the melancholia of the eighteenth-century *Lehrstand* was a group reaction to loss of status and power. Historical psychologists have often posited depressive reactions by subdued or threatened social groups, one of the most notable instances being the melancholia of the French aristocracy during the reign of Louis XIV.[84] A similar association between psychological disturbance and the social and cultural situation of the eighteenth-century German *Lehrstand* has been suggested by Hans Jürgen Haferkorn who has drawn attention to the destabilising effect of the collapse of the clerical role on men who would in more favourable circumstances have entered the church.[85]

Depression may be seen as a form of disorientation in that the depressive loses his sense of reality and identity. What he needs by way of remedy is a means to make sense of life and to reconstruct the self. Hence historical cases of epidemic depression have been adduced in explanation of the development in contemporary philosophy and literature of heroic character-ideals: the melancholia of the seventeenth-century French nobility, for example, is observed to contribute to a cult of pagan virtue.[86] There is perhaps ultimately no better evidence for the melancholia of the eighteenth-century German *Lehrstand* than its continuing quest for a source of self-understanding and self-worth. Wolff and Gottsched experimented with the stoic ideal, which may have provided some intellectual comfort to their generation but which apparently failed to satisfy the one which followed. For Wolffianism conceded little or nothing to the emotions, whereas the traditional Christianity it replaced had offered the warm feeling of assurance that came from faith in Christ. From the 1740s therefore, members of the *Lehrstand* sought a new and more potent form of psychotherapy for their followers, and indeed for themselves.[87]

One source of new ideas was the "moral sense" school of thought, of which Anthony Ashley Cooper, third earl of Shaftesbury, was a prominent spokesman.[88] Shaftesbury addressed himself to problems raised by the English civil war and seventeenth-century English political thought. Whereas Hobbes legitimated absolute government — which he saw very much as a means to end civil war — by arguing that human nature, being selfish, required firm restraint, Shaftesbury legitimated greater political liberty — which appeared to be under threat from absolute government — by arguing that men were by nature good and therefore required no such restraint.[89] He appealed to two concepts: "natural affection" and the "moral sense." According to Shaftesbury, man's natural affections, or passions, such as parental kindness, love of fellowship, compassion, and mutual succour, "lead to the good of the public." In other words, man may be relied upon to act altruistically out of instinct just as, for example, he satisfies his hunger out of instinct. Hence he is indeed naturally benevolent.[90] But being a rational creature, man can also reflect on the natural affections, so experiencing "another kind of affection towards those very affections themselves." Images of justice, generosity, or gratitude inspire liking, and their opposites, dislike: hence man possesses a natural "sense of right and wrong" or moral sense. He is drawn towards what is good and avoids what is wrong, again out of instinct, to satisfy an appetite.[91] Natural affection and moral sense enabled Shaftesbury to develop a new character-ideal. Though he by no means diminished the power and importance of reason, he insisted that the good man must at the same time be a man of feeling: one in whom the natural affections and the moral sense were fully developed. Such a man would do good without need of rational calculation, purely at the prompting of his affections and from love of right. Shaftesbury's rehabilitation of sense alongside reason enhanced the status of the artist — the aesthete and adept of feeling. Unless a man had something of the artist in him, he could not be fully human: only the *virtuoso* was truly virtuous.[92]

Within its own context the tendency of Shaftesbury's thought was emancipatory. Though a member of the aristocracy, he used his very considerable rhetorical powers to oppose traditional élites and to promote a more open society. Even the freedoms of the London clubs, the envy of many continental opponents of the old régime, did not satisfy him: he wished to introduce in England the toleration he saw in Holland.[93] Partly perhaps because of the role played by Shaftesbury in England it has been argued that the philosophy of feeling served in Germany also as a weapon in the bourgeois struggle for emancipation from traditional society.[94] Yet it was not the commercial bourgeoisie which took up and propagated the philosophy of feeling, but the academic élite, the traditional *Lehrstand*.[95] One of Shaftesbury's first German translators was the neologist cleric J. J. Spalding.[96] Many academic philosophers and teachers who responded positively to the ideas of Wolff later welcomed Shaftesbury's theories also. Such men included C. F. Gellert, J. G. Sulzer, J. A. Eberhard and J. H. Campe.[97] This development was facilitated by the circumstance that, in order to accept Shaftesbury, they had no need to reject Wolff. For Wolff's intellectualism could in fact largely accommodate Shaftesbury's emphasis on feeling, even though the latter may seem far removed from the former. Wolff himself had displayed doubt about the nature of intuitive knowledge which, though strictly part of the cognitive faculty, he had sometimes treated as a feeling — *Empfindung* — distinct from both cognition and will.[98] This ambiguity enabled Shaftesbury's ideas to be built into Wolff's system without altering its basic shape.

The relationship between Wolff's original followers and the next generation of German intellectuals was therefore one of continuity rather than conflict. The *Lehrstand* of the 1720s and 1730s evolved a rationalist orthodoxy; its successors, the neologist clergy and the faculty philosophers and schoolteachers of the 1740s and 1750s, adapted that system to produce a new orthodoxy which Gerhard Sauder has aptly called "enlightened sentimentalism" — "aufgeklärte Empfindsamkeit."[99] Whereas in English (and Scottish) philosophy reason was superseded by feeling as the arbiter of moral life, German academics kept reason in place, but set feeling alongside it. In so doing, they were essaying to supply the then perceived deficiencies of religion by means of a succedaneum better adapted to satisfy emotional needs than bare rationalism could ever have been. Enlightened sentimentalism thus contained the possibility of reassuring the traditional theoretical experts and indeed of maintaining their control over society in general.

To this end the role of theoretical expert was again remodelled. Wolff had fused clergyman with rationalist philosopher; in Gellert's generation the result was synthesised with the man of feeling and the poet.[100] The wise man was no longer simply a reasoner alone, he was also a man of sensibility. A. G. Baumgarten thus distinguished the old-style philosopher — the professional mathematical logician — and the *aestheticus* — the thinker who has also developed his power of sensory perception.[101]

G. F. Meier, who popularised Baumgarten's ideas, found that "It is impossible to describe the wretchedness of a scholar who has no aesthetic sensibility. He is a mere skeleton without flesh, a tree without leaves and without blossom."[102] Perhaps the most salient exemplar of the new ideal was the public persona of Gellert. In private a complex, hypersensitive, difficult man, and long-term sufferer from melancholia, Gellert nevertheless managed to create the appearance of successfully combining the roles of academic philosopher and poet, and his admirers assisted him in this self-stylisation until he virtually attained the status of role model for the nation. Hence Goethe's famous remark, "To believe in Gellert, in virtue and in religion is for our public practically one and the same thing."[103] Gellert's reputation as man of sensibility rested partly on his published letters, and other representatives of enlightened sentimentalism also made a point of revealing themselves and their feelings through some form of confessional writing. Thus prominent neologist clergymen including Spalding published autobiographies designed to display themselves in the character of *virtuosi*.[104]

The new sentimental philosophers remained faithful to the idea of a harmonious natural order realised in traditional community. They continued to evoke the patriarchal state with its wise philosopher king but, by stressing affective relationships, modified the abstract, rationalistic quality this institution had manifested in Wolff's system. The king who wielded power with paternal wisdom was now also credited with paternal love for his subjects.[105] But sentimental philosophers exemplified community less by the patriarchal state than by the archetype of all political communities, the family itself. This was not merely the unit into which the individual was required to fit but that in which he was held to realise himself most fully.[106] In proclaiming the obligations and celebrating the joys of family life, sentimentalism started a process which has continued into the twentieth century, whereby religion, having largely lost control of the public sphere to modernising forces, has been relocated more and more in the private sphere of the family.[107]

As advocates of community, the sentimental philosophers still upheld the norms of behaviour favoured by Wolff.[108] Sentimentalism merited its description as *Viertelstoizismus* ("semi-demi-stoicism") and Gellert, for instance, had no hesitation in preaching the familiar, self-denying private virtues of contentment and endurance.[109] But if the virtues remained the same, their dynamic did not. The stoic Wolffian had been expected to follow reason and suppress the passions. If he acted generously he did so out of rational considerations and not from a feeling of pity.[110] Now ready feeling, though not the whole of morality, became its first impetus and its guarantee. It was good to be easily moved by the sufferings of others, and whoever was so moved would never, the enlightened sentimentalists believed, seriously contravene the moral law.[111]

Sentimentalism, like much traditional religious thinking, presented man's unregenerate condition in sombre hues: indeed sentimental philosophy as a late and beleaguered faith suggests an even greater mistrust of the "world" than that postulated by many of its predecessors.[112] Left to himself in the vale of tears man endures a variety of contrasting ills. On one hand the passions, as distinct from the beneficent moral feelings, can wreck his contentment and tempt him with false goals. Yet on the other hand man is quite as likely to endure feelinglessness in all its misery, the desolation of melancholia. The way out of all these ills is to follow nature, the light of reason and the moral sense. True contentment belongs to the wise man who experiences the gentle emotions at the heart of sentimental philosophy and responds to suffering with pity and to the spectacle of virtue with affection, friendship and admiration.[113]

Thus far sentimentalist theorising largely parallels Wolff's. Unhappiness arises from unruly passion and happiness from an opposite state: the sentimentalists differ from Wolff in arguing that this opposite state involves feeling as well as the rule of reason. The regenerate state of sentimentalism is more complex than that of Wolffian rationalism but offers far greater rewards. The rationalist who submitted himself to the rule of reason might find that attainment to the state of rationality afforded a certain, somewhat abstract, gratification. The sentimentalist could expect a far more satisfying experience, notoriously involving a physical manifestation. Gentle commotion of the moral sense was expected to issue in tears, and the shedding of tears was represented as intrinsically pleasurable: suggestible contemporaries claimed to experience this pleasure in abundance.[114] Moreover one of the most striking features of the sentimental philosophy, traceable back to Shaftesbury, was the reflexive pleasure to be had from exercise of the moral sense. Not only is it pleasurable to shed tears of pity over suffering virtue but it is also and perhaps more pleasant to contemplate oneself as a compassionate and therefore truly virtuous person. This "self-approving joy" of which sentimental philosophy made so much was the greatest consolation it offered to its devotees. The mere power to produce a given reaction to specific situations restored self-esteem to the dejected, and not least to the sentimental philosophers themselves.[115]

Sentimental philosophy thus supplied the effective psychotherapy Wolffianism failed to offer and opened the possibility of integration into a strongly affective community. He who followed the sentimental norm could hope not simply to enter a meaningful order able to provide an intellectual home, but to be absorbed into a genuinely loving family, whether the biological family organised on sentimentalist principles or some larger community, such as a group of like-minded friends who treated one another as family. By comparison with Wolffian rationalism sentimentalism thus appears to offer its believers something much closer to the traditional Christian ideal of the church as family founded on the virtue of *agape*, and many eighteenth-century melancholics seem to have found their cure within the sentimental friendship-networks which flourished in the middle decades of the century.[116]

In this way the sentimental philosophy modified the Wolffian system by incorporating the affects. Nevertheless enlightened sentimentalists honoured the power of reason and wished to present knowledge to the understanding. Wolffian didacticism, in the form of precept and example, therefore kept its place in the texts of the 1740s onwards.[117] But the philosopher, now reinterpreted as the *virtuoso* man of feeling, had above all to inspire feeling in his readers and so to afford them emotional gratification. Hence the sentimentalists' characteristic contribution to aesthetics was a theory of romance, the form best able to do this. Romance does not purge but arouses and sustains feeling and aims, as Frye points out, not at *catharsis* but *ecstasis*.[118] The old heroic romancers had created an image of the ideal warrior with whom their hearers could identify so that, thus enlarged and inspired with appropriate warlike feelings, they would all the more readily commit themselves to combat. The *Chanson de Roland*, for example, is reputed to have sent men cheerfully into battle, sustained by a sense of their own martial qualities and of oneness with their fellow combatants. In this way romance was a little like rain-making: it might affect people's morale, if not their outward circumstances.[119] It might produce the effect which Edmund Burke associated with all forms of the sublime, "a sense of swelling and triumph."[120] This above all was the sentimentalists' aim.

The sentimental theory of romance was first applied to drama, which was credited with particular power over the emotions.[121] Most of the proponents of the eighteenth-century genre of domestic drama — "bürgerliches Trauerspiel" — viewed it precisely as a form of romance. Its characters were not to be "of the middling sort," as Aristotle recommended, but ideal figures shown to be "perfectly good and virtuous" ("fehlerlos gut und tugendhaft"), in Sauder's words.[122] They were to be examples, comparable with the ultimate example, Christ. The way in which such characters were to work emerges clearly from Gellert's treatise "Pro comœdia commovente"[123] of 1751, in which he argued that the leading role in sentimental comedy should belong to an image of virtue, a "Bild der Tugend." The virtue in question is of course the sentimental virtue manifested by characters like his own Caroline in *Das Loos in der Lotterie*, who are easily moved by their friends' sufferings to acts of generosity and self-abnegation. The point of the action is not to show such characters rewarded, thus stimulating either imitation in the hope of like reward or intuitions of goodness leading to disinterested desire for the same, but rather to arouse concern on the characters' behalf, leading to imaginary friendship with them. Their feelings thus become ours, and our souls respond to their souls' vibrations, so generating in our hearts a delightful inner commotion — *Rührung* — which expresses itself in tears. In short we identify with them. What they are, we feel ourselves to be also: we take on their emotional strength; we become feeling individuals. And from our new-found feeling comes self-esteem. As we contemplate our feeling selves, we experience "a sweet sensation of pride and self-love" ("eine süße Empfindung des Stolzes und der Selbstliebe").[124] Lessing, who translated "Pro comœdia commovente" into German, was apparently puzzled and disturbed by Gellert's emphasis on self-love, a sensation in which Lessing could see no moral purpose.[125] Presumably his own rather different approach to dramatic theory at this time inhibited Lessing from recognising that for certain contemporaries the enhancement of self-esteem had become a valid end in itself.[126]

In any event during the third quarter of the century members of the *Lehrstand* followed Gellert's example by promoting domestic drama as a means of arousing emotion and, through emotion, a sense of membership in an élite group of virtuous souls. As Alois Wierlacher has shown, almost all the theorists of the genre — who flourished far more abundantly in Germany than in either England or France — were clergymen, teachers, or students of theology, philosophy and the arts.[127] These men enlarged the notion of *Mitleid* — which traditionally signified the Aristotelian emotion of pity for another in his suffering — to cover almost any emotion, so long as it was felt in harmony with the dramatic characters. The audience was expected to weep at the characters' sorrows and rejoice at their joys, just as if these were its own. Indeed dramatic illusion was intended to be so complete that the spectator would tremble, despair, rave with the characters, to the point of losing himself completely in the action of the play.[128] To feel powerful emotion through the agency of the drama was to live more intensely, and the consequence of this new intensity was, the theorists believed, an access of self-confidence: in Wierlacher's words, a "Verstärkung des Ichgefühls."[129]

The theory of drama as romance envisaged an audience subjected to a kind of emotional training to which the strong collective and coercive connotations of "drill" would not seem inappropriate. Theorists favoured a dramatic compulsion which would make it difficult if not impossible for the audience either to distance itself from the action or to submit it to independent judgment.[130] The possibility not only of influencing individual audience-members but also of moulding the audience's consciousness as a group was explicitly recognised and valued by writers to whom the sense of oneness generated in the audience through a shared emotional response to events on the stage was indeed the culmination of the dramatic enterprise. All the members of the theatre audience were to merge together as if into one soul.[131] Domestic drama thus reveals a perhaps unexpectedly revolutionary potential, yet a revolutionary potential of a profoundly conservative sort. The theoretical experts who promoted domestic plays envisaged modernisation arrested by the reimposition of what Reinhart Koselleck has called "the ideological dictatorship of virtue."[132] Their approach paralleled, if to far less effect, that of the preacher and reputed practitioner of virtue Robespierre, who hoped to construct a new status society ruled by a virtuous élite comparable with Plato's philosopher élite.[133]

Perhaps because print seemed a good deal less effective than the stage as a means of stirring the emotions, and especially of affording a communal emotional experience, sentimental philosophers were relatively slow to develop a theory of narrative romance. Gellert's earliest venture into long fiction, the first part of *Das Leben der schwedischen Gräfin von G****, published in 1747, still drew heavily on the tradition of the tragic novella, and achieved its length simply by juxtaposing a negative example with a positive one.[134] The negative example may have been inspired in part by Gottsched's tale of Marianne in *Der Biedermann*, with which it shares not only the name of the heroine, rendered by Gellert as Mariane, but also the motif of a second marriage to the first husband's friend. Gellert's Mariane discovers that her second husband murdered the first — who, though she did not know it, was her own brother — in order to marry her himself. Mariane despairs, and kills herself. The Swedish countess, by contrast, copes with the problem of two husbands by resuming the first marriage during the first husband's lifetime, and the second one after his death. These contrasting stories illustrate the proposition, more Wolffian than sentimentalist, that control of the passions leads to happiness, control by them to misery and destruction. Gellert virtually confines himself to the materials of seventeenth-century storytelling, and departs from that tradition only in so far as he tries to demonstrate the power of *Gelassenheit* or equanimity to end the horrors which were its stock-in-trade.[135]

But by the middle of the eighteenth century the old *Tragica-Historien* had run their course: pieces like Gottsched's tale of Marianne belonged firmly to the past. However the story of the converted rake which Gottsched had taken from Hughes pointed the way to a new type of exemplary romance. For Hughes' simple tale of the making of a marriage prefigured Samuel Richardson's *Pamela*, which was published in 1740. Here the single action of courtship forms the basis of a story of four volumes' length. And *Pamela* set a pattern for subsequent writers both in England and abroad. Richardson, a committed Anglican, wrote with declared didactic intent. Reflecting that "when the pulpit fails other expedients are necessary," he resolved to "*steal in...the great doctrines of Christianity under the guise of a fashionable amusement.*"[136] To this end he structured his stories as romances in which a Christian hero or heroine would be tested and eventually triumph.

Pamela is the first and simplest of these stories. It is, as the subtitle proclaims, a fable of "Virtue Rewarded," and employs a comedy plot.[137] The servant-girl heroine Pamela faces a hostile world in which the bad law of Mr B., her wealthy employer, holds sway. Mr B. is a rake who corresponds to the comic humour of dramatic comedy. The resolution occurs through his reform, and the story concludes with his marriage to Pamela, which inaugurates a new, ideal order. Yet this is no classic comedy, in which the humour holds the audience's interest, while the young hero and heroine fade into the background.[138] Here humour and lover coincide, since it is the reformed Mr B. who marries Pamela. More significantly, Pamela herself is the central figure of the story: she represents goodness in a bad world, and so displaces the comedy from the ironic to the romantic sphere. Pamela's motivation reveals an ambiguity which led hostile contemporary critics to proclaim her an opportunist but which seems not to have been part of Richardson's conscious design. Having from the beginning envisaged *Pamela* as an exemplary story in which good triumphs over evil, he made his intention still clearer when he added the book's second part, which explores Pamela's family life by means of a narrative in which the emphasis has altogether shifted from the imperfect to an ideal world.[139]

While Pamela's virtue triumphs in a hostile world, *Sir Charles Grandison* shows the power of virtue in a world receptive to it. Sir Charles is a godlike hero: a reflection of the eighteenth-century Christian belief that perfection, or something very near it, is attainable by the exercise of will. However his virtue, unlike that manifested by the heroes of seventeenth-century romance, is not martial so much as social. He is no "Conqueror of Nations" but a "Friend of Mankind," a benevolent man.[140] Though his benevolence arises from fixed principle rather than feeling, Sir Charles also has a feeling heart which not only "bleeds in secret" at his friends' afflictions, but more than once causes him to shed tears of pity in company.[141] The story in which Sir Charles figures is a quest to find the right bride, a quest successfully concluded when he marries Henrietta Byron, his match in exemplary qualities. Like a knight of old, Sir Charles is temporarily diverted from his goal by other women who are not his true lady, and from these he must detach himself. The unworthy Olivia and the gentle, self-denying Emily Jervois cause him no lasting uncertainty. But Clementina della Poretta, torn between love for Sir Charles and duty to religion and family, is a woman of a different order. Passionate and haughty, she belongs to the line of "dark" heroines of romance; her eventual renunciation of Sir Charles enables him to wed the "light" heroine Harriet with a good conscience, and the book to end with a marriage which has always appeared desirable. Clementina, having sacrificed herself for her Catholic faith, thinks of entering a nunnery. But Richardson's ethic is founded on marriage and family, and the reader is left to assume that instead of taking the veil she will wed the count of Belvedere.

Pamela and *Sir Charles Grandison* end happily in the manner of romantic comedy or comic romance. The tragic inspiration for *Clarissa* generates a narrative of opposing wills engaged in a struggle which allows no reconciliation. The rape of Clarissa is the extreme expression of Lovelace's desire for dominance over her. By dying rather than marrying him she finds her freedom: the spiritual freedom of a Christian under God. The text proclaims not Grandison's enlightened Christianity at peace with an enlightened world, but what Margaret Doody calls "an ascetic, other-worldly religion" which finds its joy in heaven. Clarissa, whose innocence has been defiled, is entitled, as Clementina was not, to set this world and its conjugal obligations aside and in dying become the bride of Christ. Deprived of the earthly happiness to which she could aspire, she appears at the end of her sufferings as a figure of the martyred saint.[142] Richardson designed her as an "Example to her Sex," and believed he had shown, "for Example-sake," a "young Lady struggling nobly with the greatest Difficulties, and triumphing from the best Motives, in the course of Distresses the tenth Part of which would have sunk even manly Hearts."[143]

Richardson's fictional technique seems at first sight to conflict with his declared didactic purpose. He rejected the third-person narrator, who might guide the reader's responses, for a series of letters without connecting narrative comment. In these letters the principal correspondents not only tell their experiences but display their inmost thoughts and feelings in a manner unprecedented in English fiction. Richardson's work thus formed a striking contrast with that of his contemporary and rival, Henry Fielding. Robert Scholes and Robert Kellogg note that Fielding's characters are schematic and typical, whereas "the inner lives of Richardson's" are "much more thoroughly realized and much more complex."[144] It is this complexity, of course, which has intrigued modern readers. Ian Watt has suggested that Richardson described "the frightening reality of the unconscious life which lies hidden in the most virtuous heart": his characters are not the perfect creatures they are sometimes claimed to be.[145]

But Richardson's technique neither distances the reader from the characters nor makes him think in a detached way about them. The letters do not summarise experience in the manner of legal narrative but recreate it moment by moment. "Critical situations" are recounted together with what Richardson himself called "*instantaneous* descriptions and reflections."[146] The effect is that of a play; the situations and language are often those of drama. One review of *Grandison* spoke of "interesting scenes," "persons before our eyes," "*great drama*,"[147] and so vivid are the characters that the reader becomes caught up in them, and experiences their feelings as his own. Ian Watt argued that Richardson, by giving "a fuller and more convincing presentation of the inner lives of his characters" than earlier novelists, brought about "a much deeper and unqualified identification between the reader and these characters."[148] The satisfactions that Richardson provided were the emotional satisfactions of romance.[149]

Richardson was soon translated into German: *Pamela* in 1742 and again in 1743; *Clarissa*, by the theologian J. D. Michaelis, in 1748-53; and *Grandison*, probably by J. J. Schwabe, a friend and follower of Gottsched, in 1754-55.[150] French abridgements by the abbé Prévost were also readily available in Germany.[151] Under the title *Wege der Tugend* the Thuringian clergyman F. W. Streit published an abridged version of the three stories in 1765.[152] The *Lehrstand* quickly began to recommend the new English domestic romances to the public. Richardson convinced older Wolffians, who had hitherto expressed no sympathy with "love stories," that the form could serve their own moral-didactic purposes. When Bodmer revised the "Ladies' Library" of *Die Discourse der Mahlern* for the new edition published in 1746 under the title *Der Mahler der Sitten*, he included *Pamela*.[153] Gottsched praised Richardson in several literary journals, mentioned *Pamela* in the 1751 edition of his *Critische Dichtkunst*, and recommended *Grandison* to his niece, whom he urged to imitate the amiable characteristics of Henrietta Byron.[154] Brockes published in the final volume of his *Irdisches Vergnügen in Gott* a collection of fourteen "Poems in praise of Pamela," in which the virtuous servingmaid is given "an almost Messianic role."[155] One of these poems has Wolff setting himself up as instructor of mankind, and mankind preferring to take instruction from Pamela:

> Wenn auch Wolf gleich sagen möchte:
> Wisse menschliches Geschlechte
> Daß nur ich dein Lehrer bin;
> Spricht das menschliche Geschlechte
> Doch zur Pamela mit Rechte:
> Du bist unsre Lehrerinn!

Another poem in the collection suggests that Pamela's example is capable of shaming vice itself and converting the whole nation to virtue.[156] However it was the sentimental philosophers rather than the earlier Wolffians who did most to publicise Richardson in Germany, in the belief that he too could provide the satisfactions they expected from domestic drama. Simon, in Gellert's play *Die Betschwester*, explains to Frau Richardinn that *Pamela*, so far from corrupting its readers, is an excellent novel designed to encourage virtue and has been recommended in England from the pulpit.[157] In the *Moralische Vorlesungen* Gellert himself acknowledged that his audience might be surprised to find an academic philosopher advocating novel-reading but insisted that, if the novels were Richardson's, he had a duty so to do.[158] In private correspondence Gellert ranked Richardson's novels second only to the Bible as a work of religious instruction.[159] Many moral weeklies of the forties and fifties likewise recommended Richardson's novels as a means of teaching virtue.[160]

Anecdotal evidence confirms Richardson's powerful impact on eighteenth-century Germans, many of whom claimed to have wept over his texts. Some of these readers were women; one of Gellert's numerous female correspondents sought advice about her tearful response to *Clarissa* and *Grandison*, and was told that it did indeed seem excessive.[161] But Richardson was not simply women's reading.[162] In the 1750s and 1760s men, too, spoke of weeping over his characters' fate. K. W. Ramler described in a letter how he had shed tears over the death of *Clarissa*.[163] Gellert himself maintained that he wept copiously while reading the fifth volume of *Grandison*.[164] The critic C. H. Schmid called on Richardson's readers to weep with him over the novels.[165] And those who wept found in their weeping a copious source of self-esteem, the proof that they themselves were men of feeling, and hence belonged to a virtuous élite. Denis Diderot, reflecting on his own response to Richardson, had exclaimed: "Combien j'étais bon! combien j'étais juste! que j'étais satisfait de moi!"[166] Similarly the young C. M. Wieland, who often wrote to friends about his own sentimental response to contemporary literature including Richardson's novels, insisted that "The sentiments of which our hearts are capable show that there is an uncommon excellence in us."[167] The morale of the German *Lehrstand* might have been low, but Richardson had done something to restore the spirits of younger clerics, teachers and writers. J. K. A. Musäus, himself no supporter of Richardson, said that the novelist had generated in his German readers "a certain romantic exhilaration."[168]

In this way Richardson created the "swelling and triumph" that arise from the experience of the sublime, and his three stories provided the pattern for a new "high" romance replacing the exemplary Baroque romance in the manner of Ziegler. Despite superficial differences, the new form bore many resemblances to the old. Richardson's characters, though lower in status than — say — Ziegler's kings and princes, came in the main from the higher ranks of commoner society. Richardson's tone, though deprecated as provincial by some of his English critics, is elevated and serious: intentionally far from that of "low" or comic romance. And the epistolary form replicates in some degree the effect of the Heliodoran opening. As Norbert Miller has suggested, the reader is plunged, as it were, *mediam in personam*.[169] Bookselling history also suggests a significant continuity between the seventeenth and eighteenth-century forms of high romance. During the 1740s and 1750s, a few imitations of *Die asiatische Banise* were still being issued, addressed in antique fash-

ion to "die galante Welt."[170] Others made a last futile attempt to survive
in a modern guise: Florander's "Helden- und Liebes-Geschichte," which
had first been published in 1730 under the Baroque title *Die unver-
gleichliche Darine, Cron-Printzessin aus Creta*, was reissued in 1753 as
Die tugendhafte Darine.[171] But after 1754, when the German *Grandison*
appeared, no more of these older romances were printed.[172]

Yet German writers did not immediately produce their own imitations
of Richardson. What happened in the 1750s and 1760s was that large
numbers of English and French domestic romances, written more or less
faithfully in the manner of Richardson, were translated, usually anonymously, into German. Some of these translations were the work of
prominent clerics or teachers. Albrecht von Haller, poet, professor of
medicine and orthodox apologist, who wrote an enthusiastic review of
Clarissa, which he encouraged J. D. Michaelis to translate, himself translated Mary Collyer's *Felicia to Charlotte*.[173] Jerusalem's protégé, J. J.
Eschenburg, who eventually held a chair of philosophy at the Collegium
Carolinum in Brunswick, translated Marie Leprince de Beaumont's *Lettres
d'Émérance à Lucie*.[174] G. J. Zollikofer, one of the most successful neologist preachers and co-author, with Jerusalem and J. A. Cramer, of *Betrachtungen über die vornehmsten Wahrheiten der Religion*, translated
Maria Cooper's story, *The Exemplary Mother*.[175]

A major contribution to this development in German publishing was
made by P. E. Reich, manager of, and from 1762 partner in, the leading
Leipzig firm of M. G. Weidmann, who has been accused of doing rather
little for the cause of enlightenment, but did not fail to further enlightened sentimentalism.[176] A personal friend of Gellert, Reich travelled to
England to visit Richardson, in whom he found an exemplary father,
presiding over a harmonious family. "A noble simplicity reigns throughout and elevates the soul," observed Reich, who kissed Richardson's ink-
horn as a mark of devotion. Receiving a copy of *Grandison* from
Richardson himself, Reich claimed that Gellert would translate the
book.[177] Though the promise was almost certainly not kept, Reich did
publish the German translation, thus establishing himself as the leading
German specialist in foreign domestic romance. Among his authors were
Richardson's principal female followers, Sarah Fielding, Charlotte Lennox
and Frances Brooke, as well as the French writer Madame Riccoboni.
Reich pioneered the German publication of collections of domestic romances and moral tales in the manner of the French *Bibliothèque de
campagne*. Between 1760 and 1784 he produced five such libraries, together containing about ninety volumes of long and short stories dedicated to the propagation of virtue.[178]

In the 1760s original German domestic romances began to take the
place of translations, steadily increasing in numbers until domestic romance became the largest single category of fiction written by German-

speakers. E. D. Becker, examining German novels published around 1780, found that about one third of the total belonged to the category which she aptly called "sentimental-didactic romances of moral proving" — "empfindsam-didaktische Prüfungsromane."[179] These stories, typically written in letter form, almost invariably related virtue's trials and the earthly rewards of virtue. Courtship was the favourite theme, with more or less fabulous contingencies, from parental opposition to plots, abductions and physical violence, providing the obstacles to happy marriage. *Clarissa*, Richardson's story of martyred sainthood, had few imitators, just as there were few tragedies in the ranks of domestic drama. The letter device was used in the manner of Richardson, though usually with far less skill, as a means of displaying the characters' feelings at points of crisis. Heroes and heroines showed their instinctive love of goodness and loathing of evil both in their own tribulation and suffering and in their response to the joys and sorrows of others. The sign of a feeling heart remained the ability to shed tears. But domestic romancers also took care to incorporate into their texts a good measure of straightforward moral teaching in the form of commentary on the action, and since letter-novels lacked a narrator the job of providing this commentary fell to the characters themselves.[180]

German domestic romance, being both a highly imitable and a highly marketable commodity, might have been produced on a purely speculative basis by writers without any clerical or pedagogical background, but in fact often drew on the life of school, church and university, and was frequently dismissed by hostile critics as the work of inexperienced schoolmen. A reviewer for the *Allgemeine deutsche Bibliothek* described the authors of domestic romance as clergy, students, lecturers and tutors.[181] And among those who have emerged from their customary anonymity, many were in fact members of the *Lehrstand*.[182] These men included Andreas Riem, J. M. Schwager, the brothers C. F. and J. C. S. Sintenis and August Lafontaine, all of whom were clergymen. But the clerical writer who gained the greatest respect from reviewers as a German Richardson was J. T. Hermes. Author of the Richardsonian *Sophiens Reise von Memel nach Sachsen*, which was published between 1769 and 1773, Hermes had been encouraged to write by his theology professor in Königsberg, who felt the time had come for the church to clothe its truths in fiction.[183] By contrast J. M. Miller, who was also a clergyman, earned considerable notoriety but little critical respect with his *Siegwart: eine Klostergeschichte*, which appeared in 1776. This lachrymose tale owed nothing to Goethe's *Werther*, which predated it by two years, and everything to the French moraliser Baculard d'Arnaud. Siegwart's loss of his life as well as his lover is divine punishment for his disobedience to God, while the case of Siegwart's sister Theresa, whose story occupies about half the text, provides a counter-example of conjugal happiness as heavenly reward for patient trust in providence.[184]

Probably by the late 1760s, certainly by the 1770s and 1780s, domestic romance had ceased to serve the *Lehrstand* itself as a source of exhilaration and self-confidence. The theoretical experts had moved on, and the readers of domestic romance tended to be women and young people belonging to the educated social groups: readers who stood in the relationship of pupils to the clergy and secular moralists, but demanded something more sophisticated than traditional devotional books.[185] This audience could find in domestic romance a picture of just rewards and punishments which encouraged belief in a religious worldview or at least fostered a sense of the world as a fairytale place in which wishes are fulfilled.[186] On either reading domestic romance constituted a potential instrument of control by an authoritative group of theoretical experts. Such fiction was not, as has been claimed, a forum for discussion of bourgeois concerns and an instrument of political emancipation for the bourgeoisie,[187] but tended rather to preserve traditional values and to exert powerful pressure for a traditional society. During the later eighteenth century, the impetus towards modernisation came from a different quarter.

[1] Compare A. Tholuck, *Das kirchliche Leben des siebzehnten Jahrhunderts*, part 2 (Berlin: Wiegandt & Grieben, 1862) 96-97; Alberto Martino, "Barockpoesie, Publikum und Verbürgerlichung der literarischen Intelligenz," *Internationales Archiv für Sozialgeschichte der deutschen Literatur* 1 (1976): 140; Horst Rabe, "Autorität," *Geschichtliche Grundbegriffe: historisches Lexikon zur politisch-sozialen Sprache in Deutschland*, ed. Otto Brunner, Werner Conze and Reinhard Koselleck, vol. 1 (Stuttgart: Klett, 1972) 395.

[2] "kluge Etatsräte, listige Finanzräte, verständige Juristen": Gerd Heinrich, "Amtsträgerschaft und Geistlichkeit: zur Problematik der sekundären Führungsschichten in Brandenburg-Preussen 1450-1786," *Beamtentum und Pfarrerstand 1400-1800: Büdinger Vorträge 1967*, ed. Günther Franz, Deutsche Führungsschichten in der Neuzeit vol. 5 (Limburg/Lahn: Starke, 1972) 205.

[3] "Bekanntlich mag bei uns keine Person von einigermaßen vornehmen [sic] Stande ihren Söhnen erlauben, Theologie zu studieren": Heinrich 205.

[4] Compare Peter L. Berger, *Facing up to Modernity: Excursions in Society, Politics and Religion* (1977; Harmondsworth, England: Penguin Books, 1979) 217-220.

[5] For a brief introduction to the life and work of Christian Wolff, see Giorgio Tonelli, "Christian Wolff," *The Encyclopaedia of Philosophy*, ed. Paul Edwards, 1967. There is a fuller account in Max Wundt, *Die deutsche Schulphilosophie im Zeitalter der Aufklärung* (1945; Hildesheim: G. Olms, 1964) 122-99.

[6] See Giorgio Tonelli, "Der Streit über die mathematische Methode in der Philosophie in der ersten Hälfte des 18. Jahrhunderts und die Entstehung von Kants Schrift über die 'Deutlichkeit'," *Archiv für Philosophie* 9 (1959): 52; Gunter E. Grimm, *Literatur und Gelehrtentum in Deutschland: Untersuchungen zum Wandel ihres Verhältnisses vom Humanismus bis zur Frühaufklärung*, Studien zur deutschen Literatur 75 (Tübingen: M. Niemeyer, 1983) 402, 405-6, 449, 561; Werner Schneiders, "Der Philosophiebegriff des

philosophischen Zeitalters," *Wissenschaften im Zeitalter der Aufklärung*, ed. Rudolf Vierhaus (Göttingen: Vandenhoeck & Ruprecht, 1985) 68-69; Hans Werner Arndt, "Erste Angriffe der Thomasianer auf Wolff," *Christian Thomasius 1655-1728: Interpretationen zu Werk und Wirkung*, ed. Werner Schneiders, Studien zum achtzehnten Jahrhundert 11 (Hamburg: Meiner, 1989).

[7] *Christian Wolffs eigene Lebensbeschreibung*, ed. Heinrich Wuttke (Leipzig: Weidmann, 1841) 121. Cited by Grimm (553).

[8] Wundt 124-26, 200-201; Tonelli, "Christian Wolf," 342; Werner Schneiders, "Deus est philosophus absolute summus: über Christian Wolffs Philosophie und Philosophiebegriff," *Christian Wolff 1679-1754: Interpretationen zu seiner Philosophie und deren Wirkung*, ed. Werner Schneiders, Studien zum 18. Jahrhundert 4 (Hamburg: Meiner, 1983) 12-15.

[9] Tonelli, "Der Streit" 53.

[10] Werner Schneiders, "300 Jahre Aufklärung in Deutschland," *Christian Thomasius 1655-1728* 17.

[11] Grimm 566-67.

[12] See especially Werner Frauendienst, *Christian Wolff als Staatsdenker*, Historische Studien 171 (Berlin: E. Ebering, 1927) 92, 94-95, 100, 102-103, 104, 105-106; Christoph Link, "Die Staatstheorie Christian Wolffs," *Christian Wolff 1679-1754* 172-73, 184; Eckhart Hellmuth, *Naturrechtsphilosophie und bürokratischer Werthorizont: Studien zur preussischen Geistes- und Sozialgeschichte des 18. Jahrhunderts*, Veröffentlichungen des Max-Planck-Instituts für Geschichte 78 (Göttingen: Vandenhoeck & Ruprecht, 1985) 50-62; Bengt Algot Sørensen, "Die Vater-Herrschaft in der früh-aufklärerischen Literatur," *Tradition, Norm, Innovation: soziales und literarisches Traditionsverhalten in der Frühzeit der deutschen Aufklärung*, ed. Wilfried Barner, Schriften des Historischen Kollegs: Kolloquien 15 (Munich: Oldenbourg, 1989) 195-96.

[13] Frauendienst 108; Werner Schneiders, "Die Philosophie des aufgeklärten Absolutismus: zum Verhältnis von Philosophie und Politik, nicht nur im 18. Jahrhundert," *Aufklärung als Politisierung — Politisierung der Aufklärung*, ed. Hans Erich Bödeker and Ulrich Herrmann, Studien zum achtzehnten Jahrhundert 8 (Hamburg: Meiner, 1987) 38-41. For the concept of the patriarchal order, see Wolff, *Vernünfftige Gedancken von dem gesellschafftlichen Leben der Menschen* (Halle: Renger, 1721) par. 264-66. The "Rede von der Sittenlehre der Sineser" is reprinted in *Das Weltbild der deutschen Aufklärung: philosophische Grundlagen und literarische Auswirkung: Leibniz — Wolff — Gottsched — Brockes — Haller*, Deutsche Literatur...in Entwicklungsreihen: Reihe Aufklärung 2, ed. F. Brüggemann (Leipzig: Reclam, 1930). On China in European thought, see Paul Hazard, *The European Mind 1680-1715* (1935; Harmondsworth, England: Penguin Books, 1964) 36-40.

[14] Compare K. R. Popper, *The Open Society and its Enemies*, 5th ed., vol. 2 (London: Routledge & Kegan Paul, 1966) 4-5.

[15] "Thue was dich und deinen oder anderer Zustand vollkommener machet; unterlass, was ihn unvollkommener machet": Christian Wolff, *Vernünfftige Gedancken von der Menschen Thun und Lassen*, 2nd ed. (Halle: Renger, 1723) par. 1-12.

[16] Wolff, *Von der Menschen Thun und Lassen* par. 461-62 (Mässigkeit); 810-12 (Bescheidenheit); 538 (Vergnüglichkeit); 735 (Zufriedenheit); 582 (Fleiss); 643 (Geduld).

[17] See the articles "Ehrbarkeit" and "Wohlanständigkeit," Johann Georg Walch, *Philosophisches Lexicon...*, new ed. (Leipzig: Gleditsch, 1733) 642-44, 2923-33. Manfred Riedel,

in his article "Gesellschaft, Gemeinschaft," *Geschichtliche Grundbegriffe*, vol. 2 notes that Wolffian theory had very little to say about "die Sprache des geselligen Umgangs" (819).

[18] Christian Wolff, "Rede von der Sittenlehre der Sineser," *Das Weltbild der deutschen Aufklärung* 178, 184-85; *Von dem gesellschafftlichen Leben der Menschen*, par. 214, 227-30, 330 and "Vorrede": "...denn die gantze zeitliche Glückseelichkeit beruhet auf einem wohleingerichteten Staate"; *Frauendienst* 88, 95-97.

[19] See, for example, "Rede von der Sittenlehre der Sineser," where Wolff writes: "Auf Erden aber ist nichts Beständigers als der Unbestand" (175).

[20] On the effects of the senses, see Christian Wolff, *Vernünfftige Gedancken von Gott, der Welt und der Seele des Menschen*, 4th. ed. (Frankfurt and Leipzig, 1729) par. 434, 439, 444, 490-91, 503; *Von der Menschen Thun und Lassen* par. 183, 378.

[21] Wolff, *Von der Menschen Thun und Lassen* par. 44-45, 52.

[22] See Seneca, *Letters from a Stoic*, tr. Robin Campbell (Harmondsworth, England: Penguin Books, 1969) 18-19; Marcus Aurelius, *Meditations*, tr. Maxwell Staniforth (Harmondsworth: England: Penguin Books, 1964) 8-9. Compare E. R. Dodds, *The Greeks and the Irrational* (Berkeley: University of California Press, 1951) 247-49, 252. On Wolff's debt to stoicism see Wundt 171-73; Gerhard Sauder, *Empfindsamkeit*, vol. 1 (Stuttgart: J. B. Metzler, 1974) 103, 132-33, 208.

[23] See Wolff, *Von Gott, der Welt und der Seele des Menschen* par. 521-22, 889; *Anmerckungen über die vernünfftigen Gedancken von Gott, der Welt und der Seele des Menschen* (Frankfurt am Main: Andreae, 1724) par. 129, 154-55, 160, 327, 331; *Von der Menschen Thun und Lassen* par. 6. Compare Tonelli, "Christian Wolff" 342. See Hans M. Wolff, *Die Weltanschauung der deutschen Aufklärung in geschichtlicher Entwicklung* (Bern: Francke, 1949) 110-119 for a discussion of how far Wolff succeeds in maintaining the rational-intellectual position.

[24] Wolff, *Von Gott, der Welt und der Seele des Menschen* par. 316, 319, 321, 323, 502-3; *Von der Menschen Thun und Lassen* par. 165, 167-69. 373-74. Compare Hans M. Wolff 156.

[25] Wolff, *Von der Menschen Thun und Lassen* par. 166-67, 312, 321, 323, 373, 378.

[26] On Wolff's theory of the *Fabel*, see in particular *Von der Menschen Thun und Lassen* par. 321, 373; *Von dem gesellschaftlichen Leben der Menschen* par. 317, 328. Compare Franz Dornseiff, "Literarische Verwendungen der Fabel," *Vorträge der Bibliothek Warburg* 4 (1927): 216-218; Max Staege, *Die Geschichte der deutschen Fabeltheorie* (Bern: Paul Haupt, 1929) 22; Dietrich Harth, "Christian Wolffs Begründung des Exempel- und Fabelgebrauchs im Rahmen der Praktischen Philosophie," *Deutsche Vierteljahrsschrift für Literatur und Geistesgeschichte* 52 (1978).

[27] Compare Werner Hahl, *Reflexion und Erzählung: ein Problem der Romantheorie von der Spätaufklärung bis zum programmatischen Realismus* (Stuttgart: Kohlhammer, 1971) 14-15.

[28] Wundt 199; Tonelli, "Christian Wolff" 340, 343.

[29] Grimm 566-71.

[30] See for example Rolf Engelsing, "Der Bürger als Leser: die Bildung der protestantischen Bevölkerung Deutschlands im 17. und 18. Jahrhundert am Beispiel Bremens," *Archiv für Geschichte des Buchwesens* 3 (1960-61): 265-66.

[31] See for example the Prussian minister of state K. A. von Zedlitz on the teaching role of the "Philosophe-moraliste," *Nouveaux Mémoires de l'Académie Royale des Sciences et Belles-Lettres* 1776: 30-31.

[32] See Walter Sparn, "Vernünftiges Christentum: über die geschichtliche Aufgabe der theologischen Aufklärung im 18. Jahrhundert in Deutschland," *Wissenschaften im Zeitalter der Aufklärung*, ed. Vierhaus 19, 23; Wilhelm Schmidt-Biggemann, "Kommentar zum Beitrag N. Hammerstein, 'Der Wandel der Wissenschafts-Hierarchie und das bürgerliche Selbstbewusstsein: Anmerkungen zur aufgeklärten Universitäts-Landschaft'," *Tradition, Norm, Innovation* 293.

[33] Karl Aner, *Die Theologie der Lessingzeit* (Halle/Saale: M. Niemeyer, 1929) 22-24; Sparn 23-25, 34-37.

[34] The chief mediator here was J. C. Gottsched. See Wundt 216-18; Hans M. Wolff 155-60; Joachim Birke, *Christian Wolffs Metaphysik und die zeitgenössische Literatur- und Musiktheorie: Gottsched, Scheibe, Mizler*, Quellen und Forschungen zur Sprach- und Kulturgeschichte der germanischen Völker ns 21 (Berlin: de Gruyter, 1966) 21-48; Dieter Kimpel, "Christian Wolff und das aufklärerische Programm der literarischen Bildung," *Christian Wolff 1679-1754* 211-13.

[35] Grimm 560. The paper is to be found in Christian Wolff, *Gesammlete kleine philosophische Schriften*, ed. G. F. Hagen, vol. 2 (Halle: Renger, 1736-40) 595-687. On Wolff's view of the law see also Erich Döhring, *Geschichte der deutschen Rechtspflege seit 1500* (Berlin: Duncker & Humblot, 1953) 311-12.

[36] Döhring 311-12; Notker Hammerstein, *Jus und Historie: ein Beitrag zur Geschichte des historischen Denkens an deutschen Universitäten im späten 17. und 18. Jahrhundert* (Göttingen: Vandenhoeck & Ruprecht, 1972) 322; Hammerstein, "Christian Wolff und die Universitäten: zur Wirkungsgeschichte des Wolffianismus im 18. Jahrhundert," *Christian Wolff 1679-1754* 268-69; Horst Dreitzel, "Zur Reichspublizistik: Forschungsergebnisse und offene Probleme," *Zeitschrift für historische Forschung* 5 (1978): 344-45.

[37] Wolff, *Von der Menschen Thun und Lassen* par. 149-50, 289, 321.

[38] See Herbert Singer, *Der deutsche Roman zwischen Barock und Rokoko* (Cologne: Böhlau, 1963) 1-9, 87-103; Marianne Spiegel, *Der Roman und sein Publikum im früheren 18. Jahrhundert 1700-1767*, Abhandlungen zur Kunst-, Musik- und Literaturwissenschaft 41 (Bonn: Bouvier, 1967); Dieter Kimpel, *Der Roman der Aufklärung* (Stuttgart: J. B. Metzler, 1967) 6-37.

[39] *The Tatler*, ed. Donald F. Bond, 3 vols. (Oxford: Clarendon Press, 1987); *The Spectator*, ed. Donald F. Bond, 5 vols. (Oxford: Clarendon Press, 1965).

[40] See bibliography in Wolfgang Martens, *Die Botschaft der Tugend: die Aufklärung im Spiegel der deutschen Moralischen Wochenschriften* (Stuttgart: J. B. Metzler, 1968) 544-48.

[41] For *Der Patriot* see the edition by Wolfgang Martens (Berlin: de Gruyter, 1984).

[42] Martens, *Botschaft* 544-47.

[43] Hans M. Wolff 66-81; Martens, *Botschaft* 342-48.

[44] On the economic situation see Friedrich Lütge, *Deutsche Sozial- und Wirtschaftsgeschichte: ein Überblick*, 3rd ed. (Berlin: Springer, 1966) 334-43, 349, 355, 403; Heinz Schilling, *Höfe und Allianzen: Deutschland 1648-1763* (Berlin: Siedler, 1989) 77-84. For the symptoms of municipal malaise, see Percy Ernst Schramm, *Neun Generationen: dreihundert Jahre deutscher "Kulturgeschichte" im Lichte der Schicksale einer Hambur-

ger Bürgerfamilie (1648-1948), vol. 1 (Göttingen: Vandenhoeck & Ruprecht, 1963) 68-71; Franz Eulenburg, "Die Frequenz der deutschen Universitäten," *Abhandlungen der philosophisch-historischen Klasse der Königlichen Sächsischen Gesellschaft der Wissenschaften* 24.2 (1904) 130-31, 136, 163, 165.

[45] On Hamburg's prosperity see Wilhelm Treue, "Wirtschaft, Gesellschaft und Technik in Deutschland vom 16. bis zum 18. Jahrhundert," *Handbuch der deutschen Geschichte* by Bruno Gebhardt, 9th ed., ed. Herbert Grundmann, vol. 2 (Stuttgart: Union-Verlag, 1970) 475-77, 501, 503.

[46] For the membership of the "Patriotische Gesellschaft" see Jörg Scheibe, *Der Patriot (1724-1726) und sein Publikum: Untersuchungen über die Verfassergesellschaft und die Leserschaft einer Zeitschrift der frühen Aufklärung* (Göppingen: Kümmerle, 1973) 25-27, 50-52, 86-88.

[47] For this view, see Gerhart von Graevenitz, "Innerlichkeit und Öffentlichkeit: Aspekte deutscher 'bürgerlicher' Literatur im frühen 18. Jahrhundert," *Deutsche Vierteljahrsschrift für Literaturwissenschaft und Geistesgeschichte* Sonderheft 1975: 61*, 68*.

[48] Martens, *Botschaft* 129, and "Zur Verfasserschaft am *Patrioten* (1724-26)," *Euphorion* 58 (1964): 396-401 omits from his list the clergyman M. C. Brandenburg, who is included by Scheibe (52-53). The theologians, philosophers and arts men were Richey; J. A. Fabricius; John Thomas; J. A. Hoffmann and M. C. Brandenburg. The lawyers were Surland; Johann Klefeker; Brockes; Conrad Widow; J. J. Anckelmann and C. F. Weichmann.

[49] See Schramm 110-118.

[50] See J. M. Lappenberg, "Selbstbiographie des Senators Barthold Heinrich Brockes," *Zeitschrift des Vereines für hamburgische Geschichte* 2 (1847): 181, 200, 205, 209 and passim.

[51] On the exclusion from the city council of citizens with patents of nobility see Schramm 57. Compare the situation in Nuremberg: Hanns Hubert Hofmann, "Nobiles Norimbergenses," *Zeitschrift für bayerische Landesgeschichte* 28.1/2 (1965): 141; Hermann Kellenbenz, *Der Merkantilismus in Europa und die soziale Mobilität* (Wiesbaden: Steiner, 1965) 48.

[52] Popper, vol. 1: 184. On *Der Patriot* as a conservative organ, see von Graevenitz 65*-66*. The conservatism of the weeklies shows in their hostility to the courts and their sympathy for the *Landadel*, see Martens, *Botschaft* 342-48, 381-82.

[53] *Der Patriot* no. 1 (5 January, 1724); no. 30 (27 July, 1724); no. 72 (17 May, 1725) and no. 95 (25 October, 1725). Compare Pamela Currie, "Moral Weeklies and the Reading Public in Germany, 1711-1750," *Oxford German Studies* 3 (1968): 70-71.

[54] The writers in question are: J. G. Altmann; F. S. Bock; J. J. Bodmer and J. J. Breitinger; J. A. Cramer; J. A. Ebert; N. D. Giseke; J. C. Gottsched; J. G. Hamann; S. C. Hollmann; J. F. Lamprecht; S. G. Lange; J. G. Lindner; G. F. Meier; J. E. Schlegel; J. J. Spreng; C. J. Sucro and J. G. Sucro; J. G. Volkelt. The remaining six writers who were not or do not appear to have been members of the *Lehrstand* were J. Mattheson; Justus Möser; Christlob Mylius; G. W. Rabener; C. G. Richter; J. A. J. von Waasberghe. Martens, *Botschaft* 123-130 contains information on the authors of the weeklies and their social status.

[55] Wolfgang Bender, *J. J. Bodmer und J. J. Breitinger* (Stuttgart: J. B. Metzler, 1973) 24-27, 44, 71. Compare Martens, *Botschaft* 134.

[56] Johann Christoph Gottsched, *Erste Gründe der gesammten Weltweisheit*, 2nd ed., vol. 2 (Leipzig: B. C. Breitkopf, 1736) par. 501.

[57] Schlegel's opposition to Wolff is discussed by Hans M. Wolff (163-65); Meier's by Karl S. Guthke, *Haller und die deutsche Literatur* (Göttingen: Vandenhoeck & Ruprecht, 1962) 116-17.

[58] Both *Der Patriot* and *Die vernünftigen Tadlerinnen* sold for 6 Pf. per copy: see *Die vernünftigen Tadlerinnen* 1725, no. 23 (6 June, 1725). In Hamburg in the early eighteenth century a woman could support herself and three or four children for a week on the price of twelve copies, according to Thomas Lediard in *The German Spy* (London, 1740) 284. See also Martens, *Botschaft* 121-23.

[59] Jürgen Habermas, *Strukturwandel der Öffentlichkeit: Untersuchung zu einer Kategorie der bürgerlichen Gesellschaft*, Politica 4 (Neuwied: Luchterhand, 1962) 56-57; *The Spectator*, ed. Bond, vol. 1: xxxvi-xxxvii.

[60] *Westberliner Projekt, Grundkurs 18. Jahrhundert: die Funktion der Literatur bei der Formierung der bürgerlichen Klasse Deutschlands im 18. Jahrhundert*, ed. Gert Mattenklott and Klaus R. Scherpe (Kronberg im Taunus: Scriptor, 1974) 57-58. *Der Patriot* seems to have been unusual in that it did publish some contributions sent in by readers: see Scheibe 126-36.

[61] On advertising in an English paper, see Lawrence Lewis, *The Advertisements of* The Spectator... (Boston: Houghton Mifflin, 1909). Joachim Kirchner, *Die Grundlagen des deutschen Zeitschriftenwesens mit einer Gesamtbibliographie der deutschen Zeitschriften bis zum Jahre 1790*, part 1 (Leipzig: K. W. Hiersemann, 1928) 32 notes the absence of advertising from eighteenth-century German periodicals.

[62] Martens, *Botschaft* 213, 429.

[63] Martens, *Botschaft* 243-45; 268-69, 288-90, 318-19, 321-22, 342-54, 360-62.

[64] *Der Biedermann* no. 10 (7 July, 1727) contains the beginning of a story which is finished in no. 12 (21 July, 1727). Nos. 15, 16, 18 and 19 (11 August, 18 August, 1 September and 8 September, 1727) contain the tale of an English seaman.

[65] Martens, *Botschaft* 505; Johann Christoph Gottsched, *Versuch einer Critischen Dichtkunst*, reprint of the 4th ed., 1751 (Darmstadt: Wissenschaftliche Buchgesellschaft, 1962) 447-48.

[66] Gottsched's story appeared in *Der Biedermann* no. 26 (27 October, 1727). It resembles the story which appears as no. 257 in vol. 4 of Kirchhof's *Wendunmuth*: see Hans Wilhelm Kirchhof, *Wendunmuth*, ed. Hermann Österley, vol. 3, Bibliothek des Litterarischen Vereins in Stuttgart 97 (Tübingen: Litterarischer Verein in Stuttgart, 1869) 231-33. Mrs Behn's *The History of the Nun: or, The Fair Vow-Breaker* is contained in *The Works of Aphra Behn*, ed. Montague Summers, vol. 5 (London: W. Heinemann, 1915) 257-324.

[67] See Marce Blassneck, *Frankreich als Vermittler englisch-deutscher Einflüsse im 17. und 18. Jahrhundert*, Kölner Anglistische Arbeiten 20 (Leipzig: B. Tauchnitz, 1934) 55-57.

[68] *The Spectator*, ed. Bond, vol. 1: xxxiv-xxxvi, lx-lxi; Sir Walter Raleigh, *The English Novel: A Short Sketch of its History from the Earliest Times to the Appearance of* Waverley (London: J. Murray, 1894) 120-26; Ernest A. Baker, *The History of the English Novel*, vol. 2 (London: H. F. & G. Witherby, 1929) 253-63; Edward A. Bloom and Lillian D. Bloom, *Joseph Addison's Sociable Animal: In the Market Place: On the Hustings: In the Pulpit* (Providence: Brown UP, 1971) 11-16, 25-26.

[69] "weniger besonder als die Engelländer"; "um desto nützlicher": Guthke 113.

[70] *Der Patriot* no. 124 (16 May, 1726); *The Spectator* no. 299 (12 February, 1712); *The Tatler* no. 231 (30 September, 1710). Brockes' authorship is assumed by Scheibe (228) and Martens in *Der Patriot*, ed. Martens, vol. 4: 399. Martens does not link Brockes' paper with any English sources.

[71] *The Spectator* no. 375 (10 May, 1712).

[72] *The Spectator*, ed. Bond, vol. 3: 409, note 3.

[73] *Die vernünftigen Tadlerinnen* 1725, no. 16 (18 April, 1725). For Gottsched's sole authorship of *Die vernünftigen Tadlerinnen*, see Eugen Reichel, *Gottsched*, vol. 1 (Berlin: Gottsched-Verlag, 1908) 157.

[74] "wie schnell die Wirkung der Tugend auch an untugendhaften Seelen sey; im Fall dieselbe nicht boshaftig unterdrücket wird."

[75] Martens, *Botschaft* 492-505.

[76] *Die Discourse der Mahlern*, part 3, nos. 13 and 14. Gotthard Heidegger's *Mythoscopia Romantica: oder Discours von den so benannten Romans...* was published in Zürich in 1698. On Bodmer and Heidegger, see Wilhelm Vosskamp, *Romantheorie in Deutschland: von Martin Opitz bis Friedrich von Blanckenburg* (Stuttgart: J. B. Metzler, 1973) 125, 129 and 239, note 37.

[77] See for example *Die Discourse der Mahlern*, part 1, nos. 8 and 16; *Der Patriot*, no. 5 (3 February, 1724); *Die vernünftigen Tadlerinnen* 1725, no. 10 (7 March, 1725) and 1726, no. 3 (18 January 1726); *Der Biedermann*, no. 88 (10 January, 1729).

[78] Martens, *Botschaft* 512-20.

[79] See for example Wolf Lepenies, *Melancholie und Gesellschaft* (Frankfurt am Main: Suhrkamp, 1969) 79-83. A similar argument is put by Alberto Martino, "Barockpoesie, Publikum und Verbürgerlichung der literarischen Intelligenz," *Internationales Archiv für Sozialgeschichte der deutschen Literatur* 1 (1976): 141-44.

[80] Albrecht von Haller, see *Der deutsche Pietismus: eine Auswahl von Zeugnissen, Urkunden und Bekenntnissen aus dem 17., 18. und 19. Jahrhundert*, ed. Werner Mahrholz (Berlin: Furche-Verlag, 1921) 189-196. J. F. W. Jerusalem, see *Boswell on the Grand Tour: Germany and Switzerland 1764*, ed. Frederick A. Pottle (London: W. Heinemann, 1953) 55 and compare Schings 132. C. F. Gellert, see *Boswell on the Grand Tour* 123; Carsten Schlingmann, *Gellert: eine literarhistorische Revision*, Frankfurter Beiträge zur Germanistik 3 (Bad Homburg vor der Höhe: Gehlen, 1967) 56-58; Hans-Jürgen Schings, *Melancholie und Aufklärung: Melancholiker und ihre Kritiker in Erfahrungsseelenkunde und Literatur des 18. Jahrhunderts* (Stuttgart: J. B. Metzler, 1977) 130. N. D. Giseke, see his "Vertrauliche Briefe," *Der Anbruch der Gefühlskultur in den fünfziger Jahren*, ed. F. Brüggemann, Deutsche Literatur...in Entwicklungsreihen: Reihe Aufklärung 7 (Leipzig: Reclam, 1935) 53-72. J. G. Hamann, see Mahrholz 255-78. C. M. Wieland, see Friedrich Sengle, *Wieland* (Stuttgart: J. B. Metzler, 1949) 24-25, 31-32, 53-55, 71-73, 76, 85-86, 96-97, 107-8, 110-11, 181.

[81] See for example Sauder 150, 153; Gert Mattenklott, *Melancholie in der Dramatik des Sturm und Drang* (Stuttgart: J. B. Metzler, 1968) 32, 46; Schings 58.

[82] Schings 6, 9, 39, 73, 224-25.

[83] Schings 142, 225.

[84] Peter L. Berger, *The Social Reality of Religion* (1967; Harmondsworth, England: Penguin Books, 1973) 31; Ross Mitchell, *Depression* (Harmondsworth, England: Penguin Books, 1975) 96-98; Zevedei Barbu, *Problems of Historical Psychology* (London: Routledge & Kegan Paul, 1960) 165-66, 170, 173, 200-201; Lepenies 51-53, 58-60.

[85] Hans Jürgen Haferkorn, "Der freie Schriftsteller," *Archiv für Geschichte des Buchwesens* 5 (1964): col. 596.

[86] Barbu 173.

[87] Compare Hans M. Wolff 163; Sauder 126; Gerhard Kaiser, *Klopstock: Religion und Dichtung* (Gütersloh: Gütersloher Verlagshaus, 1963) 67.

[88] See Robert Voitle, *The Third Earl of Shaftesbury 1671-1713* (Baton Rouge: Louisiana State UP, 1984).

[89] Basil Willey, *The English Moralists* (1964; London: Methuen, 1965) 222-23.

[90] Anthony Earl of Shaftesbury, "An Inquiry Concerning Virtue or Merit," *Characteristics of Men, Manners, Opinions, Times, etc.*, ed. John M. Robertson, vol. 1 (London: G. Richards, 1900) 280-81, 286.

[91] Shaftesbury, *Characteristics*, vol. 1: 251, 258-61.

[92] Shaftesbury, "*Sensus Communis*; An Essay on the Freedom of Wit and Humour," *Characteristics*, vol. 1: 89-90; "*Soliloquy* or Advice to an Author," *Characteristics*, vol. 1: 214-17. On the term "ästhetisch" and its relationship to sense and feeling, see Friedrich Schiller, *On the Aesthetic Education of Man*, ed. Elizabeth M. Wilkinson and L. A. Willoughby (Oxford: Clarendon Press, 1967) 303-4.

[93] R. L. Brett, *The Third Earl of Shaftesbury: A Study in Eighteenth-Century Literary Theory* (London: Hutchinson, 1951) 39-41.

[94] Sauder (xii-xiii) argues that *Empfindsamkeit* was a bourgeois phenomenon. He discusses the response to this theory in "'Bürgerliche' Empfindsamkeit?" *Bürger und Bürgerlichkeit im Zeitalter der Aufklärung*, ed. Rudolf Vierhaus, Wolfenbütteler Studien zur Aufklärung 7 (Heidelberg: L. Schneider, 1981).

[95] von Graevenitz (69*) emphasises the importance of distinguishing the academic point of view from that of the *Bürgertum*.

[96] On feeling in the religion of the neologists see Kaiser 67-69, 87-90; Sparn 36-39.

[97] Sauder 185, 200, 202-3.

[98] Sauder 126-27, 200-202.

[99] Sauder 126, 137, 197.

[100] Compare Haferkorn col. 596.

[101] See Michael J. Böhler, *Soziale Rolle und Ästhetische Vermittlung: Studien zur Literatursoziologie von A. G. Baumgarten bis F. Schiller* (Bern: H. Lang, 1975) 146-56.

[102] "Man kann nicht genug sagen, wie elend ein Gelehrter ist, der kein schöner Geist ist. Er ist ein bloßes Gerippe ohne Fleisch, ein Baum ohne Blätter und ohne Blüten": cited by Leo Balet and E. Gerhard, *Die Verbürgerlichung der deutschen Kunst, Literatur und Musik im 18. Jahrhundert*, ed. Gert Mattenklott (Frankfurt am Main: Ullstein, 1973) 304.

[103] Schlingmann 10-12, 57, 63-64, 181. Goethe's remark, "An Gellert, die Tugend und die Religion glauben, ist bei unserm Publiko beinahe Eins" can be found in the *Frankfurter gelehrte Anzeigen vom Jahr 1772*, no. 15 (21 February 1772).

[104] On Gellert's letters, see Schlingmann 64. On neologist autobiographies, see Sparn 37, 51.

[105] This view appears, for example, in the context of domestic drama, see Wolfgang Schaer, *Die Gesellschaft im deutschen bürgerlichen Drama des 18. Jahrhunderts: Grundlagen und Bedrohung im Spiegel der dramatischen Literatur* (Bonn: Bouvier, 1963) 150-53.

[106] Schaer 31-33, 79-85; Lothar Pikulik, *"Bürgerliches Trauerspiel" und Empfindsamkeit* (Cologne: Böhlau, 1966) 12-18, 28, 91-6, 103-4; Alois Wierlacher, *Das bürgerliche Drama* (Munich: Fink, 1968) 72, 102.

[107] Peter L. Berger 137-38, 150.

[108] See for example Kaiser 70, 112.

[109] Sauder 103, 128-29.

[110] Compare Gottsched, *Erste Gründe* par. 520.

[111] Kaiser 87-90; Sauder 185-87, 203-4. Compare A. R. Humphreys, "'The Friend of Mankind' (1700-1760): An Aspect of Eighteenth-Century Sensibility," *Review of English Studies* 24 (1948).

[112] Sauder 103.

[113] Sauder 125-37.

[114] Schaer 15; Pikulik 84-85; Wierlacher 149, 161. Balet and Gerhard (306-13) collect some of the eighteenth-century evidence for the shedding of tears.

[115] This aspect of the sentimental philosophy is clearly formulated by David Hume, *A Treatise of Human Nature, being an Attempt to Introduce the Experimental Method of Reasoning into Moral Subjects*, ed. T. H. Green and T. H. Grose, vol. 2 (London: Longmans, Green & Co., 1886) 77-95. Self-approval is discussed by Wierlacher 132-46.

[116] On the cult of friendship see Wolfdietrich Rasch, *Freundschaftskult und Freundschaftsdichtung im deutschen Schrifttum des 18. Jahrhunderts vom Ausgang des Barock bis zu Klopstock, Deutsche Vierteljahrsschrift für Literaturwissenschaft und Geistesgeschichte*: Buchreihe 21 (Halle a. d. Saale: M. Niemeyer, 1936) 118-23, 181-93; Balet and Gerhard 181, 309-13. Giseke's "Vertrauliche Briefe" (note 80, above) are a good example of the cult of friendship.

[117] See, for example, Wierlacher 120-26.

[118] Northrop Frye, *Anatomy of Criticism: Four Essays* (Princeton: Princeton UP, 1957) 66-67.

[119] R. G. Collingwood, *The Principles of Art* (1938; Oxford: Clarendon Press, 1963) 65-77; Dieter Wyss, *Strukturen der Moral: Untersuchungen zur Anthropologie und Genealogie moralischer Verhaltensweisen*, 2nd ed. (Göttingen: Vandenhoeck & Ruprecht, 1970) 114-32; Hans Robert Jauss, *Ästhetische Erfahrung und literarische Hermeneutik*, vol. 1 (Munich: W. Fink, 1977) 233-34, 237-41; Robert Scholes and Robert Kellogg, *The Nature of Narrative* (New York: Oxford UP, 1966) 37-38.

[120] Edmund Burke, *A Philosophical Enquiry into the Origin of our Ideas of the Sublime and Beautiful*, ed. James T. Boulton (London: Routledge & Kegan Paul, 1958) 50-51.

[121] See, for example, G. E. Lessing, *Sämtliche Schriften*, 3rd ed., ed. K. Lachmann and Franz Muncker, vol. 10 (Stuttgart: G. J. Göschen, 1894) 123.

[122] Sauder 204. Compare Wierlacher 101.

[123] The German translation by Lessing was published under the title "Des Hrn. Prof. Gellerts Abhandlung für das rührende Lustspiel," *Theatralische Bibliothek* 1 (1754). See Lessing, *Sämtliche Schriften*, 3rd ed., vol. 6: 32-49.

[124] Lessing, *Sämtliche Schriften*, 3rd. ed., vol. 6: 37-38, 40, 45-49.

[125] Lessing, *Sämtliche Schriften*, 3rd. ed., vol. 6: 52-53. Compare Peter Weber, *Das Menschenbild des bürgerlichen Trauerspiels* (Berlin: Rütten & Loening, 1970) 139-58.

[126] Lessing argued that the playgoer should be induced to feel pity for suffering virtue so that he would the more readily respond with like pity, and practical action, to suffering in real life: see in particular Lessing's letter to Friedrich Nicolai, 13 November 1756, *Sämtliche Schriften*, 3rd. ed., vol. 17: 63-68.

[127] Wierlacher 11-12 and note 28. See also Wolfgang Martens, "Die deutsche Schaubühne im 18. Jahrhundert — moralische Anstalt mit politischer Relevanz?" *Aufklärung als Politisierung...* 93. J. J. Spalding encouraged the use of drama to inspire a love of virtue: see *Über die Nutzbarkeit des Predigtamtes und deren Beförderung* (Berlin, 1772) 51-52.

[128] Wierlacher 137, 151-52, 157.

[129] Wierlacher 135-36, 143-44, 151, 159-60. Compare Sauder 211-25.

[130] Compare Böhler 137-142; Horst Albert Glaser, *Das bürgerliche Rührstück...* (Stuttgart: J. B. Metzler, 1969) 23; Johann Jakob Engel, *Über Handlung, Gespräch und Erzählung*, reprint of the 1774 text, ed. Ernst Theodor Voss (Stuttgart, J. B. Metzler, 1964) 147*; Martens, "Die deutsche Schaubühne" 97.

[131] Wierlacher 139-41.

[132] Reinhart Koselleck, *Kritik und Krise: ein Beitrag zur Pathogenese der bürgerlichen Welt* (Freiburg: Karl Alber, 1959) 139; cf. 155. Benno von Wiese, who argues in *Friedrich Schiller* (Stuttgart: J. B. Metzler, 1959) 450-51 that Schiller did not share the Jacobins' enthusiasm for the dictatorship of virtue, would except him and his work from this assessment of *bürgerliches Trauerspiel*.

[133] See Sauder 206-7, and compare Roland Mousnier, *Les Hiérarchies sociales de 1450 à nos jours* (Paris: Presses Universitaires de France, 1969) 117-128; J. L. Talmon, *The Origins of Totalitarian Democracy* (1952; London: Sphere Books, 1970) 122-31.

[134] C. F. Gellert, *Das Leben der schwedischen Gräfin von G****, part 1 (Leipzig, 1747). See Christian Fürchtegott Gellert, *Gesammelte Schriften*, ed. Bernd Witte, vol. 4 (Berlin: de Gruyter, 1988).

[135] For a discussion of Gellert's novel see Eckhardt Meyer-Krentler, *Der andere Roman: Gellerts Schwedische Gräfin: von der aufklärerischen Propaganda gegen den "Roman" zur empfindsamen Erlebnisdichtung* (Göppingen: Kümmerle, 1974).

[136] "Postscript" to the final volume of *Clarissa, or, The History of a Young Lady* (1748). See Ian Watt, *The Rise of the Novel: Studies in Defoe, Richardson and Fielding* (1957; Harmondsworth, England: Penguin Books, 1972) 152, 168, 244-45.

[137] See Margaret Anne Doody, *A Natural Passion: A Study of the Novels of Samuel Richardson* (Oxford: Clarendon Press, 1974) 35.

[138] Compare Frye 166-67, 180.

[139] Frye 181-83.

[140] Samuel Richardson, *The History of Sir Charles Grandison*, ed. Jocelyn Harris, part 3 (London: Oxford UP, 1972) 383; and see also for example part 1: 413, part 2: 10, 38, 60-61, 302. The portrayal of Sir Charles is well described by Doody (242, 258-59, 272).

[141] *Grandison*, ed. Harris, part 2: 258. For an example of Sir Charles' shedding of tears see 130. See also Doody 252-53, 258, 296; Michael Gassenmeier, "Der Typus des 'man of feeling'," diss., Mannheim, 1970, 42-43, 46, 49, 37-57.

[142] Doody 106, 124-25, 179. 182; Eve Tavor, *Scepticism, Society and the Eighteenth-Century Novel* (Basingstoke: Macmillan, 1987) 104.

[143] Richardson to Lady Bradshaigh, 26 October 1748, *Selected Letters of Samuel Richardson*, ed. John Carroll (Oxford: Clarendon Press, 1964) 90.

[144] Scholes and Kellogg 101-2.

[145] Watt 267, 304.

[146] Richardson, Preface to *Clarissa*; see Watt 27.

[147] Doody 118-19, 125-26, 279, 301.

[148] Watt 228, cf. 231-32, 303, 305. Compare Richard Brinkmann's remarks on "lebende Bilder" and the spectator's emotional response, in *Wirklichkeit und Illusion: Studien über Gehalt und Grenzen des Begriffs Realismus für die erzählende Dichtung des neunzehnten Jahrhunderts* (Tübingen: M. Niemeyer, 1957) 207-8, note 1. Tavor (103-106) points out that Richardson failed to prevent the reader sometimes identifying with the wrong character.

[149] Wolfgang Iser, *Der implizite Leser: Kommunikationsformen des Romans von Bunyan bis Beckett* (Munich: UTB-Fink, 1972) 78 and 81, regards Richardson as a writer of didactic romance. For the contrary view that the Richardsonian *Briefroman* is anti-authoritarian, see Karl Robert Mandelkow, "Der deutsche Briefroman: zum Problem der Polyperspektive im Epischen," *Neophilologus* 44 (1960). Against Mandelkow, it should be said that a text may convey an unambiguous message even if the narrative voice has been suppressed, see Mikhail Bakhtin, *Problems of Dostoevsky's Poetics*, tr. R. W. Rotsel (Ann Arbor, Mich.: Ardis, 1973) 46.

[150] See Lawrence Marsden Price, "On the Reception of Richardson in Germany," *Journal of English and Germanic Philology* 25 (1926). On Michaelis as translator, see Thomas O. Beebee, Clarissa *on the Continent: Translation and Seduction* (University Park: Pennsylvania State UP, 1990) 3, 9-10, 16-24, 32-33, 51-52, 72.

[151] Marianne Spiegel, *Der Roman und sein Publikum im früheren 18. Jahrhundert 1700-1767* (Bonn: Bouvier, 1967) 56.

[152] The book was reviewed in the *Allgemeine deutsche Bibliothek* 2.2 (1766) 269-70.

[153] *Der Mahler der Sitten*, no. 76. See Th. Vetter, "J. J. Bodmer und die englische Litteratur," *Johann Jakob Bodmer: Denkschrift zum CC. Geburtstag (19. Juli 1898)*, ed. Stiftung von Schnyder von Wartensee (Zürich: A. Müller, 1900) 336.

[154] Gottsched, *Versuch einer Critischen Dichtkunst* 528; Lawrence Marsden Price, "Richardson in the Moral Weeklies of Germany," *Studies in German Literature in Honor of Alexander Hohlfeld* (Madison: University of Wisconsin, 1925) 171 and note 6; Law-

rence Marsden Price, *English Literature in Germany* (Berkeley: U of California Press, 1953) 170.

[155] Price, *English Literature in Germany* 164.

[156] B. H. Brockes, *Irdisches Vergnügen in Gott*, vol. 9, reprint of the 1748 ed. (Bern: Lang, 1970) 556-57. The stanza quoted might be roughly rendered as follows:

> Wolff the human race addressing
> And his claim to guide us pressing
> Would himself our teacher be.
> We a stronger claim are pressing
> And another name are blessing:
> Pamela — our teacher she!

The second poem reads: Man merke doch des Beyspiels Kraft / Das von der Pamela zu nehmen: / Das Laster selber lernt sich schämen; / Ein ganzes Land wird tugendhaft.

[157] C. F. Gellert, *Die Betschwester*, Act 2, Scene 1.

[158] C. F. Gellert, *Moralische Vorlesungen*, ed. Johann Adolf Schlegel and Gottlieb Leberecht Heyer, vol. 1 (Berlin: C. F. Voss, 1770) 257-58.

[159] See Wolfgang Martens, "Lektüre bei Gellert," *Festschrift für Richard Alewyn*, ed. Herbert Singer and Benno von Wiese (Cologne: Böhlau, 1967) 140-41.

[160] See Price, "Richardson in the Moral Weeklies" and Martens, *Botschaft* 512-18.

[161] An unnamed correspondent to Gellert, 22 March 1762 and Gellert's reply, 22 March 1762, C. F. Gellert, *Briefwechsel*, ed. John F. Reynolds, vol. 3 (Berlin: de Gruyter, 1991) 207-212.

[162] cf. Beebee 17, 22.

[163] Ramler to Gleim, 7 November 1750, *Briefwechsel zwischen Gleim und Ramler*, ed. Carl Schüddekopf, vol. 1, Bibliothek des Litterarischen Vereins in Stuttgart 242 (Tübingen: Litterarischer Verein in Stuttgart, 1906) 267-68.

[164] Gellert to Hans Moritz von Brühl, 13 April 1755, *Briefwechsel*, ed. Reynolds, vol. 1 (Berlin: de Gruyter, 1983) 231.

[165] Christian Heinrich Schmid, *Theorie der Poesie nach den neuesten Grundsätzen und Nachricht von den besten Dichtern* (Leipzig: S. L. Crusius, 1767) 433. Cited by Georg Jäger, *Empfindsamkeit und Roman: Wortgeschichte, Theorie und Kritik im 18. und frühen 19. Jahrhundert* (Stuttgart: Kohlhammer, 1969) 85.

[166] Roland Mortier, *Diderot en Allemagne (1750-1850)* (Paris: Presses Universitaires de France, 1954) 326.

[167] "Die Empfindungen deren unser Hertz fähig ist, sind uns Bürgen einer nicht gemeinen Vortreflichkeit die in uns ligt": *Wielands Briefwechsel*, ed. Hans Werner Seiffert, vol. 1 (Berlin: Akademie-Verlag, 1963) 43. For Wieland's interest in Richardson at this time see *Briefwechsel*, vol. 1: 8, 180, 220, 312-13. and his prose tragedy, *Clementina von Poretta* (1760).

[168] "ein gewisses romantisches Hochgefühl": Johann Carl August Musäus, *Der deutsche Grandison: auch eine Familiengeschichte*, part 1 (Eisenach: J. G. E. Wittekindt, 1781) 96-97. Cited by Sauder (229).

[169] Norbert Miller, *Der empfindsame Erzähler: Untersuchungen an Romananfängen des 18. Jahrhunderts* (Munich: Hanser, 1968) 142, 184-86; Eva D. Becker, *Der deutsche Roman um 1780* (Stuttgart: J. B. Metzler, 1964) 43-45.

[170] See for example Polimon, *Der durch Gewalt der Liebe...höchst beglückseeligte Secretarius Eginhard...* (Frankfurt und Leipzig: n. p., 1749); Christian Ernst Fidelinus, *Die Engländische Banise...* (Frankfurt und Leipzig: n. p., 1754).

[171] Hugo Hayn and Alfred N. Gotendorf, *Bibliotheca Germanorum erotica et curiosa*, 9 vols. (Munich: G. Müller, 1912-29) vol. 2: 323.

[172] Compare Herbert Singer, *Der galante Roman* (Stuttgart: J. B. Metzler, 1961) 27-31.

[173] See Mary Bell Price and Lawrence Marsden Price, *The Publication of English Literature in Germany in the Eighteenth Century* (Berkeley: U of California Press, 1934) 66. On Haller's public commendation of Richardson, see Price, "On the Reception of Richardson" 16-22; Price, *English Literature in Germany* 166; Beebee 9-10, 16-17.

[174] See Hans Fromm, *Bibliographie deutscher Übersetzungen aus dem Französischen 1700-1948*, vol. 4 (Baden-Baden: Verlag für Kunst und Wissenschaft, 1951) 150.

[175] Price and Price 70.

[176] Herbert G. Göpfert, "Bemerkungen über Buchhändler und Buchhandel zur Zeit der Aufklärung in Deutschland," *Wolfenbütteler Studien zur Aufklärung* 1 (1974) 70-71.

[177] *The Correspondence of Samuel Richardson*, ed. Anna Laetitia Barbauld, 6 vols. (London: R. Phillips, 1804) vol. 1: clxv, clxvii-clxviii; vol. 5: 297. On the firm of Weidmann see Rudolf Schmidt, *Deutsche Buchhändler: Deutsche Buchdrucker: Beiträge zu einer Firmengeschichte des deutschen Buchgewerbes*, vol. 6 (Eberswalde: R. Schmidt, 1908) 1028.

[178] On the *Bibliothèque de campagne*, see J. J. Rousseau, *La Nouvelle Héloïse*, ed. Daniel Mornet, vol. 1 (Paris: Hachette, 1925) 37. Reich's collections were: *Gesammelte Frauenzimmerbriefe zum Unterricht und Vergnügen*, 12 vols. (1760-64); *Landbibliothek zu einem angenehmen und lehrreichen Zeitvertreibe...*, 30 vols. (1762-78); *Unterricht und Zeitvertreib für das schöne Geschlecht...*, 30 vols. (1765-76); *Sammlung von Briefen und Geschichten aus fremden Sprachen*, 8 vols. (1776-78); *Lese-Cabinet zum Nutzen und Vergnügen*, at least 8 vols. (1780-?1784).

[179] The term signifies sentimental and moralising romances in which the characters' virtue is subjected to a series of trials: Becker 43.

[180] On the German domestic novel see Becker 43-50; Kimpel 80-91.

[181] *Allgemeine deutsche Bibliothek* 51.2 (1782): 432-33; see also 50.2 (1782): 451. Compare C. F. Nicolai in *Briefe, die neueste Literatur betreffend* (Berlin: Nicolai, 1762) part 4, letter 58: 207-9; part 14, letter 225: 199-200. See Wolfgang Doktor, *Die Kritik der Empfindsamkeit* (Bern: H. Lang, 1975) 33, 49.

[182] On the incidence of clerics and teachers among domestic novelists see Engelsing 249, 346, 349; Marion Beaujean, *Der Trivialroman in der zweiten Hälfte des 18. Jahrhunderts* (Bonn: Bouvier, 1964) 43; Becker 38; Hahl 70-71; Kurt-Ingo Flessau, *Der moralische Roman: Studien zur gesellschaftskritischen Trivialliteratur der Goethezeit* (Cologne: Böhlau, 1968) 37; Helmut Germer, *The German Novel of Education from 1764 to 1792: A Complete Bibliography and Analysis* (Berne: P. Lang, 1982) 181 and bibliography; Manfred W. Heiderich, *The German Novel of 1800: A Study of Popular Prose Fiction* (Berne: P. Lang, 1982) 23.

[183] See Erich Schmidt, *Richardson, Rousseau und Goethe: ein Beitrag zur Geschichte des Romans im 18. Jahrhundert* (Jena: E. Frommann, 1875) 35-45; Konstantin Muskalla, *Die Romane von Johann Timotheus Hermes* (Breslau: F. Hirt, 1912).

[184] See Heinrich Kraeger, *J. M. Miller: ein Beitrag zur Geschichte der Empfindsamkeit* (Bremen: M. Heinsius, 1893); Martin Greiner, *Die Entstehung der modernen Unterhaltungsliteratur: Studien zum Trivialroman des 18. Jahrhunderts*, ed. Therese Poser (Hamburg: Rowohlt, 1964) 45-52. On d'Arnaud and Miller see Derk Inklaar, *F.-T. de Baculard d'Arnaud, ses imitateurs en Hollande et dans d'autres pays* (The Hague: H. L. Smits, 1925) 377-80.

[185] Compare Engelsing 344-51; Hahl 63-64; Beebee 22, 182.

[186] Compare Watt 231-32.

[187] Habermas 64-65. Compare Vosskamp 179 and 255, note 12.

6: The Third Phase of Modernisation: City Society and the Comic Novel

THE IMPETUS FOR modernisation in Germany came first from certain princes who with their legal officials began to create a more modern society at the princely court. Thomasius, a law professor in a modernising state, carried the process a stage further by using his appointment at Halle to extend an originally French-based modernist culture from the courts to the universities, in the hope that it would spread out more widely still among the educated population at large. Wolff seemed to restore the initiative to the traditionalists. Yet this did not mean that Thomasius had no intellectual successors in the academic world and beyond.

The university of Göttingen, established in 1734, soon became the most influential centre of higher education in Germany, not least by following the example of Halle in several important respects. The Hanoverian government minister responsible for Göttingen's statutes, G. A. von Münchhausen, had learned his philosophy from Thomasius rather than from Wolff, and indeed suspected the latter of seeking to revive scholasticism.[1] Münchhausen wanted no "protestant popery" at his new university which he hoped would become the kind of mixed society Thomasius had tried to create in Halle. Like Halle, Göttingen should not appear narrowly academic but offer an education for men of the world, rivalling the *Ritterakademien* by teaching modern languages, dancing, sports and music.[2] In consequence Göttingen attracted many nobles, both native Hanoverians and "foreigners" from elsewhere in the *Reich*, into its student body. Historical studies flourished there as they had at Halle, and law became the new university's largest faculty: in 1774, 563 out of a total of 894 students were lawyers.[3] To this extent the tradition of Halle continued at Göttingen, yet the latter institution can not simply be regarded as the vehicle of Thomasian ideas in eighteenth-century Germany.

The new university's history faculty illustrates the complexity of the situation. Göttingen historians undoubtedly adopted Thomasius's causal-analytical approach to the subject. J. C. Gatterer, one of the faculty's first professors, won widespread acceptance for what became known in the eighteenth century as the "pragmatic" mode of history-writing: the attempt to reconstruct past events with all their contributory causes. He and his fellow pragmatists viewed events primarily as the products of human will, and therefore treated the human psyche as the principal object of their enquiries: an encyclopaedia published almost a century after Thomasius' early paper on the semiotics of personality noted that the pragmatist presented a "mirror of the human heart...with all its nuances, deviations, recesses, excuses, expedients, with all its impulses, inclinations, passions, artifices."[4] Yet though eighteenth-century pragmatic historians searched for psychological causes, and so helped keep alive a "legal" approach to events, they hardly wrote in the unmasking spirit that characterised Thomasius.[5]   Indeed their attitudes are often much less reminiscent of Thomasius' anthropology than of the metaphysics and ethics of Leibniz and Wolff. Gatterer himself aimed to integrate events into a universal system of cause and effect — the "nexus rerum universalis" — and so to enable his readers to perceive history as if with the eye of God.[6] Later Göttingen historians moralised overtly: they declared historical figures virtuous or vicious according to their contribution to human progress, and drew general lessons from their behaviour.[7] It was this approach which provoked Lord Acton's comment on the "cheap moralities of Spittler and Schlosser."[8]

Nor was Göttingen entirely Thomasian in its law. J. S. Pütter, the university's most prominent academic lawyer around the middle of the century, continued Thomasius's emphasis on law as a practical discipline, but in circumstances very different from those in which Thomasius taught.[9] Though the elector of Hanover, George II, supported the foundation of the university in order to rival his Hohenzollern brother-in-law's establishment at Halle, the costs of Göttingen were borne for the most part by the local estates, and especially the nobility, which retained much of its traditional power in a territory from which of course the electors were absent following their accession to the thrones of England and Scotland in 1714.[10] The noble influence on the university ensured that the law taught there tended to promote the interests of the local estates and the Empire, rather than those of centralising territorial rulers. Göttingen therefore inclined towards the traditionalists rather than the modernisers,[11] and like many a less overtly innovative German university continued to lag behind the pace-setting princes who had begun the modernising process and carried it forward during the eighteenth century as they enlarged their administrative apparatus in order above all to raise the taxes needed for the standing armies demanded by dynastic ambitions.[12]

Nowhere did the expansion of the state apparatus proceed more quickly than in Brandenburg-Prussia, whose capital, Berlin, consequently became the scene of significant social change. By the middle of the eighteenth century this rapidly-growing urban centre began to develop a modern mixed society on a larger scale than anything seen hitherto in the German lands. The core of this society was formed by a group of nobles and commoners in state service. For nobles continued to play a very important part in administration. Friedrich Wilhelm I carried on the Great Elector's policy of attaching the nobility to the state both as military officers and as civilian government officials. Friedrich II preferred nobles to commoners on entry to state service and promoted them more swiftly.[13] Indeed noble officials and officers became a *Staatsstand*, a social order whose special responsibility for the maintenance and defence of the state was eventually recognised in the *Allgemeines Landrecht*. Eighteenth-century Prussia has been described as a *monarchischer Adelsstaat*, where the old status-order determined by birth was overlaid by a neocorporate order determined by occupation.[14]

Meanwhile a new status group of commoner officials was establishing itself in Brandenburg-Prussia. As the administration expanded it absorbed ever more labour: hence the number of commoners in responsible government offices rapidly exceeded the totals reached in the sixteenth and seventeenth centuries. The few commoners then in government either achieved ennoblement or remained socially attached to the city patrician or notable groups from which most of them originated. Eighteenth-century commoner officials were numerous enough to form a distinct social group of their own, from which non-noble state servants were soon largely recruited.[15] Friedrich II expressly encouraged the appointment of commoner officials' sons who had, as he said, "acquired a good education and a sense of integrity."[16] J. M. von Loen noted in 1760 that officials were refusing to put their sons into any profession but their own; and much evidence supports this view.[17] In the later eighteenth century about 40 per cent of law students at Halle were sons of higher officials and of lawyers.[18]

While noble and commoner officials were forming their own neocorporate bodies in what was still to a great extent a status society, the two groups were by no means isolated from one another. The general tendency of modernisation is to level traditional social distinctions, and as political power was concentrated in central institutions, the generality of heads of household, who had formerly shared in power through their estates, were simply absorbed into the mass of private citizens. State and society — Montesquieu's *état politique* and *état civil* — separated from each other leaving all private citizens with a common status, that of subjects of the prince. Here was one factor strongly working to narrow the division between nobles and commoners in state service.[19] But much more than this increasing theoretical equality tended to unite noble and commoner officials. Both nobles and commoners could and did prepare for a career in state service at the same educational institutions. With a common training behind them, they entered occupations as *Fürstendiener* which often brought them into close day-to-day contact in the performance of similar tasks. The circumstances of the service career fostered mutual respect and a common outlook among its practitioners across the barriers of rank, and the civilian *Fürstendiener*, whether noble or commoner, began to form a single service élite.[20]

As the century progressed the noble members of this élite tended more and more often to meet their commoner colleagues socially as well as professionally. Friedrich Gedike noted in 1783 that in Berlin the educated bourgeois could thus shed his "slavish astonishment in the face of the great World, with which so many scholars are familiar only at third-hand, by hearsay."[21] The mixed service élite of nobles and commoners in turn became the nucleus of a wider educated city public which included military officers, some clerics and teachers moving outside their own traditional corporations, members of the free professions, and writers and artists attracted to Berlin as a cultural centre.[22] The Prussian state allowed its citizens considerable freedom of association in the private sphere and members of this public soon began meeting informally in clubs and societies to discuss issues of current interest.[23] These voluntary associations centred on the service élite were quite different from the contemporary friendship-networks which relied on intuited emotional kinship, included women as well as men, and very largely recruited young people at the start of careers in the *Lehrstand* or the arts. By contrast the service-centred debating clubs rested on shared intellectual interests, and were only open to men, usually men well-established in their careers.[24] One of the longest-lived of these groups, the "Montagsklub" formed in 1749, counted among its members ministers of state, high administrative officials and heads of cultural and educational institutions as well as writers such as G. E. Lessing and Thomas Abbt. Some of these men and others of similar status including several influential government officials later formed the "Mittwochsgesellschaft," which met in secret during the years from 1783 to 1797 to debate issues of the day.[25]

The Berlin public which gathered in the dining clubs and debating societies reached out beyond the city through the periodical press. Friedrich Nicolai, the Berlin bookseller and writer who became one of the most influential editors and publishers of the period, belonged to both the Montagsklub and the Mittwochsgesellschaft. He founded the *Bibliothek der schönen Wissenschaften und freyen Künste* in 1757, and from 1759 edited the *Briefe, die neueste Literatur betreffend*, to which Lessing, Abbt and Moses Mendelssohn contributed. Nicolai's largest undertaking was the *Allgemeine deutsche Bibliothek*, a journal which from 1765 to 1792 aimed to review all the publications of the German book trade with the assistance of an impressive list of contributors from all sections of the educated population of the German-speaking states. The focus of intellectual activity provided by this journal partly compensated for the absence of a single German capital city.[26] Another set of links between Berlin club society and the wider German-speaking world was developed by the *Berlinische Monatsschrift* of Friedrich Gedike and J. E. Biester, who were both members of the Mittwochsgesellschaft. The *Monatsschrift*, which spanned the last three decades of the century, had about three hundred contributors, many of them representatives of the mixed noble and commoner service élite.[27]

This new élite continued the campaigns that Thomasius had fought in his time. He proposed that lawyers be entrusted with the guardianship of the state; the service élite sought to assume just such a responsibility. For, contrary to assumptions often made about the generality of educated Germans in the eighteenth century, Prussian state servants were not apolitical.[28] They had chosen to serve the monarchic state, and as individuals were for the most part committed supporters of central authority.[29] But this did not mean that they were unaware or uncritical of the excesses of absolutism. Within the framework of the dynastic state, administrative and legal officials pursued a vigorous reformist policy designed to ensure the rule of law, to codify existing legislation, and to guarantee legal equality. At the same time they worked to curb the power and privileges of traditional corporations. They continued the princes' attack on the noble estate, and on parliamentarianism as the bastion of noble influence, and attempted to abolish the craft guilds' restrictive practices in order to promote trade and raise tax revenues.[30]

Thomasius's opposition to sectional interests brought him into especially violent conflict with the clergy since they claimed a monopoly of truth and attempted to censor the law faculty. The eighteenth-century service élite, many of whose members were trained lawyers, continued Thomasius's anticlericalism, but extended its attack on theoretical experts to include the philosophers who had risen to prominence through Wolff, and indeed the whole caste of university scholars. Men of affairs and their associates outside the universities resented the academics' persistent claims to control opinion, claims which appeared ever less acceptable as the city public gained in strength and confidence. Such resentment manifests itself in Nicolai's satirical novel *Leben und Meinungen des Herrn Magister Sebaldus Nothanker*, published in 1773. Nicolai's attacks on the narrow professionalism of German academics and the lofty, didactic tone of their publications echo the opinions of his friend and literary associate Abbt, whose experience as a teacher in German universities in the 1760s had filled him with such disgust that he exchanged the lecture hall for court service.[31] At the end of the century, the issue of academic authoritarianism was still very much alive. In 1795, the Berlin Mittwochsgesellschaft considered whether the universities ought to be reformed, or abolished altogether. On this occasion Nicolai argued that university scholars' claims to a monopoly of truth were no longer so strident as in the middle of the century. But Biester, who was librarian of the Königliche Bibliothek, objected vehemently to the stubborn pedantry, authoritarianism, and monastic practices and attitudes of German universities.[32]

Eighteenth-century men of affairs who attacked the authoritarianism of the old *Lehrstand* practised a philosophical eclecticism worthy of Thomasius. Though not untouched by Wolffian thinking — Nicolai for example always acknowledged a debt to Wolff[33] — they favoured no one system but believed in free exchange of opinion as the best approach to truth. Since such exchange depended on shared conventions of manner and speech the notions of decorum and civility were no less important to eighteenth-century city society than they had been to Thomasius. Some eighteenth-century commentators defined politeness negatively, by contrast with the manners of academics. Nicolai maintained: "Conversation in polite societies is not *onesided*, not *pedagogic*, not *authoritative*. People take care not to appear arrogant or fall into a schoolmasterly tone."[34] Positive definitions of politeness emphasised the willingness of each to respect and entertain all, through courtesy, forbearance, wit and good humour. In the clubs as at court cheerfulness was the first duty.[35] Members were expected to adopt the "cheerful and unconstrained manner" which alone could guarantee the kind of "free, enjoyable conversation" for which bodies such as the Berlin Montagsklub were formed.[36]

Thomasius took his standards of courtesy from the courts of his day; and during the later eighteenth century, the German courts remained models of conduct for the wider, educated society. Christian Garve, whose references to the "Gesellschaft der vornehmen oder der galanten Welt" echoed Thomasius, claimed in the 1790s that capital cities and princely residences displayed a naturalness and ease of manner absent from university towns and commercial centres.[37] Yet other models of civility had become better known in Germany since Thomasius's time, especially that afforded by the London club.

Besides acquainting Germans with the idea of moral sense Shaftesbury also informed them about the clubs.[38] Nicolai, Abbt and Mendelssohn found in Shaftesbury a vigorous denunciation of clerical authoritarianism, and an apologia for debate — on religion, politics and culture — conducted according to "the liberty of *the club*" and "that sort of freedom which is taken amongst gentlemen and friends who know one another perfectly well."[39] This freedom characteristically manifested itself in "wit and humour." Wit in Shaftesbury's sense had nothing in common with the destructive mockery of Restoration wits but was an avoidance of "pedantry and bigotry," a willingness to distance oneself from an opinion and allow its examination by others, a "freedom of raillery, a liberty in decent language to question everything, and an allowance of unravelling or refuting any argument, without offence to the arguer." Without this sort of wit, Shaftesbury suggested, "reason can hardly have its proof or be distinguished." For wit alone gave "the fairest hold," and allowed "an antagonist to use his full strength hand to hand upon even ground." Shaftesbury therefore endorsed the ancient idea that "humour was the only test of gravity" since "a subject which would not bear raillery was suspicious."[40] Nicolai concurred; Lessing thought Shaftesbury injured religion by exposing it to "raillery."[41]

Shaftesbury's ideal of courtesy had implications for fiction. He found wit and humour nowhere so fully realised as in the Greek dialogues, which treated "the very gravest subjects" in a "free and familiar style."[42] But courtesy was not only found among the participants in the dialogues, for the writers of dialogues were themselves courteous to their readers. The dialogists resembled poets, whose business was "imitation chiefly of men and manners." They worked in the same fashion as Homer, who presented his "actors" in such a way as to "denote their manners and distinct character" without the need for narrative comment. Homer, Shaftesbury claimed, did not give himself "those dictating and masterly airs of wisdom" characteristic of modern writers, but made "hardly any figure at all" and was "scarce discoverable in his poem." Such reticence by dialogist or poet left the reader to "judge coolly and with indifference of the sense delivered" and of the "character, genius, elocution, and manner of the persons who deliver it."[43] In this way, the writer treated his reader with civility, respecting his freedom and independence; and at the same time required a specifically intellectual exertion from him, since he was to "judge coolly" of the matter presented.

Those circles which practised free debate in Germany shared Shaftesbury's view of fiction, which they began to publicise and develop. "Legal" narrative found powerful new advocates who sought to challenge the domestic romance in the manner of Richardson, then the dominant mode of fiction-writing in Germany. Thomasius had associated romance with academic writers, Nicolai did the same. Writing in the *Briefe, die neueste Literatur betreffend*, he argued that domestic romancers showed only that minute portion of the world "which they can reach by looking out of the windows of their studies, so to speak." Having no experience of life, they relied for their characterisation on book-learning, and created types instead of individuals.[44] Other Berlin reviewers such as F. G. Resewitz and J. K. A. Musäus also criticised the domestic romancers for the colourlessness of their inventions and their didactic approach to their readers.[45]

The fullest and most considered criticism of Richardsonian romance came from C. F. von Blanckenburg, a Prussian military officer, in his *Versuch über den Roman*, published in 1774. Blanckenburg objected to the "perfect" characters in Richardson's stories, not because he denied that fiction could deal with perfection, but because Richardson presented it to the reader as given, instead of showing the process by which it was attained. A character like Sir Charles Grandison sprang perfected from the novelist's mind, and existed only on his authority. Moreover Richardson's plotting was determined by final rather than efficient causes. Clarissa Harlowe's elopement with Lovelace was arbitrarily imposed on the characters, rather than organically developed from their own experience. Finally Richardson did violence to his readers as well as his characters. He assaulted their emotions with the sufferings of virtue, forgetting that readers who are strongly aroused cannot learn from what they read. He also assaulted their intellect with the moralising reflections of his characters which forestalled his readers' own critical activity and thus denied them intellectual pleasure. Real people who set themselves up in society as moral instructors were insufferable; and characters in novels ought to observe like rules of civility.[46]

Richardson's loss in critical esteem was Fielding's gain. Thomasius died before any of the latter's works appeared; but had he known them he would surely have welcomed them, for Fielding's situation and attitudes were remarkably like his own. Fielding was a man of law: a justice of the peace and chairman of quarter sessions. As such, he had to assign responsibility, and therefore to enquire into the causes of human behaviour. His legal publications show the importance he attached to the search for causes, both in individual cases and in court procedure in general. His juridical pragmatism underlay his understanding of history and his writing of fiction. Although he published a collection of *Examples of the Interposition of Providence* he did not attribute physical effects to supernatural causes. Nor did he discern any clear design in history. Like many other eighteenth-century writers he remained loyal to the idea of an ultimately meaningful and beneficent world-order, while feeling misgivings about human nature as he experienced it. He was an optimist but a sceptic. Human history was a battle between conflicting forces of reason and unreason, in which base passions all too often had the upper hand. Fielding still believed in the traditional typology of the passions and his essay "On the Knowledge of the Characters of Men" set out the bodily and behavioural signs by which they could be identified.[47]

As a novelist, Fielding belonged to the comic tradition. He owed much to Cervantes, Scarron and stage comedy. *The History of Tom Jones, a Foundling*, published in 1749, has the comedy outline of Greek romance, in that Tom is parted from Sophia, and both endure hardships at the hands of scheming or deluded relatives, until, by a fortunate twist in the plot, they are allowed to marry. Fielding's characters in this novel come from all walks of life. Most still resemble the general types familiar from comedy: Tom is, as his name suggests, conventional and typical, as is the heroine Sophia also. Characters like the tutors Thwackum and Square, orthodox Anglican and deist, belong to the realm of satire. Only Squire Western, the heavy father of comedy, has rather more individualising characteristics as well. Fielding's careful causal motivation of his plot also owes something to the forensic minuteness of comedy and, like so many comedies, *Tom Jones* has a touch of the detective story.[48]

Fielding incorporated into *Tom Jones* his own poetics of the novel, which turned on the contrast between romance and history. The narrator, who has been described as Fielding's second self, warns the reader against "idle Romances...filled with Monsters." They are products of "distempered Brains," and bear no relation to truth. His own narrative differs from these, he claims, precisely because it is closer to history. Its title, *The History of Tom Jones*, is programmatic. The events that the narrator describes are not public events; neither are they authenticated by records. But he is, he says, no less a historian for that: the "historical" truth he tells is the truth of human nature, as seen in "every Kind of Character, from the Minister at his Levee, to the Bailiff in his Spunging-House; from the Dutchess at her Drum, to the Landlady behind her Bar." He supplies the secret history not of public but of private people. And his narrative relies for its historical authentication on experience. The narrator claims to speak the truth because he tells what he himself has seen and heard. As he argues, "the true practical System" of human nature "can be learnt only in the World."[49]

Fielding's history of human nature does not call for the same response as romance. Instead of encouraging emotional commitment and creating narrative suspense, Fielding distances the reader from the story. Tom and Sophia are sympathetic figures, but Tom in particular is shown with all his faults. Other characters are ironised, even satirised. And the narrator's comic tone dampens the fear the reader feels for hero and heroine when their enemies appear to triumph. With his feelings thus calmed, the reader follows the narrator's invitations to judge events for himself. Since Fielding's characters are not all black or white, his events do not always show the rewards of virtue and the punishment of vice, and the reader must constantly decide on the rights and wrongs of the action narrated. He is guided by the narrator but must think things through for himself.[50]

During the 1760s and 1770s, Fielding's poetics were adopted by German theorists, and his novels imitated with greater or lesser success by an increasing number of German comic novelists.[51] Thus the kind of fiction-writing which the young Thomasius had tried to foster eventually began to make headway in Germany after a gap of some three generations. Most of the German novels which acknowledged a debt to Fielding had little merit; but "legal" narrative found one major German exponent at this time in C. M. Wieland, a writer whose social origins seemed in fact most likely to mark him out as a traditionalist.

Wieland was born at Oberholzheim near Biberach on the Riss in what the eighteenth century termed the *Reich*: that assortment of small territories in south and west Germany which had formed the heartland of the medieval Empire and, unlike the more recently colonised areas of the north and east, still looked to the Empire for political leadership.[52] Wieland's father was a Lutheran clergyman, and to that extent at least a representative of the traditional order; and a great-grandfather had been burgomaster of Biberach, so that Wieland also belonged by birth to the ruling élite of this small town which had been a self-governing republic since the late Middle Ages. All in all therefore his earliest beginnings suggested he would remain within traditional society. He resisted paternal pressure to enter the church, and read law instead of theology at Tübingen university. But he threw over the law in order to establish himself as a writer, and his choice of J. J. Bodmer as literary mentor indicates that he saw writing as a form of religious expression. In Zürich he gave himself clerical airs while acting the part of cult leader for his female admirers, and at the same time he tried to recommend himself to the established church as a writer of religious verse. In both his Platonic and his Christian mystical phase he adopted traditionalist postures and taught with the voice of authority.[53]

However his biographer Friedrich Sengle finds a change in Wieland's outlook during 1756, when he was still in Zürich: the mystic became a psychologist and ironist, as witness the dialogue *Araspes und Panthea*. The change, which came with surprising suddenness, is not easily explained, though Sengle interprets it as simply a return to Wieland's true disposition, manifested during his student days at Tübingen but concealed while he enjoyed Bodmer's protection. In any event, the experiences of the next few years — his friendship with J. G. Zimmermann, his tenure of office as Senator and "Stadtschreiber" in Biberach, his visits to Warthausen and his unfortunate relationship with Christine Hagel — all confirmed Wieland in a more worldly, anti-Platonic course.[54]

Of all these experiences, Warthausen is the most interesting from the point of view of an enquirer into Wieland's social context. Warthausen was the residence of count Stadion, formerly chancellor of the Electorate of Mainz. While chancellor, Stadion had gone far towards turning Mainz into a modern state: he had fostered trade and industry, improved agricultural methods, introduced social reforms and combated superstition. A cultivated man and an admirer of Voltaire, he promoted science and the arts. In his old age he held "court" at Warthausen, surrounded by a varied group of people who combined knowledge of the world with literary tastes. One of the count's favourites was Wieland's former fiancée Sophie Gutermann, now married to Hofrat G. M. La Roche. Wieland was not a natural courtier; neither was he, the citizen of a free city, much inclined to abase himself before the count; and even in his happiest days at Warthausen, in 1761 and 1762, he was not uncritical of the life he found there. But the small courts still had few rivals in Germany as centres of a mixed society, so that at Warthausen Wieland encountered something he had not experienced before.[55] By his own account, he considered himself changed. In a letter to Salomon Gessner he said his commerce with the great world of the court had taught him that superstition and fanaticism are offensive to good society. "Humour and irony," he continues, "together with sound use of the five senses, have always been thought the best remedy for the excesses of both."[56] From the early 1760s onwards, Wieland became a spokesman of the values of the courts, the service élite and the new city public.

As such he condemned clerical dogmatism, not only within the Catholic church but among those of his own Protestant co-religionists who demanded conformity with Reformation articles of faith. He warned the secular authorities against the activities of clergy whom a less polite man — and here perhaps Wieland had Thomasius in mind — would call "hypocrites, pharisees, priests of Baal, and Tartuffes."[57] And he likewise attacked the schoolmen of his day, who claimed immunity from criticism for what he called their "definitions, sophisms and paralogisms."[58] He described the voice of infallibility adopted by academic teachers as a harsh, repellent voice, only slightly less rebarbative than that of the religious enthusiast.[59] Consistently with these criticisms, Wieland's own mature philosophical position was sceptical and eclectic. He cherished the ideal of intellectual tolerance, and considered politeness a prerequisite for the free exchange of ideas.[60] Having admired Shaftesbury's platonic idealism in his youth, Wieland now valued his thoughts on the society of the club.[61] But like Shaftesbury he found that the ideal of politeness or *urbanitas* had been most perfectly realised by the Greeks. He associated that ideal with Socrates in particular: not Plato's Socrates, but Xenophon's Socrates in the *Symposium*. Plato showed Socrates as the wise man among fools, but Xenophon showed him in a society of equals, conversing with wit and humour, the attributes of grace.[62]

Wieland's change from idealist to sceptic was at the same time a change of role from traditional clerical to modern legal expert. Instead of writing within a traditional religious discourse for a homogeneous public of friends, sympathisers or believers, as he had done in his Swiss period, he turned to the legal world of thought and wrote for the emerging mixed, general public of all who could or would listen to him. Wieland hoped at one time to solve the economic problems which beset this option by seeking a teaching post in Berlin, but eventually accepted a philosophy chair at Erfurt, offered to him through the good offices of baron von Groschlag, Stadion's successor in Mainz. While in post Wieland succeeded in addressing himself to a general rather than a specialist audience; but his unorthodox approach to his duties soon involved him in a conflict with the theology faculty, a conflict reminiscent of Thomasius' quarrels in Leipzig.[63] Hence Wieland's move, as soon as the opportunity arose, from traditionalist Erfurt to the more modern society of the princely court at Weimar. Here a three-year court tutorship, followed by a life-pension, enabled Wieland to write as he wished.[64]

Shortly after he established himself in Weimar, Wieland began work on a journal, *Der Teutsche Merkur*, which appeared from 1773 as a quarterly and from 1775 as a monthly. He had contemplated publishing a periodical when in financial difficulties many years earlier but *Der Teutsche Merkur* was not an economic necessity so much as a means of furthering public debate. Like Nicolai's *Allgemeine deutsche Bibliothek*, *Der Teutsche Merkur* was intended to serve as a forum for educated people all over the German-speaking territories. But it was a more miscellaneous periodical than Nicolai's, and in this respect followed the example of *Le Mercure de France*, to which of course Wieland's title alluded. Besides book reviews *Der Teutsche Merkur* also contained original prose and verse, much of which was by Wieland himself; essays on historical, political and literary subjects; political news; and theatre notes. Aimed at the kind of people who formed court and club society, the periodical did in fact reach a mixed readership of nobles and commoners, the male portion of which was mainly composed of officials and military officers.[65]

As a fiction-writer, Wieland is chiefly remembered for *Geschichte des Agathon*, begun in 1761 and first published in two volumes in 1766 and 1767. Wieland thought of this book as the first he had written not for a small group of like-minded friends, but for the educated general public.[66] Isaak Iselin, writing in the *Allgemeine deutsche Bibliothek*, thought the novel would appeal especially to men of affairs because it contained psychological insights worthy of the most experienced courtier.[67] The list of subscribers to the second edition, published in 1773, suggests that the novel attracted the audience Wieland reached with *Der Teutsche Merkur*. The list consists chiefly of noblemen, many in high offices of state, noblewomen, and commoner members of the service élite and includes only a small number of clerics or academics.[68] Contemporary comment indicates that *Agathon* was viewed with suspicion by some traditional experts: one Swiss clergyman confessed that it aroused in him "Stimmli des Teufels" — "little devilish voices."[69] Thus the evidence of the novel's reception suggests that *Agathon* was grounded in legal thinking and calculated to promote the legal rather than the clerical world-view. This impression is confirmed by the text of the 1766-67 edition.[70]

Barclay and duke Anton Ulrich had used the pattern of Greek romance for *Argenis* and *Aramena*, and Wieland likewise adopted it for his story of Agathon, a native of Plato's Athens. Agathon, whose name derives from *agathos*, the strongest term of recommendation in the Homeric vocabulary,[71] is in important respects a positive figure like the heroes of romance, though his qualities belong to Wieland's time rather than the ancient world. Although the terms *moral sense* and *moral taste* never appear in the text, we learn that Agathon has a "feeling for virtue" or "love of virtue."[72] He is, in other words, one of those people endowed, according to eighteenth-century thinking, with an inner sense of goodness, truth and beauty. Such people are naturally inclined do right because it gives them pleasure, and shun wrongdoing because it offends their feelings. Schiller was to call them *schöne Seelen*, and Wieland's text twice implies that Agathon belongs to this company.[73] Beauty of soul, being a gift of nature, is no merit, but Wieland represents Agathon, with his feeling for truth and goodness, as a noble figure, whereas the sophist Hippias, who lacks such feeling, is base. Agathon's moral sense is not his only claim to greatness, for he also possesses the warmth of imagination which the eighteenth century associated with heroes and especially with poets and *virtuosi*.[74] Though no poet, Agathon shares the name of an Athenian dramatist of the fifth century B.C., and comes from Wieland's pen very much as a self-portrait, and thus as the portrait of an artist.[75] Moreover Wieland writes at the moment when hero and artist fuse: his text antedates Goethe's *Werther* by a mere eight years.

The novel's preface, which mentions a Greek manuscript source for Agathon's life-story, suggests that, like the heroes of romance, he will be subjected to "various tests" through which his mind and character will be "purified," leaving him both wise and virtuous,[76] and the plot, integrated by Agathon's relationship with Psyche, his first love, from whom he is forced to part and with whom he is finally reunited, does indeed consist of a series of tests. Like all Heliodoran romances, the narrative begins *in medias res* when Agathon, who was brought up at the temple in Delphi, is banished from Athens where he has undergone his first great test as a political leader. His next test follows at Smyrna, when he is sold as a slave to Hippias, and offers himself, rather like Faust challenging Mephisto, as a living refutation of materialism.[77] The temptation Hippias puts in Agathon's way is Danae, with whom he does fall in love, but from whom he eventually parts to face a further political test as reformer in Syracuse where, a victim of intrigue, he is flung into prison. Now, when Agathon seems deserted by fortune, the Greek manuscript supplies the happy ending required by romance. The exemplary ruler Archytas appears as *deus ex machina* to rescue Agathon, whose virtue has survived all his trials, and give him a home in the ideal world of Tarentum, where he can live the life of a perfectly wise and good man.[78] Here Agathon finds Psyche, but a revelation of identity of the sort which concludes Greek romance keeps them apart for ever: Psyche, already the bride of another, proves to be Agathon's sister. He is free, should he wish, to marry Danae, who turns out to have been blown ashore at Tarentum by one of those storms so frequent in the Heliodoran narrative tradition.

Barclay and Anton Ulrich had used Heliodorus' pattern of "comic" romance to suggest the ultimate meaningfulness of a world whose immediate confusion supplied the principal content of their stories. In *Ge-*

schichte des Agathon, the gap between the ideal of meaningfulness —
the vision of absolute justice affirmed by the legal world-view — and the
starkness of the empirical world widens yet farther. *Argenis* and *Aramena* were each told in the third person by an undramatised narrator
who passed comment on the characters but not the story. Wieland, following Fielding in *Tom Jones,* uses a dramatised, self-conscious narrator
who tells the story from a legal-historical point of view, questions the
idealistic assumptions of romance to the point of denying them altogether, and concentrates the reader's attention on the sombre world of
efficient causes.

The narrator's first words in the preface set the tone of the book, for
his reference to a Greek manuscript source is ironic: here is an "editor"
who declines to assert the existence of his materials, and thus to make
the traditional truth-claims of romance, because, he says, he would not
expect to be believed. Though the narrator does not give his name, age
or station, he is evidently a contemporary of Wieland's, for besides freely
quoting ancient authors he often mentions Richardson, Fielding, and
Rousseau, as well as lesser modern writers such as de Mouhy and La
Morlière.[79] Despite this erudition, his tone is not didactic but conversational, and suggests the unemotional, witty style of club or *salon.* In fact
both Agathon and narrator are autobiographical; Wieland puts his young,
enthusiastic self into his hero, but his older, more sceptical self into the
narrator, and intends the reader's pleasure to be derived less from the
adventures of the sometimes callow Agathon than from their mediation
by an accomplished *causeur* who comments at length on human nature
and its representation in fiction.

The narrator's tongue-in-cheek reference to traditional truth-claims
indicates at the outset that Agathon's story draws on but does not respect
the Heliodoran conventions. Both in the preface and at crucial points in
Agathon's development the narrator evokes those conventions precisely
in order to distance himself from them. As perfect characters who remain
true to themselves through all vicissitudes, the heroes of romance conform to the desires of idealistic imagination, not the empirical laws of
nature.[80] Thomasius credited romance with all the realism of Plato's republic, and Wieland's narrator, whose account of Agathon's life includes
reference to Plato's political activities in Syracuse, leaves no doubt that
he also associates romance with the utopian speculations of unworldly
idealist philosophers.[81]

In contradistinction to romance as a product of pure imagination, the
narrator calls his own work a "history": the title, *Geschichte des Agathon,*
is as programmatic as *The History of Tom Jones,* to which it alludes. Late
in the book the narrator observes, lest there be any doubt, that *Geschichte* should be understood as *history* — record of truth — rather than
story.[82] Yet what the narrator offers is not mere literal veracity of re-

port — he makes it abundantly clear he is writing fiction — but the higher verity of truth both to the general principle of causality governing the real world, and to the particular laws of cause and effect which pertain to human behaviour. The narrator not only records the efficient causes of each event but claims the causal sequences he shows are invariable: given the causes, the effects must of necessity ensue.[83] The effect of Wieland's "true" story in the comic tradition is very much that of eighteenth-century pragmatic history. The narrator seeks to show what he often calls, in the causal-mechanical language of the legal world of thought, the machinery, inner workings or hidden springs of Agathon's behaviour.[84]

It has been suggested that when Wieland first conceived *Geschichte des Agathon* he intended to square the circle by showing how the mechanical laws of nature could lead to human perfection in a text which would combine the method of history with the goal of romance but that the causal factors he posited at the outset led him to a different end from that which he first envisaged.[85] If so, *Agathon* is a notable example of "telling forwards," of efficient displacing final causes in determining a narrative. In any event the narrator offers a "history" of Agathon in which this sensitive, imaginative young man is led not to perfect wisdom and virtue but to such ever increasing disillusionment with human nature that by the time he leaves Syracuse he has lost all enthusiasm for altruistic effort and has reached the brink of total cynicism.[86] Indeed it seems that wisdom and virtue are incompatible: the cool head needed for the former chilling the warm heart essential to the latter. To this extent Wieland anticipates what Schiller's *Briefe über die ästhetische Erziehung des Menschen* have to say about the antagonism between understanding on the one hand and feeling and imagination on the other.[87] Agathon may reach perfection in the fantasy world of Tarentum evoked by the "Greek manuscript," but not under the ordinary laws of causality. Despite his Faustian challenge to Hippias he is no superman but a mere deluded victim of his own imaginings,[88] whose career begins and ends under the auspices of Don Quixote.[89]

Agathon thus uses history to undermine romance and to cast doubt on the heroics and happy endings beloved of the idealising imagination. But Wieland is not simply trying to discredit the literary genre of romance and win the reading public over to the modern novel as Thomasius had sought to do more than two generations earlier. Wieland is engaged in a far more ambitious critique of the whole ethos of moral absolutism enshrined in romance. For *Agathon* is not just a superficial attempt to show how things work when analysed causally rather than manipulated by the artful romancer. Since Agathon is himself a romancer, a dreamer and an idealist the book can investigate the mentality of romance, and the effects of that mentality on the social world.

Through Agathon's experiences Wieland seeks to show the human consequences of romantic judgment based on the traditional authoritarian ethics which assesses actions in isolation, and to indicate the merits of rational judgment which takes into account all the circumstances contributing to actions.[90]

The romancing Agathon is always ready to entertain images of absolute perfection which determine his judgments of what, within the conventions of the narrative, are real people and actual events. The object to be judged is set against the absolute norm of his imagination; the terms *compare* and *comparison* — *vergleichen* and *Vergleichung* — therefore appear repeatedly.[91] If the object judged does not measure up to the absolute norm, it is rejected out of hand: judgment by absolutes knows no nuances. Neither does it know much consistency. At moments of crisis, judgments can be dramatically reversed, so that a person once judged absolutely good suddenly appears to be absolutely bad, and on such occasions the cynicism of the negative judgment is proportionate to the idealism of the corresponding positive judgment: if the earlier finding had not been so favourable, the later one would not be so harsh.[92]

This effect is caused by Agathon's earliest experiences. Delphi, with its temple, groves and statues of the gods, has determined once and for all the cast of his mind by providing his imagination with exalted images of goodness, truth and beauty. When still at Delphi he found a kindred soul in Psyche; the two imagined themselves to be sharing the love of the immortals in heaven, and henceforward Delphi and Psyche's chaste love for Agathon have remained the standards by which he judges the rest of the world.[93] The results are nowhere more striking than in his relationship with Danae, who, despite his mistrust, gains an ascendancy over him by exploiting his attachment to the image of Psyche. After a banquet at Danae's house a young dancer, miming Daphne's flight from Apollo, contrives to suggest that Daphne is mortified by the haste with which the river god answers her prayer for deliverance from her pursuer. Agathon disapproves of this performance because it does not match his mental image of Daphne, which is based on his memory of Psyche. The comparison between an ideal image and a rather complex reality condemns the latter, namely, the values revealed by the dancer in her representation of Daphne. Danae, displaying a fair grasp of philosophy, psychology and choreography, embodies Agathon's aspirations in her own mime of Daphne; the realised ideal displaces the actual woman in Agathon's mind, and the practical result Danae intends ensues. However the shocking truth about Danae's career as a courtesan is such a blow to Agathon's image of her that he almost faints and when Hippias finally admits to having been Danae's lover himself, Agathon dismisses both his supposed friend and his new mistress with contempt. This dramatic confrontation plunges Agathon into a turmoil of conflicting emotions as he compares his image of Danae with that of Psyche. Danae's sensuality, set against Psyche's spirituality, appears immoral; her mature beauty, set against Psyche's virginal slenderness, fails to please. She who lately appeared to Agathon to be the "model of every ideal perfection" — the "Urbild einer jeden idealen Vollkommenheit" — is now nothing more to him than "a calculating whore" — "eine schlaue Buhlerin."[94]

The absolute norms of so imperious an imagination play havoc with self-esteem. No sooner has Danae become Agathon's mistress than the sensualist Hippias addresses him as "one of us." Agathon, who of course regards himself in quite a different light, is thrown into confusion by the sudden confrontation of two so contradictory images of himself. In a dream his beloved Psyche points him to the temple in the sacred groves of Delphi; when he wakes Smyrna appears as a place of degradation by comparison with the Delphi he recalls. Hippias's calculating denunciation of Danae intensifies Agathon's self-abasement. By comparison with the image of his earlier, better self as the chaste admirer of Psyche, he who was so recently and unwittingly the lover of Hippias' ex-mistress is reduced in his own estimation to the most contemptible of slaves.[95]

Such violent reversals of feeling reappear in the work of Heinrich von Kleist, whom Wieland was to know and befriend many years after writing the novel.[96] The Agathon who cherishes an image of Danae as absolute perfection, nearly swoons when confronted with her past life, then almost annihilates the perfidious Hippias with a glance and condemns Danae as a whore foreshadows the Kleistian characters who lose their bearings when their imagination is called into question, and vilify what they have formerly adored. Thus the Marquise von O... imagines her "rescuer," the Russian count, as an angel, only to decide he must be a devil when she is forced to see he is the man who raped her; Gustav von der Ried imagines Toni in purest white when she has given him shelter and love, and in the blackest of black when she seems to have betrayed him.[97]

Kleist contrasts his characters' mental images, which are absolutes, and the outside world, which is contingent, but does not comment on this disparity in the narrative voice. Wieland does. His narrator contests absolute judgment, not by rehabilitating the condemned but by impugning their condemnation. When Agathon condemns Danae because she does not match up to his mental image of Psyche the narrator points out that this image is pure invention which has no basis in fact. Agathon thinks of Psyche as a model of female virtue in general and chastity in particular. While conceding that Psyche behaved more chastely than Danae, the narrator proceeds to explain why. Her chastity must be understood against the background of her youth, her upbringing in the temple at Delphi, Agathon's own youth and timidity, and the brevity of the acquaintance which preceded their forcible separation. Had circumstances been otherwise, the narrator suggests, Psyche might have acted as Danae later did; seen through his eyes, Psyche cannot serve as the norm by which to judge Danae: the cases differ; the comparison is meaningless.[98]

The narrator thus traces absolute judgments to their source in feeling and imagination, and questions their relevance to the real world. But *Geschichte des Agathon* is more than a narrative of Agathon's life and thoughts. The narrator continually engages with readers inscribed in the text: some of whom belong to the general public, some to sub-groups such as male or female, young or old, and some to quite specific types — one is a hypocritical cleric.[99] Writing at a time when fiction readers were still overwhelmingly readers of romance, Wieland has these inscribed readers judge by romantic criteria which the narrator can challenge, arguing that, like Agathon's, their norms are but products of the imagination.

When Agathon is about to succumb to Danae the narrator observes that readers "who demand perfect virtue in a hero" will now be offended by Agathon's failure to resist temptation.[100] The perfect virtue that these readers are assumed to have in mind is that represented by the heroic pattern-figures — *Muster* — of romance who exhibit courage, steadfastness and above all fidelity in love, and by contrast with whom the Agathon who is about to betray Psyche for Danae is bound to seem vile. As the narrator points out, such figures are the inventions of the romancer, who creates like Prometheus in sovereign freedom. His characters are products of pure untrammelled imagination (*Einbildungskraft*) and as such are not subject to the ordinary laws of causality. Real human beings, by contrast, are contingent and imperfect products of nature and circumstance, to whom the absolute norm of romance is irrelevant.[101] The narrator attributes the persistence of this arbitrary criterion to human vanity: imaginary heroism flatters the ego of those who believe the claim, made in all seriousness by contemporary advocates of romance in drama and the novel, that romance-readers could or might have the powers ascribed to their romantic idols.

Another striking example of absolute judgment by inscribed readers is suggested at the end of the story, when Agathon gives himself up to misanthropic reflections while imprisoned in Syracuse. The narrator imagines he hears women readers exclaim, "Is it possible? Could Agathon think such thoughts? So mean, so ignoble." What, these readers ask, is to become of the hero's virtue? What *is* virtue, but a constant struggle against the passions, against foolishness as much as vice? Once again the inscribed readers are blaming Agathon for his failure to live up to the norm of the hero of romance. But they do not stop there. Just as Agathon compared Danae with his mental image of Psyche, the inscribed readers now compare the older Agathon with their own image of his younger self. This younger self was a hero, they argue, when he resisted the advances of a concupiscent priestess at Delphi, when he fought for the persecuted innocent Lysias in Athens, and when he steadfastly endured banishment by the citizens of that city. By comparison with the young hero, the prisoner of Syracuse is a sorry spectacle.[102] In reply the narrator points out that these inscribed readers' mental picture of the perfect young Agathon is just that — a product of imagination, like Agathon's idea of the young Psyche. Agathon did indeed resist the priestess, but was assisted in so doing by his youthful innocence and love for Psyche. Help such as Agathon gave to Lysias can stem from ambition, hatred of one's friend's enemy, or even love for one's friend's wife. Finally, Agathon remained steadfast on being banished because pride in his own virtue enabled him to triumph over his enemies. Agathon the young hero of virtue is thus produced by imagination altering reality and, as such, is no fit norm against which to measure an older Agathon very much under reality's sway.

Gerd Hemmerich, noting that the narrator uses his powers of analysis negatively, showing how apparently exemplary behaviour arises from fortunate temperament, favourable circumstances, or even unworthy motives, and thus seeming on occasion even to deny the possibility of virtue, has argued that *Agathon* simply substitutes dogmatic scepticism for the Platonic, stoic and, by implication, Christian idealism which the text contests.[103] But this is to mistake Wieland's intention. His evident scepticism is but a means to a humane end; his narrator judges according to reason, viewing the individual in his own causal context, instead of comparing him with absolute norms, and considering all the circumstances before deciding on praise or blame. This method is destructive only when applied to supposed exemplars of righteousness and a system of judgment which is itself destructive, as Agathon's story indicates. Rational judgment does not abolish the distinction between right and wrong but alters our response to the doer since, if we consider all his circumstances, and understand the causes of his behaviour, we may moderate blame instead of condemning outright. Wieland's scepticism is not merely far removed from dogmatism but tends strongly towards equity, the tempering of strict judgment in accordance with individual circumstances. The terms *equity* and *equitable* — *Billigkeit* and *billig* — are so frequent in the text as to furnish key-words for Blanckenburg's reading of *Agathon*.[104] Good judgment, he observed in *Versuch über den Roman*, presupposed both knowledge of all the circumstances of an act and the capacity to weigh causes against effects. The novelist's art might help men to understand good judgment and to perceive and avoid the danger of "unjust and inequitable" treatment of one another.[105]

In *Agathon* Wieland confronts the teleological pattern-morality of the traditional world with the causal-legal morality of the modern but he does so in such a way that the reader must weigh the merits of modern morality for himself. Herein lies the real interrogative quality of the text. The narrator impugns the absolute ideals by which characters or inscribed readers make their judgments but refrains from positive judgments of his own. The reader has the task of applying the narrator's rational and equitable principles to the case in hand. When Agathon condemns Danae by comparison with Psyche, the narrator subjects Psyche's case to rational investigation, leaving the reader to arrive at a verdict on Danae, and noting simply that she might have acted differently if she had had Psyche's upbringing rather than her own.[106] Yet the reader's most complex undertaking remains that of judging Agathon himself. Judged by absolute norms Agathon is simply found wanting. He does not always act virtuously for virtue's sake, he does not remain faithful to Psyche, he is not unwavering in his beliefs. But to judge him according to all his circumstances is far more difficult, and the narrator warns against over-hasty conclusions. The reader is discouraged from forming any specific image of Agathon, as enthusiast or stoic or whatever, since to do so would be artificially to arrest events that are constantly in flux.[107] We know Agathon's heart is in the right place; beyond that we can merely say that he does as well as anyone might be expected to do in his position. This understanding of him gives a new meaning to the word *agathos*, which no longer signifies meeting a specific cultural norm, but being as good as possible according to one's own individual circumstances. Thus the Agathon who falls short according to absolute norms may be, at least to some extent, rehabilitated by rational norms, and the ultimate question for the reader is which verdict and which set of norms is most adequate to the case.[108]

Agathon is not a book that engages the emotions. The reader can come at the story only through the intermediary of the narrator and his circle of inscribed readers. There is no chance of becoming involved in the action or forgetting oneself in the characters. Indeed should this possibility ever seem imminent, the narrator prevents it by passing over a potentially emotional scene with a dismissive comment.[109] The text appeals to the intellect, and does so most powerfully. P. D. Huet in France and Thomasius in Germany had argued for a genre of fiction which would help to form the mind, but since duke Anton Ulrich, no significant German writer had attempted the task. Hence Wieland was rightly perceived by the more alert of his contemporaries as something new in the world of fiction. Blanckenburg, who expended many pages of his *Versuch über den Roman* on Wieland's virtues as a writer of interrogative fiction, differentiated *Agathon* from all other novels save only *Tom Jones*. These two, he claimed, could teach their readers to think; other fictions were intent only on indoctrinating their readers by exploiting their emotions.[110] Lessing paid Wieland briefer but, in view of his standing, far more valuable homage when he remarked that *Agathon* was "the first and only romance for the thinking man," and hence no romance at all.[111]

[1] Notker Hammerstein, *Jus und Historie: ein Beitrag zur Geschichte des historischen Denkens an deutschen Universitäten im späten 17. und 18. Jahrhundert* (Göttingen: Vandenhoeck & Ruprecht, 1972) 322, 329.

[2] "evangelisches Pabstum": Götz von Selle, *Die Georg-August-Universität zu Göttingen, 1737-1937* (Göttingen: Vandenhoeck & Ruprecht, 1937) 29; and see also 21.

[3] von Selle 108-9.

[4] "Spiegel des menschlichen Herzens...nach allen seinen Nuancen, Abwegen, Schlupfwinkeln, Entschuldigungen, Behelfen, nach allen seinen Trieben, Neigungen, Leidenschaften, Kunstgriffen": "Geschichte," *Moralische Encyclopädie*, ed. Ulrich, vol. 1, section 2 (1779) 873-74. Cited following Werner Hahl, *Reflexion und Erzählung: ein Problem der Romantheorie von der Spätaufklärung bis zum programmatischen Realismus* (Stuttgart: Kohlhammer, 1971) 51. On Gatterer and pragmatic history, see von Selle 134; Hammerstein 366-71; Hahl 51-5.

[5] cf. Hammerstein 360, 371.

[6] Hammerstein 366-67; von Selle 134; Hahl 55.

[7] See the criticism in Eberhard Kessel, ed., *Zur Theorie und Philosophie der Geschichte*, by Friedrich Meinecke (Stuttgart: K. F. Koehler, 1959) 69, 222, 224-27, 236-37, vol. 4 of *Werke.*.

[8] Herbert Butterfield, *Man on his Past* (1955; Cambridge, England: Cambridge UP, 1969) 93.

[9] Jan Schröder, *Wissenschaftstheorie und Lehre der "praktischen Jurisprudenz" auf deutschen Universitäten an der Wende zum 19. Jahrhundert*, Ius Commune: Sonderhefte 11 (Frankfurt am Main: Klostermann, 1979) 49-51.

[10] Sophie Dorothea, sister of George II, was married to Friedrich Wilhelm I of Prussia. On the part played by elector and estates, see Charles E. McClelland, *State, Society, and University in Germany 1700-1914* (Cambridge, England: Cambridge UP, 1980) 37. On the position of the nobility in Hanover, see Joachim Lampe, *Aristokratie, Hofadel und Staatspatriziat in Kurhannover: die Lebenskreise der höheren Beamten an den kurhannoverischen Zentral- und Hofbehörden 1714-1760* (Göttingen: Vandenhoeck & Ruprecht, 1963) 12-15; 22-23; "Adel und Konfession: ein Rundgespräch," *Deutscher Adel 1555-1740: Büdinger Vorträge 1964*, ed. Hellmuth Rössler, Schriften zur Problematik der deutschen Führungsschichten in der Neuzeit 2 (Darmstadt: Wissenschaftliche Buchgesellschaft, 1965) 139.

[11] McClelland 43-45; Peter Hanns Reill, *The German Enlightenment and the Rise of Historicism* (Berkeley: U of California Press, 1975) 4, 8.

[12] See Friedrich Lütge, *Deutsche Sozial- und Wirtschaftsgeschichte: ein Überblick*, 3rd ed. (Berlin: Springer, 1966) 321, 328-29, 356-60, 365-66, 397-99.

[13] On the part played by the nobility in state service under Friedrich Wilhelm I and Friedrich II, see Otto Hintze, "The Hohenzollern and the Nobility," *The Historical Essays of Otto Hintze*, ed. Felix Gilbert (New York: Oxford UP, 1975) 53, 57-58; Gerd Heinrich, "Der Adel in Brandenburg-Preussen," *Deutscher Adel 1555-1740* 299-300; Rudolf Vierhaus, "Ständewesen und Staatsverwaltung in Deutschland im späteren 18. Jahrhundert," *Dauer und Wandel der Geschichte: Aspekte europäischer Vergangenheit*, Festschrift Kurt von Raumer, ed. Rudolf Vierhaus and Manfred Botzenhart (Münster: Aschendorff, 1966)

354; C. B. A. Behrens, *Society, Government, and the Enlightenment: The Experiences of Eighteenth-Century France and Prussia* (New York: Harper & Row, 1985) 56-67.

[14] Werner Conze, "Adel," *Geschichtliche Grundbegriffe: historisches Lexikon zur politisch-sozialen Sprache in Deutschland*, ed. Otto Brunner, Werner Conze and Reinhart Koselleck, vol. 1 (Stuttgart: Klett, 1972) 23; Vierhaus 355.

[15] Reinhart Koselleck, *Preussen zwischen Reform und Revolution* (Stuttgart: Klett, 1967) 114-15.

[16] "eine gute education und sentiments von honnêteté bekommen haben": cited by Gustav Schmoller, "Der preussische Beamtenstand unter Friedrich Wilhelm I," *Preussische Jahrbücher* 26 (1870): 172.

[17] Johann Michael von Loen, *Freye Gedanken von dem Hof, der Policey, gelehrten- bürgerlichen- und Bauren-Stand, von der Religion und einem beständigen Frieden in Europa*, 2nd ed. (Ulm: J. F. Gaum, 1761) 73.

[18] J. Conrad, "Die Statistik der Universität Halle während der 200 Jahre ihres Bestehens," *Festschriften der vier Fakultäten zum Zweihundertjährigen Jubiläum der Vereinigten Friedrichs-Universität Halle-Wittenberg, den 3. August 1894: Festschrift der Philosophischen Fakultät* (Halle a. d. Saale: Waisenhaus, 1894) 36

[19] Jürgen Habermas, *Strukturwandel der Öffentlichkeit: Untersuchung zu einer Kategorie der bürgerlichen Gesellschaft*, Politica 4 (Neuwied: Luchterhand, 1962) 32-33; Erich Angermann, "Das 'Auseinandertreten von Staat und Gesellschaft' im Denken des 18. Jahrhunderts," *Zeitschrift für Politik* ns 10.2 (1963): 89-90; Manfred Riedel, "Bürger," *Geschichtliche Grundbegriffe*, vol. 1: 678-79, 681, 683; and "Gesellschaft, bürgerliche," *Geschichtliche Grundbegriffe*, vol. 2: 739, 746-47.

[20] cf. Vierhaus 355, 358; Anthony J. La Vopa, *Grace, Talent, and Merit: Poor Students, Clerical Careers, and Professional Ideology in Eighteenth-century Germany* (Cambridge, England: Cambridge UP, 1988) 281.

[21] La Vopa 234-35; cf. Johanna Schultze, "Die Auseinandersetzung zwischen Adel und Bürgertum in den deutschen Zeitschriften der letzten drei Jahrzehnte des 18. Jahrhunderts (1773-1806)," *Historische Studien* 163 (1925): 14-15.

[22] Horst Möller, *Aufklärung in Preussen: der Verleger, Publizist und Geschichtsschreiber Friedrich Nicolai* (Berlin: Colloquium-Verlag, 1974) 267, 270, 304-6, 538. On Berlin cultural life at this period, see also Ernst Kaeber, "Geistige Strömungen in Berlin zur Zeit Friedrichs des Grossen," *Forschungen zur Brandenburgischen und Preussischen Geschichte* 54 (1943).

[23] On freedom of association in eighteenth-century Prussia, see Rainer C. Baum, "Authority and Identity: The Case for Evolutionary Invariance," *Identity and Authority: Explorations in the Theory of Society*, ed. Roland Robertson and Burkart Holzner (Oxford: Blackwell, 1980) 78, 92, 99, 103; Thomas Nipperdey, "Verein als soziale Struktur in Deutschland im späten 18. und frühen 19. Jahrhundert," *Geschichtswissenschaft und Vereinswesen im 19. Jahrhundert: Beiträge zur Geschichte historischer Forschung in Deutschland*, Veröffentlichungen des Max-Planck-Instituts für Geschichte 1 (Göttingen: Vandenhoeck & Ruprecht, 1972) 9-12, 34. For a bibliography of work on voluntary associations, see Wolfgang Hardtwig, "Politische Gesellschaft und Verein zwischen aufgeklärtem Absolutismus und der Grundrechtserklärung der Frankfurter Paulskirche," *Grund- und Freiheitsrechte im Wandel von Gesellschaft und Geschichte: Beiträge zur Geschichte der Grund- und Freiheitsrechte vom Ausgang des Mittelalters bis*

zur Revolution von 1848, ed. Günter Birtsch, Veröffentlichungen zur Geschichte der Grund- und Freiheitsrechte 1 (Göttingen: Vandenhoeck & Ruprecht, 1981) 336, note 2.

[24] Möller 233-34.

[25] Möller 229-32.

[26] Möller 199, and see 197-208.

[27] Möller 251-53; *Was ist Aufklärung? Beiträge aus der Berlinischen Monatsschrift*, ed. Norbert Hinske, 3rd ed. (Darmstadt: Wissenschaftliche Buchgesellschaft, 1981).

[28] Möller 561; Hardtwig 345.

[29] See Rudolf Vierhaus, "Deutschland im 18. Jahrhundert: soziales Gefüge, politische Verfassung, geistige Bewegung," *Lessing und die Zeit der Aufklärung: Vorträge gehalten auf der Tagung der Joachim Jungius-Gesellschaft der Wissenschaften, Hamburg am 10. und 11. Oktober 1967* (Göttingen: Vandenhoeck & Ruprecht, 1968) 23.

[30] Fritz Hartung, "Studien zur Geschichte der preussischen Verwaltung 1: vom 16. Jahrhundert bis zum Zusammenbruch des alten Staates im Jahre 1806," *Abhandlungen der Preussischen Akademie der Wissenschaften: Philosophisch-historische Klasse* 17 (1941): 40-41; Fritz Valjavec, *Die Entstehung der politischen Strömungen in Deutschland 1770-1815* (Munich: R, Oldenbourg, 1951) 36-38, 77, 83; Wilhelm Störmer, "Territoriale Landesherrschaft und absolutistisches Staatsprogramm," *Blätter für deutsche Landesgeschichte* 108 (1972): 102-3; Rudolf Vierhaus, "Aufklärung und Freimaurerei in Deutschland," *Das Vergangene und die Geschichte*, Festschrift Reinhard Wittram, ed. Rudolf von Thadden, Gert von Pistohlkors and Hellmuth Weiss (Göttingen: Vandenhoeck & Ruprecht, 1973) 28-29; Möller 253 and note 77, 307-8, 313.

[31] Friedrich Nicolai, *Das Leben und die Meinungen des Herrn Magister Sebaldus Nothanker*, ed. Fritz Brüggemann, Deutsche Literatur...in Entwicklungsreihen: Reihe Aufklärung 15 (Leipzig: Reclam, 1938) 72. See Möller 75, 190; and compare 20-21, 24, 26, 72, 537-38. For a discussion of Nicolai's novel, see Maria Tronskaja, *Die deutsche Prosasatire der Aufklärung*, Neue Beiträge zur Literaturwissenschaft 28 (Berlin: Rütten & Loening, 1969) 235-55. On Abbt see Hans Erich Bödeker, "Thomas Abbt: Patriot, Bürger und bürgerliches Bewusstsein," *Bürger und Bürgerlichkeit im Zeitalter der Aufklärung*, ed. Rudolf Vierhaus, Wolfenbütteler Studien zur Aufklärung 7 (Heidelberg: L. Schneider, 1981) 225, 246-47.

[32] "diese aufgeblähte Pedanterei, dieses Alleinsprechen und Absprechen *ex auctoritate*, die ganze altfränkische mönchische Verfassung unserer Universitäten": A. Stölzel, "Die Berliner Mittwochsgesellschaft über Aufhebung oder Reform der Universitäten (1795)," *Forschungen zur Brandenburgischen und Preussischen Geschichte* 2 (1889): 218 and passim.

[33] Möller 20, 57; Wolfgang Albrecht, "Friedrich Nicolais Kontroverse mit den Klassikern und Frühromantikern (1796-1802)," *Debatten und Kontroversen: literarische Auseinandersetzungen in Deutschland am Ende des 18. Jahrhunderts*, ed. Hans-Dietrich Dahnke and Bernd Leistner, vol. 2 (Berlin: Aufbau-Verlag, 1989) 11.

[34] "Die Unterhaltung in guten Gesellschaften ist nicht *einseitig*, nicht *schulmässig*, nicht *gebietend*. Man hütet sich da Prätension zu zeigen oder in den Lehrerton zu verfallen": Friedrich Nicolai, *Beschreibung einer Reise durch Deutschland und die Schweiz*, vol. 11 (Berlin: F. Nicolai, 1796) 294-95.

[35] For the principle of cheerfulness in the eighteenth century see Hans-Jürgen Schings, *Melancholie und Aufklärung: Melancholiker und ihre Kritiker in Erfahrungsseelenkunde und Literatur des 18. Jahrhunderts* (Stuttgart: J. B. Metzler, 1977) 224.

[36] "munteres und ungezwungenes Wesen": *Friedrich Nicolais Briefe über den itzigen Zustand der schönen Wissenschaften in Deutschland (1755)*, ed. Georg Ellinger, Berliner Neudrucke, ed. Ludwig Geiger and Georg Ellinger, 3rd series, vol. 2 (Berlin: Gebrüder Paetel, 1894) 147. "freien heiteren Conversation": Möller 230.

[37] Christian Garve, *Popularphilosophische Schriften über literarische, ästhetische und gesellschaftliche Gegenstände*, ed. Kurt Wölfel, 2 vols. (Stuttgart: J. B. Metzler, 1974) vol. 2: 12*; vol. 1: 572, 575.

[38] Nicolai, Abbt and Mendelssohn together planned to translate the works of Shaftesbury into German, see Alexander Altmann, *Moses Mendelssohn: A Biographical Study* (London: Routledge & Kegan Paul, 1973) 109.

[39] "*Sensus Communis*; An Essay on the Freedom of Wit and Humour," *Characteristics of Men, Manners, Opinions, Times*, by Anthony Earl of Shaftesbury, ed. John M. Robertson, vol. 1 (London: G. Richards, 1900) 53.

[40] Shaftesbury 47-48, 49, 52.

[41] Gotthold Ephraim Lessing, *Sämtliche Schriften*, 3rd ed., ed. Karl Lachmann and Franz Muncker, vol. 8 (Stuttgart: G. J. Göschen, 1892) 27.

[42] *Characteristics*, vol. 1: 51.

[43] *Characteristics*, vol. 1: 129-30, 132.

[44] "den sie so zu sagen, aus den Fenstern ihrer Studierstube mit dem Gesichte erreichen können": letter 225, 15. April 1762; letter 58, 4. October 1759. See *Briefe, die neueste Literatur betreffend* 14 (1762): 200; 4 (1759): 207-209.

[45] See for example *Allgemeine deutsche Bibliothek* 1.2 (1765): 228; 4.1 (1767): 157; 15.1 (1771): 12-13. See also Tronskaja 114-16; Eva D. Becker, *Der deutsche Roman um 1780* (Stuttgart: J. B. Metzler, 1964) 15.

[46] Friedrich von Blanckenburg, *Versuch über den Roman*, facsimile of the 1774 ed., ed. Eberhard Lämmert (Stuttgart: J. B. Metzler, 1965) 54, 68, 85-87, 255, 297-301, 350-52, 363-64, 370-72, 409-11.

[47] See Wolfgang G. Deppe, *History versus Romance: ein Beitrag zur Entwicklungsgeschichte und zum Verständnis der Literaturtheorie Henry Fieldings*, Neue Beiträge zur englischen Philologie 4 (Münster: Aschendorff, 1965) 34, 74-78, 109-11, 137.

[48] Deppe 72, 76; R.S. Crane, "The Concept of Plot and the Plot of *Tom Jones*," *Critics and Criticism: Ancient and Modern*, ed. R. S. Crane (Chicago: U of Chicago Press, 1952) 639-40; Northrop Frye, *Anatomy of Criticism: Four Essays* (Princeton: Princeton UP, 1957) 309; Robert Scholes and Robert Kellogg, *The Nature of Narrative* (New York: Oxford UP, 1966) 101, 232; Ian Watt, *The Rise of the Novel: Studies in Defoe, Richardson and Fielding* (1957; Harmondsworth, England: Penguin Books, 1972) 298-301, 310, 312-13, 317.

[49] Henry Fielding, *The History of Tom Jones, a Foundling*, introd. Martin C. Battestin, ed. Fredson Bowers (Oxford: Clarendon Press, 1974) 1: 401-2, 150, 489, 492; 2: 687. On the implied author in *Tom Jones* see Wayne C. Booth, *The Rhetoric of Fiction* (Chicago: U of Chicago Press, 1961) 215-18.

[50] Watt 301, 310, 315, 322, 325, 328; Wolfgang Iser, *Der implizite Leser: Kommunikationsformen des Romans von Bunyan bis Beckett* (Munich: UTB-Fink, 1972) 81-93.

[51] Wilhelm Vosskamp, *Romantheorie in Deutschland: von Martin Opitz bis Friedrich von Blanckenburg* (Stuttgart: J. B. Metzler, 1973) 257; Hahl 73-75; Tronskaja 117, 217, 219, 243; Becker 55-56; Guy Stern, "Fielding and the Sub-literary German Novel: A Study of Opitz' *Wilhelm von Hohenberg*," *Monatshefte für deutschen Unterricht, deutsche Sprache und Literatur* 48 (1956): 295-307.

[52] Fritz Hartung, *Deutsche Verfassungsgeschichte vom 15. Jahrhundert bis zur Gegenwart*, 5th ed. (Stuttgart: K. F. Koehler, 1950) 159.

[53] See Friedrich Sengle, *Wieland* (Stuttgart: J. B. Metzler, 1949) 13-17, 46-52, 53-70, 70-89. On Wieland's attitude to poetry in his Swiss period see also Wolfgang von Ungern-Sternberg, "Christoph Martin Wieland und das Verlagswesen seiner Zeit: Studien zur Entstehung des freien Schriftstellertums in Deutschland," *Archiv für Geschichte des Buchwesens* 14 (1974): col. 1314, 1337, 1503-4.

[54] See Sengle 89-97, 119-50. For a contrary view, see John A. McCarthy, "Wielands Metamorphose," *Deutsche Vierteljahrsschrift für Literaturwissenschaft und Geistesgeschichte* 49 (1975): Sonderheft "18. Jahrhundert" 149*-167*.

[55] Sengle 141-50. See also Wieland's letters of 10 August 1768 to J. A. Riedel, *Wielands Briefwechsel*, ed. Hans Werner Seiffert, vol. 3 (Berlin: Akademie-Verlag, 1975) 534-35; and of 28 December 1787 to Leonhard Meister, *Ausgewählte Briefe an verschiedene Freunde von Christoph Martin Wieland in den Jahren 1751 bis 1810*, ed. Heinrich Gessner, 4 vols. (Zürich: Gessner, 1815-16) 3: 386.

[56] "Der Scherz und die Ironie sind nebst dem ordentlichen Gebrauche der fünf Sinne immer für das beste Mittel gegen die Ausschweifungen von beiden angesehen worden": Wieland to Salomon Gessner, 7 November, 1763, *Wielands Briefwechsel*, ed. Seiffert, vol. 3: 206-7.

[57] "Heuchler, Farisäer, Baalspriester und Tartüffen": C. M. Wieland, *Gesammelte Schriften*, ed. Deutsche Kommission der Preussischen Akademie der Wissenschaften, section 1, vol. 15 (Berlin: Weidmann, 1930) 166.

[58] "Definizionen...Sofismen und Paralogismen': *Gesammelte Schriften*, section 1, vol. 15: 117.

[59] C. M. Wieland, *Werke*, ed. H. Düntzer, part 32 (Berlin: Gustav Hempel, [1879]) 22.

[60] See Jürgen Jacobs, *Wielands Romane* (Bern: Francke, 1969) 9-11, 12-14, 33-42, 79-86, 96-105.

[61] Sengle 77-78, 95-96, 107, 116-18; Jacobs 54, 84, 86.

[62] Jacobs 14, 36-38.

[63] Sengle 153-55, 234-46; W. Daniel Wilson, "Wieland's *Diogenes* and the Emancipation of the Critical Intellectual," *Christoph Martin Wieland: nordamerikanische Forschungsbeiträge zur 250. Wiederkehr seines Geburtstages 1983*, ed. Hansjörg Schelle (Tübingen: M. Niemeyer, 1984) 167-71.

[64] Sengle 269-74; Wilson 174.

[65] Sengle 407-22; Hans Wahl, "Geschichte des *Teutschen Merkur*," diss., U of Berlin, 1914, 39-42, 47; Sven-Aage Jørgensen, "Wieland zwischen Bürgerstube und Adelssalon," *Bürger und Bürgerlichkeit im Zeitalter der Aufklärung* 215; Claude Miquet, *C. M. Wie-*

land, directeur du Mercure allemand *(1773-1789): un dessein ambitieux, une réussite intellectuelle et commerciale* (Bern: P. Lang, 1990) 49-52.

[66] *Wielands Briefwechsel*, ed. Seiffert, vol. 3: 163.

[67] For Iselin's review, see *Allgemeine deutsche Bibliothek* 6 (1768): 190-221, and Lieselotte E. Kurth-Voigt, "Wielands *Geschichte des Agathon*: zur journalistischen Rezeption des Romans," *Wieland-Studien* 1 (1991): 21-22.

[68] The subscription list is reprinted in *Gesammelte Schriften*, ed. Deutsche Kommission der Preussischen Akademie der Wissenschaften, section 1, vol. 8.2: 191-212. On the subscribers, see Jørgensen 213.

[69] The clergyman's comment is cited by Ungern-Sternberg (col. 1447, note 638).

[70] The text of the first edition is to be found in Christoph Martin Wieland, *Werke*, ed. Fritz Martini and Hans Werner Seiffert, vol. 1 (Munich: Hanser, 1964). My page references are to this text. For interpretations which suggest that Wieland is preaching an idealistic message, see Klaus Schaefer, "Das Problem der sozialpolitischen Konzeption in Wielands *Geschichte des Agathon* (1766/67): ein Beitrag zur Untersuchung des idealen Menschenbildes in der Literatur der deutschen Aufklärung," *Weimarer Beiträge* 16.10 (1970): 171-96; John A. McCarthy, *Christoph Martin Wieland*, Twayne's World Authors Series 528 (Boston: Twayne Publishers, 1979) 74-82.

[71] See the article "Arete/Agathon/Kakon," *The Encyclopedia of Philosophy*, ed. Paul Edwards; A. W. H. Adkins, *Merit and Responsibility* (Oxford: Clarendon Press, 1960).

[72] "Gefühl für die Tugend," *Ag.* bk. 8, ch. 6: 675; "Liebe der Tugend," bk. 8, ch. 7: 681.

[73] *Ag.* bk. 8, ch. 7: 681; bk. 10, ch. 5: 824.

[74] See "junge Leute von lebhafter Empfindung und feuriger Einbildungskraft," *Ag.* bk. 3, ch. 3: 443. "das schwärmerische Volk der Helden, Dichter und Virtuosen aller Arten," bk. 11, ch. 2: 838; and compare 424-25; 630; 543. On warmth of imagination in eighteenth-century aesthetics see Ernst Cassirer, *Die Philosophie der Aufklärung* (Tübingen: Mohr, 1932) 467-69; Victor Lange, "Zur Gestalt des Schwärmers im deutschen Roman des 18. Jahrhunderts," *Festschrift für Richard Alewyn*, ed. Herbert Singer and Benno von Wiese (Cologne: Böhlau, 1967) 155-56, 158.

[75] Wieland to J. G. Zimmermann, 5 January, 1762, *Wielands Briefwechsel*, ed. Seiffert, vol. 3: 61.

[76] "verschiedene Proben...durch welche seine Denkensart und seine Tugend erläutert... würde," "ein eben so weiser als tugendhafter Mann," *Ag.* "Vorbericht": 379-80.

[77] *Ag.* bk. 3, ch. 6: 462-67. Agathon, like Faust, is an "unbefriedigter Geist," bk. 6, ch. 4: 542; Hippias is described as "schalkhaft" (bk. 4, ch. 2: 475; bk. 6, ch. 3: 535), cf. the Lord's description of Mephisto in the Prologue in Heaven, see J. W. Goethe, *Werke*, Hamburger Ausgabe, 7th ed., vol. 3, ed. Erich Trunz (Hamburg: C. Wegner, 1964) 18.

[78] On the Greek source as authority for the ending see *Ag.* bk. 11, ch. 1: 827-31. On Archytas see book 11, ch. 1 and 2.

[79] Richardson: 824, 836; Fielding: 493, 503; Rousseau: 516; de Mouhy: 376; La Morlière: 515.

[80] *Ag.* "Vorbericht": 375. See also especially bk. 5, ch. 8.

[81] On Plato and his followers see book 9, ch. 3.

[82] *Ag.* bk. 11, ch. 1: 827. See also "Vorbericht": 375. Compare Monika Schrader, *Mimesis und Poiesis: poetologische Studien zum Bildungsroman* (Berlin: de Gruyter, 1975) 35-36.

[83] See for example *Ag.* bk. 8, ch. 1: 640; bk. 9, ch. 3: 711. Modern philosophy denies that it is possible to legislate for "invariable sequence" between conditions and events, see H. L. A. Hart and A. M. Honoré, *Causation in the Law* (Oxford: Clarendon Press, 1959) 29. Compare Lessing on inevitable sequence in drama: *Sämtliche Schriften*, 3rd ed., ed. Lachmann and Muncker, vol. 9: 308, 316.

[84] The text uses the term "pragmatisch-kritisch": *Ag.* bk. 9, ch. 2: 701. For metaphors of machinery, see bk. 4, ch. 6: 488; bk. 7, ch. 5: 596; bk. 8, ch. 3: 658; bk. 9, ch. 5: 760.

[85] See Fritz Martini, afterword, *Geschichte des Agathon*, by Christoph Martin Wieland, 1st version, Reclams Universal-Bibliothek 9933 (Stuttgart: Reclam, 1979) 663-67.

[86] *Ag.* bk. 10, ch. 5: 816-26.

[87] Friedrich Schiller, *Sämtliche Werke*, ed. Gerhard Fricke and Herbert G. Göpfert, 3rd ed., vol. 5 (Munich: Hanser, 1962) 583. Compare Benno von Wiese, *Friedrich Schiller* (Stuttgart: J. B. Metzler, 1959) 96-97.

[88] *Ag.* bk. 11, ch. 1: 827-31.

[89] *Ag.* bk. 1, ch. 2: 385; bk. 11, ch. 1: 829.

[90] cf. Erich Fromm, *Man for Himself: An Enquiry into the Psychology of Ethics* (1949; London: Routledge & Kegan Paul, 1971) 13, 32-33, 236.

[91] For *Vergleichung, vergleichen*, see especially *Ag.* bk. 4, ch. 6: 487-90; bk. 6, ch. 4: 543; bk. 7, ch. 7: 617; bk. 8, ch. 3: 652-55.

[92] See for example bk. 8, ch. 3: 654, 658.

[93] *Ag.* bk. 7, ch. 1: 551-54; bk. 7, ch. 4: 579.

[94] *Ag.* bk. 4, ch. 5: 485; bk. 4, ch. 6: 488-89, cf. 544; bk. 5, ch. 1: 491; bk. 8, ch. 2: 650-52; bk. 8, ch. 3: 653-55.

[95] "einer von den Unsrigen," bk. 6, ch. 3: 535; "Verwirrung," bk. 6, ch. 3: 536, cf. 540; bk. 6, ch. 4: 540-42; bk. 8, ch. 3: 658.

[96] Kleist stayed with Wieland in Ossmannstedt from January to March, 1803: see Sengle 517-22.

[97] Heinrich von Kleist, *Sämtliche Werke und Briefe*, ed. Helmut Sembdner, 2nd ed., vol. 2 (Munich: Hanser, 1961) 142-43, 171-76, 191-95.

[98] *Ag.* bk. 8, ch. 3: 655-57.

[99] For inscribed readers see especially bk. 5, ch. 9: 518; bk. 6, ch. 4: 542-43; bk. 8, ch. 3: 655; bk. 8, ch. 7: 680-82, 686-87; bk. 9, ch. 2: 699-701; bk. 9, ch. 3: 709-10; bk. 9, ch. 5: 757-60; bk. 10, ch. 3: 799-800; bk. 10, ch. 5: 817-26.

[100] "welche von einem Helden eine vollkommene Tugend fordern," *Ag.* bk. 5, ch. 8: 509.

[101] *Ag.* bk. 5, ch. 8: 510, 513.

[102] "Ist's möglich? Konnte Agathon so denken? So klein, so unedel," bk. 10, ch. 5: 817.

[103] Gerd Hemmerich, *Christoph Martin Wielands* Geschichte des Agathon: *eine kritische Werkinterpretation*, Erlanger Beiträge zur Sprach- und Kunstwissenschaft 63 (Nuremberg: Carl, 1979) 89.

[104] For *Billigkeit* and *billig* see *Ag.* 427, 655, 657, 740, 743, 757, 821, 866.

[105] "ungerecht und unbillig," Blanckenburg 292-93.

[106] *Ag.* bk. 8, ch. 3: 655-57.

[107] *Ag.* bk. 9, ch. 5: 758-60.

[108] cf. Iser 88 on competing norms in *Tom Jones.*

[109] *Ag.* bk. 6, ch. 5: 548.

[110] Blanckenburg "Vorbericht" and 252-53, 255, 289, 301-2, 350, 360, 362, 380.

[111] "der erste und einzige Roman für den denkenden Kopf": Lessing, *Sämtliche Schriften,* 3rd ed., ed. Lachmann and Muncker, vol. 10: 80.

7: The Traditionalist Response: Herder, Goethe and *Sturm und Drang* Romance

BY THE 1770s the traditional *Lehrstand* had all but collapsed. An address given in November 1776 by the Prussian minister of justice, baron von Zedlitz, indicates the degree to which the ordinary Lutheran clergy had forfeited authority and credibility in what was then the most modern German state. Zedlitz thought the local clergyman still had a role as schoolmaster to the common people who could not yet safely graduate from superstition to enlightenment.[1] Otherwise he should furnish the state with the services of petty officialdom: publishing decrees, filling census forms and distributing technical information.[2] Higher qualifications or more favoured social origins might enable some to exploit the partial success of Wolff's attempts to confer the cleric's traditional status and functions on the philosopher. Indeed philosophers in the Wolffian and the sentimental mould, whether clerical or lay, won explicit official recognition as apt instructors of the middle range of society; Zedlitz himself gave the *philosophe-moraliste* the job of educating the "bourgeois civilisés" on whom the state chiefly depended for its prosperity.[3] But such recognition did not ameliorate the fundamental predicament of traditional theoretical experts who, in an increasingly modern and practical world, were doing little more than surviving on its terms not their own. Their predecessors in office had been leaders exercising the higher authority of God. The Wolffian teachers of the later eighteenth century were subordinate functionaries of a secular state in which they ranked well below the administrative and judicial officials who conducted most public business.[4]

Contemporaries freely testified to the *Lehrstand*'s debilitating sense of its own inferiority to the *Weltleute* or *Geschäftsleute* who occupied secular as opposed to spiritual offices and were responsible for public affairs. The leading neologist cleric J. J. Spalding, who by 1764 had risen from humble social origins to become at the age of fifty *Probst* of St. Nicolai and *Oberkonsistorialrat* in Berlin, confessed that he continued to feel embarrassment in the social circles of the noble and commoner state officials who dominated the capital. His protégé Friedrich Gedike, director of the Friedrichswerdesche Gymnasium from 1779, recorded how many *Gelehrte* were abashed by the pretensions of Berlin society.[5] In similar vein Christian Garve, writing at the end of the century, restated the contrast between the *Weltmann* who feared no-one, always appeared at ease and made himself agreeable to all, and the scholar, philosopher, artist or poet who was tongue-tied in the *Weltmann*'s presence and felt oppressed by his social superiority.[6]

Any restoration or reconstruction of the status of the traditional theoretical expert depended on a new conception of the independent authority which had formerly belonged to the cleric as man of God but had been lost through a gradual process of modernisation to which the *Lehrstand* had so far perforce accommodated itself. So what was needed was a way of reviving that authority. Neither church nor university could thus come to the *Lehrstand*'s aid: both had served their turn in earlier generations but were now exhausted. All therefore depended on individual initiative, indeed on Weberian charisma: the role of theorist-therapist now had to pass from the clergyman and the faculty philosopher to the poet, seer or spiritual leader who could gather round himself a community of disciples and apostles. Rousseau typified such leadership, withdrawing from civil society into solitude whence with remarkable self-assurance he elicited a profound response by literary self-revelation. His readers hailed Rousseau as a supreme authority on whom they called for spiritual guidance: in short he founded a private cult which by no means lacked adherents in the German-speaking lands.[7] There too, of course, sentimental philosophy had begun to develop charismatic traits. Gellert operated within the institutional context of Leipzig university, and attempted to appeal to a general public rather than an exclusive group of sectaries but, like Rousseau, attracted a personal following through his writing.[8] And on a smaller scale the young Wieland, during his sentimental phase in Zürich, or F. M. Leuchsenring emerged briefly as charismatic leaders with a circle of like-minded followers.[9]

However the most effective German proponent of the charismatic solution to the traditional *Lehrstand*'s authority problem was J. G. Herder, a formidable critic not simply of the sentimental theorists but of most eighteenth-century philosophising. Herder was born in East Prussia in 1744 and studied theology at the university of Königsberg. After two years as pastor in Riga he held appointments as court chaplain in Bückeburg, the residence of the princes of Schaumburg-Lippe, from 1771 and in Weimar from 1776. While in Bückeburg Herder took issue with Spalding over the effects of Wolff's innovations on the clergy. Spalding's treatise *Über die Nutzbarkeit des Predigtamts* justified the existence of the clergy as philosophical "teachers of wisdom and virtue."[10] Herder's *An Prediger: fünfzehn Provinzialblätter* of 1774 condemned the Wolffians for divesting the clerical office of its traditional divine authority and breeding a generation of "fashionable, erudite, secular priests," adept at philosophical discourses and fine turns of phrase but incapable of true, godly preaching.[11] The *Provinzialblätter* and other pieces Herder published in the 1770s sought to reverse the damage done by the Wolffians by developing a counter-concept of the theoretical expert.[12]

Herder's solution to the problem of spiritual authority in modern society was based on the Hebrew prophet.[13] In effect he proposed that aspirants to the status of theoretical expert, whether clerical or lay, should look to the Old Testament, where the ancient institution of group-prophecy evolves, from Elijah onwards, into a series of distinctively literary religious teachers of whom Isaiah is perhaps the greatest. The concept of the prophet as the man from God declaring the holy word of judgement enabled Herder to reconstruct the divine authority of the theoretical expert in a literary form. The Old Testament prophet utters the word of God in language the people can understand because it speaks to the heart: this language is poetry.[14] God's word to Israel was poetry; given the historical priority still assigned to the Bible, the earliest poetry was the word of God. From these data Herder inferred a momentous result, that the prophet must be a poet, and anyone worthy of the name of poet must be a prophet. The "noblest, the highest poetry," he declared, "will always remain, like music, essentially *theology*."[15] "Poet" is not a role until identified as such.[16] The sentimental enlightenment made the philosopher a poet and the poet a philosopher; now cleric and poet coalesced as Herder rediscovered the *poeta vates*, "Bote der Götter," messenger of the gods.[17] Herder's prophet-poet is of course none other than the "genius" who, in Herder's usage as much as in J. G. Hamann's or J. K. Lavater's, receives the divine spark: through him God speaks to men.[18] In thus reviving ancient ideas of dæmonic possession this *Sturm und Drang* concept of genius transfers all the awe and reverence formerly attaching to the religious sphere to the aesthetic.[19]

Herder's cognitive scheme relies on a profoundly communitarian notion of genius. It is the patriarchal community which most perfectly reflects God's will in a divinely-ordered universe.[20] And it is the prophet-poet who combines in his own person all the leadership-roles of that community: patriarch, priest and king. The prophet who has power over words wields power, through his words, over the world around him. He shapes the community by his decree, presides over it, and ministers to it. "A poet," Herder wrote, "is the creator of a people around him, he shows them a world and has their soul in his hand, to lead them there."[21] The transforming power of words enabled Herder to link poetry to magic: poetry had a "wundertätige Kraft"; it was reckoned by primitive peoples to be "der Zauberei zunächst."[22] Herder's concept of genius thus reverses the separation of the secular from the religious sphere which initiated modernisation. As genius the theoretical expert takes the political world back to himself with the power of the word rather than the sword. Hence he regains the status which had passed to the *Weltmann* and the humiliation of the *Lehrstand* ceases. Whereas Wolff had argued that the monarch should be a philosopher, and that the philosopher should therefore rule, but with the necessary assistance of others in the large contemporary state, Herder opened a distinctly more radical project in proposing to give the genius absolute control over a simple patriarchal community.[23]

It is of course the duty of the individual to integrate himself into this God-ordained community and to fulfil its purposes. Herder therefore holds that to live well is not to obey laws but to attain virtue: to conform to the practices of a particular and specific social organism. Contrasting law (*Gesetz*) with custom (*Sitte*), he maintains that "to have no customs is as wretched as to have no instincts."[24] Accordingly Herder's code requires life to be lived for and ultimately surrendered to the community. He more than any of his predecessors, whether orthodox Lutherans or Wolffian philosophers, extols heroic self-sacrifice — an enterprise he exemplified from the lives of Socrates, Brutus or, more recently, Ulrich von Hutten and Franz von Sickingen.[25]

The social integration Herder advocated would sustain the individual while protecting the community, the former objective being no less urgent than the latter in the judgement of one who rarely if ever enjoyed a blithe or even simple relationship with his fellow man. As a young man Herder suffered bouts of severe melancholia such as those recounted in his travel diary of 1769.[26] His acquaintance with the ancient theory of the temperaments which associated melancholia with senility led Herder to describe himself as "old in my youth"[27] and to characterise his contemporaries in similar terms as "aged souls, young ancients, ancient youths."[28] "The eye is extinguished," he maintained, "the body flaccid, the gaze uncertain, the brain consumes itself."[29] According to earlier religious theorists this unfortunate condition resulted from rejection of God or, more generally, the rule of reason: Herder carried the diagnosis much further, blaming excessive cerebration for such cases of melancholia and decrepitude. But contemporary education encouraged precisely those long periods of abstract thought ("langen Abstraktionen") which he isolated as the cause of black depression. Young minds were wrenched from the world of objects, of everyday activities and social relationships, and filled with meaningless abstract concepts.[30] Hence universal unhappiness. "The young man is to learn to abstract and to speculate, and if he learns these things, he is made *miserable*."[31]

But eighteenth-century educational practices were only part of a much wider social phenomenon. Society as a whole was in transit from concreteness and specificity to ever greater abstraction, manifesting, to Herder's dismay, the phenomena of universalism, performance, functional specificity and ego-orientation identified by nineteenth and twentieth-century sociology.[32] Herder viewed the large administrative apparatus of the centralised state, the growth of urban populations and the competitive market economy as so many threats to the happiness of his contemporaries, who were required to integrate themselves into the anonymous structures of modern society, not as living organisms but as mechanical parts.[33] Rational, abstract society was thus dehumanising the individual even as it "released" him from traditional bonds: perhaps this effect was intended by rulers who promoted rationalism to maximise social conformity. It seemed, Herder suggested, as if "day by day" people were being increasingly encouraged to "feel like machines": i.e. not to feel at all.[34]

Defective feeling could only be remedied by a return to the primitive community which, by its very closeness to instinct and nature could rejuvenate modern man and restore health and happiness to the mind sickened by overmuch thought. Herder describes the life of the Old Testament patriarchs or the ancient Greeks as rooted in nature and not merely youthful but invulnerable by time. His images for the ancient patriarchal, pastoral world are organic and spatial: the Hebrews and Greeks are planted in the landscape as spreading cedars or as slender olive trees around a spring; and these scenes survive in the theatre of history, bearing visible witness to God's purpose for mankind.[35] The poet-prophet's task is therefore clear. He must rouse his hearers from apathy and inspire them to create a new world — or rather to recreate the old world of youth and community. Hence Herder's almost exclusive concern with the invigorating power of poetry: in eighteenth-century terminology, its embodiment of the sublime.[36]

Heroic romance was the archetype of such poetry. The earliest poets, Herder argued, were at one and the same time religious leaders who rehearsed in song the ancestral deeds that inspired the people with new confidence and new vigour; as Hesiod recorded, "No sooner does the bard strike up the praise of gods and ancient heroes than whoever feels a secret, gnawing sadness in his soul forgets his sorrow and feels his pain no more."[37] The nordic peoples provided particularly striking examples of the inspirational cult of heroes. Herder was well acquainted with scholarly discussion of the effect of poetry, sagas and myths on the ancient Norse warriors who could be roused to fight "fearlessly and gloriously" by "the examples of their forefathers, their songs, the headstones on their graves."[38] But he also sought heroic song elsewhere, finding in the medieval romances considered by the educated as childish fantasies a "manly spirit of enterprise; generosity; compassion; tender, wondrous love" which could not fail to do good whatever the literary guise in which these sentiments appeared.[39]

Herder's theory of poetry led the rising generation of men interested in theology, philosophy and the arts to insist that poetry must transform its hearers by confronting them with heroic images like those of romance. J. M. R. Lenz proposed to judge plays according to "the effect they make as a whole," and hoped that G. A. Bürger's projected translation of Homer would "live and work and perform miracles on its readers, as the Greek Homer did on his hearers."[40] F. L. Stolberg likewise credited poetry with transforming power. "You lift the heart on eagles' wings," he wrote, "and shape it for everything great and noble."[41] Bürger hoped to make poetry popular once more and intended that it should regain its vivifying power over the hearts of men, by becoming the "Breath of God, which awakens us from sleep and death."[42] These writers expected poetry to derive its inspirational effect from heroic imagery even if they failed to identify the exact process by which such an effect would be achieved. Stolberg looked back to the beginning of the Christian era. "Young man," he declared, "you who are revelling in the divine Plutarch, you whose heart is pounding at the noble deeds of ancient times,...how great you can become."[43] But Lenz, who proclaimed Shakespeare as one who made the heroes of past ages live again, so that the astonished spectator was moved to cry, as if in the presence of Christ, the greatest exemplar of all, "blessed are the eyes that have seen thee," reserved his highest praise for his own contemporary Goethe, who had created in Götz von Berlichingen a figure as inspiring as the greatest ancient heroes. Lenz urged his readers: "let us take on the character of this old-fashioned German...so that we may make ourselves again the Germans from whose example we have so far departed."[44]

Götz transformed German drama yet could not match the influence exerted by Goethe's most important work of the *Sturm und Drang* period, his prose fiction *Die Leiden des jungen Werthers*, published in 1774.[45] Goethe seems to have conceived *Werther* in theatrical terms, for a "five-act" structure can still be discovered in the text.[46] But by abandoning drama for prose narrative, Goethe seemed to be accepting rather than rejecting the romance form valued by Herder; in any event Goethe's contemporaries found little difficulty in placing *Werther* in the context of Herder's aesthetic of the sublime alongside the far more obviously exemplary *Götz*.

Lenz completed this exercise in his "Briefe über die Moralität der Leiden des jungen Werthers." The Germany in which he lived was a society marked by timidity, gravity and pedantism, a Herderian world of men, old before their time, whose natural feelings had been stifled by calculation and convention. Goethe had confronted this world with a young, brave, vital hero in the shape of Werther, who embodied everything that his contemporaries so fatally lacked, above all the capacity to feel, to love what is worth loving, and fearlessly to do what one believes to be right. Lenz identified Werther as a saint ("heiliger Werther"), an iconic figure against which the reader might measure himself; indeed as "a crucified Prometheus" ("ein gekreutzigter Prometheus") Werther might be seen as completing both the classical and the Christian traditions of heroic suffering. There was nothing discreditable or cowardly in Werther's death. Devoted to Lotte but mindful of the sanctity of marriage, he accepted death for her sake, and even in expiation of his guilt — if such it was. Werther did not fear death, which might be said to have crowned his life; in death he was a colossus, like Samson under the ruins.[47]

Not surprisingly Lenz hoped that *Werther* would rouse contemporaries from their torpor, not to emulate Werther's suicide, but to be stirred by his example into an emotional and spiritual activity capable of creating a society where so noble an existence could find a true home. Such aspirations were fulfilled at least to the extent of the *Wertherfieber* which roused so many young readers of the 1770s to exhibit the best-documented instance of mass ecstasy centred on a hero of high literature. Reviews and private correspondence show how readers projected themselves on to Werther and experienced a sense of enlarging or improving themselves through him. Christian Stolberg was one young reader who immediately found Werther in himself and himself in Werther. "Oh I can not tell you," he wrote to J. H. Voss, "how I love that little book, it wraps itself right around my heart and it is in such harmony with me that I recognise myself in every thought and in every observation."[48] Voss wrote to Ernestine Boie of the sense of oneness with Werther that he felt when he heard the book read aloud: "It was no wonder, I thought all the time of you and felt Werther's sorrows as my own."[49] David Hartmann asked Lavater: "Did you find no similarity between me and Werther?"[50] As earlier audiences had related their lives to those of the characters of domestic drama, so Goethe's readers identified themselves with Werther. Wilhelm Heinse sympathised so intensely with the hero that he was, he said, hardly able to comment on the book: "Anyone who has felt, and feels, what Werther felt will find his thoughts vanish like a slight mist in the heat of the sun, if he has to do anything so prosaic as reviewing it."[51]

Lenz was fully aware of the process by which sensations and aspirations that were only half understood before the book appeared were thereafter recognised by Goethe's young contemporaries as part of their own identity. "Werther is valuable," Lenz argued, "precisely because he makes us aware of passions and emotions which we all feel obscurely but cannot name."[52] Such conscious discovery of latent feeling often occasioned a great access of self-confidence: once the reader had equated his hero's attributes with his own, he could easily identify himself as a hero. In his autobiographical novel *Anton Reiser* K. P. Moritz described how the struggling apprentice Reiser gained from *Werther* a sense of his own dignity as a human being that enabled him to ignore the world's unflattering judgements:

> Meanwhile through his reading of *Werther* he felt himself raised above
> his circumstances; the increased consciousness of his own existence

that he drew from the thought of himself as a creature in whom heaven and earth were pictured as in a mirror made him proud of his humanity, no longer the unimportant, cast-off creature he felt he was in other people's eyes.[53]

Other readers took a similar gratification from feeling themselves to be Werther's emotional kinsmen. F. H. Jacobi thanked God for creating Goethe, the world of Werther, and his own capacity to respond thereto.[54] Lenz himself vowed that "I will at least try to make myself immortal through my ability completely to appreciate the worth of this my contemporary."[55] The sense of oneness with Werther was so life-enhancing that many readers claimed to value it beyond any worldly distinction. C. F. D. Schubart concluded his review of the book by stating that "I would rather be poor all my days, lie on straw, drink water and eat roots, than fail to share the feelings" of such a writer.[56]

While Goethe's text thus recreated the *Hochgefühl* an earlier generation derived from Richardson, it also helped constitute a group identity for its readers. Those who felt as Werther regarded themselves as members of a select band of noble souls, an aristocracy of the heart: one reviewer addressed the enthusiastic reader with the words, "Happy man, you who can sympathise with Werther,...I salute you as one of the few noble souls!"[57] Disparagement of outsiders reinforced such group identity. People with no feeling for Werther were blind, said Hartmann: "Is it worth the effort of printing things for such scoundrels?"[58] Lenz thought the book's critics must be wicked men: "schlechte Seelen."[59] The community of Werther's devotees used the book as a kind of breviary; it was regularly re-read, carried about everywhere, and consulted in time of need.[60] Some even adopted Werther's costume of blue jacket and yellow waistcoat and breeches as the emblem of loyalty to the cult. F. M. Klinger and his friend Ernst Schleiermacher had "Werther's uniform" made for themselves, with "everything so alike that you might mistake each of us for the other."[61] Klinger's remarks are paradigmatic: by adopting Werther's identity many readers enhanced their sense of individual worth yet simultaneously, by "putting on uniform," offered to merge their consciousness in that of a group where individuals were indistinguishable.

Herder's notion of inspirational literature met the cultural demands of an endangered *Lehrstand,* and those who most publicly and unequivocally hailed Werther as saint or hero tended to have personal experience of the decline of the theoretical expert, since they were usually young men trained in theology, philosophy or the arts, reduced to scraping a more or less precarious living in low-status occupations such as school teaching or tutoring. Schubart, Heinse, Voss, Lenz, Moritz and Hartmann all come in this category.[62] But their adulation of Werther did not go unchallenged. The orthodox clergymen and Wolffian clerics and teachers in the older generation of the *Lehrstand* distanced themselves from the "little book" because they considered Werther's suicide to be a dangerous example. Men like Bodmer and Sulzer hoped some suitable person, such as Eberhard, Spalding or even Jerusalem *père*, the father of the young man whose fate suggested Goethe's plot, would write an antidote to the book, showing Werther recovering from a suicide attempt, moderating his "enthusiasm," and living happily and usefully thereafter.[63] These hopes were realised, if not precisely in the form desired, by Friedrich Nicolai's *Freuden des jungen Werthers. Leiden und Freuden Werthers des Mannes*, which used the device of parody to discredit Werther.[64] Other representatives of the sceptical *Aufklärung* sought to defuse Goethe's text by reading it as "legal" narrative, specifically as the history of a psychopathological case. Wieland outlined this approach in a review for *Der teutsche Merkur* in which he suggested that excessive emotion and an over-heated imagination caused the suicide of Werther, whom Goethe had represented as an object of pity rather than admiration.[65] Blanckenburg went further, arguing that Goethe's story revealed in minutest detail the sequence of efficient causes which ultimately led to Werther's suicide. Readers would pity Werther in his sufferings — but would also learn from this case-history how others might be counselled against ending their lives.[66]

Modern readers of *Die Leiden des jungen Werthers* have followed Goethe's contemporaries by dividing into two antagonistic groups. One has construed the book as a romance, and Werther himself as a heroic figure fated to destruction by a hostile world; Marxists in particular have made Werther into a class hero playing a part in the inevitable progress of history towards proletarian revolution. Georg Lukács and Peter Müller see him as a bourgeois opponent of feudalism; Klaus Scherpe considers him a rebel against an ossified bourgeois society.[67] Other modern readers, usually western, "bourgeois" critics, have interpreted Werther not as hero but as patient: some think the book a study in individual psychopathology, others point to a general malaise of the eighteenth-century middle class. Thomas Saine calls attention to the vindictiveness of Werther's neurotic personality; Reinhart Meyer-Kalkus offers a Freudian analysis of Werther's narcissism within the context of the historical evolution of the conjugal family. Stefan Blessin regards Werther as typical of his class because he wants too much too soon; Hans Vaget sees him as a representative of middle-class dilettantism.[68] Many western writers agree that Werther's wretched, lingering death excludes the possibility of any heroic or romantic reading of the text. Heinz Schlaffer has suggested that the two opposite readings that have persisted since the book was first published were both part of its author's design: Werther as hero is the exoteric meaning of the text; Werther the neurotic is the true, esoteric meaning.[69] But contestable readings do not close contests, and even if

Schlaffer is to be followed in positing alternative meanings to Goethe's text two moves would remain legitimate as well as possible: the meanings may still be disputed; so may their relationship. *Die Leiden des jungen Werthers* may be heroism without, neurosis within, the surface of romance sugaring a bolus of admonition, but it is worth considering another interpretation: that Goethe takes an evident but complex pathological condition to exemplify at a deeper level of understanding what he apprehends as a noble if forlorn aspiration.

The pathology is evident enough since Werther deviates from "normal" human behaviour in fairly obvious ways. Instead of seeking the society of his peers — young university-educated commoners — he leaves the town where he has been living with his mother for a solitary country retreat. There he makes no friends of his own age, sex and social status: on the contrary he discourages the conversational overtures of young V..., who seems a perfectly suitable companion, and takes ostentatious pleasure in the company of children and unlettered country folk. So far from reproaching himself with failure to enter adult, educated society Werther congratulates himself on his easy condescension to social inferiors and, from his rural sanctuary, disparages the conventional career in public office for which his education has prepared him, and in which his mother would like to see him reach the rank of privy counsellor or ambassador.[70] Rejecting this kind of life, which he scathingly dubs *Aktivität* as opposed to good honest German *Tätigkeit*,[71] Werther tries to turn himself into an artist, unsuccessfully sketching from nature, and vainly attempting a portrait of Lotte. He explains the resultant failures with a series of excuses: extreme happiness, the wrong medium, etc.[72] When he is at last moved to take a job, as legation secretary, it proves predictably uncongenial and he blames his inevitable resignation on those who originally urged him to apply. His emphasis on the insult he has received at the noble assembly and his failure to keep his confidant Wilhelm informed about his abrupt departure from office indicate a more or less conscious intention to extricate himself from a repugnant service career while preserving at least something of his self-esteem.[73]

Marriage and family hold as few attractions for Werther as does a conventional career. Just before his correspondence with Wilhelm begins, Werther has left home to escape a marriageable young woman who has fallen in love with him; the women with whom he forms close relationships are all for some reason unavailable as marriage partners. The woman he describes as the friend of his youth has already died of old age by the time that the correspondence with Wilhelm begins.[74] Lotte is of course engaged to Albert, as Werther well knows from the start of his friendship with her. Fräulein von B..., whom Werther meets and likes while in his legation post, is titled and hence also inaccessible to him, as the incident at the noble assembly indicates.[75]

Such avoidance of society, career and marriage bespeaks a discontent with ordinary human possibilities confirmed in Werther's self-analysis. He regards that part of personality which functions consciously in the commonsense world of everyday reality as a poor, restrictive thing, indeed a form of psychic captivity. As early as 22 May 1771 Werther reflects on man's sense of freedom, and his ability to quit the "prison-house" of life at will; the unnamed means of escape is clearly suicide.[76] On 6 December 1772, far gone in despair but unable to face self-annihilation, he complains that, however much man may strive for freedom, he is constantly forced back to "dull, cold consciousness." The letter of 12 December records a heartfelt desire that freedom may yet be granted to the wretched "imprisoned" self: "dem Eingekerkerten."[77]

This sense of inadequacy as a separate self alternates with Werther's belief in the almost godlike greatness he can have through fusion with and reinforcement by something above and beyond himself. This rather special capacity so to enhance his self-esteem first manifests itself in Werther's relationship with nature: he is filled with joy to find the heavens and indeed God mirrored in his soul.[78] The relationship with Lotte continues the process. The conviction that Lotte loves him makes him adore himself: if she favours him he must be a god; conversely if she favours another, he feels like a man stripped of his honour[79] and endures the sensation that a part of him is missing — he refers to a gap in his being which he could fill only by pressing her to his heart.[80]

The relationship with Lotte thus fails to sustain Werther's sense of godlike greatness but, as he sinks into deepening despair, another relationship gradually pervades his consciousness. Werther breaks his journey back to Lotte after his brief period of employment to revisit his birthplace and recall the happy childhood he enjoyed before his father's death. Such reminiscences concentrate Werther's mind on the eternal father in heaven and the divine passion which comes to reflect his own experience. Heterodoxy beckons. Instead of seeking Christ the mediator, Werther aspires to direct sonship of the Father, whom he addresses with the words from the cross: "My God, my God, why hast thou forsaken me?"[81] He regards the parable of the prodigal son as the story of the lost father, before whose face the returning offspring may live for ever more.[82] Werther's death is thus his means of reconciliation with the father, his return to the protection of the divine *pater familias*.[83]

Freudian psychoanalysis affords a possible interpretation of these fictive data. Werther's responses are infantile. His sense of his soul as mirror of the world and the world as mirror of his soul parallels the infant's narcissistic inability to distinguish between self and other; the constant desire to merge in the totality of nature, to swim as it were in the elements, suggests the infant's longing for oneness with the mother, such as it experiences at the breast or, still more fully, when immersed in the womb. Werther's relationship with Lotte is consistently fixed in the pattern of the young child's diadic relationship with a mother who means everything to it.[84] Lotte, who first appears to Werther in the role of substitute mother to her siblings, becomes a mother-figure for him, while his image of himself is that of a rather sophisticated child: he romps with her young brothers and sisters and welcomes chastisement at her hands.[85] Lotte's favour is as necessary to Werther's sense of self-esteem as the mother's is to the child's. Meanwhile physical desire for Lotte causes Werther acute anxiety: he recoils from accidental contact as if burned or struck by lightning, and generally exhibits a well-developed sense of Lotte as mother-figure protected by the incest taboo.[86]

The Freudian paradigm explains Werther's fixation in the infantile phase by the early death of his father and Werther's subsequent upbringing by his mother. During a highly significant period of life he had no father to transmit and exemplify the cultural norms necessary for his own successful development to manhood. His pilgrimage to his birthplace and subsequent quest for God are intelligible as the search for a lost father. Historical psychology would link this personal search with developments in eighteenth-century society: modernisation, the separation of public and private spheres, and the consequent specialisation of parental roles. These changes inaugurate the conjugal family in which the father's role is largely confined to the public sphere, the mother's to the private. While the father engages in economic activity outside the home, the mother takes sole charge of domestic arrangements and, more particularly, of child-rearing. This becomes the principal focus and justification of the mother's existence; and the paternal influence in the family is so diminished as to create the historical-psychological problem of the inhibited, "fatherless" son who, on the road to manhood, experiences great, and perhaps insurmountable, difficulties. Werther could be said to exemplify this problem.[87]

This Freudian reading of *Die Leiden des jungen Werthers* emphasises the pathological nature of the central character far more strongly than any hostile contemporary readings did: and it is difficult to see Werther the case of arrested development in a positive light. However Freud's categories were not Goethe's and may only offer clues to Goethe's thought. Freud was concerned with psychological development and its pathologies: he regards mother-fixation as a failure of normal development. Goethe did not share Freud's aetiological perspective and saw mother and father relationships not as stages in an ascending developmental scale but as antithetical orientations of the individual within the universe. Hence the special importance of Freud's description of the mother-child relationship in the understanding of Goethe's symbols. In early infancy, Freud suggests, the child does not distinguish self and mother — self and world — and so can not form relationships with objects. A mother-fixation is thus a pathological failure to form object-relationships, a failure of "object-cathexis"; it is the intervention of the father on the diadic mother-child relationship which eventually forces the child to distinguish self from other and enables it to enter the world of objects.[88] The theory rests on profoundly patriarchal assumptions which are nevertheless scarcely unknown from the history of ideas. Indeed the near-universality of such sexual hierarchies must support the conclusion that, if the figures of mother and father play a central part in the symbolism of Goethe's text, they do so because he was using them in a way which does broadly anticipate Freud while remaining firmly within the structure of eighteenth-century thought, and in particularly close relationship to those notions of distance from and nearness to objects which underlie the great antithesis of idealism versus realism.[89]

Both Herder's and Goethe's symbols identify the sphere of the adult male with the "real world." Man in his prime, the pater familias, leads an active life close to objects in which he works to support himself and his dependents; the key-words of the father-world are *Welt, tätig, Realität*. Thus Herder, meditating in his travel diary on childhood, maturity and old age, concludes that once the child becomes a man, "this is truly the level of reality": "dies ist eigentlich die reelle Stufe." Now his passions do not lift him out of the world, instead they enable him to involve himself in it: "sich in die Welt hineinzuleben." The mature male is therefore "the true philosopher of action": "der wahre Philosoph der Tätigkeit."[90] Goethe, throughout his mature work, likewise associates adult maleness above all with activity in the world of objects, hence Faust's vision of his colonists able "to live in freedom through activity": "tätig-frei zu wohnen." This, says Wilhelm Emrich, is Goethe's idea of the male attitude: "männliche Haltung."[91]

Herder was best able to envisage adult male activity not in a hypothetical Faustian colony but within the small patriarchal communities in which ancient Hebrews or Greeks led their lives close to the earth, among their beasts or crops. The smaller the sphere of activity, the closer the actors' involvement with the world of objects.[92] And in *Die Leiden des jungen Werthers*, too, the father-world is manifest in ancient civilisation mediated through the poetry of Homer. Werther imagines that he is integrating aspects of patriarchal life: "Züge patriarchalischen Lebens" into his own experience when he picks and shells peas and cooks them with his own hands.[93] Homer provides practically the only image in the text of man as husband and father of an intact family. For it is no doubt with Ulysses in mind that Werther exclaims on man's instinct for home, wife and children, and work in support of them:

> So in the end even the most restless vagabond longs for his homeland
> and finds at his wife's bosom, in the circle of his children, and in the

work of supporting them, the happiness for which he searched the wide world in vain.[94]

The paternal life in close proximity to objects also appears through Werther's home town, where he lived as a boy during his own father's lifetime. Werther calls the town a "dear, familiar place," and his return immediately recalls the Homeric patriarchs since his childhood feelings resembled those of the childhood of the race.[95]

Active, manly self-sufficiency in the concrete Homeric world has ceased to be a possibility long before Werther's childhood which, following his father's death, is itself hardly more accessible than the world of the *Iliad* and the *Odyssey*. Reality itself has become a lost ideal for the exile from *Gemeinschaft*, driven into the amorphous, abstract world of *Gesellschaft* represented by the "unbearable town" to which his mother took him after his father died,[96] there to suffer from the modern condition, which Herder defined as seeing shadows instead of feeling real objects.[97] Werther thus perceives his world as one which offers not *Tätigkeit* but mere *Aktivität*, epitomised by employment in impersonal, abstract institutions.[98] Hence the resolute avoidance of the forms of integration this world offers the adult male: *Wilhelm Meisters Lehrjahre* tells the story of a young man, with very much the Wertherean cast of mind, nevertheless accepting his father's will and adopting an active life in the world of objects, in the interests of his own son; *Die Leiden des jungen Werthers* offers but one possibility of integration into a paternal world — that of sonship to God the Father in the life after death.[99]

In contrast to the real male world of action on objects, attachment to the female signifies pursuit of the ideal. Many details of Goethe's text suggest in a very straightforward way that Werther's Lotte is an ideal: not the flesh-and-blood woman known to everyone else, but a creation of his own mind, existing only on a higher-than-earthly plane. Werther uses epithets like *himmlisch* and *heilig* of her, calls her "Engel des Himmels" and develops a cult of Lotte worthy of a saint: making an image of her — if only a silhouette — which he keeps and venerates, and collecting relics of her, such as the pink ribbon she wore at the ball.[100] All this detail belongs firmly within the realistic framework of the story: what Werther does can plausibly be done by a German commoner living in the late eighteenth century. But the symbolism which surrounds Lotte points far beyond any specific context to Goethe's later journeys into the mysterious realm of the ideal; the continuity of his preoccupations throughout his long life justifies an interpretation of at least certain circumstances of Werther's and Lotte's relationship in the light of later developments in Goethe's work.

For instance the letter of 30 August 1771, written shortly before Werther resolves to leave Lotte, describes the infinite passion — "endlose Leidenschaft" — he feels for her. After meeting her he is sometimes so

oppressed that he must go out into the open air in search of release. At
such times he ranges far and wide across the landscape — "weit im
Felde umher"; climbs a precipitous rock — "einen jähen Berg"; and
forces his way through a trackless wood — "einen unwegsamen
Wald" — where he falls asleep exhausted in the middle of the night,
with the moon bright above him — "in der tiefen Nacht, wenn der hohe
Vollmond über mir steht": his soul is so troubled he longs for the loneli-
ness of a hermit's cell — "die einsame Wohnung einer Zelle."[101] In describing Werther's parting from Lotte the letter of 10 September 1771,
which ends the first book of the novel, repeats some of the motifs of 30
August. Albert and Lotte meet Werther at his request by night in the garden he has always loved at a most romantic and thrillingly lonely spot
enclosed by trees.[102] The moon rises as they arrive and their talk soon
turns to death and the life beyond.

The symbolism of moonlight in wild, lonely places returns with intensified force at the end of Book Two, when Werther's passion for Lotte
has become well-nigh intolerable. On 12 December 1772 an unknown
inner turmoil — "ein inneres, unbekanntes Toben" — has driven Werther out into the dark once again. Floodwaters hurtle down the valley
under the moon; and yet again a thrill — "ein Schauer" — runs through
him.[103] Finally when Werther has at last covered Lotte's lips with passionate kisses, he rushes from her house into the night and climbs a
steep rock overlooking the valley: there after his death his hat is found,
arousing astonishment that he did not fall from so precipitous a place in
the darkness.[104] This landscape of Werther's experience is replicated, in
the final phase of his life, by that of Ossian's lays. The letter of 12 October 1772, recording the transfer of Werther's loyalties from Homer to
Ossian, characterises the Ossianic world: mists, mountains, caves, storms,
night and moonlight, the spirits of dead heroes.[105] When Werther finally
visits Lotte in breach of her command to wait until Christmas, it is Ossian
from whom he reads aloud. Each passage unfolds the vast, turbulent,
mist-swathed landscape anew: a landscape unutterably lonely because
the active males who once populated it are in their graves, and the objects on which they acted are obscured.[106]

As Wilhelm Emrich has shown, Goethe's late work repeatedly uses
the features of both the Ossianic landscape and Werther's own wintry
valley to evoke an awesome ideal world beyond that of reality. Thus the
final climactic passage of the *Zweiter römischer Aufenthalt* evokes the
Capitol appearing in the moonlight, looking like a fairy palace in the
midst of desolation: "wie ein Feenpalast in der Wüste." In the solitude —
"Einsamkeit" — of the Via Sacra, familiar objects seem strange and
ghostly: "fremdartig und geisterhaft." The Coliseum is barred, and when
Goethe peers into its enclosed interior space, he feels a thrill of awe:
"darf ich nicht leugnen, daß mich ein Schauer überfiel."[107] Here, Emrich

suggests, Goethe universalises the ideal of the classical world.[108] In similar fashion a passage written for *Wilhelm Meisters Wanderjahre* situates Wilhelm's discovery of his ideal, Natalie, in a lonely landscape strewn with massive rocks. Wilhelm finds himself on a precipice above rushing waters; the atmosphere of the place makes him thrill. Far away on the other side of the chasm he suddenly spies, through a magic telescope, the figure of Natalie.[109] However Goethe's most famous and influential image of the ideal in a vast, lonely, awe-inspiring landscape occurs in the course of Faust's search for Helen. The guardians of the ideal to whose realm Helen belongs are themselves female figures, the Mothers, whose very multiplicity puts them beyond the real biological world. These goddesses, round whom is neither space nor still less time, "rule on high in isolation": they are "formation, transformation, eternal mind's eternal constitution." "Have you any idea," asks Mephistopheles, "of such solitude and desolation?" "The sense of awe," counters Faust, "is the best side of mankind."[110] But plainly he has no idea for the Mothers' sphere is unbounded, insubstantial, other-worldly and as such, utterly opposed to the masculine sphere of individuated, concrete objects.

Seen on this vast stage Werther's love for Lotte is indeed a passion for the ideal beyond the world of objects, and his kisses are no less than an attempt to seize the ideal and force it into the sphere of reality. Hence the fearful price Werther feels he must pay for what he has done. For his suicide is not easily explained by more mundane interpretations of the text. It can not be that Werther dies to uphold the sanctity of marriage, or because the religion of love has failed him, or because he is sunk in depression. The idea of kissing Lotte and dying comes to him long before she is another man's wife, and before his mood turns to despair. As early as 16 July 1771 he reflects on the possibility of disturbing her peace, intruding on her "heaven," as he puts it, and hints at the fearful consequence of doing so.[111] When he spells out this consequence — which is suicide — in his letter of 24 November 1772 he thinks of a wall of partition — "Scheidewand" — standing, it seems, for the division between ideal and real.[112] Other texts appear to confirm this interpretation. More than once Goethe creates a situation in which a character transgresses the division between ideal and real only to pay, or almost pay, with actual or symbolic death. Tasso who, Goethe agreed, was Werther raised to a higher power, idealises his princess, tries to embrace her as Werther does Lotte, and is punished by an enforced parting from his friends: and parting, in the words of "An Werther," is death.[113] So too the Wilhelm Meister who spies Natalie through the magic telescope reaches out to grasp her and narrowly escapes the precipice at his feet.[114] Finally when Faust tries to embrace the Helen he has conjured from the realm of the Mothers, an explosion hurls him swooning to the ground: one of the pseudo-deaths that end successive phases of his career.[115]

Thus the Werther who is diagnosed by modern psychoanalysis as a lover of a mother-figure and seeker after a father is better described, from Goethe's own eighteenth-century point of view, as a man obsessed with the ideal world which he is fatally tempted to possess, though he knows his salvation lies in integration into the world of reality. This Werther links the cultural and social concerns of two epochs. He recalls the early modern man of intellect, the devotee of the *vita contemplativa*, as contrasted with the man of action, the *politicus*; at the same time he foreshadows Schiller's sentimental man and all those artist and intellectual figures of nineteenth and twentieth-century literature who stand in antithetical relationship to the denizens of life. Werther, with his education in the classics, his love of the arts and his distaste for a career in administration, represents the *Lehrstand* in transition from the old-fashioned scholar in theology, philosophy or the arts to the poet and literary intellectual. Goethe uses the character of Werther to explore the situation of his own group, the theoretical experts or would-be theoretical experts in a world increasingly controlled by lawyers and administrators: hence the text's contemporary appeal for that very group. *Die Leiden des jungen Werthers* provides striking evidence for Northrop Frye's observation that in the romantic period the poet — artist and intellectual — himself becomes a hero of romance.[116]

The young man who sets his sights on an ideal which he cannot realise is not a pathetic failure but a true hero, and his story is a romance, albeit a tragic one. Some readers have dismissed Werther as a whiner: Friedrich Engels called him a "Tränensack."[117] But he is not intended as such. Both Herder and Goethe were quick to criticise whatever was vapid, decadent or effete in the sentimental culture of their time. Herder denounced J. G. Jacobi's sectaries as milksops: "Milch- und Käseseelen von Sankt Jacobi"; and Goethe satirised J. M. Leuchsenring as Father Pap: Pater Brey.[118] Werther, on the contrary, is Lenz's "fiery youth" — 'feuriger Jüngling' — who closely resembles the picture Herder gives of life's early vigour when describing the ages of man in the *Reisejournal*: Werther has the wealth of imagination which Herder describes as the chief talent of youth, and this imagination takes fire from love and from solitary communion with the poets.[119] Werther is nothing if not passionate, and singleminded in his passion. His words still have the power to move modern readers as demanding as Roland Barthes whose *Fragments d'un discours amoureux* has been described as "a tribute to Werther's uncompromising sensibility."[120] It is not weakness, but strength of erotic desire which drives Werther to the gesture he makes, just as strength of desire, seen as a positive force, drives Faust to try to seize the Helen he has brought from the realm of the Mothers.[121]

Such singlemindedness recalls both the romance hero's obsessive quest and the dæmonic quality of his character. Werther seems to be guided by fate working through his own nature: his story has what Storz calls "a hidden, suprapersonal teleology."[122] The doomed quest also has the elegiac atmosphere characteristic of tragic romance. The story is permeated by regret for the lost world of patriarchal simplicity, by the "dream of herds, pastures and fields of corn" of which Werther speaks from the depths of melancholy.[123] Goethe also associates Werther with the heroes of tragic romance by synchronising his experiences with the seasons of the year. Many romance heroes resemble the dying and rising nature-divinities of myth, in that they flourish in the spring of the year, and die with its decline. So, too, in the spring of 1771 Werther experiences an exultant happiness which fades with the advance of summer. His life with Lotte begins again in the summer of 1772, and with the autumn of that year comes his decline. As nature herself grows weary, so too does he. He himself recognises their congruence. "Mourn then, nature!" he exclaims: "Your son, your friend, your lover is nearing his end."[124] He shoots himself on the longest night of the year, 22 December, the winter solstice, when nature's light and life are at their feeblest.

Such consonance with myth might suggest that Goethe intended his readers to discover in Werther something not merely heroic but godlike, and Werther of course blurs the distinction between himself and Christ. But the connection between Werther and the saviour has seemed to most readers to be the mere product of Werther's unhinged mind, and his death, narrated in stark physical detail, is usually held to give the lie to all such delusions: having failed to kill himself outright with a shot through the head Werther lingers, paralysed, for twelve hours, his brains half blown out, his lungs rattling. Moreover, Werther's story also seems to lack that final, indispensable element of the divine myth, the bodily resurrection of the dead god. So Werther tends not to be read as a Christ-like figure.

Yet the title of the book, which is not a product of Werther's mind, immediately suggests to the reader a parallel between Werther's sufferings and Christ's, since *Leiden* is Luther's term for Christ's passion. The starkness of Werther's earthly end approximates to that of cross, nails, sweat and blood. And there is a sense in which Werther's death is not the end, any more than was Jesus' death on the cross. Werther has no bodily resurrection, neither does he ascend from earth to heaven, but he does become the object of a cult. The story is not linear, and does not conclude in Werther's death; it is circular, in that the "ending" — Werther's death — is succeeded in time by the editor's work, and leads back to the editor's Foreword, which initiates the cult. The editor invites the reader's "admiration and love" — "Bewunderung und Liebe" — for Werther: the responses appropriate to a hero of romance. But he goes further by speaking in a pastoral voice both to a putative community of Werther's devotees, whom he addresses as *Ihr*, and more particularly to

the individual soul in anguish such as Werther's: "you, good soul, who
are feeling the same urge as he."[125] But the editor's choice of words suggests something more than the discourse of a simple preacher addressing
his flock, since the words "take comfort from his suffering" ("schöpfe
Trost aus seinem Leiden") echo those of Paul in the second epistle to the
Corinthians.[126] In the Foreword, therefore, the editor appoints himself the
apostle of a Werther who is a new Christ. The dead hero is shared
among his devotees: Werther's resurrection is a resurrection in the hearts
of those who learn of him through the "sacrament" of the word and
Goethe as author offering Werther — an *alter ego* — to the world is
playing the role of prophet, priest and comforter of souls: as indeed he
seems sometimes to have done in private around this time.[127] His initiative in writing *Werther* thus resembled Rousseau's offering of himself
through his texts, and won a like response from readers who saw themselves in Werther and wrote seeking Goethe's advice and comfort.[128]

Die Leiden des jungen Werthers is the testament of a new cult of
Werther: so much is clear from the Foreword. But in what does Werther's power consist? Paul's words to the Corinthians to which the Foreword makes allusion — "For as the sufferings of Christ abound in us, so
our consolation also aboundeth by Christ" and "our hope of you is
steadfast, knowing that as ye are partakers of the sufferings, so shall ye
be also of the consolation" — are rendered by Luther as "Denn gleichwie
wir des Leidens Christi viel haben, also werden wir auch reichlich
getröstet durch Christum," and "dieweil wir wissen, daß, wie ihr des
Leidens theilhaftig sind, so werdet ihr auch des Trostes theilhaftig sein."
Christ suffered and died, and his followers share in his sufferings in that
they, too, are despised and rejected of men; but they also take consolation from his sufferings in that through Christ's death, they may have life.
The sense in which Werther's sufferings can give consolation is that revealed by the grateful testimony of contemporary readers. Werther dies a
martyr to the mind's detachment from reality in the modern world. His
suffering is exemplary: he drinks this particular cup to the dregs. And the
reader who is in the same situation as Werther can identify with him,
understand himself through him, and in so doing, acquire a new sense
of dignity and self-worth. Thus Werther does indeed die so that others
may live. Once he has done so his readers have no need of dying as he
did. He procures for them that "swelling and triumph" that all heroes
arouse in those who contemplate them and gives courage to bear the
cross of the alienated man of knowledge in the modern world. Contemporary enthusiasts for Werther did not misread him. He belongs to the
line of ideal figures that begins with his beloved Homeric heroes and
passes through medieval and seventeenth-century romance to the domestic romance of the earlier eighteenth century; and Werther, with his
blue coat and yellow breeches, his love for Lotte of the white dress and

pink bows, and his solitary grave under the limes, is not the least of those that figure in this long genealogy.

[1] Karl Abraham von Zedlitz, address delivered on 7 November 1776, *Nouveaux Mémoires de l'Académie Royale des Sciences et Belles-Lettres* 1776: 30-31. Compare Paul Drews, *Der evangelische Geistliche in der deutschen Vergangenheit*, Monographien zur deutschen Kulturgeschichte, ed. Georg Steinhausen 12 (Jena: E. Diederichs, 1905) 130.

[2] Paul Drews, "Der Einfluss der gesellschaftlichen Zustände auf das kirchliche Leben," *Zeitschrift für Theologie und Kirche* 16.1 (1906): 64, 68-69; Karl Aner, "Zwei märkische Landgeistliche aus der Aufklärungszeit," *Jahrbuch für Brandenburgische Kirchengeschichte* 18 (1920): 23-24; John Stroup, *The Struggle for Identity in the Clerical Estate: Northwest German Protestant Opposition to Absolutist Policy in the Eighteenth Century*, Studies in the History of Christian Thought 33 (Leiden: E. J. Brill, 1984) 82-5.

[3] Zedlitz 30-31.

[4] On the declining prestige of theology and related disciplines compared with the law see Anthony J. La Vopa, *Grace, Talent, and Merit: Poor Students, Clerical Careers, and Professional Ideology in Eighteenth-century Germany* (Cambridge, England: Cambridge UP, 1988) 40, 67, 221, 326-27.

[5] La Vopa 234-35.

[6] Christian Garve, *Über Gesellschaft und Einsamkeit*, vol. 2 (Breslau, 1800) 55; cited by Hans Gerth, "Die sozialgeschichtliche Lage der bürgerlichen Intelligenz um die Wende des 18. Jahrhunderts," diss., U Frankfurt am Main, 1935, 58. Compare Garve, "Über die Maxime Rochefaucaults: das bürgerliche Air verliehrt sich zuweilen bey der Armee, niemahls am Hofe," *Popularphilosophische Schriften über literarische, ästhetische und gesellschaftliche Gegenstände*, by Christian Garve, ed. Kurt Wölfel, Deutsche Neudrucke: Reihe Texte des 18. Jahrhunderts, ed. Paul Böckmann and Friedrich Sengle, vol. 2 (Stuttgart, J. B. Metzler, 1974).

[7] See Jean Starobinski, *Jean-Jacques Rousseau: la transparence et l'obstacle* (Paris: Plon, 1957) 70-71, 217-18, and rev. of *Correspondance complète de Jean Jacques Rousseau*, ed. R. A. Leigh, *The Times Literary Supplement* 13 February 1976: 154-55.

[8] For instances of correspondents appealing to Gellert for advice on the conduct of their lives see Christian Fürchtegott Gellert, *Briefe, nebst einigen damit verwandten Briefen seiner Freunde*, ed. Johann Adolph Schlegel and Gottlieb Leberecht Heyer (Leipzig: Weidmanns Erben & Reich, 1774) 186-87, 193, 204, 224, 266, 270, 289, 368-69.

[9] For Wieland see Friedrich Sengle, *Wieland* (Stuttgart: J. B. Metzler, 1949) 70-72. For Leuchsenring see J. W. Goethe, *Werke*, Hamburger Ausgabe, 3rd ed., vol. 10 (Hamburg: C. Wegner, 1963) 562, 578; Wilhelm Dobbek, *Karoline Herder: ein Frauenleben in klassischer Zeit* (Weimar: H. Böhlaus Nachfolger, 1967) 17-21.

[10] "Lehrer der Weisheit und Tugend": see J. G. Herder, *Sämmtliche Werke*, ed. Bernhard Suphan, 33 vols. (Berlin: Weidmann 1877-1913) 7: 229. Subsequent references to Herder's works by volume and page numbers are to Suphan's edition.

[11] "galanter, gelehrter, *Civilpriester*," 7: 295.

[12] cf. Stroup 36, 38-39, 41, 124-8.

[13] See "An Prediger," 7: 265, 295, 312; "Über die Würkung der Dichtkunst auf die Sitten der Völker in alten und neuen Zeiten," 8: 344-65.

[14] 7: 265.

[15] "die edelste, höchste Dichtkunst wird wie die Tonkunst ihrem Wesen nach immer *Theologie* bleiben," 7: 300.

[16] cf. Michael Böhler, *Soziale Rolle und ästhetische Vermittlung: Studien zur Literatursoziologie von A. G. Baumgarten bis F. Schiller* (Bern: H. Lang, 1975) 57-59, 107-8.

[17] 8: 369.

[18] For Herder's ideas on the genius see for example 4: 454-55; 5: 218, 600-610; 8: 230-31. On Hamann and Lavater, see Bruno Markwardt, *Geschichte der deutschen Poetik*, vol. 2 (Berlin: de Gruyter, 1956) 361-62, 418-19.

[19] cf. Angus Fletcher, *Allegory: The Theory of a Symbolic Mode* (Ithaca: Cornell UP, 1964) 249; Böhler 44.

[20] 5: 513, 559.

[21] "Ein Dichter ist Schöpfer eines Volkes um sich, er gibt ihnen eine Welt zu sehen und hat ihre Seelen in seiner Hand, sie dahin zu führen," 8: 433. cf. 8: 365-66 and 7: 295, 297-99, 234-35.

[22] 5: 164; 8: 390.

[23] cf. Böhler 198-220.

[24] "keine Sitten haben, ist so unglücklich, als keine Instinkt Kräfte haben," 4: 468; cf. the observation "Geschriebenes Gesetz ist ein Schatten, lebende Sitte und Gewohnheit ist ein Körper," *Johann Gottfried von Herders Lebensbild*, ed. Emil Gottfried von Herder, vol. 2 (1846; Hildesheim: G. Olms, 1977) 352.

[25] Socrates and Brutus, 28: 22, 24; Hutten and Sickingen, 9: 476-97. On heroic sacrifice see 5: 576; 8: 230.

[26] 4: 447, 451.

[27] "alt in meiner Jugend," 4: 447. For the link between melancholy and old age see for example Thomasius' typology in *Ausübung der Sittenlehre*, reproduced in Hans-Jürgen Schings, *Melancholie und Aufklärung: Melancholiker und ihre Kritiker in Erfahrungsseelenkunde und Literatur des 18. Jahrhunderts* (Stuttgart: J. B. Metzler, 1977) 43.

[28] "veraltete Seelen, junge Greise, greise Jünglinge," 4: 450, cf. 4: 451-52, 456; 8: 218.

[29] "Das Auge ist verlöscht, der Körper welk, der Blick unstät, das Hirn sich selbst verzehrend," 8: 215.

[30] 4: 451.

[31] "Der Jüngling soll abstrahieren und spekulieren lernen, lernt ers, so wird er *elend*," 8: 218.

[32] For these phenomena see Talcott Parsons, *The Social System* (Glencoe, Ill.: Free Press, 1970) passim.

[33] See for example 4: 455, 5: 555-56 on the modern state; 8: 430, 434 on the market economy.

[34] "man breitet Denken vielleicht unter sie aus – …damit sie sich von Tage zu Tage mehr als Maschine fühlen…," 5: 538; cf. 5: 554-6.

[35] For organic images see 4: 447; 5: 479-80, 495. For the theatre of the world see 5: 513, 559, 565-66, 585.

[36] cf. Fletcher 244-49.

[37] "Ist jemand, der in seiner Seele einen geheimen nagenden Kummer fühlt, der Sänger...hebet nur an das Lob der Götter und alten Helden, sogleich vergißt er seinen Kummer und fühlt sein Leid nicht mehr," 8: 368.

[38] "die Vorbilder ihrer Väter, ihre Gesänge, der Stein auf ihrem Grabe"; "furchtlos und ruhmvoll," 8: 390.

[39] "der männliche Geist von Unternehmung, Freigebigkeit, Erbarmen, zarter, wunderbarer Liebe," 8: 398.

[40] "die Wirkung, die sie im ganzen machen": Jakob Michael Reinhold Lenz, *Werke und Briefe in drei Bänden*, ed. Sigrid Damm, vol. 2 (Munich: Hanser, 1987) 639; "lebe und wirke und Wunder tue auf seine Leser, wie ehemals der griechische auf seine Zuhörer": Jakob Michael Reinhold Lenz, *Gesammelte Schriften*, ed. Franz Blei, vol. 4 (Munich: G. Müller, 1910) 267.

[41] "Du erhebst das Herz auf Flügeln des Adlers, und bildest es zu allem, was groß ist und edel": Christian and Friedrich Leopold Grafen zu Stolberg, *Gesammelte Werke*, 20 vols. (Hamburg: F. Perthes, 1820-25) 10: 371.

[42] "Odem Gottes, der vom Schlaf und Tod' aufweckt!": Gottfried August Bürger, *Sämtliche Werke*, ed. Günter and Hiltrud Häntzschel (Munich: Hanser, 1987) 692.

[43] "O Jüngling der da schwelget im göttlichen Plutarch, dem das Herz schlägt bei den Edeltaten der Vorzeit,...wie groß kannst du werden": C. and F. L. Stolberg 370.

[44] "selig sind die Augen, die dich gesehen haben"; "laßt uns den Charakter dieses antiken deutschen Mannes...uns eigen machen, damit wir wieder Deutsche werden, von denen wir so weit weit ausgeartet sind": *Werke und Briefe*, ed. Damm, vol. 2: 669, 639-40.

[45] For the 1774 text, see *Der junge Goethe*, new ed., ed. Hanna Fischer-Lamberg, vol. 4 (Berlin: de Gruyter, 1968) 105-187. This edition will be referred to as *JG*.

[46] "Act 1": 4 May to 16 June 1771, before the meeting with Lotte; "Act 2": to 30 July, the eve of Albert's return; "Act 3": to 10 September, Werther's leave-taking; "Act 4": Werther's seven-month absence at court and on his travels; "Act 5": the six months to Werther's death. See Gerhard Storz's similar analysis, *Goethe-Vigilien oder Versuche in der Kunst, Dichtung zu verstehen* (Stuttgart: Klett, 1953) 29.

[47] *Werke und Briefe*, ed. Damm, vol. 2: 681, 685, 687.

[48] "O ich kann Ihnen nicht sagen, wie ich das Büchelchen liebe, es legt sich ganz um mein Herz herum, und so sehr *harmonirt* es mit mir daß ich in jedem *raisonne*ment und in jedem Gesicht mich erkenne," *Goethe-Jahrbuch* 33 (1912): 14.

[49] "Es war kein Wunder, ich dachte beständig an Dich und fühlte Werthers Leiden als meine": Wilhelm Herbst, *Johann Heinrich Voss*, vol. 1 (Leipzig: B. G. Teubner, 1872) 145.

[50] "hast du keine Aehnlichkeit zw. mir u: Werther gefunden?" *Goethe-Jahrbuch* 9 (1888): 133.

[51] "Wer gefühlt hat, und fühlt, was Werther fühlte; dem verschwinden die Gedanken, wie leichte Nebel vor Sonnenfeuer, wenn er's bloß anzeigen soll," *Iris* 1.3 (1774): 78. Reprinted in *Goethe im Urteil seiner Kritiker. Dokumente zur Wirkungsgeschichte Goethes in Deutschland*, ed. Karl Robert Mandelkow, vol. 1 (Munich: Beck, 1975) 23.

[52] "Eben darin besteht Werthers Verdienst, daß er uns mit Leidenschaften und Empfindungen bekannt macht, die jeder in sich dunkel fühlt, die er aber nicht mit Namen zu nennen weiß," *Werke und Briefe*, ed. Damm, vol. 2: 682.

[53] "Indes fühlte er sich durch die Lektüre des 'Werthers'...über alle seine Verhältnisse erhaben; das verstärkte Gefühl seines isolierten Daseins, indem er sich als ein Wesen dachte, worin Himmel und Erde sich wie in einem Spiegel darstellt, ließ ihn, stolz auf seine Menschheit, nicht mehr ein unbedeutendes weggeworfenes Wesen sein, das er sich in den Augen andrer Menschen schien": Karl Philipp Moritz, *Werke*, ed. Horst Günther, vol. 1 (Frankfurt am Main: Insel Verlag, 1981) 247.

[54] To Goethe, 21 October 1774: *Briefwechsel zwischen Goethe und F. H. Jacobi*, ed. Max Jacobi (Leipzig: Weidmann, 1846) 43.

[55] "will mich wenigstens damit unsterblich zu machen suchen, daß ich den Wert dieses meines Zeitverwandten ganz zu fühlen im Stande bin," *Werke und Briefe*, ed. Damm, vol. 2: 677.

[56] "Wollte lieber ewig arm seyn, auf Stroh liegen, Wasser trinken, und Wurzeln essen, als einem solchen sentimentalischen Schriftsteller nicht nachempfinden können": Christian Friedrich Daniel Schubart, *Deutsche Chronik auf das Jahr 1774*, ed. Hans Krauss (Heidelberg: L. Schneider, 1975) 575-76.

[57] "Glücklicher Mann! der du mit Werthern sympathisieren...kannst,...sey mir gegrüßet unter den wenigen Edeln," *Frankfurter Gelehrte Anzeigen* 1 Nov. 1774. Reprinted in Julius W. Braun, *Goethe im Urtheile seiner Zeitgenossen: Zeitungskritiken, Berichte, Notizen, Goethe und seine Werke betreffend, aus den Jahren 1773-1786* (Berlin: F. Luckhardt, 1883) 54.

[58] "Ists wohl noch der Mühe werth, für solche Schurken was drucken zu lassen," *Goethe-Jahrbuch* 9 (1888): 133.

[59] *Werke und Briefe*, ed. Damm, vol. 2: 682.

[60] See for example Hartmann to Lavater, 22 February 1775, *Goethe-Jahrbuch* 9 (1888): 133; Heinse 81; Mandelkow 24.

[61] "Ich und Ernst haben uns Werthers Uniform machen lassen, haben alles so gleich daß man einen mit dem andern verwechseln möchte": *Der junge Goethe im zeitgenössischen Urteil*, ed. Peter Müller (East Berlin: Akademie-Verlag, 1969) 215.

[62] For Schubart, Heinse, Voss, Lenz and Moritz see Richard Newald, *Von Klopstock bis zu Goethes Tod 1750-1832: Erster Teil, Ende der Aufklärung und Vorbereitung der Klassik*, Geschichte der deutschen Literatur von den Anfängen bis zur Gegenwart, ed. Helmut de Boor and Richard Newald, vol. 6.1 (Munich: C. H. Beck, 1967) 223, 293, 209, 268-69, 289-90. For Hartmann see La Vopa 165.

[63] Bodmer to Schinz, 20 Nov. 1774 and 8 Feb. 1775, *Goethe-Jahrbuch* 5 (1884): 189, 191; Sulzer to Bodmer, 24 Dec. 1774: *Briefe der Schweizer Bodmer, Sulzer, Gessner*, ed. Wilhelm Körte (Zürich: H. Gessner, 1804) 425-26.

[64] Friedrich Nicolai, *Freuden des jungen Werthers. Leiden und Freuden Werthers des Mannes. Voran und zuletzt ein Gespräch* (Berlin; F. Nicolai, 1775). Reprinted Mandelkow 27-39.

[65] C. M. Wieland, *Gesammelte Schriften*, ed. Deutsche Kommission der Preussischen Akademie der Wissenschaften, section 1, vol. 21 (Berlin: Weidmann, 1939) 405-6.

[66] *Neue Bibliothek der schönen Wissenschaften und der freyen Künste* 18.1 (1775) 46-95. Reprinted Mandelkow 65-86.

[67] Georg Lukács, *Deutsche Literatur in zwei Jahrhunderten* (Neuwied: Luchterhand, 1964) 57-66, vol. 7 of *Werke*; Peter Müller, *Zeitkritik und Utopie in Goethes* Werther (East Berlin: Rütten & Loening, 1969) 29, 119-21, 132; Klaus R. Scherpe, *Werther und Wertherwirkung: zum Syndrom bürgerlicher Gesellschaftsordnung im 18. Jahrhundert* (Bad Homburg vor der Höhe: Gehlen, 1970) 45, 52, 66, 71, 73, 88.

[68] Thomas P. Saine, "Passion and Aggression: The Meaning of Werther's Last Letter," *Orbis Litterarum* 35 (1980): 327-56. Reinhart Meyer-Kalkus, "Werthers Krankheit zum Tode: Pathologie und Familie in der Empfindsamkeit," *Urszenen: Literaturwissenschaft als Diskursanalyse und Diskurskritik*, ed. Friedrich A. Kittler and Horst Turk (Frankfurt am Main: Suhrkamp, 1977) 91-96, 110-16. Stefan Blessin, *Die Romane Goethes* (Königstein im Taunus: Athenäum, 1979) 282, 289, 297-98. Hans Rudolf Vaget, "Die Leiden des jungen Werthers (1774)," *Goethes Erzählwerk: Interpretationen*, ed. Paul Michael Lützeler and James E. McLeod (Stuttgart: Reclam, 1985) 37-72.

[69] Heinz Schlaffer, "Exoterik und Esoterik in Goethes Romanen," *Goethe-Jahrbuch* 95 (1978): 217.

[70] Letters of 15 and 17 May 1771 and 24 March 1772, J. W. Goethe, *Werke*, Hamburger Ausgabe, 6th ed., vol. 6, ed. Benno von Wiese and Erich Trunz (Hamburg: C. Wegner, 1965) 10-13, 71. Page references to the text of *Werther* are to this edition (HA), which reproduces the revised text of 1787. The corresponding text of the 1774 edition may be found by way of the dates attached to the letters. Where the 1774 text differs from that of the Hamburg edition, page references to *Der junge Goethe*, vol. 4 (*JG*) are given. Further references to the Hamburg edition of Goethe's works are given in the form HA, followed by volume and page number.

[71] 20 July 1771: 40; 24 December 1771: 62.

[72] 10 May 1771: 9; 24 July 1771: 41.

[73] 20 July 1771: 40; 24 December 1771: 61-62; 15 March 1772: 67; 24 March 1772: 71.

[74] 17 May 1771: 12; last letter to Lotte: 116 (*JG* 181).

[75] 16 June 1771: 20; 15 March 1772: 67-69.

[76] "das süße Gefühl der Freiheit, und daß er diesen Kerker verlassen kann, wann er will" (22 May 1771): 14.

[77] "zu dem stumpfen, kalten Bewußtsein" (6 December 1772): 92. 12 December 1772: 99 (*JG*, 8 December 1772: 168).

[78] 10 May 1771: 9.

[79] 13 July 1771: 38. For the similar situation in *Torquato Tasso* see Walter Hinderer, "'Torquato Tasso'," *Goethes Dramen: neue Interpretationen*, ed. Walter Hinderer (Stuttgart: Reclam, 1980) 180.

[80] "sie nur *einmal*, nur *ein*mal an dieses Herz drücken" (19 October 1772): 83.

[81] "Mein Gott! mein Gott! warum hast du mich verlassen?" (15 November 1772): 86.

[82] 30 November 1772: 90-91, cf. Meyer-Kalkus 129.

[83] Last letter to Lotte: 117 (*JG* 182).

[84] Meyer-Kalkus 97-105, 116-124.

[85] 16 June 1771: 21-22, 27; 29 June 1771: 30.

[86] 16 July 1771: 39; 24 November 1772: 87-88.

[87] Meyer-Kalkus 116-30, 137-38.

[88] cf. Starobinski, *Jean-Jacques Rousseau* 222, note 1.

[89] For Goethe's comments on the problem of distance from objects and lack of activity in the real world, see for example *Dichtung und Wahrheit*, HA 9: 577-84; letter to Riemer, August 1808, J. W. Goethe, *Gedenkausgabe der Werke, Briefe und Gespräche*, ed. Ernst Beutler, 24 vols. (Zürich: Artemis-Verlag, 1948-1960) 22: 498. cf. Erich Trunz, notes to "Die Leiden des jungen Werther," HA 6: 548; Paul Requadt, *Die Bildersprache der deutschen Italiendichtung von Goethe bis Benn* (Bern: Francke, 1962) 63-5.

[90] Suphan 4: 449.

[91] *Faust: Part 2*, line 11564 (HA 3: 348). Wilhelm Emrich, *Die Symbolik von Faust II: Sinn und Vorformen*, 3rd ed. (Frankfurt am Main: Athenäum Verlag, 1964) 403; cf. *Torquato Tasso*, lines 2954, 3406 (HA 5: 153, 166).

[92] Suphan 5: 568-69.

[93] 21 June 1771: 29.

[94] "So sehnt sich der unruhigste Vagabund zuletzt wieder nach seinem Vaterlande und findet in seiner Hütte, an der Brust seiner Gattin, in dem Kreise seiner Kinder, in den Geschäften zu ihrer Erhaltung die Wonne, die er in der weiten Welt vergebens suchte" (21 June 1771): 29.

[95] "den lieben, vertraulichen Ort" (5 May 1772): 72. The patriarchs, 9 May 1772: 73 (*JG* 155).

[96] "unerträgliche Stadt" (5 May 1772): 72.

[97] "Schatten zu sehen, statt würkliche Dinge mir zu erfühlen," Suphan 4: 446.

[98] cf. Goethe in *Dichtung und Wahrheit* on the plight of young men in the Werther period (HA 9: 583).

[99] On *Wilhelm Meisters Lehrjahre* see Chapter 8.

[100] For *saint, angel* etc. see for example 16 July 1771: 39; 30 August 1771: 55; 21 January 1772: 64; 20 February 1772: 67. For the cult of Lotte see 20 February 1772: 67; 28 August 1771: 54.

[101] 55.

[102] "ein geschlossenes Plätzchen..., das alle Schauer der Einsamkeit umschweben": 56; cf. Werther's first visit to the garden, 4 May 1771: 8.

[103] 12 December 1772: 98-99 (*JG*, 8 December 1772: 167-68.)

[104] 115 (*JG* 180-81).

[105] 12 October 1772: 82.

[106] 108-114 (*JG* 175-80).

[107] HA 11: 555.

[108] Emrich 220.

[109] J. W. Goethe, *Werke* , 133 vols. (Weimar: H. Böhlau, 1887-1918) 1: 25.2: 130. (Subsequent references to this edition of Goethe's works are given in the form WA, followed by section, volume and page number.)

[110] *Faust: Part 2,* "Finstere Galerie," and "Rittersaal" lines 6427-6452 (HA 3: 190-94, 197-98). Emrich 215. On the terms Goethe uses to suggest a thrill of awe, see the articles "Schaudern" and "Schauer" (Section 8), Jacob and Wilhelm Grimm, *Deutsches Wörterbuch,* vol. 8, ed. Moriz Heyne (Leipzig: S. Hirzel, 1886-93) col. 2306-09, 2324-27; "Schaudern" and "Schauer," *Duden Etymologie: Herkunftswörterbuch der deutschen Sprache,* ed. Paul Grebe, Der Grosse Duden vol. 7 (Mannheim: Bibliographisches Institut, 1963) 596-97.

[111] 16 July 1771: 39.

[112] 24 November 1771: 87.

[113] HA 1: 381.

[114] WA 1: 25.2: 131. Emrich 222.

[115] Emrich 222; Dorothea Lohmeyer, *Faust und die Welt: der Zweite Teil der Dichtung: eine Anleitung zum Lesen des Textes* (1940; Munich: C. H. Beck, 1975) 153.

[116] Northrop Frye, *Anatomy of Criticism: Four Essays* (Princeton: Princeton UP, 1957) 60.

[117] Karl Marx and Friedrich Engels, *Historisch-kritische Gesamtausgabe,* ed. V. Adoratskij for the Marx-Engels-Lenin Institute, Moscow, section 1, vol. 6 (Berlin: Marx-Engels Verlag, 1932) 59.

[118] Herder to Caroline Flachsland, 25 May 1771, *Herders Briefwechsel mit Caroline Flachsland,* ed. Hans Schauer, vol. 1 (Weimar: Verlag der Goethe-Gesellschaft, 1926) 228; Goethe, "Ein Fastnachtsspiel vom Pater Brey," WA 1: 16: 57-73.

[119] Suphan 4: 448-49.

[120] Martin Swales, *Goethe: The Sorrows of Young Werther* (Cambridge, England: Cambridge UP, 1987) 67.

[121] Lohmeyer 152.

[122] Storz 24, cf. Emrich 70.

[123] "ein Traum von Herden, Wiesen und Ährenfeldern" (8 December 1772): *JG* 168. The 1787 text, dated 12 December 1772, has "Ehrenämtern" instead of "Ährenfeldern" (99).

[124] "So traure denn, Natur! Dein Sohn, dein Freund, dein Geliebter naht sich seinem Ende" (last letter to Lotte): 116 (*JG* 181).

[125] "du gute Seele, die eben den Drang fühlst wie er": 7.

[126] 2 Cor. 1: 5, 7. For Goethe's knowledge of the Pauline material see for example "Brief des Pastors zu*** an den neuen Pastor zu ***," HA 12: 228-39, 671-73.

[127] cf. Goethe's letter to Lavater, WA 4: 3: 109 and Emrich 403-4.

[128] See the case of F. V. L. Plessing, recounted by Goethe in *Campagne in Frankreich,* HA 10: 321-22, 328-33, and that of the young man who wrote in French to Goethe in Italy in 1787, HA 11: 443.

8: Traditionalism Triumphant

THE END OF the *ancien régime* saw great changes in the pattern of challenge and response which had characterised successive phases of clerical and legal culture in Germany after the peace of Westphalia. Neither Herder's call for a revival of Protestant spirituality nor the literary outpouring of the *Sturm und Drang* seemed to provoke commensurate efforts from the legal-administrative élite or its supporters and followers, such as they were in the last two decades of the eighteenth century, when revolution came to France, and when German intellectual life came so completely under the sway of Kant's undertaking to "deny *knowledge*, in order to make room for *faith*," in the bold formulation he adopted in 1787 for the preface to the second edition of the *Critique of Pure Reason*.[1]

Kant's project continued that of Wolff, whose efforts he regarded as having fallen short of what the contemporary cultural crisis required.[2] Kant, like Wolff, wanted the philosopher to assume the traditional theologian's work as teacher of the people, and argued for the primacy of philosophy over the "higher" professional faculties of theology, law and medicine because whereas all three came under the control of the secular authorities philosophy knew no rule but reason's. Philosophy's task was, therefore, to examine, criticise and correct all other forms of mental activity.[3] Of course Kant might also have revived the age-old demand that the servant of reason should rule but, moved by the conviction that power corrupts, simply envisaged the philosopher influencing the conduct of affairs as the statesman's friend and adviser.[4] This was by no means a crudely neo-clerical programme. Again like Wolff, Kant insisted that the philosopher should resist dogmatism and fearlessly examine the foundations of knowledge and belief. Philosophy was to be justified not by the clergy's traditional and now discredited appeal to divine authority, but by critical thought.[5] Yet this approach did not imply intellectual uncertainty or acquiescence in doubt: Kant dismissed sceptics as "a species of nomads, despising all settled modes of life"[6] and indeed spoke with no less authority, under the rule of reason, than the clergy claimed for themselves under God. His philosophising subordinated the empirical world to the world of the mind and aspired to a theoretical and systematic completeness worthy of traditional theology. He equated philosophical empiricism with pessimism and intended the critical philosophy to restore a sense of awe before the starry heavens above and the moral law within. Hence "Der Streit der Fakultäten" defines the conflict between lawyers and philosophers as one between empiricist *Politiker* who perceive life as a meaningless farce, and academic theorists who see meaning and progress in the world.[7]

Reading Kant as a successor to Wolff directing the *Lehrstand*'s ideological enterprise goes against the grain of the well-constructed Kant of autonomous selfhood, the founding father of liberal individualism who rejects state paternalism as an interference with individual freedom, reduces the functions of secular authority to the maintenance of law and order and desires the law to leave the individual free to choose whatever rational goals he pleases.[8] But Kant was by no means an advocate of an atomistic modern society based on the calculation of self-interest and integrated only by the cash nexus and legal contract. To think of him as providing the philosophical underpinning for modern concepts such as human rights and respect for persons, or as liberating the individual to do as he likes, provided only that he respect the freedom of others, is to mistake the nature of Kant's enterprise: the freedom he maintains is the positive freedom to obey an inner authority which Kant himself spoke of as autocracy.[9]

Moreover despite the evidence that MacIntyre and others have adduced to identify Kant's morality of rules as a decisive break with the traditional religious ethics which emphasises virtue within the divinely-ordained community,[10] Kant does clearly set the categorical imperative within such a framework of Aristotelian and Christian ethical concepts as excludes any very convincing interpretation of the man as not attempting to maintain traditional religion in a changed intellectual climate. The similarity of Kant's and the theologians' enterprise has not passed unnoticed. Fritz K. Ringer noted that "Idealism was a creed as well as a philosophy from the very beginning."[11] Benjamin Nelson described the rationalism of the Enlightenment as "illuminism detached from its mystical source and symbolism...leaving the sober afterglow of a reason freed of irrational constraints and declaring the truth by the sole authority of its inner light."[12] But perhaps the most significant testimony to the nature of Kant's thought is that offered by MacIntyre himself who, when persuaded by the debate on *After Virtue* to alter his view of Kant as liberal individualist, conceded that Kant's closely interrelated concepts, "the moral law, moral worth, the kingdom of ends, moral desert,...and the *summum bonum*" were "fully intelligible only when understood as a late and secularized rational moral theology."[13]

Christian moral theology considers human nature as it is and could be and posits virtue as a means whereby man achieves his true end or realises his essence. Kant also distinguishes actual and ideal man. The former is a physical being like the animals, a creature of sense subject to natural impulses and the laws of the physical universe: as mere object in the "kingdom of means," he is acted on rather than acting. The latter is a spiritual or even godlike being, obeying only the voice of reason in himself, subject in the "kingdom of ends," active and fully autonomous.[14] So striking is Kant's contrast between these two states that he almost seems to deny the possibility — central to traditional ethics — of passing from one to the other through virtue: he seems to demand the eradication rather than the refinement of lower nature. But Kant remained true to the Aristotelian doctrine that nothing natural is vain, maintaining that man's lower nature in fact contains in itself a potential for good which ought to be developed.[15] The ethical writings thus speak the traditional language of virtue.[16] The *Grundlegung zur Metaphysik der Sitten* presents right action as an outer manifestation of a constant inner character or *Gesinnung*. The *Metaphysik der Sitten* provides "Metaphysische Anfangsgründe der Tugendlehre" as well as a discussion of the individual virtues.[17] As Onora O'Neill points out, Kant offers not so much rules for determinate action as a character ideal, a general concept of moral worth which will direct behaviour in particular situations.[18]

Kant makes two points about that character ideal. Man is to develop his faculties so that he can "rise above the rudeness of nature and at the expense of the animal in him develop the humanity, whereby alone he is capable of choosing ends for himself";[19] virtue controls feelings and inclinations, and brings them into conformity with reason.[20] Furthermore man is to cultivate his will, until he arrives at a purely virtuous temper of mind,[21] of which Kant uses the phrase "moralisches Gefühl." Man's nature contains the element of moral sense, a capacity to respond with pleasure to the moral law, which is strengthened in the cultivation of the will. Kant often speaks of "moralische Stärke," which he sometimes equates with *Tapferkeit*, the traditional virtue of courage.[22]

A theory of moral worth attained through reform of original nature must say something about education. The *Kritik der Urteilskraft* explains how experience of beauty enables man to free himself from the domination of the senses and attain a certain liberality of thought; beauty thus helps us shed our animality and become more fully human. The sublime by contrast appeals to our moral sense, fills us with enthusiasm, and strengthens our will.[23] These observations — specifically about the effects of beauty and sublimity in nature — suggest the foundations of a theory of education through art. Kant's early essay on the sublime and the beautiful finds sublimity in tragedy, and beauty in comedy.[24] *Die Religion innerhalb der Grenzen der bloßen Vernunft* recommends frequent stimulation of the moral sense, presumably through the sublime in art rather than nature.[25] The *Kritik der Urtheilskraft* declares that art does "much to overcome the tyrannical propensities of sense, and so prepare man for a sovereignty in which reason alone shall have sway."[26] Thus Kant is no less open than Wolff or Herder to the possibility of harnessing the powers of imaginative literature to ethical and ultimately religious ends.[27]

However Kant might seem to differ from traditional ethical and religious attitudes to community. Traditional ethics defined virtues as the
qualities required to maintain traditional communities and held that individual happiness depended on community membership. Kant seems to
abandon the concept of community by treating the individual as
autonomous and an end in himself, and apparently loses sight both of
the community's needs and of its contribution to the individual's welfare.
Caird observed of Kant's theory of the relations of individuals in society
that "Each remains permanently external to the other; and though all
may surrender themselves to the law, this only produces a similar life in
each, but not a community of the same life in all."[28] Yet, as Caird himself acknowledged, there is a principle of community in the Kantian
system. Recognising that universal morality does not realise itself in any
actual domestic, civic or national community, Kant posited the ideal of a
kingdom of ends, a perfect social order in which nature serves spirit and
men are members one of another; and this conception is but a part of
the whole Leibnizian vision of a God-given harmony between means
and ends, facts and values, happiness and virtue, nature and grace which
Kant intended to sustain by his own theorising.[29] In a universe so constituted, the individual's freedom as end in himself is compatible with his
determination by an objective end, the good of the whole. He "becomes
conscious that he can realise his own end only as he makes himself the
voluntary servant of the social end, which is realising itself in the world
without him."[30]

The kingdom of ends is an idea that can never become reality and
can act purely as a regulative principle of moral life. But in *Die Religion
innerhalb der Grenzen der bloßen Vernunft* Kant introduced the possibility of an ethical community or *Tugendbund* which he described as
"corresponding in character to the Christian Church," an invisible union
which labours "for the removal of all the hindrances, which prevent the
moral law from becoming the subjective principle of the life of all
men."[31] Another treatise, "Idee zu einer allgemeinen Geschichte in
weltbürgerlicher Absicht," represents the larger grouping of civil society
as a community which, despite its tendency to *bellum omnium*, is necessary to man's moral perfection. For

> it is only in a society in which there is the greatest freedom and there-
> fore a thorough antagonism of all the members, and at the same time
> the most exact determination and secure maintenance of the limit of
> this freedom in each, so that it may consist with equal freedom in all
> the rest, that the highest end of nature in man, i.e., the full develop-
> ment of all his natural capacities can be attained.[32]

As Caird remarks, in thus asserting that man's moral culture depends on
the society to which he belongs, Kant "practically abandons the merely
subjective principle of morals," a move which brings him very close to

the historicist position later adopted by Kantians such as Wilhelm von Humboldt, who regarded the state as an organic community essential to the moral growth of its members.[33]

Kant thus gave further and powerful impetus to the movement for intellectual and spiritual revival within the *Lehrstand* as a whole. What many contemporaries took from his complex system was a Leibnizian vision of individual monads striving to perfect themselves within a harmonious universe, a notion of self-cultivation originating in the mystical ideal of *cultura animi*. The Kantian idea of *Kultur*, as distinct from superficial worldly politeness or *Zivilisation*,[34] gave timely support to the so-called neohumanists, led by J. M. Gesner and C. G. Heyne in Göttingen and F. A. Wolf in Halle, who were already promoting a revival of classical studies in the universities. Kantian neohumanists maintained that the way to ethical self-perfection lay through classical education, specifically through the study of Greek rather than Latin texts. They held, as Anthony La Vopa points out, that language synthesised "the concreteness of vocabulary and the abstraction of grammar" into a model of harmonious self-cultivation or *Bildung*. Greek "deserved special reverence because it had achieved this fusion to a unique degree and hence was the most appropriate medium for achieving an equivalent unity in the individual personality."[35] The young Humboldt suggested that the study of Greek culture required the student to marshal all his energies and "stretch all his powers equally," so cultivating himself as a human being.[36]

Kant's and Herder's ideas, together with those of the neohumanists, gave the *Lehrstand* a new *raison d'être* during the last two decades of the eighteenth century. As the church's prestige dwindled, clergy and teachers increasingly presented themselves as providers of *Bildung* rather than religious instruction: some practising clergymen adopted the new ideas, some theologians abandoned their studies for philosophy, the classics or ancient history.[37] People caught up in these developments, which paralleled changes effected by Wolffianism earlier in the century, did not regard themselves as being involved in a utilitarian compromise with the trend of the times, but as being engaged in an impassioned crusade, in which the utopian element of the new ideal compensated for the loss of traditional religious substance.[38] As Ringer claimed, higher education "acquired a tremendous moral and spiritual significance...and the intellectual leaders of the cultivated élite filled the role of intermediaries between the eternal and temporal realms."[39] *Bildung* was a new faith, its exponents a new priesthood in succession to the old. Thomas Nipperdey describes philosophers and philologists as "a new sort of priests and mentors," and suggests that "the grace of the human spirit replaced the grace of God, and the word of the Greeks His word."[40] F. I. Niethammer, a contemporary educational theorist, talked of a "favoured class of individuals" called by fate "to be the priests of reason" and "to preserve its holy fire on earth."[41]

The idealist-neohumanist ideology offered the late eighteenth-century *Lehrstand* the possibility of victory over the lawyers in the two hundred-year battle for control of German cultural life, a victory which would assert the theoretical over the empirical, and the traditional over the modern world-view.[42] Imaginative literature had played a significant part on both sides of this battle, and continued to do so in the years of "Weimar classicism," despite the fact that Schiller's and the classical Goethe's allegiances have been obscured, not least by their own claims to represent timeless values which transcend the party strife of localised cultural tendencies. Schiller is sometimes remembered more for differences from than similarity to Kant.[43] Yet as a Kantian philosopher and university professor he was a *Lehrstand* figure whose philosophical and literary work makes sense only as a contribution to the Kantian and neohumanist programme, a contribution of unusual weight and power, motivated by Schiller's compelling need to justify himself against Goethe as he understood him.

Schiller's Kantianism appears in his argument that man's highest goal is to fulfil himself as spirit.[44] As a creature of sense, Schiller argues, man is animal; as a creature with a dual nature, compounded of sense and reason, he is human; and as a rational creature, he is spirit: man's human nature should transcend the animal, his spiritual nature the human. This conviction is clearly stated in the enclosure to Schiller's letter of 11 November 1793, to the duke of Augustenburg. There Schiller refers to "three different epochs or stages...that man must pass through, before he is what nature and reason destined him to be." At the first stage, that of *Sensualität*, man is "nothing but a passive force"; at the second stage, he begins to use a higher faculty, namely that of *Rationalität*; while at the third stage, he leaves his sensory nature behind, to attain "to the freedom of pure spirits."[45] The argument reemerges in *Über die ästhetische Erziehung des Menschen*, where man is said to have to pass, both as individual and as species, through the same three stages, from the "*physischen* Zustand" to the "*moralischen*."[46] This developmental sequence leading to the kingdom of reason is fundamental to Schiller's thought: the establishment of the "Monarchie der Vernunft" would render all aesthetic endeavours superfluous and he himself, he told the duke of Augustenburg, would be content to bid farewell to the Muses.[47]

Über die ästhetische Erziehung des Menschen outlines man's ascent much as Kant had done in his "Idee zu einer allgemeinen Geschichte in weltbürgerlicher Absicht." Man begins as "raw nature," as an animal or "savage" subject to the power of nature, entirely dominated by sense, and hence unfree.[48] But progress is possible even under the aegis of nature. Where favourable conditions release man from the struggle for bare existence, he can play. He is unconstrained by sense or reason since the two work together in harmony to produce man as pure nature, or perfect natural man, the state of development represented by the Greeks, the happy, carefree children of nature.[49] In the next stage of human development, man leaves nature behind, and enters the epoch of culture. Though sense and reason no longer harmonise, Schiller, like Kant, accepts this "fall" into conflict as the necessary precondition of further development.[50] The lower form of harmony represented by pure nature must be destroyed so that a higher one may be attained through the epoch of culture which is synonymous with history, since both lower and higher harmony are conceived by Schiller as timeless: only the intervening conflict takes place in and through time. Through this conflict man may develop *Vernunft* or *Geist*, which Schiller describes as historically as well as biologically *männlich*, "adult" as opposed to "childish," since they characterise both the adult individual and modern man in general, the representative of the adulthood of the race. Schiller's final stage of human development belongs to the ideal, the new state of oneness of which pure nature's blissful oneness was an image. Each individual bears within him the model of "pure, ideal man," who is characterised by "immutable unity"[51] which, like the unity of nature, harmonises sense and reason, so that "through all the fluctuations of fantasy" the latter "maintains its rule."[52] This new harmony — "nothing but light, nothing but freedom, nothing but power"[53] — is "the ultimate extension of being," which transcends time[54] and hence humanity and brings about a "transformation of man into god"[55] reminiscent of Schiller's "Die Götter Griechenlands," where the gods retreat to an Elysium "removed from the flux of time."[56]

The movement towards the ideal could occur in history through the refinement of man's human nature into virtues corresponding to the qualities Kant identified as fundamental to self-cultivation: harmony between man's lower and higher nature, and reverence for the ideal. These virtues characterise the perfected human, the "beautiful soul" in whom instinct is so refined that it conforms to the moral law, without any sense of strain.[57] Such harmony between the two natures obtains when reason leads and sense gladly follows. Yet life presents situations where sense attempts to lead against the dictates of reason and morality, as when a person tries to save himself by sacrificing another. In such a situation, Schiller argues, the truly beautiful soul, who is a natural and not yet a purely spiritual creature, a virtuous human being not a god,[58] will nevertheless become sublime: in other words, will rise above the promptings of instinct.[59] For human nature as such has something much like Kant's sense of reverence for the moral law, a sense of the sublime or an appetite for spiritual things which draws it to the world of spirit.[60] Cultivation of this "idealistic inclination" or "germ of idealism" produces the "strength of will" that, according to Schiller, distinguishes the genuinely beautiful soul, the truly virtuous human being, from those whose will is weak and who merely appear to enjoy inner harmony.[61] Such strength of will, arising from a lively sense of the sublime, issues in actions that are themselves sublime in that they subjugate the instincts to the will. Since they arise from a moral sense, rather than from obedience to the moral law for its own sake, they are not moral acts: in Schiller's terms they are aesthetically rather than morally sublime.[62] But they reveal a moral capacity in human nature, the virtue of the beautiful soul, which is the condition of true morality. For while strength of will need not issue in moral acts, there can be no moral acts without strength of will.[63]

Art and literature help to cultivate such virtue, in so far as beauty of soul requires both harmony of sense and mind, and strength of will, qualities which are developed, respectively, by those two resources of aesthetic education, the beautiful or "melting beauty," and the sublime or "energetic beauty." A beautiful object induces a state in which "senses and mind are both active,"[64] but sense does not dominate mind, nor mind sense, because the beautiful object simultaneously satisfies our senses' striving for content and our mind's striving for form.[65] The action of a sublime object is rather different. It rouses us from apathy and renews our energies by embodying the conflict of sense and mind, and revealing the independence of the latter from the former.[66] The spectacle of a dramatic character who acts contrary to instinct can make us aware of our own capacity to do the same: it can summon us to action, give us strength for great deeds, and make heroes of us.[67] Schiller suggests that love alone may have a like effect.

Thus far Schiller's theory specifies an ideal, the virtues which lead thereto, and the forms of art which stimulate those virtues, but has nothing to say about particular empirical works of literature, and still less about their relative values. He attempts this task in the text of, and his letters on, *Über naive und sentimentalische Dichtung*, which moves beyond specifically literary matters to present Schiller's reckoning with the two cultural traditions that had been disputing for primacy in Germany since early modern times.

Although *Über naive und sentimentalische Dichtung* does not employ the categories of the beautiful and the sublime, it attributes to naive poetry the effect Schiller ascribed to melting as distinct from energetic beauty, which he equated with the sublime. For naive poetry creates a harmony of sense and reason, leaves the reader "calm, relaxed, at one with himself and completely contented," and, beyond a certain point, reduces him to a state of excessive relaxation or *Erschlaffung*.[68] Though the category of the beautiful therefore includes all ancient Greek literature of whatever genre, whether epic, lyric or dramatic, Schiller seems to have regarded comedy as the archetype and apogee of beauty in literature.[69] Conversely Schiller attributes to sentimental poetry the effect of the sublime. For sentimental poetry alerts the reader to the disharmony between sense and reason; it energises the psyche, sets it "in motion," braces it, and causes it to fluctuate "between conflicting feelings," and if taken to excess will cause "hypertension" — *Überspannung*.[70] If "playful satire" be discounted because of its proximity to comedy and the naive, the properly sentimental modes of writing seem to be "punitive satire" and elegy, with its subdivisions of elegy proper and idyll. Punitive satire is represented by tragedy, elegy by *Gedankenlyrik*.[71] Tragedy as conceived by the modern idealist poet seems to Schiller the most effective form of the sublime. "Tragedy does not make us into gods," he wrote, "because gods can not suffer; it makes us into heroes, that is, into god-like men or, if you like, into suffering gods, into titans."[72]

These propositions were not developed in a spirit of detachment. On the contrary, the writing of *Über naive und sentimentalische Dichtung* was affected by intensely personal concerns. The contrast between naive and sentimental poets, realists and idealists, stated the distinctions Schiller drew between himself and Goethe. Schiller's notion of Goethe as a creature of sense rather than of mind runs through all the former's comments about the latter, from early, hostile remarks made to Körner to the sensitive analysis which Schiller offered Goethe himself in 1794. Schiller remarked on Goethe's "reliance on his five senses"; complained that "His way of looking at things is altogether too sensuous and does too much *touching* for my liking"; and observed to Goethe himself that "Your sound instinct contains everything that analysis seeks so laboriously, and contains it in far greater completion."[73] Goethe's reliance on the senses made him, in the terminology of *Über naive und sentimentalische Dichtung*, the "thoroughly hardened realist" Schiller once called him.[74] Schiller regarded himself as a man of the mind rather than a creature of sense; as just over a month before his death he wrote to Wilhelm von Humboldt, "we are both of us idealists and would be ashamed to have it said that objects shaped us, rather than that we shaped objects."[75]

Psychological categories and sociological categories can coincide.[76] In defining Goethe and himself as realist and idealist, Schiller was also contrasting the rival groups of lawyer-statesmen and academics to which the two of them — at least superficially — belonged. More than once Schiller explicitly links the realist with the man of affairs or *Geschäfts-mann*, the idealist with the academic philosopher.[77] *Über die ästhetische Erziehung des Menschen* refers, like *Über naive und sentimentalische Dichtung*, to the antagonism between intuitive and speculative understanding which marks the modern world, and characterises intuitive understanding as a "practical attitude" — *Geschäftsgeist*. In *Über naive und sentimentalische Dichtung*, Schiller uses various antithetical pairs. There are the "working part" ("arbeitender Teil") of the population and the "contemplative part" ("kontemplativer Teil"); there are the "Mensch im praktischen Leben" and the "Philosoph"; and there are the "Geschäfts-mann" and the "Gelehrte."[78] Schiller's realist thus represents the whole social group which concerned itself with public affairs, the group the historian Mack Walker called "movers and doers."[79] Conversely when drawing the idealist Schiller had in mind those scholars who, far from in-volving themselves in public affairs, pursued their discipline in the uni-versities or devoted themselves to solitary speculation. Kant himself, the monkish figure who acted as lawgiver to the people, the "Draco of his time," was probably never far from Schiller's thoughts when he described the philosopher.[80]

Schiller therefore gave the realist the characteristics of the lawyer-statesmen and administrators who worked towards modernisation. The realist is an empiricist opponent of system-building who takes a low view of human nature, though this does not prevent him from promoting the earthly happiness of his fellow creatures. He is in fact a benevolent utilitarian, content with material wellbeing for himself and others. His low expectations of humanity lead to tolerance, but he values participa-tion and co-operation and cannot abide extravagance or eccentricity. His attitudes are precisely those which underlie the comic tradition, with its low view of human nature, its attack on eccentricity, and its vision of a workable society based on acceptance of rules.[81] By contrast the idealist displays the characteristics of theoretical experts, whether clergy or phi-losophers, who upheld the values of tradition and community. The ideal-ist is a rigorist system-builder who demands conformity with immutable laws. Since temporal welfare and happiness mean nothing to him beside man's spiritual calling, he strives not to improve the earthly lot of others but to perfect them as moral beings, and his exalted view of mankind as a species may make him high-handed and intolerant in his dealings with fellow human beings. He worships heroism and will reconcile himself with the extravagance that arises from greatness of soul. Contempt for the average man sets the idealist apart from society and inclines him to solitude, reclusiveness, even melancholia; rigidity of principle makes his differences irreconcilable; he readily sacrifices earthly happiness for higher values. Such attitudes underlie all forms of exemplary writing which concern themselves with human greatness, its struggles with fate or circumstance, and its ability to rise above earthly defeat.[82]

Schiller's typology indicates his awareness of the opposition in his own society between "lawyers" and "philosophers," modernisers and traditionalists. But he did not attempt a mere inventory of the character-istics of realist and idealist; he made a reckoning which is itself *parti pris*, a contribution to the struggle. Yet the issue was so delicate, and so much bound up with his personal relationship to Goethe, that Schiller could

not make his partisanship absolutely plain. His attitude to the two conflicting groups must be read between the lines, and the reader will
search *Über naive und sentimentalische Dichtung* in vain for a final decision in favour of either realist or idealist. Neither, according to Schiller,
represents complete humanity. The ideal is split between the two, and
would become reality could they unite.[83] Hence Schiller approved of
much that belongs to the realist side of his dichotomy. He often heaped
praise on whatever was natural and instinctive, finding in nature a state
of original wholeness and completeness best represented in the modern
world by the integrity and innocence of the child. The human race as a
whole experienced a childhood which Schiller associated with the ancient Greeks, who enjoyed the blessings of a golden age and an earthly
paradise.[84] Children and Greeks apart, the realist is closest to nature and
in his highest form, the "schöne Seele" whose instinct infallibly leads him
to do what is right, the "seal of perfected humanity."[85] The natural, instinctive writer, the naive poet who manifests the qualities of genius,
seems to command Schiller's greatest respect. Comedy, the province of
naive poets and "schöne Seelen," has a greater goal than tragedy, in
striving after the highest state of man, freedom from passion: a letter to
Humboldt describes comedy as "the highest form of poetry" yet
achieved.[86]

Yet Schiller's praise of the realist is deeply equivocal. The antithetical
presentation of realist and idealist provides a metaphor of horizontality
which constitutes his essay's exoteric meaning, the public message which
would avoid offence to readers in general and Goethe in particular. But
read in conjunction with Schiller's general scheme of human evolution
Über naive und sentimentalische Dichtung yields an esoteric meaning to
which Schiller gave frank expression only in his correspondence with
Humboldt, whom he regarded as a fellow-spirit. Schiller's sub-text inevitably assigns to the realist a lower rung on the ladder than that occupied
by the idealist, for the realist represents perfected humanity, whereas
man's destiny is to rise beyond mere humanity to the realm of mind.
Writing to Humboldt about Goethe, Schiller maintains that the realist's
closeness to nature and the Greek childhood of the race necessarily en-
tails a proportional deficiency in *Geist*.[87] The idealist, in whom the modern, adult prerogative of mind is more fully developed, alone has the
potential to realise the ideal of harmony under the rule of reason; only
he can recognise the maxim of "duty for duty's sake" and create the
moral world within the physical.

Schiller's evaluation of literary modes ultimately depends upon his
"vertical" schema of human development. Different sorts of writing matter to him in so far as they assist the moderns' further progress towards
the rule of reason. Naive poetry, "the completest possible *imitation of
reality*,"[88] therefore occupies a less exalted position in Schiller's canon

than might be expected from a simply "horizontal" reading of *Über naive und sentimentalische Dichtung*. Such poetry serves in the first instance to relax the force of nature in the savage, a process analysed at length in *Über die ästhetische Erziehung des Menschen*.[89] But savagery in the modern world was confined to the lower social orders, to whose further development Schiller gave little attention, while among the cultivated classes relaxation of the senses had already gone far enough.[90] Schiller did posit the existence of a category of "barbarians": cultivated modern men, suffering from the constraint of mind over sense, whose principles threaten to crush their emotions. But he never analyses the process by which naive poetry might set them free.[91] Indeed he never seems to take the problem of excessive rationality as seriously as that of excessive sensuality. The concept of constraint by reason hardly figures in the Augustenburg letters, and probably owes its prominence in *Über die ästhetische Erziehung des Menschen* only to the promptings of Goethe;[92] Schiller does not in fact give naive poetry a serious function to perform in the modern world: so far as he is concerned, its time would seem to be past. Hence perhaps the suggestion, in his letter to J. W. Süvern, that Sophoclean tragedy is not appropriate to the needs of his contemporaries.[93]

These reservations about naive or realistic writing account for Schiller's equivocal assessment of the great comic writers. He describes Cervantes, Fielding, Sterne and Wieland as naive and uses them as examples of genius.[94] But they are not properly naive, since they figure in Schiller's discussion under the heading of playful satire, which is a mode of modern, sentimental poetry. The obvious implication is that they are straightforward realists, mere approximations in modern times to ancient naive poets.[95] Moreover it is not the most conspicuously comic aspects of their work that Schiller chooses to praise: he seems instead to be seeking some idealistic element which will rescue them from condemnation. Having noted that playful satire requires beauty of soul, he tests this quality by these authors' ability to rise to difficult and demanding subject-matter. When subject-matter grows serious, the trivial writer will fail abjectly, while the beautiful soul will rise to the sublime. He will not of course approach a great theme as the idealist would, in full consciousness of the disparity between reality and the ideal, but he will nevertheless be moved by his instinct to treat his material with dignity. Thus Schiller credits Cervantes with having displayed a "great and beautiful character" on every appropriate occasion. Fielding is said to possess the beautiful soul's capacity to achieve sublimity: "What a magnificent ideal must have lived in the soul of the poet who created a Tom Jones and a Sophia."[96] Wieland, "the immortal author of *Agathon*," shows the same "seriousness of sentiment" — "Ernst der Empfindung" — which marks Fielding. The "grace of his heart," Schiller continues, "inspirits and ennobles even his caprices; this grace impresses itself even on the rhythm of his song, and he never lacks momentum when it is a question of lifting us up to the heights."[97] Schiller values Wieland for his sense of the sublime, not for the realist qualities that link him with the sceptical tradition of Thomasius.

The honorific title of naive poet thus serves to conceal a fundamental criticism of the major comic novelists. Schiller simply dismissed many lesser comic fiction-writers of eighteenth-century Germany as mere realists "in the narrow sense of the term."[98] Though he contrasted comedy as an intellectual exercise and tragedy as an appeal to the emotions, he did not follow the sceptical *Aufklärer* in crediting comic fiction with power to enlarge the intellect; presumably such a purpose appeared to Schiller to be strictly extra-aesthetic, and so no part of his concern as a poet. Hence he ranked modern comedy for the most part as an unsuccessful attempt to emulate the naive model: its authors had transported the raw material of the imperfect modern world directly into their work, without first raising it to the poetic level through their own resources, and thus sinned by allowing their fictions to become a product rather than a portrait of their times, a shortcoming Schiller also found in the work of the poet G. A. Bürger.[99] Such writers presented their readers with distasteful scenes of immorality and squalor and, at the extreme of naturalism, merely reverted to matter.[100] The appeal of a naturalistic approach was entirely sensory. It could satisfy a need for relaxation, and was therefore in Kant's terminology agreeable — to a very large audience — but could not be aesthetic. Those who read with pleasure the many inferior comic novels of the time were succumbing to the pressures of modern life. Wearied by constant exercise of one or another faculty, they sought mere relaxation through literature,[101] an entirely unworthy function for something which Schiller regarded as the means to human greatness.

M. A. von Thümmel's *Reise in die mittäglichen Provinzen von Frankreich*, a novel in the manner of Sterne's *Sentimental Journey*, illustrated the difference between great comedy and entertaining fiction. Thümmel's "light and jovial nature" did not suffice to raise his work to the aesthetic level; lacking any real wealth of ideas, he failed to satisfy the needs of the mind, and his admittedly diverting novel remained "almost contemptible when judged against the ideal." This was a harsh verdict on a book which enjoyed considerable popularity with contemporary readers, and whose immediate appeal Schiller did not deny. But Thümmel did not represent the depths of the German comic tradition, Friedrich Nicolai was even worse. Nicolai's *Geschichte eines dicken Manns* proved him to be a caricature of his times; his work was entirely material and thus irredeemably unaesthetic.[102]

Schiller's criticism of sentimental poetry strikes a different note. Naive poetry imitates reality, sentimental poetry represents the ideal.[103] Thus it draws attention to the discrepancy between real and ideal, lacks harmony, is not strictly poetry at all, and so ranks below the naive: as Schiller admitted to Humboldt, sentimental poetry "is represented by me only as *striving* towards the ideal...so that effectively I allow it less poetic quality than I allow the naive."[104] The sentimental, that is, the idealist poet is therefore in effect but a philosopher. Yet inferior though it may be, sentimental poetry is the form for which the age cries out, since sentimental poetry can promote the will-power the cultivated classes need to translate knowledge into action. Read in the context of his philosophy of history, Schiller's aesthetic theory thus makes a reasoned plea for the kind of writing Herder was advocating in the 1770s, a heroic literature which could rouse contemporaries from lethargy by inspiring them with a sense of their own potential for heroism. But Schiller goes beyond Herder in distinguishing between ancient and modern literature, and parts company with the neohumanists who saw Greek culture as an adequate source of materials for a modern education. Schiller believed, as his letter to the classicist schoolmaster Süvern shows, that Greek tragedy was beautiful not sublime. What was wanted was a modern tragedy capable of bracing rather than relaxing its audience. To this end Schiller built into the idealist-neohumanist scheme of moral education a theory of a modern *German* literature which he saw himself as creating by precept, example, and encouragement.[105]

Though himself almost exclusively a lyricist and tragic playwright, Schiller commented on the tradition of European prose romance, which he treated far more leniently than comic fiction. Here he very much agreed with Herder, who forgave romance its excesses on account of its noble ideals. Schiller was willing to overlook sentimental, idealistic novelists' loss of contact with reality, because he credited them with genuine belief in values he himself held dear. Despite his aesthetic of harmony between senses and mind, he inclined once more to the side of mind: better by far to exaggerate an ideal than to overstate a reality. Exaggerated sentiment most frequently appeared in fiction as love for an ideal woman; the object was unreal — the woman was a creature of the imagination — the feeling was not. It came from the heart and could touch the heart. "This exaggeration deserves to be corrected, not condemned," he warned cynical detractors of high sentiment, "and anyone who ridicules it should examine himself, to see whether it is not heartlessness that makes him so clever, and lack of reason that makes him so knowing."[106] Thus Schiller justified the tradition of exemplary romance, beginning with the *Ritterromane* which derived their admittedly "exaggerated delicacy in the matter of gallantry and honour" from a genuine moral sentiment that alone could account for these works' power to move their readers, and continuing in the best modern French and English sentimental novels, such as Richardson's *Grandison*, which Schiller cited as an example of moral greatness.[107]

Even one of the most lachrymose novels of enlightened sentimentalism won Schiller's approval. Like Kant, who criticised contemporary romances for trifling with noble sentiments and encouraging public
decadence, Schiller insisted that "delicate sensitivity and melancholy"
could not alone make for successful elegy, and that the tearful pieces of
the 1770s merely caused enervation.[108] But he defended J. M. Miller's
Siegwart, because the feeling expressed in it, though exaggerated, was
nevertheless genuine. What Siegwart felt for his Marianne resembled
Petrarch's feeling for Laura, St. Preux's for Julie, or Werther's for Lotte.
Miller's book, though "a little ridiculous when judged against experience," was therefore far more worthwhile than Thümmel's "almost contemptible" *Reise*.[109] A sin against the ideal was always much greater in
Schiller's eyes than a sin against reality.

Schiller's commitment to the values of the *Lehrstand* is further evidenced in his evaluation of Goethe, whom he saw as realist poet, man of
affairs and representative of a contrasting, empiricist tradition. Goethe's
novels aroused Schiller's unease and set him looking for redeeming
idealist features. In *Über naive und sentimentalische Dichtung* he described *Die Leiden des jungen Werther* as the first example of something
impossible before his own epoch, the naive treatment of a sentimental
theme, but left his personal response to this phenomenon to be conjec-
tured from what he said earlier about naive representations of affecting
subject-matter, such as Homer's account of Glaucus' and Diomedes'
resolution to avoid injuring each other in battle because of the ancient
friendship between their houses: an episode which Schiller thought
Homer narrated as if he had no heart, such was his coolness and detachment.[110] Schiller was deeply disturbed by this lack of pathos, which
he also detected in other great naive writers such as Shakespeare and,
presumably, Goethe,[111] who had drawn in Werther a remarkable portrait
of the sentimental character in its extreme form, and assembled with un-
erring instinct all the influences which Schiller thought conducive to excessive sentimentalism: unhappy love, a passion for nature, religious
yearnings, a philosophical bent. Schiller recognised Werther as a young
man "who clings to an ideal with ardent feeling and flees from reality"
but in the end remained silent on the central interpretative question of
whether this character was to be read normatively, with moral effect, or
simply descriptively as a psychopathological study.[112]

A question mark has also to be put against Schiller's reaction to *Wilhelm Meisters Lehrjahre*, still in progress when *Über naive und sentimentalische Dichtung* appeared, and so far as Schiller was concerned, a
naive work with sentimental potential. Setting the *Lehrjahre* in the comic
tradition, Schiller understood Wilhelm as an idealist falling into the excess of "Phantasterei," who would form airy schemes without any
thought for their practicability and who in the course of the story was

cured of this failing, and finally integrated as a functioning member of society, much as any comic figure might be.[113] Indeed the comic spirit — "der leichte Humor" — presided over the story, so that finally "the seriousness and pain of the world fade as if they were a shadow-play," with Friedrich acting at the last the part of one who "wakes us from an anxious dream through laughter."[114] Schiller described the effect of the first two books of the story as that of comedy or of naive poetry, "so joyous, so full of life, so harmoniously relaxed and so true to human nature," and felt moved to reflect uncomfortably on his own shortcomings and those of idealists and philosophers generally, who seemed to be, by contrast with a poet like Goethe, "so strict, so rigid and abstract and so very unnatural."[115] Yet none of this prevented Schiller from trying to manœuvre Goethe into making the *Lehrjahre* more "philosophical" and so closer to romance.[116]

In Schiller's reading of the story, Wilhelm was not so much a comic figure who should be cured, as the hero of sentimental man's spiritual odyssey, a bourgeois philosopher living in the mind and lacking the confidence to make a position for himself in the real world, who in the course of the story acquired more and more of the realist's easy confidence and ability to act, and was finally accepted into a company of noblemen — archetypal representatives of this-worldly power and accomplishment — without forfeiting the quality of mind with which he began, a quality that for Schiller was no disadvantage but a precious possession. "He moves," Schiller wrote to Goethe, "from an empty and indefinite ideal to a definite, active life, but" — and this was the crucial thing for Schiller — "without losing his idealising power in the process."[117] If Wilhelm could be rewritten as taking on Goethe's qualities, while retaining Schiller's intellectual and spiritual advantages, the former's creation could embody the latter's theories. Schiller therefore resisted everything which might suggest that Wilhelm's progress was fortuitous, and advocated using the novel to represent in almost programmatic fashion the education of the idealist.[118]

He suggested, for example, that Goethe should show how Wilhelm's aesthetic sense develops through experience by contrasting his youthful response to his grandfather's pictures with a more mature interest to be shown on the occasion of his visit with Natalie to the "Saal der Vergangenheit." Schiller also wanted Goethe to give Wilhelm a proper philosophical education since this would be essential for an idealist, whose instinct was by itself less reliable than a realist's.[119] Above all Schiller urged Goethe to establish a clear relationship between the events of the novel and its "philosophical concept" — "philosophischen Begriff" — of apprenticeship and mastery, "Lehrjahre" and "Meisterschaft." The "fable is perfectly true," Schiller told Goethe, "and the moral of the fable is perfectly true, but the relationship of one to the other does not yet leap clearly enough to the eye."[120] Here Schiller uses the vocabulary of didactic literature as he tries to steer the *Lehrjahre* in the direction of allegory and romance. Three months later, on receiving Goethe's revised version of the final book, Schiller expressed satisfaction with certain alterations of detail, but indicated that his desire for a clearer statement of what he wished to be the meaning of the text remained unsatisfied.[121]

Though his comments on Goethe's novels show the tensions in the relationship between the two Weimar classicists plainly enough, Schiller's understanding of those tensions was not itself entirely clear. He presents the difference between the two friends as if it did indeed correspond with that between the legal and clerical traditions, with Goethe the *Geschäftsmann*, empiricist and realist, and himself the academic philosopher, theoretician and idealist. But despite Goethe's training as a lawyer, his position as minister of state, and the degree to which he gravitated away from Herder towards Wieland,[122]it is difficult to see him, even in his classical phase, as a writer within the "legal" tradition. It is true that *Wilhelm Meisters Lehrjahre* was no romance but something much more akin to comedy, as Schiller rightly perceived; the book has even been interpreted as a vision of modern society, in which Wilhelm entrusts himself to free market forces and finds happiness in a self-regulating system of risk-taking and reward.[123] Yet the story is ultimately one of integration into a patriarchal world. Though unfilial defiance characterises Wilhelm's early life, he finally keeps faith with his father by abandoning the theatre, and his apt fascination with Hamlet is duly if somewhat mystically satisfied by receipt of a paternal blessing from the mouth of Hamlet's father's ghost, speaking with the voice of Wilhelm's own father.[124] His paternally approved new life is that of the adult male, involving wife, child, and the practical economic activity — "Tätigkeit" — needed to support them. By taking on these obligations, Wilhelm integrates himself into a line which reaches back through many generations, and will, through Felix, presumably continue for generations to come; the prospect of his wealth passing to his child and his child's children gives Wilhelm particular pleasure.[125]

Goethe's next work of fiction, the *Unterhaltungen deutscher Ausgewanderten*, published in *Die Horen* in 1795, reemphasises the theme of family continuity. Writing in a periodical pledged to abstain from political comment, Goethe aroused controversy by referring to the unhappiness which the French revolutionary army caused German nobles "branded as criminals because they honoured their fathers and enjoyed the many advantages that a right-thinking parent bestows on children and descendants."[126] His text concerns the renewal of a society disrupted not only by war but by internal political conflict. As Ulrich Gaier points out, this renewal depends on renunciation — *Entsagung* — by individual members of that society; but Gaier's claim that Goethe's social philosophy belongs to the tradition of Thomasius and the "common sense" Enlightenment fails to reckon with the intensity of Goethe's commitment to the very different tradition expressed in the noble ideal of the family.[127]

Die Wahlverwandtschaften, written after the Prussian defeat at Jena in 1806, may be read as a lament for the loss of that very ideal. Eduard is a nobleman who, unlike Wilhelm Meister, fails to assume his responsibility as *pater familias*. Indifferent to sexual relations with his legitimate spouse, he is ready to consign their one child, a child conceived in mental adultery with a phantasy of sexless motherhood, to the care of that personification of sexless fatherhood, the professional educator.[128] Meanwhile traditional noble patterns of procreation and nurture collapse into sterility as modernity spreads: religion and piety fall into neglect, personal rule gives way to rational administration, new technologies bring mass-produced goods on to the market and improved communications break down the barriers between ancient communities.[129]

Thus whatever Schiller may have thought, Goethe was not a realist as defined in *Über naive und sentimentalische Dichtung*, a pragmatic, sceptical figure in the tradition of Thomasius or Wieland.[130] Though minister of state in a small principality, he was not the modernising public lawyer so much as the traditionalist Frankfurt burgher. His co-operation with Schiller may be seen as yet another instance of the old alliance of *Reichsstadt* notables and the *Lehrstand*. Goethe and Schiller most certainly differed from one another, but not in the way Schiller suggested. Goethe shared Herder's reverence for specific, historical communities and Plato's orientation to the past rather than the future.[131] Schiller shared Wolff's and Aristotle's belief in an ideal world yet to be constructed by man's powers of reason and feeling. In short both Goethe and Schiller contributed to idealist neohumanist thinking and threw their weight on the side of clergy, philosophers and philologists in the cultural conflict with the modernising lawyer-statesmen.

Hence the great preponderance of intellectual ability on the side of the *Lehrstand* in the last two decades of the eighteenth century, when economic and political events were anyway shaking the confidence of pragmatic *Aufklärer* connected with the service élite. In 1786 the death of Friedrich II of Prussia and the accession of the far more conservative Friedrich Wilhelm II filled men like Nicolai and Biester with fears of repressive measures against the Enlightenment, and these fears were intensified when von Zedlitz was replaced as minister of justice by Wöllner, whose *Religionsedikt* of 1788 aimed to rid the established Lutheran church of rationalist influence.[132] Moreover as the French Revolution, though very largely a rebellion by conservative forces against the modernising reforms of an Enlightenment alliance of nobles and commoners in state service, was generally seen in Germany as an attack by

progressive, enlightened forces on a traditionalist regime, the revolutionary Terror turned both intellectuals and rulers against the sort of reform-
ism represented, for example, by Berlin *Aufklärer* such as Nicolai.[133]

The combined effect of intellectual and political developments in the
last two decades of the eighteenth century was to end the long-running
conflict among educated Germans between practical *Politiker* and men
of affairs on the one hand and theoretical experts — clergy and philosophers — on the other. Some voices were raised against the abstraction of
Kant's system; in 1795 the Berlin official J. E. Biester was still arguing that
the universities should be abolished because of their remoteness from
public debate; and Goethe's and Schiller's *Xenien*, published in 1797,
astonished contemporaries by the intemperance of their onslaught on
Nicolai in particular.[134] But the tone adopted by Goethe and Schiller suggests confidence rather than fear, and Nicolai's response, though spirited,
amounted to little more than a restatement of *Aufklärung* belief in common sense and well-mannered public debate.[135] By 1800 the *Lehrstand*'s
idealist-neohumanist-classicist ideology was rapidly gaining ground
among educated Germans in all walks of life, and no serious alternative
thinking presented itself. For two hundred years the clerical group had
been obliged to compete for intellectual supremacy with public lawyers
active in the world of politics and administration. Now the competition
had collapsed, and a new, united élite was emerging under clerical leadership.[136] After many vicissitudes, the unified medieval *Gelehrtenstand*
was being replaced by a unified *Bildungselite*. Thus Fritz Ringer writes of
an "aristocracy of cultivation" embracing clergy, bureaucrats, humanist
scholars and idealist philosophers alike; Koselleck refers to a "nobility of
service and culture" superseding the old learned estate in Prussia.[137]

The unity of the new educated élite shows nowhere more clearly
than in the changed stance of academic lawyers from the 1790s onwards.
Law, which had been for Thomasius a practical discipline above all else,
had during most of the eighteenth century successfully resisted the en-
croachments of the philosophers, among whom Wolff had been especially aggressive. But with Kant's theory of knowledge gaining
acceptance in the universities, academic lawyers rapidly succumbed to
the new intellectual climate, drastically reducing the resources devoted to
practical training and transforming jurisprudence into a philosophically-
based *Geisteswissenschaft*.[138] As Kant's *Critiques* appeared, law lost its
critical impetus.[139] The public lawyers who had led the movement toward modernisation in the territories, using both Roman and natural law
as instruments for social change, whether against the ancient privileges
of the estates or monarchical despotism, gave way to historicist legal
philosophers like Gustav Hugo and F. K. von Savigny, who defended the
pre-modern legal order.[140] The historicists, who were indebted to
Herder's theory of language, taught that law developed organically as a

creation of the *Volksgeist*. Hence there was "no possibility of it 'standing apart' in some way and 'acting upon' society," and the function of the academic lawyer was simply to act as guardian and interpreter of the legal tradition or, as Cotterrell puts it, "distiller of abstract concepts from age-old doctrine."[141] The erstwhile opposition to *Lehrstand* thought became its conservative ally.

Thomasian fiction was engulfed by Kantian idealism along with the Thomasian tradition of jurisprudence. Thomasius, and Wieland after him, belonged to the "unmasking trend" of *moralistes* such as Montaigne, La Rochefoucauld and Gracián.[142] Their wisdom was the wisdom of the man of the world. Though Kant seemed to admit the validity of this *Weltleute-Weltkenntnis* in his *Anthropologie in pragmatischer Hinsicht*, which not only employed the then current terminology of *Welt haben*, *Welt kennen*, and *die große Welt*, but outlined the traditional temperaments, and recommended Molière as a source of character-knowledge, Kantian *Weltkenntnis* is a typically theoretical affair: the sage of Königsberg's remoteness from the real thing may be gauged from his suggestion that knowledge of the world is to be acquired by immersion in the life of — Königsberg.[143] Practical anthropology, which Odo Marquard concluded was at most peripheral to the critical philosophy, could be said to have been crushed by it.[144]

Consequently practical anthropology played only a limited part in the fiction of the last two decades of the eighteenth century. Jörg Schönert's study of the relationship between novel and satire distinguished a line of "empirical" writers following Wieland, including J. G. Müller and Adolph Freiherr von Knigge, who rejected the satirist's overt moralising for an inductive approach to characterisation which applied practical anthropological principles.[145] But J. K. Wezel and others among this group of empirical novelists barely conceal a moralising intent much more in tune with the Wolffian *Aufklärung* than with Wieland.[146] Schönert's empirical-sceptical tendency in late eighteenth-century German fiction culminates — or rather collapses — in the humour of T. G. Hippel, who questioned the existence of general principles of psychology and presented his characters as unique individuals, to be judged individually.[147] Hippel, a lawyer who attained the offices of *Stadtpräsident* of Königsberg and Prussian *Geheimer Kriegsrat*, might seem to be an heir to the Thomasian tradition but is described by Richard Newald as a hyperidealist and forerunner of Jean Paul and in fact offers a striking example of the way in which the empirical tendency in eighteenth-century fiction was engulfed by idealism and romanticism.[148] G. C. Lichtenberg, one of the most acute late eighteenth-century German *moralistes*, made various plans for novels set in his own society but never completed any of them.[149] In any event as medical man rather than lawyer, Lichtenberg perhaps hints at the quarter from which the anthropological thought of the future was largely to come.[150]

Two remarkable features of the seventeenth and eighteenth centuries were the persistence with which the German *Lehrstand* struggled to hold its own against modernising princes, lawyers and statesmen, and the success with which it ultimately reincorporated graduates of all faculties into a unified idealist-neohumanist *Bildungselite*. Only an examination of nineteenth-century élites could discover to what extent this success had lasting influence on German culture and society. The recent historiography of the period has emphasised the notion that Germany followed a different path from France and Britain.[151] Many versions of this *Sonderweg* theory stress the supposed failure of the nineteenth-century German bourgeoisie to gain social and economic power and to establish liberal political institutions.[152] Against this it has been argued that the bourgeoisie occupied much the same socio-economic position in all three countries; all three experienced a process of modernisation in which the bourgeoisie played a significant part. David Blackbourn writes of "the substantial achievements of a silent bourgeois revolution in nineteenth-century Germany, in the fields of property relations, economic organization, the law, and free public association."[153] Nevertheless in Britain, France and Germany alike strong central government was the principal agent of modernisation, the aristocracy remained the dominant class, and the bourgeoisie did not transform so much as interact with existing power structures. Blackbourn argues: "If one looks at nineteenth-century Europe it is difficult to identify an unambiguous instance where the bourgeoisie ruled as a class, without the help of an élite or oligarchy, without a strong man or allies from some other class or classes."[154] Thus if there was a difference of ideology in Germany compared with Britain or France, it can not simply be traced to a difference in the socio-economic situation of the German bourgeoisie.

Yet commentators on the whole agree that there was such a difference, of which Ralf Dahrendorf's description has never been seriously assailed even if his socio-economic aetiology has been questioned. Antimodern thinking existed in certain quarters in Britain and France, but Dahrendorf observes that throughout the nineteenth century it dominated the intellectual life of Germany where, he argues, there was no serious intellectual opposition to "a German ideology of the classless community," and where cultural pessimism was more highly developed and widely represented than its opposite.[155] While society was increasingly modernised, intellectual and cultural leaders continued to propagate an unmodern world-view. If so, might the explanation not lie precisely in the fact that Germany's principal intellectual élite throughout most of the century was a "clerical" rather than a legal-administrative or technological élite? Seventeenth and eighteenth-century clerics, philosophers and arts men had won their fight to impose their world-view on their rivals and maintain their own status. Their nineteenth-century successors managed to impose themselves, in an almost priestly role, in a society which was in fact moving farther and farther away from traditional structures. The history of the German *Lehrstand* and *Bildungselite* serves to illustrate the theory that élites may not merely act as spokesmen for dominant social groups, but, once in being, may take on an independent life of their own, and successfully fight to preserve a role for themselves in a world where, it would seem, they ought no longer to find a place.

[1] "Ich mußte also das *Wissen* aufheben, um zum Glauben Platz zu bekommen" (preface to 2nd ed., *Kritik der reinen Vernunft*), Immanuel Kant, *Gesammelte Schriften*, ed. Königliche Preussische Akademie der Wissenschaften (Berlin: G. Reimer, 1902-) 1: 3: 19. My references to Kant's works by section, volume and page number are to this edition (*GS*).

[2] For Kant's view of Wolff, see *GS* 1: 3: 22.

[3] "Der Streit der Fakultäten," *GS* 1: 7: 27-29.

[4] "Zum ewigen Frieden," *GS* 1: 8: 368-69.

[5] "Der Streit...," *GS* 1: 7: 67.

[6] "eine Art Nomaden, die allen beständigen Anbau des Bodens verabscheuen," *GS* 1: 4: 8. The translation is Norman Kemp Smith's.

[7] "Der Streit...," *GS* 1: 7: 80-88.

[8] See for example Alasdair MacIntyre, *After Virtue: A Study in Moral Theory*, 2nd ed. (London: Duckworth, 1985) 268; Edward Caird, *The Critical Philosophy of Immanuel Kant*, 2nd ed., vol. 2 (Glasgow: Maclehose, 1909) 315, 318, 352; Michael Stolleis, "Untertan – Bürger – Staatsbürger: Bemerkungen zur juristischen Terminologie im späten 18. Jahrhundert," *Bürger und Bürgerlichkeit im Zeitalter der Aufklärung*, ed. Rudolf Vierhaus, Wolfenbütteler Studien zur Aufklärung 7 (Heidelberg: L. Schneider, 1981) 82.

[9] Robert Tucker, *Philosophy and Myth in Karl Marx* (Cambridge, England: Cambridge UP, 1969) 33-36.

[10] This is the thrust of MacIntyre, *After Virtue*: see especially 43-47, 51-53, 236.

[11] Fritz K. Ringer, *The Decline of the German Mandarins: The German Academic Community, 1890-1933* (Cambridge, Mass.: Harvard UP, 1969) 96.

[12] Benjamin Nelson, "Self-Images and Systems of Spiritual Direction in the History of European Civilization," *The Quest for Self-Control: Classical Philosophies and Scientific Research*, ed. Samuel Z. Klausner (New York: Free Press, 1965) 72.

[13] Alasdair MacIntyre, "Moral Rationality, Tradition, and Aristotle: a Reply to Onora O'Neill, Raimon Gaita, and Stephen R. L. Clark," *Inquiry* 23 (1983): 450.

[14] See for example *Kritik der praktischen Vernunft*, *GS* 1: 5: 28-29, 43.

[15] See *Die Religion innerhalb der Grenzen der blossen Vernunft*, *GS* 1: 6: 50; *Die Metaphysik der Sitten*, *GS* 1: 6: 387, 441.

[16] See Caird, vol. 2: 351-75.

[17] *GS* 1: 4: 435; *GS* 1: 6: 375-474.

[18] Onora O'Neill, "Kant after Virtue," *Inquiry* 26 (1983): 396-97.

[19] "sich aus der Rohigkeit seiner Natur, aus der Thierheit..., immer mehr zur Menschheit, durch die er allein fähig ist sich Zwecke zu setzen, empor zu arbeiten," *GS* 1: 6: 387. The translation is Caird's, vol. 2: 353.

[20] *GS* 1: 6: 408.

[21] "Die Cultur seines Willens bis zur reinsten Tugendgesinnung," *GS* 1: 6: 387.

[22] *GS* 1: 5: 250, 262; *GS* 1: 6: 390, 394, 399-400, 405.

[23] *GS* 1: 5: 268, cf. 266-67, 297; *GS* 1: 5: 271, 274; cf. *Die Religion innerhalb der Grenzen der blossen Vernunft*, *GS* 1: 6: 49-50.

[24] "Beobachtungen über das Gefühl des Schönen und Erhabenen," *GS* 1: 2: 212.

[25] *GS* 1: 6: 50.

[26] "gewinnen der Tyrannei des Sinnenhanges sehr viel ab und bereiten dadurch den Menschen zu einer Herrschaft vor, in welcher die Vernunft allein Gewalt haben soll," *GS* 1: 5: 433.

[27] cf. Donald W. Crawford, "The Place of the Sublime in Kant's Aesthetic Theory," *The Philosophy of Immanuel Kant*, ed. Richard Kennington, Studies in Philosophy and the History of Philosophy 12 (Washington, D.C.: Catholic U of America Press, 1985).

[28] Caird, vol. 2: 372.

[29] *Grundlegung zur Metaphysik der Sitten*, *GS* 1: 4: 433; cf. Caird, vol. 2: 208-9, 222, 557. Charles M. Sherover, "Kant's Evaluation of His Relationship to Leibniz," *The Philosophy of Immanuel Kant*, ed. Kennington 202, 213, 218-20, 227.

[30] Caird, vol. 2: 221; cf. 561.

[31] Caird, vol. 2: 566-67.

[32] "Da nur in der Gesellschaft und zwar derjenigen, die die größte Freiheit, mithin einen durchgängigen Antagonism ihrer Glieder und doch die genauste Bestimmung und Sicherung der Grenzen dieser Freiheit hat, damit sie mit der Freiheit anderer bestehen könne, – da nur in ihr die höchste Absicht der Natur, nämlich die Entwickelung aller ihrer Anlagen, in der Menschheit erreicht werden kann...," *GS* 1: 8: 22. The translation is Caird's.

[33] Caird, vol. 2: 513, 516. Georg G. Iggers, *Deutsche Geschichtswissenschaft: eine Kritik der traditionellen Geschichtsauffassung von Herder bis zur Gegenwart*, 2nd ed. (1968; Munich: Deutscher Taschenbuch Verlag, 1972) 19, 27, 32, 34, 75-77.

[34] "Idee zu einer allgemeinen Geschichte in weltbürgerlicher Absicht," *GS* 1: 8: 26.

[35] Anthony J. La Vopa, *Grace, Talent, and Merit: Poor Students, Clerical Careers, and Professional Ideology in Eighteenth-century Germany* (Cambridge, England: Cambridge UP, 1988) 209-12, 265-66, 269, 308-16, 311-17.

[36] "alle Kräfte gleichmässig anzuspannen," Wilhelm von Humboldt, *Werke*, ed. Andreas Flitner and Klaus Giel, 5 vols. (Stuttgart: J. G. Cotta, 1960-81) 2: 7.

[37] Hans Heinrich Gerth, "Die Struktursituation der bürgerlichen Intelligenz im ausgehenden 18. Jahrhundert," *"Die Bildung des Bürgers": die Formierung der bürgerlichen Gesellschaft und die Gebildeten im 18. Jahrhundert*, ed. Ulrich Herrmann, Geschichte des Erziehungs- und Bildungswesens in Deutschland 2 (Weinheim: Beltz, 1982) 341;

Thomas Nipperdey, *Deutsche Geschichte 1800-1866: Bürgerwelt und starker Staat* (Munich: C. H. Beck, 1983) 473-74; John Stroup, *The Struggle for Identity in the Clerical Estate: Northwest German Protestant Opposition to Absolutist Policy in the Eighteenth Century*, Studies in the History of Christian Thought 33 (Leiden: E. J. Brill, 1984) 36, 38-39, 41, 124-28; La Vopa 345-49.

[38] Gerth 341.

[39] Ringer 113.

[40] "Universität und Gymnasium werden Quasi-Tempel, die Philosophen und Philologen eine Art neue Priester und Lebensführer, die Gnade des Geistes löst die Gnade Gottes, das Wort der Griechen Sein Wort ab," Nipperdey 59; cf. 440-53. See also Michael Naumann, "Bildung und Gehorsam: zur ästhetischen Ideologie des Bildungsbürgertums," *Das wilhelminische Bildungsbürgertum: zur Sozialgeschichte seiner Ideen*, ed. Klaus Vondung (Göttingen: Vandenhoeck & Ruprecht, 1976) 35-38.

[41] Friedrich Immanuel Niethammer, *Der Streit des Philanthropinismus und Humanismus in der Theorie des Erziehungs-Unterrichts unserer Zeit* (Jena, 1808) 105-106, quoted by R. Steven Turner, "The *Bildungsbürgertum* and the Learned Professions in Prussia, 1770-1830: The Origins of a Class," *Histoire Sociale Social History* 13, no. 25 (May 1980): 127.

[42] For the anti-modernism of idealism-neohumanism see Charles E. McClelland, *State, Society, and University in Germany 1700-1914* (Cambridge, England: Cambridge UP, 1980) 61; Nipperdey 453; La Vopa 283-86, 321.

[43] See for example Ulrich Gaier, "Soziale Bildung gegen ästhetische Erziehung: Goethes Rahmen der 'Unterhaltungen' als satirische Antithese zu Schillers 'Ästhetischen Briefen' 1-9," *Poetische Autonomie?: zur Wechselwirkung von Dichtung und Philosophie in der Epoche Goethes und Hölderlins*, ed. Helmut Bachmaier and Thomas Rentsch (Stuttgart: Klett-Cotta, 1987) 237-38; Bernd Leistner, "Der Xenien-Streit," *Debatten und Kontroversen: literarische Auseinandersetzungen in Deutschland am Ende des 18. Jahrhunderts*, ed. Hans-Dietrich Dahnke and Bernd Leistner, vol. 1 (Berlin: Aufbau-Verlag, 1989) 472-73.

[44] cf. Jost Hermand, "Schillers Abhandlung 'Über naive und sentimentalische Dichtung' im Lichte der deutschen Popularphilosophie des 18. Jahrhunderts," *PMLA* 79 (1964): 437-38.

[45] "drey verschiedene Epochen oder Grade,...die der Mensch zu durchwandern hat, ehe er das ist, wozu Natur und Vernunft ihn bestimmten"; "nichts als eine leidende Kraft"; "zu der Freiheit reiner Geister," Friedrich Schiller, *Briefe*, ed. Fritz Jonas, 7 vols. (Stuttgart: Deutsche Verlags-Anstalt, 1892-96) 3: 386-388. This edition of Schiller's letters is subsequently cited as Jonas. (Spellings have been modernised.)

[46] Friedrich Schiller, *Sämtliche Werke*, ed. Gerhard Fricke and Herbert G. Göpfert, 3rd ed., 5 vols. (Munich: Hanser, 1962) 5: 646. References to Schiller's works by volume and page numbers are to this edition (*SW*).

[47] Jonas 3: 332.

[48] *SW* 5: 650-51.

[49] *SW* 5: 716-17.

[50] *SW* 5: 586-87.

[51] "einen reinen idealischen Menschen"; "unveränderlicher Einheit," *SW* 5: 577.

[52] "bei allem Wechsel der Phantasie die Vernunft ihre Regel behauptet," *SW* 5: 695-96.

[53] "lauter Licht, lauter Freiheit, lauter Vermögen" (to Wilhelm von Humboldt, 30 Nov. 1795), Jonas 4: 338.

[54] "die höchste Erweiterung des Seins," *SW* 5: 606.

[55] "Übertritt des Menschen in den Gott" (to Humboldt, 30 Nov. 1795), Jonas 4: 338; cf. *SW* 5: 696.

[56] "Aus der Zeitflut weggerissen," *SW* 1: 173, cf. 5: 618-19.

[57] *SW* 5: 461, 468, 477.

[58] "Siegel der vollendeten Menschheit," *SW* 5: 468; "edleres Naturwesen" (enclosure to the letter of 11 Nov. 1793 to duke Christian Friedrich von Augustenburg), Jonas 3: 382.

[59] *SW* 5: 474-75.

[60] *SW* 5: 794, 796-97, 806.

[61] "idealistischen Anlage," *SW* 5: 794; "Same des Idealismus" (to Goethe, 17 Aug. 1797), Jonas 5: 241; "Energie des Willens," *SW* 5: 794; *SW* 5: 474-75.

[62] For this distinction see *SW* 5: 528-37.

[63] See the discussion of "Kraft" and "Richtung der Kraft," *SW* 5: 535-36.

[64] "Sinnlichkeit und Vernunft *zugleich* tätig sind," *SW* 5: 633.

[65] See "Über die ästhetische Erziehung des Menschen in einer Reihe von Briefen," letters 11-15, *SW* 5: 601-19.

[66] See enclosure to the letter of 11 Nov. 1793 to the duke of Augustenburg, Jonas 3: 378; *SW* 5: 620-21, 796-99, 807.

[67] *SW* 5: 535.

[68] "ruhig, aufgelöst, einig mit sich selbst und vollkommen befriedigt," *SW* 5: 752. On *Erschlaffung* see *SW* 5: 759-60. Compare the effect of beauty, *SW* 5: 619-22.

[69] For the idea that Greek tragedy is beautiful see Schiller's letter of 26 July 1800 to J. W. Süvern, Jonas 6: 175-76. For the position of comedy see Schiller to Humboldt, 30 Nov. 1795, Jonas 4: 338; cf. Benno von Wiese, *Friedrich Schiller* (Stuttgart: J. B. Metzler, 1959) 542-43; Friedrich Schiller, *Werke*, Nationalausgabe, ed. J. Petersen, G. Fricke et al. (Weimar: H. Böhlau, 1943-) 21: 301.

[70] "Daher ist hier das Gemüt in Bewegung, es ist angespannt, es schwankt zwischen streitenden Gefühlen," *SW* 5: 752. On *Überspannung* see *SW* 5: 759.

[71] "Strafende Satire," see *SW* 5: 721-24; "Elegie" and "Idylle," see *SW* 5: 728-38. Compare Hermand 440.

[72] "Die Tragödie macht uns nicht zu Göttern, weil Götter nicht leiden können, sie macht uns zu Heroen, d. i. zu göttlichen Menschen, oder, wenn man will, zu leidenden Göttern, zu Titanen," *SW* 5: 1018.

[73] "Resignation in seine fünf Sinne" (to Gottfried Körner, 12 Aug. 1787), Jonas 1: 381. "Überhaupt ist seine Vorstellungsart zu sinnlich und *betastet* mir zu viel" (to same, 1 Nov. 1790), Jonas 3: 113. "In Ihrer richtigen Intuition liegt alles und weit vollständiger, was die Analysis mühsam sucht" (to Goethe, 23 Aug. 1794), Jonas 3: 472.

[74] "ganz verhärteter Realist" (to Humboldt, 9 Jan. 1796), Jonas 4: 389; cf. letter to Goethe, 17 Aug. 1797, Jonas 5: 241.

[75] "Und am Ende sind wir ja beide Idealisten und würden uns schämen, uns nachsagen zu lassen, daß die Dinge uns formten und nicht wir die Dinge" (to Humboldt, 2 April 1805), Jonas 7: 226.

[76] Compare Michael Böhler, "Die Freundschaft von Goethe und Schiller als literatursoziologisches Paradigma," *Internationales Archiv für Sozialgeschichte der deutschen Literatur* 5 (1980): 60-64.

[77] The "Geschäftsmann" is, in the usage of the period, not the businessman but the official, the man who transacts the business of the state. Schiller referred to Goethe, the statesman, as a "Geschäftsmann" (to Körner, 12 Aug. 1787), Jonas 1: 383, and to other Weimar state officials as "Ihr Herren Staats- und Geschäftsleute" (to Wilhelm von Wolzogen, 4 Sep. 1803), Jonas 7: 69.

[78] *SW* 5: 583-87. *SW* 5: 768, 769, 766.

[79] Mack Walker, *German Home Towns: Community, State and General Estate, 1648-1871* (Ithaca: Cornell UP, 1971) 119.

[80] On Kant see *SW* 5: 465-66, 587-88, and Schiller, *Werke*, Nationalausgabe 21: 326.

[81] *SW* 5: 770-79, 724-25.

[82] *SW* 5: 772-79. Schiller certainly thought of the idealist as the proper author of tragedy. "Pathetische Satire," which requires the idealistic temperament, embraces tragedy, *SW* 5: 723.

[83] *SW* 5: 778.

[84] *SW* 5: 695, 697, 709, 711, 716-17, cf. 5: 655 and 1: 163; to Christian Friedrich von Augustenburg, 3 Dec. 1793, Jonas 3: 406.

[85] "Siegel der vollendeten Menschheit," *SW* 5: 468, cf. 5: 772.

[86] *SW* 5: 704-6, 726; "das höchste poetische Werk" (to Humboldt, 30 Nov. 1795), Jonas 4: 338.

[87] To Humboldt, 26 Oct. 1795, Jonas 4: 301. Cf. Dieter Borchmeyer, "Über eine ästhetische Aporie in Schillers Theorie der modernen Dichtung: zu seinen 'sentimentalischen Forderungen' an Goethes 'Wilhelm Meister' und 'Faust'," *Jahrbuch der deutschen Schillergesellschaft* 22 (1978): 328.

[88] "die möglichst vollständige *Nachahmung des Wirklichen*," *SW* 5: 717.

[89] See for example *SW* 5: 579, 623-24, 633, 641, 645.

[90] *SW* 5: 580, 621, cf. 5: 1041; Jonas 3: 378.

[91] *SW* 5: 579, cf. 624.

[92] Compare the definition of barbarism in the letter to the duke of Augustenburg, 13 July 1793, Jonas 3: 334; and to same, 21 Nov. 1793, Jonas 3: 392. For "Zwang der Begriffe" see *SW* 5: 609-11 (footnote), 623 and 1140, note to 609, line 31.

[93] To Süvern, 26 July 1800, Jonas 6: 175-76.

[94] *SW* 5: 705, 727, 744 note 1, 756 note 1.

[95] cf. Schiller's letters to Humboldt of 26 Oct. 1795, Jonas 4: 299-302, and to Goethe of 14 Sep. 1797, Jonas 5: 255-57.

[96]SW 5: 726-27; "großen und schönen Charakter," "Welch ein herrliches Ideal mußte nicht in der Seele des Dichters leben, der einen Tom Jones und eine Sophia schuf," SW 5: 727.

[97] "den unsterblichen Verfasser des 'Agathon'," SW 5: 744 note 1; "selbst die mutwilligen Spiele seiner Laune beseelt und adelt die Grazie des Herzens; selbst in den Rhythmus seines Gesanges drückt sie ihr Gepräg, und nimmer fehlt ihm die Schwungkraft, uns, sobald es gilt, zu dem Höchsten empor zu tragen," SW 5: 727.

[98] "in beschränkter Bedeutung des Worts" (to Goethe, 14 Sep. 1797), Jonas 5: 256.

[99] On Bürger, see SW 5: 981-82.

[100] SW 5: 755. Cf. 5: 458 note 1.

[101] SW 5: 758-59.

[102] "leichte und joviale Gemütsart," "dem Ideale gegenüber beinahe verächtlich," SW 5: 739-40. SW 5: 758.

[103] SW 5: 717.

[104] "wird von mir nur als nach dem Ideale strebend vorgestellt…daher ich ihr auch in effectu weniger Poetisches zugestehe als der naiven" (to Humboldt, 25 Dec. 1795), Jonas 4: 366.

[105] cf. Borchmeyer 353.

[106] "Diese Überspannung verdient also Zurechtweisung, nicht Verachtung, und wer darüber spottet, mag sich wohl prüfen, ob er nicht vielleicht aus Herzlosigkeit so klug, aus Vernunftmangel so verständig ist," SW 5: 762.

[107] "überspannte Zärtlichkeit im Punkt der Galanterie und der Ehre," SW 5: 762, cf. 5: 426, 1027.

[108] Kant, GS 1: 5: 273; "zärtliche Weichmütigkeit und Schwermut," SW 5: 739.

[109] "der Erfahrung gegenüber ein wenig lächerlich," "beinahe verächtlich," SW 5: 740; cf. 5: 762.

[110] SW 5: 738-39, 715, cf. 712-13.

[111] A letter of 1 Nov. 1790 to Körner suggests as much. Here Schiller described Goethe as lacking the passion to commit himself to a cause: "Es fehlt ihm ganz an der herzlichen Art, sich zu irgend etwas zu bekennen" (Jonas 3: 113).

[112] "der mit glühender Empfindung ein Ideal umfaßt und die Wirklichkeit flieht," SW 5: 738.

[113] To Goethe, 3 July 1796, Jonas 5: 11.

[114] "Ernst und Schmerz durchaus wie ein Schattenspiel versinken," "uns aus einem bänglichen Traum durch Lachen aufweckt" (to Goethe, 28 June 1796), Jonas 4: 467-68.

[115] "so heiter, so lebendig, so harmonisch aufgelöst und so menschlich wahr," "so strenge, so rigid und abstrakt und so höchst unnatürlich" (to Goethe, 7 Jan. 1795), Jonas 4: 96.

[116] cf. Borchmeyer 307; Gaier 219.

[117] "Er tritt von einem leeren und unbestimmten Ideal in ein bestimmtes tätiges Leben, aber ohne die idealisierende Kraft dabei einzubüßen" (to Goethe, 8 July 1796), Jonas 5: 92.

[118] To Goethe, 8 July 1796, Jonas 5: 19-23.

[119] To Goethe, 9 July 1796, Jonas 5: 24-30.

[120] "die Fabel ist vollkommen wahr, auch die Moral der Fabel ist vollkommen wahr, aber das Verhältnis der einen zu der andern springt noch nicht deutlich genug in die Augen" (to Goethe, 8 July 1796), Jonas 5: 23.

[121] He talked of his "Grille mit etwas deutlicherer Pronunziation der Hauptidee" (to Goethe, 19 Oct. 1796), Jonas 5: 89.

[122] cf. Friedrich Sengle, "Wieland und Goethe," *Wieland: vier Biberacher Vorträge 1953*, by Friedrich Beissner, Emil Staiger, Friedrich Sengle and Hans Werner Seiffert (Wiesbaden: Insel-Verlag, 1954) 56, 62-66, 68.

[123] Stefan Blessin, "Die radikal-liberale Konzeption von 'Wilhelm Meisters Lehrjahren'," *Deutsche Vierteljahrsschrift für Literaturwissenschaft und Geistesgeschichte* 49 (1975): *Sonderheft* "18. Jahrhundert" 205*-210*, 213*, 216*, 219*-21*.

[124] J. W. Goethe, *Werke*, Hamburger Ausgabe, 6th ed., 14 vols. (Hamburg: C. Wegner, 1965) 7: 495. Subsequent references to this edition are given in the form HA, followed by volume and page number.

[125] HA 7: 501. On Wilhelm's relationship with his father, see Ulrich Stadler, "Wilhelm Meisters unterlassene Revolte," *Euphorion* 74 (1980).

[126] "denen man zum Verbrechen machte, daß sie sich ihrer Väter mit Freuden und Ehren erinnerten und mancher Vorteile genossen, die ein wohldenkender Vater seinen Kindern und Nachkommen so gern zu verschaffen wünschte," HA 6: 125.

[127] Gaier 269-70, 234.

[128] See Friedrich A. Kittler, "Ottilie Hauptmann" and Wolf Kittler, "Soziale Verhältnisse symbolisch dargestellt," *Goethes* Wahlverwandtschaften: *kritische Modelle und Diskursanalysen zum Mythos Literatur*, ed. Norbert W. Bolz (Hildesheim: Gerstenberg, 1981); David E. Wellbery, "'Die Wahlverwandtschaften'," *Goethes Erzählwerk: Interpretationen*, ed. Paul Michael Lützeler and James E. McLeod (Stuttgart: Reclam, 1985).

[129] See for example Wellbery 292-93, 298-301, 307-9, 312.

[130] Friedrich Sengle, "Die klassische Kultur von Weimar, sozialgeschichtlich gesehen," *Internationales Archiv für Sozialgeschichte der Literatur* 3 (1978): 78-79 notes that Goethe disliked Wieland's ironic-satirical style.

[131] On Goethe, history and historicism, see Karl Mannheim, *Ideology and Utopia: An Introduction to the Sociology of Knowledge* (1936; London: Routledge & Kegan Paul, 1960) 209-212; Iggers 280-87.

[132] cf. Hans-Dietrich Dahnke, "Was ist Aufklärung?" *Debatten und Kontroversen*, vol. 1: 97-98, 101; Hans-Jürgen Schings, *Melancholie und Aufklärung: Melancholiker und ihre Kritiker in Erfahrungsseelenkunde und Literatur des 18. Jahrhunderts* (Stuttgart: J. B. Metzler, 1977) 143-44.

[133] On the Revolution as a revolt by traditionalists see Alfred Cobban, *The Social Interpretation of the French Revolution* (Cambridge, England: Cambridge UP, 1964) 10, 59-61, 67, 79, 84-85, 89-90, 170-73; William Doyle, *Origins of the French Revolution* (Oxford: Oxford UP, 1980) 132-35. On German responses to the Revolution see Helmut Koopmann, *Freiheitssonne und Revolutionsgewitter: Reflexe der Französischen Revolution im literarischen Deutschland zwischen 1789 und 1840* (Tübingen: M. Niemeyer, 1989) 1-6 and bibliography.

[134] On criticism of Kant see for example Monika Ammermann, *Gemeines Leben: gewandelter Naturbegriff und literarische Spätaufklärung: Lichtenberg, Wezel, Garve*, Abhandlungen zur Kunst-, Musik- und Literaturwissenschaft 239 (Bonn: Bouvier, 1978) 96; Hans-Dietrich Dahnke and Bernd Leistner, "Von der 'Gelehrtenrepublik' zur 'Guerre ouverte'," *Debatten und Kontroversen*, vol. 1: 23. On Biester's view of the universities see A. Stölzel, "Die Berliner Mittwochsgesellschaft über Aufhebung oder Reform der Universitäten (1795)," *Forschungen zur Brandenburgischen und Preussischen Geschichte* 2 (1889): 218. On the response to the *Xenien* see Leistner, "Xenien-Streit" 467-68, 494-97, 521.

[135] Leistner 501-504.

[136] cf. Stroup 127.

[137] Ringer 21. Koselleck is cited by Turner, "The *Bildungsbürgertum*" 125; see also 135.

[138] Nipperdey 510; Christoph Link, "Rechtswissenschaft," *Wissenschaften im Zeitalter der Aufklärung*, ed. Rudolf Vierhaus (Göttingen: Vandenhoeck & Ruprecht, 1985) 140-41; Jan Schröder, *Wissenschaftstheorie und Lehre der "praktischen Jurisprudenz" auf deutschen Universitäten an der Wende zum 19. Jahrhundert*, Ius Commune: Sonderhefte 11 (Frankfurt am Main: Klostermann, 1979) 80, 131, 212, 252.

[139] Link 141; Stolleis 83.

[140] cf. Roger Cotterrell, *The Sociology of Law: An Introduction* (London: Butterworth, 1984) 46-47, 22-25; Nipperdey 510-12; Iggers 58, 89-90, 98.

[141] Cotterrell 49, 27.

[142] Lionel Trilling, *Sincerity and Authenticity* (London: Oxford UP, 1972) 141; Ammermann 158-59; Odo Marquard, "Zur Geschichte des philosophischen Begriffs 'Anthropologie' seit dem Ende des achtzehnten Jahrhunderts," *Collegium Philosophicum: Studien Joachim Ritter zum 60. Geburtstag* (Basel: Schwabe, 1965) 227, note 36.

[143] Kant, *GS* 1: 7: 120-21 and note, 286-91.

[144] Marquard 211-214.

[145] Jörg Schönert, *Roman und Satire im 18. Jahrhundert: ein Beitrag zur Poetik* (Stuttgart: J. B Metzler, 1969) 79-80.

[146] Ammermann 46-47, 169.

[147] Schönert 95-96, 168-69.

[148] Richard Newald, *Von Klopstock bis zu Goethes Tod 1750-1832: Erster Teil, Ende der Aufklärung und Vorbereitung der Klassik*, Geschichte der deutschen Literatur von den Anfängen bis zur Gegenwart by Helmut de Boor and Richard Newald, vol. 6.1 (Munich: C. H. Beck, 1967) 288-89. See also Joseph Kohnen, *Theodor Gottlieb von Hippel 1741-1796: l'homme et l'œuvre* (Berne: P. Lang, 1983) 1377-91.

[149] Ammermann 102.

[150] On medical anthropology in the nineteenth century see Marquard 215.

[151] See for example Geoff Eley, "The British Model and the German Road: Rethinking the Course of German History Before 1914," David Blackbourn and Geoff Eley, *The Peculiarities of German History: Bourgeois Society and Politics in Nineteenth- Century Germany* (Oxford: Oxford UP, 1984) 39-43.

[152] Blackbourn and Eley 6.

[153] David Blackbourn, "The Discreet Charm of the Bourgeoisie: Reappraising German History in the Nineteenth Century," Blackbourn and Eley 164. Compare Nipperdey 264-67 on modernisation in nineteenth-century Germany.

[154] Blackbourn 174, and see 169-175; Eley 135-36.

[155] Ralf Dahrendorf, *Society and Democracy in Germany* (1965; London: Weidenfeld & Nicolson, 1968) 131-32, 127-32. Blackbourn (216) agrees that expressions of cultural despair were probably sharper in Germany than elsewhere.

Index